Higher Education at a Crossroad:
The Case of Estonia

Ellu Saar / René Mõttus (eds.)

Higher Education at a Crossroad: The Case of Estonia

PL ACADEMIC RESEARCH

Bibliographic Information published by the Deutsche Nationalbibliothek
The Deutsche Nationalbibliothek lists this publication in the Deutsche Nationalbibliografie; detailed bibliographic data is available in the internet at http://dnb.d-nb.de.

Gratefully acknowledging support byEuropean Union European Social Fund and program Primus, implemented by Archimedes Foundation.

European Union
European Social Fund

Investing in your future

Cover illustration:
© Andres Tennus, University of Tartu.

Library of Congress Cataloging-in-Publication Data

Higher education at a crossroad : the case of Estonia / Ellu Saar, René Mõttus (eds.).
pages cm
ISBN 978-3-631-63784-5
1. Education, Higher—Estonia. I. Saar, Ellu.
LA850.4.H54 2013
378.4798—dc23

2013008753

ISBN 978-3-631-63784-5

PL Academic Research is an Imprint of Peter Lang GmbH

Peter Lang – Frankfurt am Main · Bern · Bruxelles · New York · Oxford · Warszawa · Wien

www.peterlang.de

Content

HIGHER EDUCATION AT A CROSSROAD: THE CASE OF ESTONIA

Foreword

This is a very timely publication, coming as it does during a period of continuing changes in higher education landscape and policies in Estonia. While much has been written about different aspects of higher education in Western European countries, less is known about the developments within this sector in the new European accession countries, such as Estonia. What are the challenges for higher education in Estonia? Is the sector experiencing similar or different challenges from other countries? This volume provides the reader with a useful understanding of some of the issues confronting the Estonian higher education sector today, as well as providing an insight into how institutional processes and practices shape the lives of students within these institutions and beyond.

Higher education in Estonia has a long history. In 1617, during the Swedish-Polish war, Estonia became incorporated into a Swedish province called Livonia and came under the rule of the Swedish king, Gustav Adolf II. Following the foundation of Uppsala University, in 1632, the *Academia Gustaviana* was established in Estonia as the second university founded in the Swedish Empire. At that time, the only students were of Swedish and Finnish origin and the *Academia Gustaviana* was not open to Estonian students. However, the *Academia Gustaviana* was to be the predecessor of the University of Tartu, which is now recognized as one of the oldest universities in Northern Europe.

Over the centuries, the Estonian education landscape has been shaped and re-shaped by the turbulent historical developments in the region. In 1918, Estonia emerged as an independent country and, in the following year, established Estonian as the principal language of instruction at the University of Tartu. During the period of political independence (1918–1940), education became highly valued and many higher education institutions began to emerge that provided a number of different disciplines.

The events of the Second World War and the Soviet occupation resulted in further changes in higher education in Estonia. For over 40 years, until the end of the 1980s, Estonia was influenced by the Soviet education system. Following the country's independence from the Soviet Union in 1991, Estonia has undertaken several extensive reforms in the field of higher education, which have aimed at integrating Estonia into European models and practices of education and research.

This volume focuses on these and subsequent developments and challenges in higher education that have taken place in Estonia. However, these changes have not been implemented without problems and the current situation has received criticisms for issues such as uneven development of higher education policies and practice, over-supply of higher education institutions for the population size (approximately 1.3 million citizens), mismatching of fields of study for the needs of the labour market, insufficient international cooperation and academic mobility, and limited funding, among others. That said, for years, Estonia has continued to rank among the top countries internationally with a high proportion of people achieving higher educational qualifications.

This book provides a comprehensive outline of various developments and challenges in higher education in Estonia. It covers a wide range of issues, including the development of higher education policy, access to higher education, changes in the profile of higher education students, the experiences of students in higher education institutions and their subsequent transition to the labour market. It also addresses key questions about quality improvement and inequity in higher education.

This very comprehensive collection is directly relevant to higher education professionals working within the Estonian system and will be useful for international readers with an interest in comparative perspectives of developments of higher education systems. It is a wonderful resource for researchers, policy makers and practitioners and a welcome addition to the emerging literature in the field of higher education.

Dr. Merike Darmody

Research Officer, Department of Social Research, the Economic and Social Research Institute, Ireland

Assistant Professor, Department of Sociology, Trinity College, Ireland

Chapter 1.
Introduction: A brief overview of the Estonian higher education system and its challenges

Ellu Saar, René Mõttus

Higher education in Estonia: broad trends

Following independence from the Soviet Union, Estonian higher education underwent rapid changes during the 1990s. These changes, which took place against a background of a general shift from a socialist planned economy to a market-based economy, were characterised by an increasing number of higher education institutions and developments in areas including funding, quality assurance, equity and links to the job market. The changes continued into the following decade, however, by then many aspects of the changes were different. We start the chapter by giving a brief overview of the developments in Estonian higher education since the early 1990s to the present, as it is our view that much of what will be written in this and the following chapters has to be understood in the context of these developments.

Since 1991 there have been two types of higher education establishments: universities that offer academic programmes and institutions of professional higher education that offer professional higher education programmes. At the end of the 1990s, the Bologna Declaration was implemented, the '3+2' curriculum was adopted and provisions for professional higher education studies were drafted. Since then higher education has been divided into two categories:

- professional higher education, requiring three years of study based on a professional higher education curriculum (ISCED 5B);
- academic higher education, in which three years of study are required for a Bachelor's degree (ISCED 5A), two years for a Master's degree (ISCED 5A), and four years for a doctoral degree (ISCED 6).

Due to a liberal higher education policy, the number of higher education institutions grew very fast to 49 institutions in 2002 but is now somewhat lower than this at 34 institutions (see Figure 1). This expansion of higher education occurred through (1) the establishment of new private universities and professional higher education schools; (2) the reorganisation of specialised secondary schools as public professional higher education schools; and (3) new legislation allowing foreign universities to establish branches in Estonia. With the aim of maximising revenue and keeping costs low, the private higher education institutions tend to concentrate on programmes in the more lucrative professions, such as law, business management, and psychology, which do not require expensive infrastructure.

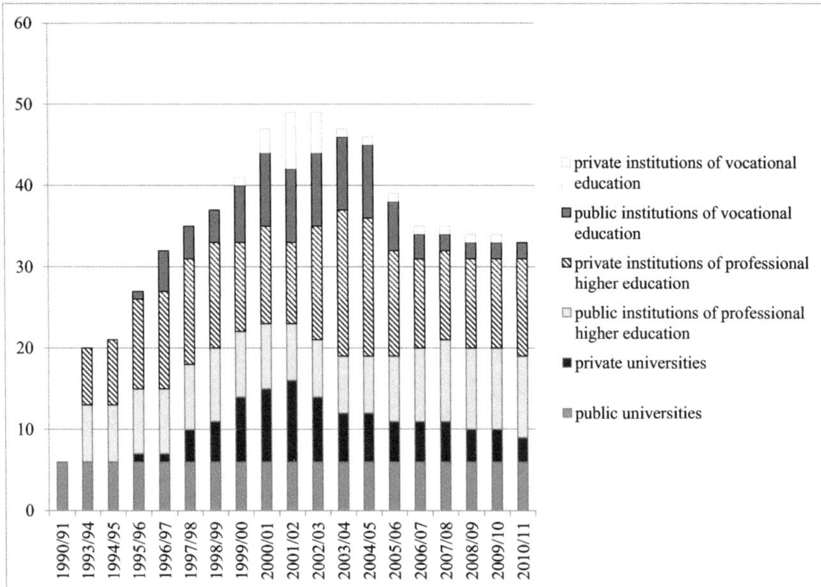

Figure 1. Number of higher education institutions, 1990–2010

Source: Tõnisson, 2011

The number of students enrolled in higher education increased 2.7 times between the academic years 1994/1995 and 2008/2009, growing from 25,000 to 68,000 (Tõnisson, 2011). In 2009 36 per cent of people aged between 25 and 64 had undertaken tertiary education (OECD 2007 average: 28 per cent). Over the past decade the number of higher education graduates has doubled as well.

The proportion of students who had enrolled in professional higher education increased until 2001, then it started to slightly decrease. Since the academic year 2005/06 the proportions of students in academic and professional higher education (66 per cent and 34 per cent respectively) have remained the same (Tõnisson, 2011).

This rapid expansion might have lead to inequalities. On the one hand, the expansion opened up more places in tertiary education institutions, and these should have increased the opportunities for under-represented students to attend. On the other hand, given the pattern of the expansion, socially disadvantaged or otherwise less prepared students might have gained access to lower-status institutions, including those in smaller towns, and to fee-paying places either in the public or the private sector. As the OECD Review of Tertiary Education in Estonia (2007:63) indicates 'as is the case in many other countries, vocationally-oriented tertiary studies still suffer from a lack of parity of esteem relative to university studies'. Chapter 14 of this book also indicated that vertical differentiation exists in higher education in Estonia.

Subject area is important in horizontal differentiation in higher education. In a similar way to other Central and Eastern European countries, Estonia experienced a substantial decrease in enrolment in engineering, manufacturing and construction; the proportion of students in these areas fell from 20 per cent in 1994 to 14 per cent in 2009. The agricultural fields also declined in popularity from 5 to 3 per cent in the same period. Enrolment also declined, but less significantly, in arts and humanities, and education. The number of students studying business increased dramatically between 1994 and 1999 and then levelled out at about 23 per cent (Saar and Lindemann, 2008; Tõnisson, 2011). Enrolment in social sciences and media can be looked at as a U-shape, with higher proportions of students enrolling during the mid-1990s and mid-2000s. An inverted U-shape is evident for law specialities, with almost 10 per cent of all students choosing this subject area in 1999.

Among the most notable tendencies in higher education is the increasing number of female students; in the 1993/94 academic year 51 per cent of all students were women and this figure had grown to 60 per cent by 2010/11 (Tõnisson, 2011). Of those who graduated from university in 2009, more than two thirds (69 per cent) were women, which is more than in any other developed country (50–60 per cent). There is also a strong gender differentiation in terms of subject area. Men still dominate in engineering, manufacturing and technology (although the proportion of women has been increasing), and in sciences, where the proportion of men has remained more or less static over the past twelve years. Although the proportion of women studying agriculture and services is inferior to the proportion of men, women dominate the rest of the subject areas. In recent years the proportion of women in services and in health and welfare has been increasing particularly rapidly. However, the rankings of popularity of different fields, in terms of the proportions of female graduates, were very similar for Estonia and other developed countries, suggesting that, although women were more likely to graduate in Estonia than men, they generally choose the same fields as their peers in other countries.

One of the most striking features of the development of Estonian higher education since independence is the rapid growth in the numbers of tuition-fee paying students, both in terms of absolute numbers and as a proportion of all students. In the early 1990s the majority of students were publicly funded; the situation now is that half of all students are fee-paying. The proportion of students paying tuition fees has increased from 7 per cent in 1993 to 49 per cent in 2011 (Tõnisson, 2011).

Some important challenges

This development raises some fundamental issues for funding policies, particularly regarding the appropriateness and impact of a funding model which results in half of all students receiving no public support. Support for students is provided in the form of grants for living costs and a student loan scheme, but eligibility for grants is restricted to students in state-commissioned places. With the exception of a small proportion (5 per cent) of grants that are distributed on the basis of financial need, grants are generally allocated on the basis of academic performance. Furthermore, the existing loan scheme does not fully remove the risk that some students with the ability to successfully undertake higher education will be prevented from doing so due to lack of funds. Loans are only available to full-time students to cover tuition and living costs, but the amounts available do not cover the tuition fees for most of the fee-paying students. In addition, because access to a loan is conditional on a student's credit worthiness taking out a loan is not an option for students from poor backgrounds.

The recently adopted reform of higher education will make all full-time study places free from 2013/2014 onwards and will also introduce a system of means-tested income support. However, full time study is required to maintain the free study place and support. As a result, this reform might make students from poor backgrounds and non-traditional students (for example adult students) worse off because the proposed value of 135 EUR for the means-tested grant is likely to mean that students without parental support and older students with their own families will need to work to support themselves while studying (OECD, 2012; Saar et al., 2012).

So, the expansion has led to a number of challenges which are demanding a priority shift from growth to quality improvement and equality. With respect to access to higher education in Estonia, the policy has emphasised the overall expansion of enrolment rather than equity of access, which relates more to differences in participation rates among groups of students (OECD, 2007). The Estonian Higher Education Strategy 2006–2015 does not put enough emphasis on the equity dimension. In an interview, an official from the Ministry of Education and Research indicated the following (Tamm and Saar, 2010):

> I mean that we must be aware of the problem. For example, the support system based on students' needs and social fairness. Two years ago we participated in an

> OECD study and the experts were amazed that our higher educational institutions do not recognise that there is a problem. They – both the staff and the management – do not see it as a problem and neither do the students. The currents system of state commissioned education is considered normal – people believe that if you have finished a so-called elite school (one of the best schools in Tallinn or Tartu that accept 7 year olds to year one on the basis of entrance tests) then you have the right to a state funded study place, because you are better than others. Nobody seems to realise that the advantages of an elite school graduate may be the result of his/her better starting position compared with a graduate from a secondary school in the countryside or a small town. Our society does not recognise that social fairness is a problem. People do not want to see it.

Previous studies indicate that the impact of social origin on access to higher education has increased since the 1990s (Saar, 2010; Saar and Unt, 2011). The enrolment in higher education of students from poor backgrounds is particularly low (OECD, 2012). An OECD Review (OECD, 2007) also indicated that Estonian higher education was inequitable in its overall admissions policy and access to state-commissioned places (especially in the best institutions) were disproportionately granted to students from families with well educated parents. In Estonia the main demographic group that is under-represented in higher education is the Russian-speaking population because the language of instruction in public higher education institutions is mainly Estonian. However, although it is possible to study in Russian at several private universities, the students enrolled in these institutions have to pay tuition fees. In total, 11 per cent of all students in higher education are studying in Russian, predominantly in private higher education institutions. The OECD (2007) finds that Russian-speaking school leavers find themselves at a disadvantage accessing the main higher education institutions as these institutions give instruction mainly in Estonian. Statistics for secondary school graduates who continued to higher education are provided by the Estonian Ministry of Education and Research. In 2007, 55 per cent of Estonian-language secondary school leavers secured a state-commissioned place in tertiary education, while only 49 per cent of Russian-secondary school leavers did so. In 2010 the differences have decreased (66 and 64 per cent respectively) (Tõnisson, 2011). Previous analyses also indicated that higher education opportunities for people not proficient in Estonian are limited because they have a limited choice of courses to choose from and they have to pay for their studies (Lindemann and Saar, 2012). Chapter 7 examines a very acute problem that is the provision of higher education to non-native speaker students in the face of their lower command of the language of instruction.

The age structure of students has changed. In the middle of the 1990s less than 10 per cent of students were over 30 years old but now this figure is 20 per cent (Tõnisson, 2011) and most adults pay for their studies themselves (Tamm and Saar, 2010). Despite the expansion of higher education and the different age structure of students, the lifelong education offerings from higher education institutions are underdeveloped and the needs of adult learners have not been focused on by the institutions. There are no provisions to allow for entry into higher education on the basis of a person's assessed competencies instead of formal qualifications. In Estonia, earlier studies can only be of use (e.g., for obtaining credit points) after the person has been admitted to the higher education institution. Currently, about 40 per cent of students are working and learning simultaneously (Beerkens, Mägi and Lill, 2011; Kirss et al., 2011). The OECD Review (2007) states that it is important to provide support to these students by making available more flexible programmes. An extract from an interview with an official from the Ministry of Education and Research describes the situation very well (Tamm and Saar, 2010):

> As regards the access of adults to higher education, it has not been recognized as a problem yet. The mainstream understanding is that if a person is hard working enough he/she will manage without any help. The studies of people over 30 years old should not be supported financially. There is even no discussion in the society. We don't talk about it; we do not have comprehensive policies. …We do not know what the problems of people over 40 years old who work full-time and study half-time are.

Therefore, one challenge for higher education is the development of strategies for promoting lifelong learning. The aim of Chapter 17 – to analyse the institutional barriers perceived by adults participating in higher education programmes and the impact of institutional factors on the formation of these barriers – is directly connected with this challenge.

Quality assurance

The growth of the higher education system has led Estonians to realise that the quality of higher education varies depending both on the type of institution and the subject area. Estonia started to build its national higher education quality assurance system in the mid-1990s, following the rapid expansion of the higher education sector. Since 1996, the *Standard of Higher Education* has regulated the establishment of higher education institutions and has determined the requirements that they and their programmes must meet in order to obtain an appropriate education licence. The *Strategy for Higher Education 2006–2015* also places considerable emphasis on quality and the means of assuring it. However, an OECD Review (2007) indicates some problems in the existing quality assurance system (see also Tomusk, 1997; Kroos, 2010). First, there is a risk of developing a formal quality assurance system based on quantitative indicators rather than a qualitative system. Second, the standards for programme evaluation are general and do not refer to the requirements of specific programmes. Third, the quality criteria applied to the programmes fail to take into account the views of stakeholders or any specific national requirements. The system is based on the work of international evaluators. It makes it difficult to systematically take account of any national priorities, be they at the institutional or the programme level. The review also emphasises the importance of learning outcomes. 'The learning outcomes would thus provide the core of contents, abilities and attitudes that should be developed during the teaching and learning process' (OECD, 2007:78). Chapters 8 to 11 examine problems connected with the quality of learning in higher education institutions.

Higher education and labour market

Despite the expansion of higher education, the demand for it remained strong in the 2000s. Unemployment rates were lowest for individuals with higher education and have remained relatively stable at between 3 and 6 per cent in the period 1997–2008 (Statistics Estonia). However, the recession in 2008 somewhat changed this situation. The unemployment rate of people with higher education increased to 8 per cent whereas the unemployment gap between educational groups increased, suggesting that higher education nevertheless offered a relatively better protection against unemployment. In 2010 (i.e. during a time of economic hardship), people with a higher education qualification were 50 per cent less likely to be unemployed than people with upper secondary or post-secondary vocational education qualifications and 67 per cent less likely to be unemployed than people who had not undertaken secondary education. In the other developed countries (OECD members), the respective percentages were 38 and 63, which suggests that having a higher education qualification was slightly more protective against unemployment in Estonia than in many other developed countries (OECD, 2012). However, while the relatively low unemployment rate of graduates suggests that their qualifications are well recognised by employers, the return to higher education in terms of wage premiums is low when comparing internationally (OECD, 2012). Some analyses indicate that a significant proportion of graduates appear not to find employment in an area matching the competencies and skills that they acquired in higher education (Saar and Unt, 2012). Also, a growing number of graduates are not obtaining high-level positions (see Chapter 13). Chapter 15 points to another potential issue that higher education graduates face: that the value of Bachelor's degrees may have decreased.

Another general problem, according to the OECD Review (2007), are the limited opportunities for practical training experience for students because companies are not interested in providing these places for students.

The objectives of this book

In this book we aimed to cover a comprehensive range of topics pertaining to Estonian higher education. First, we focused on various aspects of the learning process and learning environment. For instance, one study investigated the degree to which peer comparisons can influence students' self-concepts and showed that students' expectations for their own performances may depend on their peer groups and ultimately influence their evaluations of progress. Another study looked at the association between fatigue and academic performance, comparing students who undertake employment while studying with those who do not. The study found that fatigue was unrelated to academic performance once a number of psychological and demographic variables were taken into account. However, academic performance was predicted by the personality trait conscientiousness, by academic self-esteem, and by high-school performance. Other studies have investigated perceptions of the class-room environment, students' roles in society in general, and, on the more practical side, the language needs of minority students. Second, various aspects of the teaching process were investigated from the point of view of teachers. For instance, teacher's views of themselves and their teaching processes are considered, and issues relating to planning and organising teaching are studied. Third, the book has addressed the transition from higher education to the job market. In particular, the relationships between higher education and employment and unemployment, professional success, income and male-female income differences have been studied. The changes in higher education and the effects of these on the labour market were also investigated. Finally, as a somewhat separate topic, Chapter 2 presents an overview of the strategy documents that steer Estonian higher education policy.

The book benefits from contributions from a range of scientific disciplines, including educational sociology, educational sciences, psychology and econometrics, and we believe that this multidisciplinarity is one of the strengths of the book. Below we summarise each of the chapters.

Chapter 2, Estonian Higher Education and Research Strategy: A Systematic Review and Policy Discussion, had three interrelated goals. The first aim was to map the content of the Estonian higher education and research policy documents together with their goals, measures and actions. The second aim was to assess the extent to which the policy met the reasonable expectations, framed within the rational-comprehensive policy paradigm, that these goals, measures and actions should be equipped with at least one indicator that would allow the evaluators to assess the policy progress and its outcomes. The final aim was to make indirect inferences about the policy process that produces the strategic documents. The author concluded that Estonian higher education policy is fragmented across many documents. Numerous strategic documents have been approved to steer higher education and research, as have the goals, measures and actions that allow the justification of almost any policy decision. In addition, there is a lack of local policy analysis and evaluation of the measures and actions described in the strategic documents. This situation suggests that, rather than problems looking for solutions, it is the other way around in the Estonian higher education and research policy process – the ideas expressed in the policy documents are looking for issues to tackle and problems to solve.

Chapter 3, **Does a research-oriented university really have a negative effect on students' self-evaluations?**, investigates differences in students' self-evaluations in a research oriented university and in institutions of professional higher education. Evidence was found to support the hypothesis that actual grades at university, not estimates of students' intellectual levels, are linked to students' self-evaluations, after controlling for the influence of cognitive ability. Although the choices for students are limited in a small country like Estonia, aspects of the Big Fish Little Pond Effect (equally able students have lower levels of academic self-concept in high-ability schools than in low-ability schools) are evident. The implications of the Big Fish Little Pond Effect for the students' futures (lowering career aspirations, dropping out from university) are discussed.

Chapter 4, **Fatigue does not predict academic performance among university students**, found that higher levels of self-rated fatigue were linked to lower academic performance at university. However, the association disappeared after controlling for a number of psychological traits, demographic factors and high-school performance. Structural equation modelling revealed that better academic performance was associated with higher levels of the personality trait Conscientiousness, higher academic self-esteem and higher high-school performance. Therefore, fatigue might have an apparent correlation with low university performance but this may be because the kinds of people who tend to perform better in university may simply experience less fatigue.

Chapter 5, **Experiencing learning at university: making the best of lifelong learning?**, concentrated on how students experience learning and teaching practices at university. The results confirmed that universities are still dominated by teaching practices where little consideration is given to the learning experiences of students and where the understanding that students are adult learners is not common. Learning is primarily experienced in situations where teachers impart knowledge, which results in passive learning. More specific limitations of teaching practices in typical study situations at university include, for example, a lack of support from academics for the students' development and learning. The analysis suggested that academics should see dealing with adult learners and their learning experiences as a great opportunity to develop their teaching practice.

The aim of **Chapter 6, What makes a good classroom environment for an adult learner? A comparative perspective**, was to study the differences in classroom environment perceptions in Estonia compared to other European countries. The particular objective was to show which aspects of the classroom environment were seen more positively by adult learners in higher education, and which of those aspects related most strongly to confidence in completing studies and satisfaction with the learning process and outcomes. The results indicated that adult learners in Estonia were positive about the classroom environment, and this was the case in other European countries as well. However, the adult learners were less positive about their potential to achieve their personal goals and here the Estonian adult learners were more critical than learners in other countries. Adult learners are not a homogenous group and, depending upon their learning stage, they might need different approaches: at the beginning of their studies they might benefit from a more supportive, and thus teacher-centred, learning environment, whereas in the later stages a more independent, learner-centred environment might be appropriate.

Chapter 7, How non-native speaker students cope in higher education: a case study of ethnic minority students in Estonia, examined how Estonian non-native speaker students cope in various higher education situations and what kind of support they need and get. The study demonstrated that the universities' language courses partially met the students' academic language needs. It also showed that the question of whether subject instructors should provide language support in their courses is controversial (opinions differ about whether coping is just the student's responsibility or whether mature expression skills in the language of instruction constitute part of the general education quality that speciality subject instructors should provide). However, most instructors still use a range of support measures. There is room for development in moving from merely helping the student pass the content requirements of speciality subject courses, to deliberately supporting the development of their academic language skills.

Chapter 8, From teaching to guiding learning: novice university teachers' conceptions of teaching, aimed to develop the understanding of Estonian early-career university teachers' ideas about teaching and the factors that influence their teaching practice. The results of the study showed that novice teachers' teaching practices are mostly based on their own learning experiences and on teaching traditions in their discipline. Pedagogical courses might motivate novice teachers to change their teaching practice. However, problems in implementing methods that value more learner participation, the discipline's prevailing conceptions of teaching, and pressure from colleagues, might influence novice teachers to turn to traditional teaching.

The aim of **Chapter 9, The impact of Estonian research, development and education policies on value conflicts in universities**, was to show which of the goals and processes set out in Estonian research, development, and education policies created value conflicts among university employees. The authors concluded that pressure to publish, which is linked to budgeting policy, was found to be detrimental to excellence and co-operation. University employees felt that insufficient and project-based funding, favouring applied research, jeopardizes academic values, most notably those of academic freedom, being science-based, and being committed. Finally, a distinct policy area that has caused much discontentment among academic employees is the 'massification' of higher education.

Chapter 10, Supervisors' activities in supporting PhD students in the supervisory process, examined the supervisory practice of supervisors of educational studies' PhD students in the context of the changes taking place in higher education in Estonia. The results showed a connection between finding a supervisor and the course of the supervisory process. The role of the supervisor was considered to be very important in the planning stage of a doctoral thesis, in helping to find appropriate resources, and in supporting the PhD student in the process of writing. The PhD supervisors' activities to support PhD students to become fully-fledged members of the academic community were described, including passing on contacts and participating in different academic events with the PhD students.

Chapter 11, Defining the determining element of content mastery as the key aspect in congruence between learning outcomes and assessment, was based on research undertaken in the Estonian Academy of Security Sciences about the alignment of intended learning outcomes and assessment. Research on police and border guard curricula indicated that learning outcomes and assessment were not well aligned, and, in addition, there was almost no information about assessment in the syllabuses. The analyses of the assessments of the 2009/2010 and 2011/2012 school-year subjects indicated that the main differences appeared in defining and aligning assessment both toward greater clarity and alignment. Examples of the congruence of the learning outcomes and assessments with the Determining Element of Content Mastery, and the reasons for deviations, were also presented and examples were given about how the Determining Element of Content Mastery was expressed in the final grade of the subject.

The aim of **Chapter 12, The trends and problems of planning outcome-based courses in e-learning**, was to study the actual practices of outcome-based e-learning at Estonian universities, focusing on the courses where personal learning environments (e.g. blogs and portfolios) were used as a medium. The frequencies and co-usage of the learning outcomes, activities and assessment types were described, which enabled the trends and critical problems in planning outcome based e-courses to be illustrated. Based on the study results, the authors suggested design guidelines to help in the planning of learning activities and assessment types for e-learning courses held in personal learning environments, taking into account the different types of learning outcomes prescribed by the Higher Education Standard.

Chapter 13, **From bust to boom and back again: Social positions of graduates during last decade in Estonia**, gave an overview of the occupational position of graduates during the last decade in Estonia, a decade marked by educational expansion, two severe economic recessions and one exceptional boom. The authors also explored gender and ethnic effects and their interaction with educational level in predicting employment status. The analyses indicated that it is possible to observe the differentiation in graduates' occupational positions and the downward substitution process that was taking place during the 2000s. The likelihood of insecure employment and the risk of unemployment have risen most rapidly for graduates with professional higher education qualifications. There was also a clear tendency for every succeeding cohort of BA graduates to start their careers from a lower position than the previous cohort. An increasing proportion of BA graduates continue on to study at the Master's level without entering the job market. Master's degrees still seem to hold distinct value in the job market. There is also clear horizontal differentiation – except for MA graduates, graduates belonging to ethnic minorities have a significantly higher risk of being unemployed and have less chance of securing atop position than Estonians.

In **Chapter 14**, **Why do social science graduates earn more than natural science graduates in Estonia?**, the authors compared the labour market performance of hard science and social science graduates. Their aim was to analyse whether there is any evidence of an over-supply of social science graduates. The wage analysis, based on data from the Estonian alumni survey 2010, indicated that there is a wage-premium for social science graduates, but only at the master's/doctoral level, not at the bachelor's level.

Chapter 15, The expansion of higher education: devaluation or differentiation? The Estonian case, examined the perceptions of employers, graduates and representatives of higher education institutions of the potential devaluation of higher education in Estonia as a consequence of the expansion of the sector. Going to university or an applied higher education institution has become the norm and not having a higher education qualification may give a negative signal and result in de-selection in job applications. Vertical differentiation exists in the sector, indicating some devaluation of higher education in Estonia. Differentiation within the sector has also increased. The expansion of higher education has meant that the qualifications from some private higher education institutions have lost their capacity to 'make a difference'.

The focus of **Chapter 16, The graduate gender pay gap in Estonia**, was on gender segregation in subject areas in Estonian higher education, the male-female wage gap among recent graduates and the main reasons for the gap. The results indicated that the Estonian higher education sector is clearly gender segregated. On average the gender wage gap was around 25 per cent, but vast discrepancies exist across subject areas, for example, in health and welfare on average men earned 40 per cent more than women, while in the service sector the wages were almost equal. The wage discrepancies are largely explained by labour market segregation by gender – occupation and sector are the most important determinants of the gender wage gap. The expansion of higher education and the falling birth rate have changed the profile of the student population, amongst other things the number of adult students has increased.

Chapter 17, Wishing welcome to the non-traditional student: barriers to returning to and learning in higher education, examined the barriers to the participation of adults in higher education, concentrating on the impact of supply side factors such as access, flexibility and affordability of higher education programmes. The analysis was based on a comparative international data set. Among the countries analysed, Estonia has one of the highest levels of perceived institutional barriers to learning. Estonian non-traditional students are paying the highest tuition fees, and the proportion of students who pay for their studies themselves (two thirds) is high. Lack of financial means is a serious barrier to accessing higher education, financial support is inadequate and the current system for applying for this support is demeaning.

We would like to thank Alison and Marcus of Derettens OÜ for the language editing, and Epp Reiska for technical assistance. This book was written as part of the research projects funded by Primus. Primus is a Programme for Higher Education Quality Enhancement in Estonia (2008–2014), which aims to improve the quality of higher education and increase the competitiveness of graduates. The programme is financed by the European Social Fund and the Estonian state budget, and is implemented by the Archimedes Foundation (Primus office – Centre for Higher Education Development).

References

Beerkens, M., Mägi, M. and Lill, L. (2011). University studies as a side job: causes and consequences of massive student employment in Estonia. *Higher Education*, 61, 679–692.

Kirss, L., Nestor, M., Haaristo, H.-S., Mägi, E. (2011). *Eesti üliõpilaste eluolu 2010* [Being a Student in Estonia. 2010]. Tallinn: Praxis.

Kroos, K. (2010). *Kõrghariduse kvaliteet kehtivates riiklikes strateegia dokumentides* [Higher Education Quality in the Existing National Strategy Documents]. Unpublished report.

Lindemann, K. and Saar, E. (2012). Ethnic inequalities in education: second-generation Russians in Estonia. *Ethnic and Racial Studies.*

OECD (2006), *OECD Factbook 2006: Economic, Environmental and Social Statistics*. Paris: OECD.

OECD (2007). *OECD Reviews of Tertiary Education. Estonia.* Paris: OECD.

OECD (2012). *OECD Economic Surveys: Estonia*. Paris: OECD.

Saar, E., Tamm, A., Roosalu, T. and Roosmaa, E.-L. (2012). *Mittetraditsiooniline tudeng kõrgkoolis* [Nontraditional student in university]. Tartu: Archimedes Foundation.

Saar, E. (2010). Changes in intergenerational mobility and educational inequality in Estonia: comparative analysis of cohorts born between 1930 and 1974. *European Sociological Review*, 26, 367–383.

Saar, E. and Lindemann, K. (2008). Estonia. In Kogan, I., Gebel, M. and Noelke, C. (Eds.), *Europe Enlarged: A Handbook of Education, Labour and Welfare Regimes in Central and Eastern Europe*. Bristol: Policy Press, 151–181.

Saar, E. and Unt, M. (2011). Education and labour market entry in Estonia: closing doors for those without tertiary education. In Kogan, I., Noelke, C. and Gebel, M. (Eds.), *Making the transition: Education and Labour Market Entry in Central and Eastern Europe*. Stanford: Stanford University Press, 240–268.

Saar, E. and Unt, M. (2012). Labour Market Returns to Tertiary Education in Post-Socialist Countries. In Lambert, P., Connelly, R., Blackburn, R.M. and Gayle, V. (Eds.), *Social Stratification: Trends and Processes*. Farnham UK: Ashgate Publishing, 209–219.

Tamm, A. and Saar, E. (2010). Projekt LLL2010. *SP5 Estonia country report.*

Tomusk, V. (1997). External quality assurance in Estonian higher education: its glory, take-off and crash. *Quality in Higher Education*, 3, 173–181.

Tõnisson, E. (2011). *Kõrghariduse valdkonna statistiline ülevaade 2011* [Statistical overview of higher education 2011]. Tartu: Estonian Ministry of Education and Research. Available online and only in Estonian: http://www.hm.ee/index.php?048183

Chapter 2.
Estonian Higher Education and Research Strategy: A Systematic Review and Policy Discussion

Karmo Kroos

The problem was not in the first place the nature of the consultation, but rather the vagueness of the White Paper which achieved consensus, as with all policy documents produced in this period, by providing all things to all people (Cloete and Maassen, 2002:454).

Introduction

Higher education and research (HE&R) policy is fragmented across a number of strategy documents in Estonia. More specifically, at the end of 2010, the effective number of HE&R policy documents in Estonia, (which is a country of just 1.3 million people, with a student body of 67,607 in the academic year 2011–2012) were spread over more than 500 pages (see Table 1 and Appendixes 1–3). In addition to these policy documents, there was a growing number of HR&R programmes and documentation developed for the implementation of specific policy tasks. After careful selection, explained in the Population and Sampling section of this paper, 12 documents listed in Table 1 and specified in Appendix 2 and 3, remained for closer analysis in this paper. A meta-analysis was undertaken to get an overview of the various goals and measures, as well as to determine how well they were connected to the metrics and data sources. On the basis of the systematic overview and as the argument of the paper developed, we showed that Estonian HE&R is steered by a huge number of policy goals, measures, and actions. In total, there were 22 different major goals and 37 subgoals, 34 measures[1] and 193 activities[2] related to HE&R in these policy documents. Contrary to the proposal from the Estonian Ministry of Finance (2007), 'Proposal for the Method of Selecting the Aims and Indicators', which states that each goal mentioned in the state policy document should be associated with at least one indicator that would allow the assessment of progress and evaluation of results, it was found that two-thirds of the existing state HE&R policy docu-

1 There were 40 measures before the obvious duplicates in various policy sets were excluded. See Table 2 and its notes for details.

2 There were 220 activities before the obvious duplicates in various policy sets were excluded. See Table 2 and its notes for details.

ments met the formal criteria only if the meaning of 'indicator' is stretched to include, in addition to metrics, the descriptions of intended results. Furthermore, it was surprising to learn that none of these strategy documents contained the major goals that were worded explicitly to tackle the challenges in the traditional policy areas, such as 'Curriculum & Studies', 'Study & Library Materials', 'Infrastructure', 'Financing' or 'Life-long Learning'.

The observed content of the Estonian HE&R policy papers, explained in details in the forthcoming coming sections, allowed us to make indirect inferences about the process and the steering mechanism that produce such documents. As will be argued in more detail below, the uncoordinated and unstructured time frame of adoption of the policy documents related to tertiary education at different levels, as well as the number of policy aims, measures and activities in these documents, suggested that this Estonian public policy area cannot be classified into any of Olsen's state steering mechanisms (Olsen, 1988:236–237) but can be better described along the lines of the 'garbage can model' developed by Cohen, March and Olsen (1972).

It must be stressed that this study interpreted policy as a strategic plan and did not consider the politics around it or limit the analysis to the laws related to HE&R. In English there is a clear conceptual difference between the words policy and politics, but no such difference exists in Estonian where both words are '*poliitika*'. To keep the conceptual clarity, whenever the word 'policy' is used in this paper only its English meaning is implied (which in Estonian would correspond to such terms as strategies, development plans or action plans). That is, this paper was about these documents and not about the political struggles or legislation of Estonian HE&R. Furthermore for the sake of clarity that this study concentrated only on the strategic plans advanced at the national level and, hence, left out of the analysis those policy papers that were developed and agreed among the member states of the EU, or the development plans adopted by the particular institutions of HE&R in Estonia.

The paper consists of the following four parts: (i) brief notes on the scholarly literature of HE&R policy-making, (ii) the research method, (iii) a description of the Estonian HE&R policy documents, and (iv) the Estonian HE&R policy process (including the discussion and policy suggestions).

Brief Notes on the Scholarly Literature of Higher Education and Research Policy-Making

Mainstream political science treats policy as an outcome of the formal distribution of power that is determined through free and fair elections in a democratic system. As a result, policy is presented all too often in political science text-books as the outcome of a rational and well-structured process. In these models, labelled the 'rational-comprehensive process' (see e.g. Heineman, Peterson and Rasmussen, 1995:257), the policy process starts with setting the aims, followed by specifying the goals; enumerating the alternative policies; selecting the policy; implementing the chosen policy; and finally, evaluating the policy outcomes, which also serves as preparation for the next policy process. The latter clarifies why some scholars like to present the policy-making and its implementation as cyclical instead of hierarchical and top-down process. In both approaches, the (unnaturally) systematic and well-structured policy process is assumed, which is why this over simplistic view is challenged from various angles.

Political sociology, with its models of democratic pluralism, incrementalism, élitism and bureaucracy, which describe policy as an outcome of the political struggles among the competing interest groups, arguably better captures the empirical reality. Concerning the latter model, Salter and Tapper (1981:87–114), for instance, argue that it is a mistake to assume that the implementing 'state educational apparatus' is itself policy neutral. More specifically, they make the point that the 'struggle over educational policy takes place in a bureaucratic context which is far from passive in its policy preferences, and which, in fact, sets the parameters within which the policy debate is conducted' (Salter and Tapper, 1981:88). Therefore, they support a closer analysis of the role played by the bureaucratic power holders in the educational policy-making process. This is the analytical position taken by Voldemar Tomusk in some of his comments about Estonian HE&R policy. The conclusions of his analysis might be disturbing to some as he is very sceptical about any positive policy impact of an HE&R strategy developed at the national level by the responsible Ministry (see Tomusk, 2004:50) under the influence of the closely related academic oligarchy[3] (see Tomusk, 2003). But since, in the mid-1990s Tomusk was the Head of the Higher Education Division and Acting Director of Higher Education and Research in the Estonian Ministry of Education and is currently the Director of Policy and Evaluation on the Open Society Foundation's International Higher Education Support Program, there is little doubt that he knows something about the Estonian HE&R policy (process) from the comparative perspective[4].

3 A related term, 'oligopoly', has later also been used by Masso and Ukrainski (2009:693) to describe the Estonian competitive project funding for research.

4 Although for different reasons, Tomusk's view on the ineffectiveness of HE&R public policy-making is, interestingly, similar to the assessment of the current Minister of Education and Research, Jaak Aaviksoo, of the Estonian R&D policy from the same time period (when he was still the Rector of the Tartu University). For details, see Aaviksoo (2003).

However, the problem with the otherwise rather realistic models of political sociology is that they seem to assume that policy is identifiable in strategic decisions or in law. More specifically, there is a tendency in the literature about HE&R steering to simplify and to understand the policy as something that can be found in a single strategic document or in a (handful of) legal act(s). This mistake seems to be to do with two interconnected developments: the ambiguous legal position of the 'development plan' type of policy documents within the Estonian legal structure, and the fact that policy deviations and violations bring hardly any sanctions on those who simply ignore it or who pursue strategic goals determined independently and outside the formal policy-making framework. In fact, it was not until the end of 2005, when the Estonian Government (2005) introduced the Governmental Regulation no. 302 which classified the different types of strategic development plans and set out the procedures for their drafting, revision, implementation, evaluation and reporting, that there was legal regulation for strategic planning in Estonia. Before this, Keit Kasemets (2006), the former Director of Strategy of the State Chancellery (i.e. the Government Office), responsible for the coordination of the policy drafting and implementation at the highest level in Estonia[5] considers that the lack of legal regulation led to a situation where a large number of strategies were approved at various levels, with hardly anyone caring whether the goals were consistent with each other, if the content duplicated another strategic document or if there was any money for implementation. Heli Aru (2001, 1.4), who later became the Advisor to the Minister of Education and Research, considers that in addition to the public policy decisions, approved at different levels, being in conflict with one another to a greater or lesser extent, it was not uncommon to work actively against orders, to take up an inactive 'wait and see' position, or to consciously ignore or distort their meaning in areas where the policies affected many organisations.

The current understanding of policy instruments seems to be largely limited to understanding policy as mandates and rules (i.e. legal regulations) as the primary (if not the only) elements. Although there are some important exceptions, such as the review of Estonian tertiary education policy undertaken by the OECD (see Huisman et al., 2007), in most cases, both locally and internationally, there is a tendency to limit the study and analysis of policy to the legal aspects. Indeed, some of the most active tertiary education policy researchers in Estonia as well as in Europe take the approach that limits policy analysis to legal regulations. Among the local observers, Aaviksoo (2001:27)

5 For a more detailed discussion of the problems related to the strategic planning and policy process, including the impact assessment, at the national level in Estonia see Pruks (2000), Kasemets, K. (2006 and 2009), PRAXIS (2008), Kasemets A. (2006 and 2009) as well as Järve and Võrk (2009).

emphasises, and the Estonian Ministry of Education and Research (2006:5–8) reports, that Estonian HE&R policy developments are only about formal legal changes. Even the afore-mentioned Tomusk, a well-read and widely travelled expert of tertiary education, a critical intellectual, who is not influenced by local funding, institutional or political pressures, takes a legalistic perspective in his principle publications on Estonian tertiary education policy (see Tomusk, 1996, 2001). More recently, Vilgats (2008) has continued within the same analytic frame and complained about the wide use but little conceptual clarification of the term 'quality' in Estonian legislation, which regulates tertiary education. Within the international context, the legalistic approach has also been followed in the pan-European policy studies on tertiary education that have been directed by Velt, Füssel, and Neave (1996), CHEPS Consortium (2006) as well as de Boer and File (2009).

Although limiting policy studies to legal aspects conforms to developments in Estonia[6], where strategy documents can easily be ignored unless they take the form of mandates or formal rules, one should not disregard the different types of policy documents that have been adopted. Indeed, Estonian multidimensional HE&R policy deserves to be analysed and understood because it is one of the key strategies that should secure the transfer of the country to a knowledge-based society and economy. As the OECD (2001:191) review of Estonian tertiary education policy emphasises:

> The challenge for Estonia – as it is for all OECD Member countries – is to establish the means for nation-wide strategic direction for higher education – while at the same time supporting a highly decentralised, flexible and responsive network of institutions. Higher education is perhaps the most important national resource for developing the human and intellectual resources of a small country to compete in the global economy.

To make sense of the many and varied HE&R strategies, adopted at different levels and time periods, we needed to undertake a systematic overview of all of the policy documents that have been developed to steer Estonian HE&R. To conceptualise the processes that lead to these documents we needed to look beyond the theoretical frames of mainstream political science and public administration about the policy-making and its implementation. As will be suggested below, the 'garbage can model' developed by Cohen et al. (1972) is more appropriate than the traditional steering mechanisms developed for Western democracies. Although it was initially proposed for conceptualising decision making in complex organisations, such as universities, it has recently been employed

6 As the current Chief Justice of the Supreme Court of the Republic of Estonia, states: 'There is no politics outside the law and no law outside politics' (Rask, 1998:167).

more widely to describe the irrational nature of the policy-making process (see Peters, 2005 for details) by showing that rather than policy problems looking for solutions, it is policies that are looking for problems to solve.

It could be expected that within the 'garbage can model' all political or institutional interests can find support within the existing strategies. Within this context, it is not surprising to learn that the Estonian Ministry of Finance's (2007) 'Proposal for the Method of Selecting the Aims and Indicators', originating from the framework of normative thinking about policy-making as a 'rational-comprehensive process,' is hardly followed in the Estonian HE policy process. Instead of the systematic evaluation-planning-execution-evaluation cycle we can expect to find that Estonian HE&R policy has been developed and implemented on an ad hoc basis. More specifically, given the abundance of the Estonian HE&R policy documents, we can expect in line with the thesis statement of the 'garbage can model' that at some level they contain aspects, which can be used to support or even justify almost any political agenda or proposal for changes.

Research Method

In order (i) to find out what the Estonian HE&R policy consists of, (ii) to learn to what extent it follows the above mentioned Estonian Ministry of Finance's (2007) 'Proposal for the Method of Selecting the Aims and Indicators' and (iii) to investigate what kind of process (steering mechanism) produces (i) and (ii), a policy study has been undertaken. Based on Hogwood and Gunn (1981), who distinguish between different kinds of policy studies (study of policy content, study of policy process, study of policy outputs, and evaluation) and policy analysis (evaluation, information for policy-making, process advocacy and policy advocacy), this research aimed to describe the substance of the multi-dimensional HE&R policy in Estonia and identify its steering mechanism. The assumption was that the analysis of the structure of and interrelationships between the different HE&R related strategy papers reflected the policy-making process and studying the content of these documents allowed us to identify the type of the steering mechanism that is being used in Estonian HE&R policy implementation.

To achieve the research aims we undertook a systematic review of the Estonian HE&R policy documents particularly looking at their goals, measures, activities and metrics, and we used methodological tools developed for meta-analysis. As far as possible with this kind of meta-study, we followed the QUOROM[7] quality

7 This acronym stands for The Quality of Reporting of Meta-analyses. For details, see Moher et al. (1999).

standard, which specifies the criteria for conducting systematic overviews. The authors of the QUORUM standard, Moher et al. (1999), state that the meta-analysis has to be sufficiently detailed and include specific information, from objectives to data collection, and review methods as well as reporting the results and including a discussion section. For instance, it has to be explicit about the research aim (question), the inclusion and exclusion criteria of the selection of the primary studies (in this case the policy documents), data abstraction methods used and processes followed. As for the sampling, which is the basis of data collection and meta-analysis, a summary of the selection and exclusion process in the form of a flowchart has to be provided. In the final discussion section, in addition to summarising the main results and validity threats, which might lead to different interpretations of the results, suggestions should also be made for future research. To meet the QUOROM's requirements and make the methodological choices transparent, the following sections give details of the aim, population, sampling, data collection and analysis.

Population and Sampling

An aim of the systematic review was to map what the Estonian HE&R policy consists of and clarify to what extent the goals mentioned in the strategic documents met the criteria of the Estonian Ministry of Finance (2007). To do this all the valid Estonian state policy documents (including the national strategies, development and implementation plans) that are directly applicable to HE&R were collected. Although it is often almost impossible to collect all of the existing documents (Cooper and Lindsay, 1998), an attempt was made to compose the complete sample in this systematic overview. As an absolute minimum, the searching methods and selection criteria should enable the identification of all of the important policy documents for steering Estonian HE, together with the goals, measures and actions, as well as the metrics used for the evaluation. The sample was considered to be representative once the saturation point had been reached – recognition that additional data collection and analysis does not lead to new or additional findings about Estonian HE&R policy documents. The inclusion and exclusion criteria should be explicitly stated as this allows other researchers to validate the analysis (King, 1995) or update the results (Patrick et al., 2004).

As new policy documents are often added and existing ones updated before they expire, a clear search window had to be set. Given the time when the data collection was undertaken, to be included in the analysis the policy document had to be in effect on 27.04.2009 and because the state registry that should include all of the national strategies and their implementation plans did not exist, the sample frame had to be composed by the author following the logic of snowball sampling. First, the list of the existing development plans available on the website of the State Chancellery was compared to that of the Estonian Ministry of Education and Research and the Estonian Ministry of Economic Affairs and Communications. On 27.04.2009 the State Chancellery listed 134 public policy documents, the Estonian Ministry of Education and Research 51 and the Estonian Ministry of Economic Affairs and Communications 22. Altogether this meant 207 strategic documents and from these 162 remained after duplicates were excluded. The titles and the author's prior knowledge enabled the identification of 27 documents from the sample frame, which were directly relevant to HE&R. However, the initial analysis showed that some of these 27 documents did not fit into the sample either because they had expired (n=8) or because they were still in the process of development (n=2). Also, a decision was made to exclude the Academic Programme for Teaching Estonian Language and Culture Abroad (2005–2010) because it represents one of the programs that Estonian Ministry of Education and Research has developed to implement specific tasks of the HE&R policy[8]. So, the total number of policy documents was therefore 16 which were grouped into 12 policy sets (see Appendix 1) in order to avoid double counting strategies and their implementation plans.

The sample was checked again while undertaking the meta-analysis. The list was sent to Tiina Annus, Head of the Analysis Department, and her colleagues at the Estonian Ministry of Education and Research on 12.05.2009. As they did not suggest any additions, it was concluded that the saturation point had been reached in the sampling. However, it was discovered later, when an attempt was made to collect the evaluation reports of the policies that had been implemented for a sufficient amount of time, that the 'Estonian e-Learning Strategy in Vocational and Higher Education 2007–2012' cannot be referred to as a strategic document. Similarly, neither can the document entitled 'National higher education program on ICT "Tiger university+" (2009–2012)', which was approved by the board of the Estonian Information Technology Foundation, be viewed as an official policy document. Both documents concerned semi-private policy initiatives (Aru, 2009) and were, therefore, excluded from the sample. Furthermore, taking into account that not all of the remaining policy documents dealt solely with HE, the sample was further refined by filtering out from the strategies only

8 There is no publicly available list of programs implemented by either or both the Estonian Ministry Education and Research and its policy implementing agencies. The HE&R policy documents analysed in detail in this paper mention 20 different programs among the planned activities. At least six of these programs are also mentioned among the 34 programs implemented by the Archimedes Foundation from the EU Structural Funds. (For details, see Archimedes Foundation, 2012).

the components that were directly related to HE&R. In the process of doing so, it also turned out that in two instances the specific objectives, measures and actions related to HE&R were only specified at the level of the implementation plan[9] or programmes[10]. Therefore, the National Strategy for the use of Structural Funds 2007–2013, and Estonian Integration Strategy 2008–2013 were left out from the sample, or to be more precise, included only through their implementation plans or programmes. The final list of policy papers (N=12) that were included in the meta-analysis is listed in the Table 1 and their exact components that relate directly to HE&R are given in Appendix 2. In order to provide a schematic picture of the sampling process, the following flowchart suggested by the QUOROM statement was created.

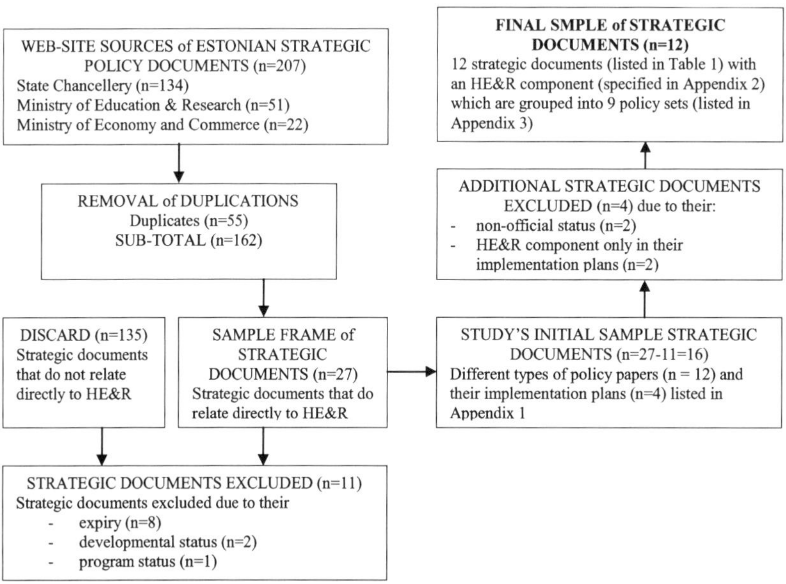

Figure 1. Sampling of the Estonian Higher Education and Research (HE&R) policy documents

Composed by the author

---

9 An element of the Estonian Integration Strategy 2008–2013 and its implementation plan for 2008–2010.

10 Elements of the National Strategy for the use of Structural Funds 2007–2013 and its Operational Programme for Human Resource Development, CCI number: 2007EE051-PO001.

Data Collection

Data collection from the Estonian HE&R policy documents (with the special emphasis on their goals, measures, activities and metrics) followed the procedures identified by Forster (2006:91) who divides the *modus operandi* of document research into five stages: (i) securing access, (ii) controlling for authenticity, (iii) understanding documents, (iv) evaluating (the usability) of data and (v) further application (actual analysis) of data. Access to the data was secured in several stages of data collection and went hand-in-hand with the specification of the population and use of the selected (snowballing) sampling procedure, as described in detail in the previous section. Checking the authenticity of the documents did not present a major challenge. In the case of the policy documents that required the approval of parliament or the government, the electronic version of the State Gazette was used. This ensured that the final and valid version of the document was used for the analysis. In the case of the development plans, it was assumed that the versions available through the websites of the State Chancellery and the Estonian Ministry of Education and Research were the most recent and valid versions of the documents[11].

The first step in undertaking the systematic overview of the Estonian HE&R policy documents with special emphasis on the goals, metrics and data sources was the compilation of a separate factsheet (an overview table) on each of the policy sets listed in Appendix 1[12]. In addition to the basic information (such as the title, author(s), responsible ministry, contacts, source and its reference, date of issue and expiry, type of policy document, the concentration on HE and parts that were included in the analysis) an attempt was made to abstract the following information from the documents whenever available: (i) major goal(s); (ii) subgoal(s); (iii) measure/course of action; and (iv) activities. In addition, whenever possible components relating to all of these (i–iv) were registered: indicators/metrics and method of measurement, base-lines of measurement, intended results, and data sources.

In the second stage of data collection we had to overcome the challenges of understanding the data. The first had to do with the language and our interpretation abilities (Scott, 2006:32). As all of the documents were fairly recent and written in Estonian, this did not present a challenge such as those faced by

11 Although this may sound trivial, the National Audit Office (2008:11–13) reports that the working versions of the documents can be misleading, not only for the auditors but also for the Ministry.

12 During the course of data collection, some policies were eliminated from the analysis for the reasons mentioned in the previous section. The final list of policy sets, about which an overview Table was composed, is listed in Appendix 3.

scholars working on historic documents in foreign, extinct or dead languages. However, the interpretation of the policy documents' basic terminology (such as goals, expected results, measures, and courses of actions) was not always very easy.

As Scott (2006:39) highlights, there are three aspects of the understanding of the text: (i) intended content – what the author wanted to say; (ii) received content – how readers understood it; and (iii) internal meaning – semiotic meaning of the text. In other words, one should not forget, according to Scott (2006), the reasons why the text was formed and the identity of the intended reader. The fact should not be ignored that the objective meaning of the text is actually wider than the one intended by the author. Although the various authors of the HE&R policy documents use different terminology, the (intended) meaning can be expected to be rather similar. The opposite also occurs – despite the use of the same concepts and terms in the strategy papers, the anticipated meaning of these by the authors in the given context differs. So, it is imperative to get a good sense of the context, otherwise it is difficult to understand the intended meaning. To overcome these challenges, we double-checked our interpretation of the terminology with the authors of the implementation plans as well as evolutions, whenever they were available[13]. This additional data collection effort enabled us to harmonize our interpretation of the terminology used in the policy documents with respect to the following aspects: goal(s) at various levels, measures (courses of action) and activities. The re-coding of the components of the strategy is documented in the notes of the Table 2. Last but not least, an effort was made to extract from the policies and the accompanying documents, such as the implementation plans and evaluation reports, the metrics and their data sources.

13 At the time, midterm evaluations were available for the Higher Education Strategy (n=1), Knowledge-based Estonia (n=2), Operational Programme for Human Resource Development (n=1), Integration Strategy (n=1), and Development Strategy of the Estonian Language (n=2).

A Description of the Estonian Higher Education and Research Policy Documents

The fragmentation of Estonian HE&R policy is almost overwhelming – especially given the size of the country and the total number of students enrolled in the institutions of tertiary education. More specifically, there are 12 strategic documents (listed in Table 1) with HE&R components (specified in Appendix 2) which can be grouped into 9 policy sets (listed in Appendix 3). As shown on Table 1, in addition to the five sectoral policies and one implementation plan, relating just to HE&R, there are six other strategic documents, which cover additional public policy issues but include HE&R in Estonia. After elimination of duplicates (because the implementation plans repeat in some cases the content of the strategy that they relate to), we identified in total 22 different major goals and 37 sub-goals, 34 measures[14] and 193 activities[15] related to HE&R in these policy documents. In the following sections the content of the Estonian HE&R policy documents is discussed in more detail.

Using the Governmental Decree no. 302 that differentiates hierarchically between the Central Strategic Plan (CSP), Sectoral Development Plan (SDP) and Organisational Development Plan (ODP), for the classification of the strategy documents listed in the Table 1, it can be concluded that there is a single CSP to steer HE&R, five sectoral policies and one ODP. In addition to these, there are four implementation plans (IP) that coordinate issues relevant to HE&R. Last but not least, a separate programme document has been developed to plan and guide the channelling of EU funds to Estonian HE&R. Although this programme document is difficult to classify into the hierarchical structure of the governmental decree, it was nevertheless included in the sample as the document specifies the very general ideas of the strategy[16] into specific goals, measures and activities (together with their indicators).

Most of the reviewed policy documents, listed in Table 1, were launched quite recently. There were three that started in 2007, five that started in 2008 and four that were put into effect in 2009. The strategic document concerning Estonian language policy was older; they were introduced in 2004. The most important strategy paper in this context – the Estonian Higher Education Policy – was also older; it was approved in November 2006. Of the 12 documents reviewed in this analysis the expiry dates of 3 occurred in 2010, 1 each in 2011

14 There were 40 measures before the obvious duplicates in various policy sets were excluded. See Table 2 and its notes for details.

15 There were 220 activities before the obvious duplicates in various policy sets were excluded. See Table 2 and its notes for details.

16 National Strategy for the use of Structural Funds 2007–2013.

and 2012, 5 in 2013 and 2 in 2015. The point to be made here is that the dates when the policy documents came into effect, as well as when they expire, do not suggest a systematic planning approach. Systematic planning would presuppose that the CSP is set first, along with its major goals, which would be translated into specific goals in the sectoral, organisational and institutional strategies and in the implementation plans. During the period reviewed it appeared that the 'Action Plan for Growth and Jobs' – the state's CSP (of which there are only three) – had been set for the years 2008–2011, while many of the lower level policies were set to last few years longer. For instance, two SDP are in effect until 2013, and another two until 2015, and the ODP until 2012, while the programme document developed for channelling EU funds to HE&R is in effect until 2013. All this suggests that there is a long way to go in Estonian HE&R policy-making to meet the intentions of the Governmental Decree no. 302 which structures the strategic documents approved at different levels of decision-making into different types, and sets a hierarchical relationship between them and determines the procedures for their drafting, revision, implementation, evaluation and reporting.

Table 1. *Strategic Estonian Higher Education and Research (HE&R) policy documents: Central Strategic Plan (CSP), Implementation Plan (IP), Organisational Development Plan (ODP), Sectoral Development Plan (SDP), of the Ministries of: Culture (MoC), Economy and Commerce (MoE&C), Education and Research (MoE&R)*

Name of the policy document	**Respon-sible Ministry**	**Source**	**Starting year**	**Expi-ry year**	**Type of the stra-tegic docu-ment**	**Does this re-late only to HE&R?**	**Included in the review**
Higher Education Strategy	MoE&R	State Gazette	2006	2015	SDP	Yes	Com-pletely
The implementa-tion plan of the Higher Education Strategy	MoE&R	MoE&R, State Chancel-lery	2008	2010	IP	Yes	Com-pletely
Higher education internationalisa-tion strategy	MoE&R	MoE&R	2007	2015	SDP	Yes	Com-pletely
Action Plan for Growth and Jobs	MoE&C MoE&R	State Chancel-lery	2008	2011	CSP	No	Partially
Knowledge-based Estonia	MoE&C MoE&R	State Gazette, MoE&R	2007	2013	SDP	No	Partially
The implementa-tion plan of the Knowledge-based Estonia	MoE&C MoE&R	State Gazette, MoE&R	2009	2013	IP	No	Partially
Estonian Teacher Education Strate-gy	MoE&R	MoE&R	2009	2013	SDP	No	Partially
The implementa-tion plan of the Estonian Teacher Education Strate-gy	MoE&R	MoE&R	2009	2013	IP	No	Partially
Operational Pro-gramme for Hu-man Resource Development	MoE&R	MoE&R	2007	2013	Uncate-go-rizable	No	Partially
Development Strategy of the Estonian Lan-guage	MoE&R	MoE&R, State Chancel-lery	2004	2010	SDP	No	Partially

Table 1. Continued

Name of the policy document	Responsible Ministry	Source	Starting year	Expiry year	Type of the strategic document	Does this relate only to HE&R?	Included in the review
The implementation plan for the Integration Strategy	MoC	State Chancellery	2008	2010	IP	No	Partially
Smart and Active People	MoE&R	MoE&R	2009	2012	ODP	No	Partially

Source: Composed by the author

During the course of data collection the goals, measures, actions and metrics (together with data sources if available) of the Estonian HE policy documents were registered. It is more difficult to count the goals, measures and activities of the Estonian HE&R policies than it may seem at the outset because the actual policy documents use very different styles, structure, terminology and vary greatly in their detail. The documents not only use the preferred terminology style and structure of the authors of the different policy papers, the documents do not use any referencing system, which would allow one to identify how the goals, measures, or actions relate to other strategies. An additional complication is that even the style and structure of different parts of the same policy paper may vary a great deal (like for instance in the case of the Estonian Higher Education Strategy) – reflecting, in all probability that different contributors have authored different parts. Therefore, a great effort was put into producing the overview tables that would describe the policies in the common structure. This allowed counting the frequencies presented in the Table 2 (see the cross-totals for a summary).

A normative policy interpretation would allow one to exclude (automatically) from the total frequency counts the items related to the CSP (Action Plan for Growth and Jobs) and ODP (Smart and Active People). It could be argued that they represent strategies for different hierarchical positions (in the sense of the Government's Decree no. 302) which, if they were in total harmony with the content of all the HE&R related policies and their implementation plans, would lead to the double or triple counting some components of the policy documents. Following this logic, the sub-totals of the Table 2 show the total number of goals, measures and actions in the strategy papers (excluding the items of CPS and ODP). Furthermore, an attempt was made in this analysis to identify the double (or triple) entries individually. As shown in Table 2 and explained in its notes, the results of this exercise allowed us to establish that there are 22 different major goals and 37 sub-goals, 34 measures and 193 actions that relate to HE&R in the selected Estonian policy documents. Altogether this means that there are 286 items that should be measured to assess the progress of the Estonian HE&R strategies. We shall return to this in the section that gives an overview of the metrics employed in Estonian HE&R strategies.

Table 2. The number of Higher Education and Research (HE&R) related goals, measures and activities in the selected Estonian policy documents

Name of the policy document	**Major goals (n)**	**Sub-goals (n)**	**Measures / courses of action (n)**	**Activities (n)**	**Activities – duplicates in the policy & its implementation plan excluded (n)**	**Items to be measured total (n)**
Higher Education Strategy	6	0	4	*45*	(34[a]-32)+(33-32)+32=35	57
The implementation plan of the Higher Education Strategy	0	12		*33*		
Higher education internationalisation strategy	1	3	3	*21*[b]	21	28
Action Plan for Growth and Jobs[c]	2[d]	6	10	*37*	37	55
Knowledge-based Estonia	3	0	4	*36*	36	43
The implementation plan of the Knowledge-based Estonia				*36*		
Estonian Teacher Education Strategy	6[e]	6[f]	6	*32*[g]	(29[h]-18)+(23-18)+18=34	52
The implementation plan of the Estonian Teacher Education Strategy	0	0		*23*[i]		
Operational Programme for Human Resource Development	0	5[j]	4[k]	*8*	8	17
Development Strategy of the Estonian Language	1	1	1	*4*	4	7

Table 2. Continued

Name of the policy document	Major goals (n)	Sub-goals (n)	Measures / courses of action (n)	Activities (n)	Activities – duplicates in the policy & its implementation plan excluded (n)	Items to be measured total (n)
The implementation plan for the Integration Strategy	0	1	0	*0*	0	1
Smart and Active People[l]	3	3[m]	8[n]	*45*[o]	45	59
Cross-total	22	37	40	*321*	220	319
Sub-total (without Action Plan for Growth and Jobs & Smart and Active People)	17	28	22	*239*	138	205
TOTAL (duplicates individually identified & excluded)	**22**	**37**	**34**	*220*	**193**	**286**

[a] Since the implementation plan merges the 15 activities listed under the 2nd field of action of the strategy into 5, and 2 activities listed under the 4th measure into 1, 34 (instead of 45) activities are used in this calculation. [b]Although within the 2nd and 3rd measures (called chapters in the strategy) the activities are also grouped and titled under the common nominators, the figure in the table above includes only the specific actions. [c]This strategy uses the structure which lists aims, sub-goals and measures with no activities. However, the 8th aim groups the measures into 5 categories and subtitles these under the common nominators. For the purposes of this research, the latter were interpreted as courses of action and therefore, the Table lists 10 measures (of which 5 are titled and 5 untitled in the strategy) as well as 37 activities (which are called measures in the strategy). [d]Although the strategy mentions in the introduction 3 measurable goals, there are also 9 aims (of which 2 are directly relevant to HE&R) that are listed in the table of content and are used as the sub-headings/structural components in the strategy. The figure in the table above refers to the latter. [e]These major goals are called 'strategic visions' in the strategy. [f]These sub-goals are called 'aims' in the strategy. [g]The strategy lists these under the courses of action as sub-measures. [h]In one instance the implication plan merged 2 actions mentioned in the strategy into 1, in another instance 3 were merged into 1 and in the third instance only a third of the action mentioned in the strategy was mentioned in the implementation plan. Therefore, 29 (instead of 32) activities are used in this calculation. [i]The operational programme calls these 'goals/actions'. [j]These are aims attached to the 'priority directions' in the operational programme. [k]The implementation plan calls these 'priority directions'. [l]This strategy uses a structure which identifies 3 general goals and 4+1 'fields of activity', to which sub-goals (called strategic aims) along with the indicators and measures (divided further into sub-measures and sub-sub-measures) are related. Basically these 4 fields of activity should cover the strategies that MoE&R is responsible for. [m]These relate to the aims of the 'fields of activity' that have a HE&R component in the strategy. [n]These are listed as sub-measures under specific measures in the strategy. [o]These are listed as sub-sub-measures in the strategy.

Source: Data collated by the author

In order to get a better idea of the content of the Estonian HE&R policy papers, the data was recoded, allowing the same major goal, sub-goal or measure to be classified into more than one category (i.e. major policy theme listed in the first column of Table 3). Multiple entries were allowed because the Estonian HE&R policy documents have been worded so that each of its functional component (such as aim, measure or action) may include more than one suggestion about the strategic direction of the specific policy item. Table 3 shows the results of the recoding by listing the frequencies of Estonian HE&R strategy in different policy themes[17]. The fact that the 'Knowledge Based Society/Economy' came up as the most frequent category within the major goals was to be expected by anyone familiar with the Estonian context. Yet, the finding that indicates 'Access & Equity' as the second most frequent category within the Estonian HE&R policy documents while important categories within HE&R policy studies and public discussions, such as 'Curriculum & Studies,' 'Study & Library Materials,' 'Infrastructure,' 'Financing' and 'Life-long Learning' remained completely empty at the major goals level of all of the strategic documents. The case of 'Life-long Learning' can be explained by the fact that a separate strategy was being developed, but it was surprising that during the period reviewed here traditionally central HE&R policy issues were not prioritised in Estonian HE&R policy documents. Moreover, the effects of the major infrastructure developments, as well as the reform of HE&R funding and the introduction of learning outcome-based curricula have been characterizing the internal life of many HE&R institutions in recent years. But as the effects have impacted without having any explicit prioritization in the national strategies at the level of major goals, they reflect that these themes might be seen as means rather than ends of the policy. In addition to the 'Knowledge Based Society/Economy', HE&R polices place a lot of emphasis on the 'Curriculum & Studies,' 'Students (including doctoral students),' and 'Quality' at the level of sub-goals, as shown on Table 3. On the basis that 'Quality' and the 'Knowledge Based Society/Economy' appeared at the sub-goal level amongst the most frequent categories reflects that these policy themes have been introduced and used in Estonian policy discussions as imperatives that no right-minded individual should oppose[18]. Also, similar to the major-goals, 'Study & Library Materials,' 'Infrastructure' and 'Financing' get very little attention at the level of sub-goals.

17 It was not practical to list the exact content of the classifications. However, these lists that contain all the Estonian HE&R policy goals, sub-goals and measures in different categories, are available upon request.

18 For a critical discussion concerning the 'Quality' theme within the West European context see Neave (1994) and concerning the 'Knowledge Society' theme within the East European context see Tomusk (2004:145–166).

At the measures level, the most frequent categories were 'System Management of Higher Education, R&D and Innovation' as well as 'Curriculum & Studies' while the courses of action that could be associated with 'Study & Library Materials,' 'Estonian Language & Culture' as well as 'Access & Equity' proved to be the least frequent themes. Last but not least, at the level of actions it was interesting to learn that after most frequent category after the 'Curriculum & Studies', with which actions could be associated, came 'Financing,' followed by 'Research & Development,' 'Internationalization,' and 'System Management of Higher Education, R&D as well as Innovation.'

Table 3. Priorities of the Estonian Higher Education and Research Policy Documents

Policy Category	**Major goals (n)**	**Sub-goals (n)**	**Measures (n)***	**Activities (n)***	**Total (n)***
1. Curriculum & Studies	0	9	11 (11)	55 (56)	75 (76)
2. Research & Development (R&D)	2	5	6 (9)	44 (55)	57 (71)
3. Internationalization	3	5	3 (3)	42 (47)	53 (58)
4. Faculty & Scientists	1	3	2 (4)	20 (23)	26 (31)
5. Students (including doctoral students)	1	8	5 (7)	31 (33)	45 (49)
6. System Management of Higher Education, R&D as well as Innovation	1	5	10 (12)	42 (49)	58 (67)
7. Study & Library Materials	0	0	0 (0)	9 (11)	9 (11)
8. Infrastructure	0	2	3 (3)	17 (19)	22 (24)
9. Financing	0	1	4 (4)	49 (57)	54 (62)
10. Estonian Language & Culture	3	3	1 (1)	13 (14)	20 (21)
11. Access & Equity	4	6	1 (1)	11 (13)	22 (24)
12. Quality (including both Higher Education and Research & Development)	3	8	3 (3)	23 (26)	37 (40)
13. Knowledge Based Society/ Economy	6	9	7 (9)	32 (40)	54 (64)
14. Life-long Learning	0	5	2 (3)	15 (17)	22 (25)
15. Other	8	6	6 (6)	27 (32)	47 (52)

Source: Data collated by the author

* *Number in the brackets reflects the frequencies before duplicates were individually identified and excluded*

These results show that there was not a single theme that is systematically well represented among all the strategy components – aims, measures and actions – in Estonian HE&R policy documents. More specifically, 'Curriculum & Studies' and 'Knowledge Based Society/Economy' came closest but the former had no emphasis on the level of major goals while the latter was moderately represented at the level of actions. However, 'Study & Library Materials' as well as 'Estonian Language & Culture' were quite systematically under-represented in all of the policy components. Examining the total scores, the 'System Management of Higher Education, R&D as well as Innovation' and the 'Research & Development (R&D)' themes come out as the most frequently identifiable themes in Estonian HE&R policies after the 'Curriculum & Studies'. HE&R 'Financing' is mentioned largely only at the level of actions, which explains its quite high overall frequency – equal to that of 'Knowledge Based Society/Economy'. The least frequently mentioned themes amongst the functional components of the Estonian HE&R policy papers are the 'Study & Library Materials' and 'Access & Equity'. Although it would be interesting to learn how well these policy prioritisations correspond with the state financing decisions about the resources originating either from Estonian or EU taxpayers. The aspect that is important within this analysis is that this looks like a 'garbage can model' of policy-making and implementation. This is so, because not one theme was completely neglected, which leaves the real possibility of picking from the abundance of policy documents and their strategy components any references, which support the desired agenda. We shall return to this issue in the section that discusses the Estonian HE&R policy process and makes suggestions for improvement.

Overview of the Indicators Employed in Estonian Higher Education and Research Policy Documents

The systematic overview of the Estonian HE&R policy papers was partly also undertaken in order to learn the extent to which the strategy documents met the expectations of the Estonian Ministry of Finance's memorandum entitled the 'Proposal for the Method of Selecting the Aims and Indicators' (04.06.2007). This document set out the criteria according to which each aim mentioned in the policy document should be related at least to one indicator and introduced their classification into impact, result and outcome indicators along with the required information about the description of the metric, data source, their base-lines and target values. As shown in Table 2 in the form of cross totals, there were 22 major goals, 37 sub-goals, 40 measures, 220 activities before excluding the duplicates of different polices and after excluding the ones present both in the strategy and in its implementation plan. This means that there were 319 strategy components (including the goals, sub-goals, measures and activities) that could or should be measured. Out of these 22 major goals, 7 can be associated with intended descriptive results or indicators revealed in the strategy documents or in their implementation plans. The corresponding frequencies were sub-goals – 37 and 22; measures – 34 and 11; activities – 193 and 154. In total, 194 components, of the 286, were equipped with at least one indicator. So, roughly two-thirds of all the measurable policy components can be associated with intended descriptive results or metrics (statistic for measurement) in the Estonian HE&R strategy documents. But the gap between what the Estonian Ministry of Finance's memorandum intended to achieve and the reality of the HE&R policy documents could easily be even larger. Particularly, if it is taken into account that the rate was improved by merging the content of the strategies and their implementation plans as well as interpreting the intended descriptive results (if provided) as indicators. But the fact that the metric has been identified does not say anything about the appropriateness of the selected method of measurement or indicator[19].

Furthermore, as it is easiest to register whether or not an activity took place, it is not surprising that in absolute numbers, impact was most frequently measured at the level of activities. Unfortunately, more often than not, the indicators were not classified into outcome, result or impact indicators. Excluding the multiple metrics that were proposed to measure the same goal, measure or activity, 186 of the 194 indicators listed in the Estonian HE&R policy documents were unclassified. Last but not least, there is not much to report about the method of measurement, base-lines of measurement, intended results, or data sources as, in the vast majority of cases, these were simply left unspecified. The only exceptions to this trend are the 'Action Plan for Growth and Jobs', and 'Knowledge-based Estonia', which made the base-line measurements and the intended results explicit. Also the 'Operational Programme for Human Resource Development' stood out as a strategy paper, which had disclosed detailed information about the outcome, result or impact indicators for the planned actions. But generally speaking there was much to be desired in the Estonian HE&R policy papers with respect to the measures. This confirmed the truth of the OECD expert team's impression that in Estonian tertiary education 'policy evaluation studies seem to be sporadic' (Huisman et al., 2007:38), as well as Aru's (2009) comment that the Estonian Ministry of Education and Research has been investing its energy in the development and implementation of the policy documents rather than in the evaluation.

19 See PRAXIS (2008) as well as Järve and Võrk (2009) on this issue.

The fragmentation of policy, on the one hand, and the abundance of strategic documents coordinated by the Estonian Ministry of Education and Research, on the other, was noticeable even in comparison with other ministries in Estonia. Keit Kasemets (2006:61) finds that, among Estonian ministries, the Estonian Ministry of Education and Research is often given as an example of policymaking practice that has developed a separate strategy for each sub-field. Unfortunately, comparative statistics about the number of policy documents steering HE&R in other countries were not readily available as the mapping initiatives of the national policies at the EU level, such as Velt et al. (1996), CHEPS Consortium (2006) and de Boer and File (2009), are limited to meeting legal requirements; they offered few relevant points of comparison. To identify all the effective HE&R policy documents of a country (together with their aims, measures, actions and so forth) is a separate and labour-intensive research task, as this paper about Estonian HE&R shows.

Furthermore, because the strategy documents of Estonian HE&R hardly meet the expectations of the memorandum of the Estonian Ministry of Finance (2007), the results of the overview indicated a more general shortcoming in public policy development and measurement in Estonia. That is, the systematic overview added to the findings of Pruks (2000), Kasemets K. (2006, 2009), Kasemets A. (2006, 2009), and Järve and Võrk (2009:16) about the problems relating to strategic planning, setting objectives and conducting policy measurements at the state level generally, as well as the National Audit Office's (2008:12) and PRAXIS's (2008:19–21) observations about the limitations of the Estonian HE&R policy, more specifically.

The Estonian Higher Education and Research Policy Process – Discussion as well as Policy Suggestions

In order to make indirect inferences about the policy process (i.e. to identify its steering mechanism) that produced the observed characteristics of the Estonian HE&R policy documents, in this section policy-making in a broader theoretical context was analysed and some policy lessons that could be learned from this exercise were suggested.

The observed tendency in the literature on the HE&R policy studies, to limit the analysis just to the mandates (legal regulations), has hampered the quality of research and its results. McDonnell and Elmore (1987) identify five possible mechanisms of intervention – mandates (rules), inducements (money/ procurement), capacity-building (money/investments) and system-changing (authority) – but such a broad spectrum of possible policy instruments has hardly been used in HE&R policy studies. Rather, Clark's (1983:143) triangle of coordination, which models the governance of different national systems of tertiary education as a mixture of three powers of integration, has dominated the HE&R research field internationally. These three forces of integration are: state authority, academic oligarchy and market. While the first dominated the steering mechanism in the USSR, the second in Italy, and third in the US, Clark suggests that all other countries have mixed their own cocktails from these three components for governing their higher education systems.

Indeed, Clark's heritage is profound, even if the leading European scholars do not find his model sophisticated enough to capture the complexity of contemporary systems of tertiary education and their governance mechanisms. For instance, it serves as the basis of the analysis put forward by van Vught (1989), Neave and van Vught (1991), Maassen and van Vught (1994) and Gornitzka and Maassen (2000) on the comparative analysis of West European tertiary education and its steering, as well as the diagnosis of the Eastern European higher education system made by Tomusk (1997 and 2004:89–104). Commonly, they all suggest, along the lines of Neave (1998), that Clark's triangle of coordination is too simplistic to capture the complexities of the socio-economic and political realities of the higher education systems in different countries. Therefore, a number of the above-mentioned authors, such as Maassen and van Vught (1994), as well as Gornitzka and Maassen (2000), suggest the use of the typology of state steering models, developed by Olsen (1988:236–242). Olsen identifies on a theoretical basis, (using assumptions about the rationality of actors/role of the environment and method of conflict resolution/values), the following four 'ideal types': (i) the sovereign, rationality-bounded steering model; (ii) the institutional steering model; (iii) the corporate-pluralist steering model; and (iv) the state supermarket model (classical liberal state). Gornitzka and Maassen's (2000:270–272) interpretation of these models for the higher education policy context is summarised in Table 4.

Table 4. Main characteristics of Higher Education (HE) governance and steering models

Characteristic / Steering model	**The sovereign, rationality-bounded**	**The institutional**	**The corporate-pluralist**	**The supermarket model**
Relationship between state & HE institution is based on	State's direct intervention & tight control over HE	Shared understanding between élite universities	Multiple interest groups & centres of authority	State withdrawal & market coordination
HE institution accountable to/for	Political authorities	Protecting academic values & traditions	Stakeholder society	?
HE institution assessed on the basis of	Political effectiveness	Effects on the structure of meanings & norms	Meeting the interests of the members of the stakeholder society	Efficiency, economy, flexibility & survival
Interaction rules between state & HE	Superior (state) – subordinate (HE)	Non-interference	Dependent on the power relationships between stakeholders as the legislative & executive power of the state reduced & authority / control shared with others.	State takes the role of a bookkeeper & 'night-watchman' – making sure that the market mechanism runs smoothly
Social participation through	'Numerical channel'	-	Organised interest groups	Market action
Decision-making	Centralised & top-down	Specialised & traditionalist	Negotiation & consultation	Individual
Steering	Hierarchical	Isolated / protected from political and market forces as well as short term interest of interest groups	Segmented & dominated by clusters of interest groups	Minimal & limited to self-regulating capacity of the market
Main policy arena	'The parliamentary chain of command' – elected assemblies & neutral but politically loyal civil service	Dominated by élite universities leaders	Corporate network of public boards, councils & commissions	Non-existent (because of extreme decentralisation)

Table 4. Continued

Characteristic / Steering model	The sovereign, rationality-bounded	The institutional	The corporate-pluralist	The supermarket model
Goal setting by	Majority rule	Élite universities leaders	All members of the stakeholder society	Stakeholders of the market that have 'earned' their position because of the resources they have available
Basis of the HE autonomy	Governmental overload which leaves 'technical' decisions for HE inst.	Shared norms of non-interference	Negotiations – result of a distribution of interests & power	Depends on their ability to survive
Typical organizational form of HE institution	An agency embedded in a governmental hierarchy	'Independent court' embedded in a moral order	Not harmonised as there is little co-ordination across policy sub-systems	Corporation embedded in a competitive market
Change as a result of	Changes in political leadership	Historical processes & evolution	Changes in power, interests & alliances	Changes or stability of the environment

Source: Gornitzka and Maassen (2000:270–272)

In a similar way to research on welfare regimes, the above-described typology has attracted some scholars, such as van Heffen, Verhoeven and de Wit (1999), as well as Gornitzka and Maassen (2000), to compare and contrast countries by classifying them into the corresponding categories. Another similarity between the higher education governance literature and the research on welfare regimes are the limits of how the typology can be applied, as it was originally developed for classifying the Western democracies, to consider the countries of Central and Eastern Europe and the former Soviet Union. Indeed, as the summarised Olsen models and their reinterpretations for the higher education sector indicate, none of the models describe Estonian tertiary education policy well enough. While Estonian higher education policy is part of the more general neoliberal agenda (see Laar, 1996) that has been pursued throughout the post-communist era, and it might seem to fit with most of the features of the above summarised state supermarket model at first glance, it actually does not describe the complexity of the approach used to steer Estonian HE&R. Far from being totally decentralised, its governance partially resembles the sovereign, rationality-bounded steering model. More specifically, in terms of political leadership and public (including EU) funds, the Estonian government, together with its Estonian Higher Education Quality Agency and various commissions, has an increasing will to intervene, as well as the power to do so. It should also be clear to anyone familiar with Estonian HE&R, which policy-making and distribution of research funding has been described as oligopolistic (Tomusk, 2003; Huisman et al., 2007:48, 72; and Masso and Ukrainski, 2009:693), that some of its institutions are more equal than others, as reflected, for instance, by having their own laws passed by parliament[20] in order to regulate their relationships with the state or to protect their special status or to do both. In this context it is not surprising that their leaders have an important role in the policy arena, from agenda setting to political leadership in the implementation of reforms – far beyond the intimate relationship between élite institutions and government that is suggested by the institutional steering model.

Furthermore, it would also be incorrect to say that Estonia has been totally immune to the long-term developments in some of the Western higher education systems, which have increased the role of the stakeholder society in steering the tertiary education systems there (see Neave, 2002) as suggested by the corporate-pluralist model. For instance, Estonian universities have been asked to describe their relationships with their stakeholder societies in the on-going institutional assessments[21]. Likewise, 'the importance of the research theme to science and to the economy and culture of Estonia and the EU, including its conformity with national strategic development plans' (Estonian Research Council, 2012:2) is one of the six aspects, about which applicants for the highly competitive institutional research funding are expected to supply information. The socio-economic and cultural relevance of research is also criteria according to which local evaluators should assess and which the expert panel should take into account in their funding decisions in Estonia[22]. Last but not least, the state has been looking for ways to increase the relevance of HE&R to the economy (and possibly to escape from the institutional pressures), by selecting priority areas for

20 There are two institutions in Estonia, which have their own laws: The University of Tartu and The National Institute of Chemical Physics and Biophysics (for details see University of Tartu Act, and National Institute of Chemical Physics and Biophysics Act).

21 This seems to be a response to OECD reviews that strongly expressed concern about the lack of social relevance and role of the stakeholder society in Estonian tertiary education (see Huisman et al., 2007, 3.8, 4.8 and 5.8). Unfortunately, what has been copied as a result of international policy transfer to the strategic documents at the national level in Estonia, reflects little comprehension of why HE&R needs to be socially relevant and how to achieve that aim (see e.g. Estonian Higher Education Quality Agency 2011, 7.4 – including the Evaluation Criteria and Indicators in the Appendix). The result of the policy transfer ridicules the idea behind the stakeholder society while the actual Estonian HE&R policy-making continues to take 'place informally and formally within a small network of higher education stakeholders' (Huisman et al., 2007:72).

22 For details see Estonian Research Council (2012 – especially the V.5).

HE&R funding, which in alphabetical order are: biotechnology, energy technology, ICT and material technology[23]. As if this was not sufficiently concentrating HE&R funds to the selected sectors[24], a recent action has replaced the Minister, as the head of the Commission distributing government-commissioned study places for tertiary education in Estonia. The replacement is a corporate representative – Tarmo Kriis, who also chairs The Estonian Employers' Confederation. Critics may interpret Kriis' first public statement that institutions of higher education, despite the threat to academic autonomy, have been given too much freedom to open study programmes and accept (fee paying) students (Estonian Public Broadcasting, 2011). Nevertheless, as a Commission is only now being reformed in Estonia indicates more about the historical roots of higher education financing (an inherited system still exhibiting features of a planned economy) than about the government's attempt to correct the market failures[25]. This practice does not understand the nature of market failures nor tries to find fixes (that would allow the Estonian higher education steering system to be classified under the classical liberal model, referred above as the supermarket model). Instead, this interventionist practice looks much more like market distortion, if not government failure, as the National Audit Office (2008) report to parliament suggests. Indeed, as Huisman et al. (2007:42) point out in their review of

23 These are the priority areas mentioned in several strategy documents. In addition to these, Minister Aaviksoo says that environmental protection and public health are also priorities (see Sõerunurk, 2011). Indeed, in addition to the fact that 'Knowledge Biased Estonia' mentions explicitly only three focus areas (all but the energy technology mentioned above), it also lists three national R&D programs. One of these is for the three focus areas, one for solving the socio-economic problems (among which energy, defense, health-care and welfare, environmental protection and information society are mentioned as examples), and finally one for Estonian national culture, language, history and nature as well as Estonian statehood.

24 Minister Aaviksoo makes such a comment in his interview to Sõerunurk (2011).

25 Legal changes that have been passed by the Estonian Parliament on 10.05.2012 and signed by the President on 21.05.2012 (i.e. the Act of Changing the University Act, Institutions of Professional Higher Education Act and Other Acts), will introduce fundamental changes to Estonian higher education funding starting from 2013 but the immediate and long-term impacts of this reform on EH&R remain ambiguous for the time being. One the one hand, it remains to be seen how the institutions of higher education will solve the market failures (including the asymmetric information problems in which their strategic interest are contrary to students) in the new funding and contractual relationship with the state. On the other hand, numerous concerns have been expressed in the press that this reform will make together with the new system for the science funding (that is already in the first face of introduction) some disciplines extinct in Estonia, (for an example of such a concern see Estonian Association of Sociologists, 2012).

the current funding mechanism, due to expire in 2012, there are two key issues. First, the misunderstanding of the modern 'knowledge' economy in Estonian policy-making in general, and secondly the public funding focus on the allocation of state commissioned study places to the 'hard sciences' (while giving inadequate emphasis on the service sector).

All these deviations from the ideal types indicate that Estonian HE&R policy does not resemble any of the governance or steering mechanisms summarised in Table 4. That is, these models do not capture the richness of its policy, even if produced just for political consumption, or even if the Estonian Ministry of Education and Research lacks the capacity to implement these strategies and the institutions are allowed to do as they please (Tomusk, 1996, 2001; Sutrop, 2003:4) without being accountable either to the state or to the wider stakeholder society (Tomusk, 2004:50).

The difficulty of categorising an empirical case into one of the ideal types could be associated with the more general problem of relating theory with reality – actual HE&R policy tends to be a hybrid of different models, as has been shown on the example of some of the Western European countries by Gornitzka and Maassen (2000:272–284). Instead of arguing that a bureaucracy can adopt one model or another, depending on the situation, as proposed by Olsen (1988:236–237), an extension of this typology could be suggested with the 'garbage can model'. This model states that complex organisations (Cohen et al., 1972) and contemporary public policy-making (Peters, 2005) 'can be viewed for some purposes as collections of choices looking for problems, issues and feelings looking for decision situations in which they might be aired, solutions looking for issues to which they might be an answer, and decision makers looking for work' (Cohen et al., 1972:1). The observed lack of a clearly coordinated time frame between the different strategies adopted at different levels, the abundance of documents from which one can find support for almost any policy issue (either at the level of goals, measures or activities), and the lack of will or capacity to evaluate these suggests that 'garbage can model' by Cohen et al. (1972) could potentially describe the Estonian HE policy process more adequately than any mechanism of governance and autonomy identified by Olsen (1988:236–237).

This argument rests on the assumption that the observations about Estonian HE&R policy described in previous sections are sufficient to indicate that the 'garbage can model' kind of policy process could be behind the Estonian HE&R policy development and implementation. More specifically, for this theory to hold, three general properties about the policy process should be met, according to Cohen et al. (1972:1). First, preferences should be problematic in the sense that there are a 'variety of inconsistent and ill-defined preferences, which can be better described as a loose collection of ideas than as a coherent structure'. Second, preferences should be discovered through action rather than acts being defined on the basis of preferences; technology should be unclear in the sense that despite the ability of the policy process to function, its 'processes are not understood by its members. It operates on the basis of simple trial-and-error procedures, the residue of learning form the accidents of past experience, and pragmatic inventions of necessity'; and it is characterised by fluid participation in the sense that '[p]articipants vary in the amount of time and effort they devote to different domains; involvement varies from one time to another. As a result, the boundaries ... are uncertain and changing; the audiences and decision makers for any particular kind of choice change capriciously'. Although all three elements seem to be present in either or both Estonian HE&R strategy and its policy-making process, in order to say firmly that it follows the 'garbage can model', future research needs to employ more direct methods of observation.

Even if more exact research is indeed necessary to confirm the indirect evidence presented here, the observations are in line with one of the three major conclusions about Estonian tertiary education of the OECD expert team, which is that the local policy-process must become more rational-comprehensive if the desired ends and challenges of building the knowledge economy, are to be met. This is what Huisman et al. (2007:93) state:

> Another priority is the reinforcement of the steering capacity of the Ministry of Education and Research in the effort to build a coherent system. Taking on responsibilities such as policy steering and performance evaluation should entail changes in its competencies and organisation. In particular, it needs to strengthen its capacities with respect to data collection and analysis, policy experimentation, and policy analysis. This requires the ability to judge whether higher education is meeting expectations and the improvement of the formal processes of informing, reporting and follow-up.

This brings the discussion to the policy lessons learned from the overview, which might be more important than the exact label of the steering mechanism of the Estonian HE&R policy process. More specifically, one may ask:

a) How to improve policy development and the compatibility of the strategic documents?
b) What would strengthen the connections between situational analysis, goals, indicators and evaluation?
c) What would improve the planning of the strategies and the interconnections between policy documents at the various hierarchical levels?
d) What should be kept in mind with respect to the planning of new and amendment of existing development plans?

e) What should evaluators do if no goals have been identified, or when the activities cover different or additional aspects to those mentioned in the policy documents?
f) What kind of indicators should be selected to evaluate specific goals?
g) What would improve the data collection and evaluation of the policies implemented according to the strategy documents?

Although it is difficult to answer to these questions just on the basis of the systematic overview, it is possible to share ideas which could give impetus for additional analysis and for the improvement of the evaluation of the HE&R policy documents. To take the questions above in order, one could consider:

a) Standardisation of policy documents – including their basic terminology, cycle, structure, involvement of the evaluators in the preparation, harmonisation of supervision and evaluation criteria, as well as learning from the best practice;
b) Creation of a clear hierarchical structure for the documents (including those composed for the use of EU funds) and a reduction in the total number of public polices developed for steering HE&R;
c) Introduction of a public policy planning process that copies the financial perspective of the EU seven-year framework and collection of all the strategic documents, as well as their evaluation reports, into a state registry. (For instance, the list available on the State Chancellery website needs to be regularly updated and should include all the strategies and their implementation plans);
d) Involvement of evaluators, not only in the final assessment, but also in the preparation and review phases (including the selection of the indicators and method of measurement);
e) Acknowledgment that there are other evaluation techniques available in addition to objective- and goal-based evaluation, which can be used in certain contexts;
f) Collection of primary and/or secondary data (e.g. from the state registers) for measurement purposes depending on the evaluation needs as well as the pros and cons of different types of data;
g) Improvement of the quality of HE&R policy evaluation by:
    - Enhancement of and easier access to the registries, or development of a comprehensive solution to data collection by introducing a regular HE survey (executed, for example by Statistics Estonia);
    - Following the European Commission (2006:9–10) suggestions on impact evaluation and, if necessary, commissioning a separate study for the policy to be evaluated;

- Setting a monetary value for the goals, sub-goals, measures and activities above which impact evaluation is required;
- Using social cost-benefit analysis more widely for the selection and evaluation of the policy instruments;
- Collecting information from the (financial) beneficiaries in forms that facilitate its easy and meaningful use in the evaluations;
- Tidying the strategy documents – reformulating the existing and developing the new documents in a unified structure and using common terminology.

Conclusion

Despite the ambiguous position of development plans and other strategic documents in the Estonian legal structure, one should look beyond laws to understand Estonia's HE&R policy. This section summarises the main lessons learned from the review of these documents, spells out the validity threats that might lead to different interpretations of the results and makes suggestions for future research.

Given the number of HE&R policy documents in Estonia, the first task in this study was to make sense of what they cover by undertaking a systematic review. To that end, meta-analysis, within which the methodological tools for undertaking systematic reviews have been developed, was followed as far as possible within the policy study area. More particularly, the overview followed the QUOROM quality guidelines in the sampling procedures as well as in the data collection. As a result, the Estonian HE&R policy documents, together with their aims, measures and activities were identified. Furthermore, in structuring and summing up the data, simple descriptive statistics in the commonly used categories in this research field enabled Estonian HE&R policy to be described in simple terms. Although as many as 22 different major goals could be counted, it was surprising that none of the strategy documents set major goals in traditional higher education policy areas such as 'Curriculum & Studies', 'Study & Library Materials', 'Infrastructure', 'Financing' or 'Life-long Learning'. This did not mean that these policy areas were totally neglected by the Estonian HE&R policy makers. As was expected, coverage of almost any policy issue can be found within the existing strategic documents – if not at the major goals level, then within the sub-goals, measures or activities – leaving room for the well informed to justify basically any HE&R policy decision or reform agenda with reference(s) to strategic documents.

The second aim of this study was to find out to what extent the documents met the Estonian Ministry of Finance's (2007) policy planning and evaluation criteria which represent the normative understanding of policy-making and implementation as a 'rational-comprehensive process'. Using the structured review, it was found that two-thirds of the existing HE&R policy documents met the Ministry's proposal, which states that strategies should be equipped with indicators to allow the assessment of progress and evaluation of results. But this is true only if the meaning of 'indicator' is stretched to include, in addition to metrics, descriptions of intended results. If the narrow meaning of indicator as the statistical measure would have been applied, only the policy documents that have been developed to channel the EU funds to the Estonian HE&R could be said to meet the expectations of the Ministry. (For instance, the final (approved) version of the Operational Programme for Human Resource Development often identifies more than one indicator and classifies these into impact, result and outcome metrics as well as includes the required information about base-lines, targets and data sources).

The third aim of this study was to make indirect inferences about the policy process that produces the observed outcomes. The large number of policies together with their goals, measures and activities suggested that the 'garbage can model' of Cohen et al. (1972) could potentially describe the Estonian HE&R policy process more adequately than any other mechanism of governance and autonomy identified by Olsen (1988:236–237). This suggestion rests on the assumption that the large number of policy documents, together with their goals, measures and actions, on the one hand, and the lack of metrics to plan and evaluate these, on the other, were sufficient to indicate that the 'garbage can model' could best describe Estonian HE&R policy. Since this inference was based on indirect observations and strict assumptions, it could be argued that a different research design, one which is able to study the features of the 'garbage can model' more directly, is needed to verify the hypothesis generated in this study. That is, further research, which adopts a more direct method of observation than this study, might investigate the applicability of the 'garbage can model' to the empirical reality of the HE&R policy process in Estonia (and possibly beyond it into the former socialist block).

In addition to more direct validation of the 'garbage can model', future research could update this overview with the latest policy documents and possibly arrive at a slightly different conclusion. Other evaluation-research efforts could also help the Estonian Ministry of Education and Research to review and assess the outcomes of the policies and/or undertake the missing policy assessments as required by the Estonian Governmental Decree no. 302. Last but not least, each of the policy themes from 'Curriculum & Studies' to 'Lifelong Learning', listed in Table 3, deserve a separate analysis within the Estonian context. The international review of Estonian tertiary education undertaken by the OECD expert team (Huisman et al., 2007) has been ground-breaking in the local policy context, covering, for example, such themes as 'Governance, steering and planning,' 'Funding,' 'Quality assurance,' 'Equity,' 'Research and innovation,' 'Links to the labour market,' and 'Internationalisation.' The first steps to follow their direction have been taken, for instance, with respect to the 'quality' theme (see Kroos, 2010) and one would like to hope that more would follow, either as a result of the Ministry's in-house analysis or by independent policy evaluators. However, (i) past experience about the willingness of insiders in Estonian HE&R to express their views openly may be discouraging (see Sutrop, 2003:3–4), (ii) any policy analysis is subject to validity threats caused by the funder's agenda setting and author's self-censorship – 'inevitably blunted by sensitivity to the demands of the commissioning agency' (Neave, 1996:408) – and (iii) although they can be seen as nothing more than part of a political struggle for survival (Tomusk, 2007:26), it is still regrettable that the decision-makers behind the LÜKKA[26] and PRIMUS[27] programmes failed to take advantage of the opportunity to use the designated research funds to commission independent and critical evaluations of the major sub-fields of the policy and their implementation in Estonia (or they did this only very indirectly for a handful of issues – see Pilli and Valk (2008) for details). This would have benefited the Ministry in their required policy assessments, data collection and enhanced the capacity of the HE&R policy evaluators that Estonia is lagging behind. To quote once again the policy recommendation made by the OECD expert team (Huisman et al., 2007:72):

> The Review Team suggests improving the information base needed for policy development, particularly in the areas of education and policy evaluation. The Team has identified a number of important gaps in the data base that should be available for evidence-based policy-making… A key step is to systematically collect data at the system and institutional level in areas relevant for policy. The Ministry should also commission research on a number of key issues such as equity or labour market outcomes of students. This could draw on Estonian research groups with an interest in educational policy.

26 LÜKKA was a programme supported by the European Union Social Fund in Estonia with the aim 'to increase the competition capacity of university graduates and of the competence for working on the labour market of a knowledge based society through the collaboration of universities and other parties developing study activities' (Project LÜKKA, 2006).

27 PRIMUS is the 'Program for Higher Education Quality Enhancement in Estonia' of the Priority Axis 'Development of the Human Resources of Research and Development Activities' of the Operational Programme for Human Resource Development.

It is hoped that this study makes a small contribution towards the understanding of the need to make Estonian HE&R policy more systematic and well-structured. As the argument of the paper developed, we showed on the basis of the systematic review that Estonian HE&R is steered by a huge number of policy documents and the goals, measures, and actions set out in them. It can be concluded that the overview gave additional support for the need to take real actions to undertake the required policy evaluations, as well as the need to improve the HE&R policy process by making it more systematic and well-structured. If this is the policy-making model that Estonian HE&R policy-makers would like to move in, the next steps should include an acknowledgement that the evaluation of the existing policies enables the identification of the problems that need to be solved. Knowing these, alternative policy solutions could be identified and instruments considered before the political commitment to implement election promises are made.

Acknowledgments

Publication of this article was granted by the Archimedes Foundation's PRIMUS programme created under the auspices of European Union Social Fund. Project code RIHU09. The author would like to thank Tiina Annus and Heli Aru from the MoE&R as well as Aare Kasemets from the project team for the inspiring exchange of information and ideas. Special thanks also go to the editors – Ellu Saar and René Mõttus – for their valuable feedback. The regular limited liability applies. That is, the author is solely responsible for any mistakes and misinterpretations.

References

Aaviksoo, J. (2001). Teadusreformide aastakümme [Decade of Science Reforms]. Eesti teadusreform – plussid ja miinused [Estonian science reform – pluses and minuses]. Materials of the 5 October 2001 conference. Tallinn: Estonian Academy of Sciences, 25–28.

Aaviksoo, J. (2003). Estonian R&D policy – still to be defined. *Trames*, 7, 32–39.

Act of Changing the University Act, Institutions of Professional Higher Education Act and Other Acts (2012). [Ülikooliseaduse, rakenduskõrgkooli seaduse ja teiste seaduste muutmise seadus]. Available online and only in Estonian: https://www.riigiteataja.ee/akt/130052012001

Archimedes Foundation (2012). Toetused ja programmid [Assistance and Programs]. Available online and only in Estonian: http://str.archimedes.ee/et/struktuurifondid/toetusedjaprogrammid

Aru, H. (2001). Strateegiline juhtimine avalikus sektoris [Strategic Management in Public Sector]. Study Material. Tallinn: State Chancellery of the Republic of Estonia and Estonian Institute of Public Administration. Available online and only in Estonian: http://www.riigikantselei.ee/arhiiv/atp/Koolitus/oppematerjal/pdfid/stratjuht.pdf

Aru, H. (2009). Personal correspondence with the author 18.06.2009.

Boer, H. de and File, J. (2009). *Higher Education Governance Reforms Across Europe*. Brussels: European Centre for Strategic Management of Universities.

CHEPS Consortium (2006). The Extent and Impact of Higher Education Governance Reform across Europe. Part 1: Comparative Analysis and Executive Summary. Enschede: Center for Higher Education Policy Studies.

Clark, B. R. (1983). *The Higher Education System. Academic Organization in Cross-National Perspective*. Berkeley, LA & London: University of California Press.

Cloete, N. and Maassen, P. (2002). The Limits of Policy. In Cloete, N., Fehnel, R., Maassen, P. A. M., Moja, T. and Gibbon T. (Eds.), *Transformation in Higher Education. Global Pressures and Local Realities in South Africa*. Lansdowne, SA: Juta and Company, 447–491.

Cohen, M. D., March J. G. and Olsen J. P. (1972). A Garbage Can Model of Organizational Choice. *Administrative Science Quarterly*, 17, 1–25.

Cooper, H. M. and Lindsay, J. J. (1998). Research synthesis and meta-analysis. In Bickman, L. and Rog, D. J. (Eds.), *Handbook of applied social research methods*. Thousand Oaks: Sage, 315–337.

de Boer, H. and File, J. (2009). *Higher Education Governance Reforms Across Europe*. Brussels: European Centre for Strategic Management of Universities.

Estonian Association of Sociologists (2012). Eesti Sotsioloogide Liidu avalik pöördumine Riigikogu kultuurikomisjoni, Eesti Teaduste Akadeemia, Haridus- ja teadusministeeriumi ja Eesti Teadusagentuuri poole [Estonian Association of Sociologists' Public Petition to The Cultural Affairs Committee of the Parliament of Estonia, Estonian Academy of Sciences, Estonian Ministry of Education and Research, and Estonian Research Council], Tallinn: Estonian Association of Sociologists' Mission Conference 17.09.2012, Sotsiaalteaduste s(t)aatus Euroopas ja Eestis [The Faith and Status of Social Sciences in Europe and Estonia]. Available online and only in Estonian: http://www.sotsioloogia.ee/?lang=et

Estonian Government (2005). Vabariigi valitsuse määrus nr. 302. Strateegiliste arengukavade liigid ning nende koostamise, täiendamise, elluviimise, hindamise ja aruandluse kord [Degree Nr 302 of the Government of the Republic of 13 December 2005. Types of strategic development plans and the procedures for their drafting, revision, implementation, evaluation and reporting], 13.12.2005, *Riigi Teataja*, 67, 522. Available online and only in Estonian: https://www.riigiteataja.ee/akt/968099

Estonian Higher Education Quality Agency (2011). Conditions and Procedure for Institutional Accreditation (01.04.2011). Available online: http://ekka.archimedes.ee/files/IA_tingimused_kord_01.04.11%5B1%5D_ENG%20(23.05.12).pdf

Estonian Ministry of Education and Research (2006). OECD Thematic Review of Tertiary Education. Country Background Report for Estonia. Tartu: Estonian Ministry of Education and Research.

Estonian Ministry of Finance (2007). Ettepanek eesmärkide-indikaatorite määratlemise meetodi kohta [Proposal for the Method of Selecting the Aims and Indicators], 04.06.2007.

Estonian Public Broadcasting (2011). Koolitustellimuse komisjoni juhiks kinnitati Tarmo Kriis [Tarmo Kriis was approved as the Head of the Commission of the Government-commissioned study places]. Available online and only in Estonian: http://uudised.err.ee/index.php?06227544

Estonian Research Council (2012). Guidelines for evaluating institutional research funding applications. Available online: http://www.etag.ee/wp-content/uploads/2012/05/IUT-taotluste-hindamisjuhendi-kinnitamine-LISA.pdf

European Commission (2006). Indicative Guidelines on Evaluation Methods: Monitoring and Evaluation Indicators. *Working Document No. 2*, Brussels: Director General Regional Policy.

Foster, N. (2006). The Analysis of Company Documents. In Scott, J. (Ed.), *Documentary Research,* Vol. 4. London: Sage, 86–106.

Gornitzka Å. and Maassen P. (2000). Hybrid steering approaches with respect to European higher education. *Higher Education Policy*, 13, 267–285.

Heineman, R. A., Peterson, S. A. and Rasmussen, T. H. (1995). *American Government*, 2nd ed. New York: McGraw-Hill Inc.

Hogwood B. W. and Gunn, L. A. (1981). *The Policy Orientation.* Glasgow: Centre for the Study of Public Policy, University of Strathclyde.

Huisman, J., Santiago, P., Högselius, P., Lemaitre, M. J., and Thorn, W. (2007). *OECD Reviews of Tertiary Education. Estonia.* Paris: Organization for Economic Co-operation and Development.

Järve, J. and Võrk, A. (2009). Strateegiate mõjude hindamise võtmekohtade kaardistus valitud valdkondlike arengukavade kaasuste analüüsi põhjal [Mapping of the Key Aspects of the Impact Measurement of Strategies on the Basis of the Development Plans of Selected Fields], Tallinn: The Estonian Center for Applied Research (CentAR) and Praxis Center for Policy Studies. Available online and only in Estonian: http://www.riigikantselei.ee/failid/Strateegia_MH_kaardistus_kaasuste_pohjal_final.pdf

Kasemets, A. (2006). Teadmistepõhise ja säästliku avaliku poliitika institutisionaalsed eeldused Eestis [The institutional preconditions for knowledge-based and sustainable public policy in Estonia]. *Riigikogu Toimetised*, 14, 152–160.

Kasemets, A. (2009). Lõhe õigusloome normide ja faktide vahel 1998-2009 mõjude hindamise ja kaasamise teabe esitamisel [The gap between law-making norms and facts (1998–2009) in the field of impact assessment and civic engagement]. *Riigikogu Toimetised*, 19, 104–115.

Kasemets, K. (2006). Strateegiline planeerimine Eestis eile ja täna [Strategic planning in Estonia, yesterday and today]. *Riigikogu Toimetised*, 14, 58–61.

Kasemets, K. (2009). Kuidas strateegilisi valikuid Eestis tehakse ja kuidas neid tuleks teha? [How Strategic Choices Are Made in Estonia and How They Should Be Made?] Tallinn: EBS JKK Kõrgemate riigiametnike koolitus.

King, K. (1995). Replication, Replication. *PS: Political Science and Politics*, 28, 443–499.

Kroos, K. (2010). Kõrghariduse kvaliteet kehtivates riiklikes strateegiadokumentides. [Higher Education Quality in the Existing National Strategy Documents]. Unpublished research report.

Laar, M. (1996). Estonia's Success Story. *Journal of Democracy,* 7, 96–101.

Maassen, P. and van Vught F. (1994). Alternative Models of Governmental Steering in Higher Education. An analysis of steering models and policy-instruments in five countries. In Goedegebuure, L. and van Vught F. (Eds.), *Comparative Policy Studies in Higher Education*. Utrecht: LEMMA, 35–65.

Masso, J. and Ukrainski, K. (2009). Competition for public project funding in a small research system: the case of Estonia. *Science and Public Policy*, 36, 683–695.

McDonnell, L. and Elmore, R. (1987). Getting the Job Done: Alternative Policy Instruments. *Educational Evaluation and Policy Analysis*, 9, 133–152.

Moher, D., Cook D. J., Eastwood, S., Olkin, I., Rennie, D. and Stroup, D. F. (1999). Improving the quality of reports of meta-analyses of randomized controlled trials: the QUOROM statement. *The Lancet*, 354, 1896–1900.

National Audit Office. (2008). Kõrghariduse riiklik koolitustellimus. Kas riik saab, mida soovib? [Government-commissioned higher education. Does the government get the desired result?], Tallinn: National Audit Office's Report to the Parliament, 19.06.2008. Available online and only in Estonian:
http://www.riigikontroll.ee/DesktopModules/DigiDetail/FileDownloader.aspx?FileId=10687&AuditId=2044

National Institute of Chemical Physics and Biophysics Act. Available online:
http://www.kbfi.ee/?id=27.

Neave, G. and van Vught, F. A. (Eds.) (1991). *Prometheus Bound: The Changing Relationship Between Government and Higher Education in Western Europe*. Oxford: Pergamon Press.

Neave, G. (1994). The Politics of Quality: developments in higher education in Western Europe 1992-1994. *European Journal of Education*, 29, 115–134.

Neave, G. (1996). Higher education policy as an exercise in contemporary history. *Higher Education*, 32, 403–415.

Neave, G. (1998). The Evaluative State Reconsidered. *European Journal of Education*, 33, 265–284.

Neave, G. (2002). The Stakeholder Perspective Historically Explored. In Enders, J. and Fulton, O. (Eds.), *Higher Education in a Globalising World*. Dordrecht: Kluwer Academic Publishers, 17–37.

OECD. (2001). *Reviews of National Policies for Education. Estonia*. Paris: Organization for Economic Co-operation and Development.

Olsen, J. P. (1988). Administrative reform and theories of organization. In Campbell C. and Peters, B. G. (Eds.), *Organizing Governance; Governing Organizations*. Pittsburgh: University of Pittsburgh Press, 233–254.

Patrick, T. B., Demiris, G., Folk, L. C., Moxley, D. E., Mitchell, J. A. and Tao, D. (2004). Evidence-based retrieval in evidence-based medicine. *Journal of the Medical Library Association*, 92, 196–199.

Peters, G. (2005). Governance: A Garbage Can Perspective. In Grande, E. and Pauly, L. W. (Eds.), *Complex Sovereignty: Reconstituting Political Authority in the Twenty-first Century*. Toronto, Buffalo and London: University of Toronto Press, 68–92.

Pilli, E. and Valk, A. (Eds.) (2008). *Quo vadis, Eesti kõrgharidus? Uuringud 2005–2007*. [*Quo vadis*, Estonian higher education? Research 2005–2007]. Tartu: Tartu University Press.

PRAXIS. (2008). Strateegiate mõjude hindamise hetkeolukorrast ja selle peamistest kitsaskohtadest Eestis [State of the Affairs and the Major Limitations of the Impact Assessment of Strategies in Estonia]. Tallinn: Praxis Center for Policy Studies. Available online and only in Estonian: http://www.riigikantselei.ee/failid/Strateegiate_mojude_hindamine_Praxise_raport.pdf

Project LÜKKA. (2006). Official website. Available online: http://www.ut.ee/lykka/set_lang_id=2

Pruks, P. (2000). On Formation of Policy Analysis and Legal Policy in Estonia. *Juridica International*, 5, 3-10.

Rask, M. (1998). Erakondlikkusest õiguspoliitikas [Political Affiliations and Law], *Juridica*, 4, 166–167.

Salter, B. and Tapper, T. (1981). *Education, Politics and the State. The Theory and Practice of Educational Change*. London: Grant McIntyre Ltd.

Scott, J. (2006). Assessing Documentary Sources. In Scott, J. (Ed.), *Documentary Research*, Vol.4. London: Sage, 23–41.

Sõerunurk, S. (2011). Minister Aaviksoo: Eesti-sisene kõrgkoolide konkurents on naeruväärne [Minister Aaviksoo: Competition among Institutions of Higher Education within Estonia is a Joke]. *Universitas Tartuensis* 01.06.2011. Available online and only in Estonian: http://www.ajaleht.ut.ee/1020196

Sutrop, U. (2003). Science Policy (in Estonia). Preface to the special issue of Trames. *Trames*, 7, 3–5.

Tomusk, V. (1996). Republic of Estonia. In Velt, R., Füssel, H-P., and Neave, G. (Eds.), *Relations between State and Higher Education*. The Hague, London and Boston: Kluwer Law International, 151–161.

Tomusk, V. (1997). External Quality Assurance in Estonian Higher Education: its glory, take-off and crash. *Quality in Higher Education*, 3, 173–181.

Tomusk, V. (2001). Higher Education Reform in Estonia: a legal perspective. *Higher Education Policy*, 14, 201–212.

Tomusk, V. (2003). Aristoscientists, Academic Proletariat and Reassembling the Megamachine: 21st century survival strategies of the Estonian academia. *International Studies in Sociology of Education*, 13, 77–99.

Tomusk, V. (2004). *The Open World and Closed Societies. Essays on Higher Education Policies "in Transition"*. New York: Palgrave Macmillan.

Tomusk, V. (2007). Big Freeze in Vodkobuzia: the Path of Past, and Involution in the Post-Communist Academia. In Pausits, A. and Pellert, A. (Eds.), *Higher Education Management and Development in Central, Southern and Eastern Europe*, Münster, New York, München and Berlin: Waxmann, 26–50.

Velt, R., Füssel, H-P., and Neave, G. (Eds.) (1996). *Relations between State and Higher Education.* The Hague, London & Boston: Kluwer Law International.

Tartu Ülikooli seadus. [University of Tartu Act]. Available online: http://www.legaltext.ee/et/andmebaas/tekst.asp?loc=text&dok=X70009K4&keel=en&pg=1&ptyyp=RT&tyyp=X&query=Tartu+%FClikooli+seadus

van Heffen, O., Verhoeven, J. and de Wit, K. (1999). Higher education polices and institutional response in Flanders. Institutional analysis and cultural theory. In Jongbloed, B., Massen, P. and Neave, G. (Eds.), *From the Eye of the Storm. Higher Education's Changing Institution.* Dordrecht: Kluwer Academic Publishers, 263–293.

van Vught, F. A. (Ed.) (1989). *Governmental Strategies and Innovation in Higher Education.* London: Jessica Kingsley.

Vilgats, B. (2008). Quality Conception in Higher Education Legislation – The Estonian National Profile, *Problems of Education in the 21st Century*, 8, 153–161.

Appendix 1. Study's Initial Sample of Estonian Higher Education Policy Documents

1. Estonian Higher Education Strategy, 2006–2015 and its implementation plan for the years 2008–2010 (*Eesti kõrgharidusstrateegia aastateks 2006–2015 & selle rakendusplaan aastateks 2008–2010*);
2. Estonian higher education internationalisation strategy, 2006-2015 (*Eesti kõrghariduse rahvusvahelistumise strateegia aastateks 2006–2015*);
3. National higher education program on ICT 'Tiger university+' (2009–2012) (*Riiklik IKT kõrgharidusprogramm 'Tiigriülikool+' (2009–2012)*);
4. Estonian e-Learning Strategy in Vocational and Higher Education 2007–2012 (*Eesti e-õppe strateegia kutse- ja kõrghariduses 2007–2012*);
5. Estonian Research and Development and Innovation Strategy 2007-2013 'Knowledge-based Estonia' and its implementation plan (for years 2009-2013) (*Eesti teadus- ja arendustegevuse ning innovatsiooni strateegia 'Teadmistepõhine Eesti' 2007–2013 ja selle rakendusplaan (aastateks 2009–2013)*);
6. Action Plan for Growth and Jobs, 2008-2011, for the implementation of the Lisbon Strategy (*Eesti majanduskasvu ja tööhõive tegevuskava 2008–2011 Lissaboni strateegia rakendamiseks*);
7. National Strategy for the use of Structural Funds 2007–2013 (*Riiklik struktuurivahendite kasutamise strateegia 2007–2013*);
8. Operational Programme for Human Resource Development, CCI number: 2007EE051PO001 (*Inimressursi arendamise rakenduskava CCI 2007EE051PO001*);
9. Estonian Teacher Education Strategy for 2009-2013 and its implementation plan (*Eesti õpetajahariduse strateegia 2009–2013 ja selle rakenduskava*);
10. Estonian Integration Strategy 2008–2013 and its implementation plan for years 2008–2010 (*Eesti lõimumiskava 2008–2013 ja selle rakendusplaan 2008–2010*);
11. Development Strategy of the Estonian Language (2004–2010) (*Eesti keele arendamise strateegia 2004–2010*);
12. 'Smart and Active People' – a development plan of the area of government of the Estonian Ministry of Education and Research (*HTMi valitsemisala arengukava 'Tark ja tegus rahvas' 2009–2012*).

Appendix 2. Components of Strategic Documents that Relate to Higher Education

1. Estonian Higher Education Strategy, 2006–2015 – completely;
2. Implementation plan of the Estonian Higher Education Strategy (2006–2015) for years 2008–2010 – completely;
3. Estonian higher education internationalisation strategy, 2006-2015 – completely;
4. Action Plan for Growth and Jobs, 2008–2011, for the implementation of the Lisbon Strategy – partially: aim no. 4 (completely) & aim no. 8 (partially: sub-goals 1, 2 & 4);
5. Estonian Research and Development and Innovation Strategy 2007–2013 'Knowledge-based Estonia'– selectively:
   aim no. 1,
   measure 1 completely,
   measure 2 partially (2.2; 2.3; 2.4; 2.11; 2.13; 2.14; 2.15; 2.16; 2.17; 2.18),
   measure 3 partially (3.6; 3.8;),
   measure 4 partially (4.1; 4.6; 4.7);
6. The implementation plan (for years 2009–2013) of the Estonian Research and Development and Innovation Strategy 2007–2013 'Knowledge-based Estonia' – selectively:
   aim no. 1
   measure 1 completely,
   measure 2 completely,
   measure 3 partially (3.6; 3.8;),
   measure 4 partially (4.1; 4.4; 4.6; 4.7; 4.8);
7. Estonian Teacher Education Strategy 2009–2012– selectively:
   4.2.1 all except 4.2.1.5,
   4.2.2 all except 4.2.2.12,
   4.2.3 partially (4.2.3.2; 4.2.3.3; 4.2.3.4),
   4.2.4 partially (4.2.4.1),
   4.2.5 partially (4.2.5.1; 4.2.5.3; 4.2.5.8; 4.2.5.9b),
   4.2.6 partially (4.2.6.6; 4.2.6.7),
8. The implementation plan of the Estonian Teacher Education Strategy 2009–2013 – selectively:
   1. completely,
   2. all except 2.4 and 2.10,
   3. partially – 3.3; 3.4; 3.6,
   4. partially – 4.1,
   5. partially – 5.7; 5.8,
   6. partially – 6.4; 6.5,
9. Operational Programme for Human Resource Development, CCI number: 2007EE051PO001 – selectively:
   priority direction 4.1 (aim no. 1 only),
   priority direction 4.2 (completely),
   priority direction 4.4 (aim no. 4 only),
   priority direction 4.5 (aim no. 2 only),
   priority direction 4.5 (aim no. 1 & 2);
10. Development Strategy of the Estonian Language (2004–2010) – selectively (only 3.4.3 Higher education)

11. The implementation plan for the Integration Strategy (2008–2010) – selectively (only V1.5 1.);
12. 'Smart and Active People' – a development plan of the area of government of the Estonian Ministry of Education and Research – selectively:
    2.1 (measures 1.3.1. and 1.4.),
    2.2 (measures 2.1.1.1, 2.1.1.8. and 2.1.1.9),
    2.4 completely.

Appendix 3. Strategy Sets of Estonian Higher Education Policy Papers

1. Estonian Higher Education Strategy, 2006–2015 and its implementation plan for the years 2008–2010 (*Eesti kõrgharidusstrateegia aastateks 2006–2015 ja selle rakendusplaan aastateks 2008–2010*);
2. Estonian higher education internationalisation strategy, 2006-2015 (*Eesti kõrghariduse rahvusvahelistumise strateegia aastateks 2006–2015*);
3. Estonian Research and Development and Innovation Strategy 2007–2013 "Knowledge-based Estonia" and its implementation plan (for years 2009–2013) *(Eesti teadus- ja arendustegevuse ning innovatsiooni strateegia „Teadmistepõhine Eesti" 2007–2013 ja selle rakendusplaan (aastateks 2009–2013)*);
4. Action Plan for Growth and Jobs, 2008–2011, for the implementation of the Lisbon Strategy (*Eesti majanduskasvu ja tööhõive tegevuskava 2008–2011 Lissaboni strateegia rakendamiseks*);
5. Operational Programme for Human Resource Development, CCI number: 2007EE051PO001 (*Inimressursi arendamise rakenduskava CCI 2007EE051PO001*);
6. Estonian Teacher Education Strategy for 2009–2013 and its implementation plan (*Eesti õpetajahariduse strateegia 2009–2013 ja selle rakenduskava*);
7. Implementation plan of Estonian Integration Strategy 2008–2013 for years 2008–2010 (*Eesti lõimumiskava 2008–2013 rakendusplaan 2008–2010*);
8. Development Strategy of the Estonian Language (2004–2010) *(Eesti keele arendamise strateegia 2004–2010*);
9. 'Smart and Active People' – a development plan of the area of government of the Estonian Ministry of Education and Research *(HTMi valitsemisala arengukava 'Tark ja tegus rahvas' 2009–2012*).

PART 1

LEARNING AT HIGHER EDUCATION INSTITUTION

Chapter 3.
Does a research-oriented university really have a negative effect on students' self-evaluations?

Karin Täht, Liina Adov, Mari-Liis Mägi, Olev Must

Introduction

Modern cultures stress the importance of education both for individual and for societal development. In order to prepare their children for top universities, parents attempt to put them into élitist high schools; which are believed to improve a talented child's prospects for getting into the best colleges, a step on the way to the most sought-after careers (Attawell, 2001). It is a widespread belief that students gain a lifetime advantage if they get into a prestigious university or college which has a high proportion of research active academic staff, laboratories with vigorous research programmes and impressive campus facilities. Research evidence demonstrates something different – that graduates of élite universities do not earn more and they are not more satisfied with their jobs compared to graduates from other educational institutions (Zhang, 2003, 2005; Pascarella and Terenzini, 2005). So, there is no unequivocal support for the belief that studying at a prestigious university gives an advantage later in life. We were interested to find out how undergraduates of the relatively more prestigious universities felt about themselves, as well as how – if at all – their self-evaluations differed from students from relatively less prestigious higher education institutions.

Traditionally this controversy – selective schools and low student aspirations – is considered in terms of social comparison (Festinger, 1954). The Big-Fish-Little-Pond Effect (BFLPE) explanation proposed by Marsh and Parker (1984) is the best theoretical scheme to look at how the process might work. Recently Zell and Alicke (2010) took a step forward as they emphasized the dominant role in the formation of self-evaluation of comparisons in the immediate local environment. This paper investigates differences in students' self-evaluations in a research oriented university (ROU; a highly selective university) and in institutions of professional higher education (IPHEs; less selective).

The history of Pond theories

Davis (1966) described the Frog Pond effect suggesting that students in high-ability schools have lower grade-point averages (GPAs), which negatively influence their self-evaluations and, subsequently, their career decisions. In his study, Davis found that students' GPAs were more strongly related to their career aspirations than to the school-average ability. Davis applied the theory of relative deprivation to explain why a highly selective academic environment decreases students' future aspirations. Since then many researchers have supported this theory (Werts and Watley, 1969; Drew and Astin, 1972; Alwin and Otto, 1977). Alexander and Eckland (1977) reported evidence that partly supported the Frog Pond effect. They found that attendance at selective institutions lowered the freshmen's GPAs and their academic self-concepts. However, Thistlethwaite and Wheeler (1966) provided an alternative explanation; they suggested that peer pressure from high-achieving and highly motivated classmates enhances one's desire to achieve and may increase one's future aspirations.

There is more support for the theory of relative deprivation, although there is empirical evidence to support both the relative deprivation and the peer pressure explanations. (Drew and Astin, 1972).

Big-Fish-Little-Pond Effect (BFLPE)

Almost twenty years later Marsh and Parker (1984) supported Davis' findings: that academically selective schools are intended to affect students' academic self-concepts positively, but in reality the opposite is found to be true – students in high-ability schools have lower levels of academic self-concept than students in low-ability schools. Marsh has been studying what he calls the BFLPE for almost thirty years. The BFLPE hypothesises that equally able students have lower levels of academic self-concept in high-ability schools than in low-ability schools (Marsh, 1987). Marsh and Hau (2003) in the *American Psychologist* confirmed this statement with data from 26 countries presenting the BFLPE as a robust universal phenomenon in very different cultural settings. Some years later the same conclusion was reached for a further 41 countries (Seaton, Marsh and Craven, 2009).

It could be argued that students who attend high-ability schools have lower self-concepts before going to the selective school. A study that compared West German students who moved from non-selective, heterogeneous primary schools to high schools that were streamed on the basis of academic achievement proves the argument to be wrong (Marsh, 1987). When the students were first selected to enter the high or low-ability schools, those entering high-ability schools had substantially higher academic self-concepts than those entering the low-ability schools, but the two groups did not differ in academic self-concept by the end of their first year in the new schools. This shows that the selective environment had a negative effect regardless of previous positive self-evaluations.

In addition to investigating the validity and generalization of the BFLPE, Marsh, with colleagues, has also studied different aspects of the effect and showed that school-average ability also has a negative effect on self-efficacy (Marsh et al., 2007). The authors proposed that the effect could be due to the wording of the questions in the questionnaire and brought out the importance of further studies on that subject. Marsh (1987) proposed that the BFLPE should be greatest amongst younger students because they have no standard of comparison except the performance of their classmates and may not even know how the average ability level of their classmates compares with a broader frame of reference. Older students typically have some other basis for the assessment of their own academic skills, which is independent of the performances of their classmates.

That being said, selective schools may also have some positive effect on students' self-concepts (Marsh, Kong and Hau, 2000). In addition to the negative effect of the school-average achievement on self-concept, they found that a more highly perceived school status had a counterbalancing positive effect on self-concept. They referred to the positive effect as a reflected-glory or an assimilation effect – attending a prestigious high school is valued and has a positive effect on self-evaluation.

In addition to the relative deprivation theory there have been studies that point out different influences that may bias the occurrence of those effects. McFarland and Buehler (1995:1068) proposed that it is not always 'better to be a big fish in a little pond than a little fish in a big pond'. Rather, 'although everyone feels good about being a big fish in a little pond, not everyone feels bad about being a little fish in a big pond'. In their study they found that the frog-pond effect was strongest among individuals with lower collective self-esteem, with an individualistic cultural heritage, or with a weaker bond with a particular social group. Those who valued their group highly were immune to the negative effect of group achievement.

The BFLPE in universities

Astin (1968) argues that the traditional indicators of the institutional quality of colleges and universities do not appear to contribute to the students' achievements. Astin recognizes that at the level of raw output of the achievement indicators élite colleges are really better, but controlling for student input parameters has significant consequences the contribution of the institution of higher education is close to zero. Later, based on longitudinal data, Astin (1993) shows that the institutional characteristics of colleges have little direct effect on the students' educational outcomes once the students' peer group characteristics are taken into account. Astin considers that the student's peer group is the single most potent source of influence on their growth and development during the undergraduate years. Astin's findings have been supported by other researches (e.g. Alwin and Otto, 1977; Phan, 2010) who find that the social influence of peers, teachers and family members, particularly parents, contribute to the formation of college plans and future occupational aspirations.

Astin (1993) finds that attending a college with a high proportion of research oriented academic staff increases the students' dissatisfaction with various aspects of the college and has negative impacts on most measures of cognitive and affective development. Research orientation is defined primarily by the publication rate of the academic staff, time spent conducting research, and personal commitment to research and scholarship. It is also important to note that research orientation is strongly correlated with the size and selectivity of the institution. Research orientation is highly negatively correlated with student orientation. By 'student orientation' we mean that the academic staff is interested in the students and their academic and personal problems. Student orientation has a positive effect on the students' satisfaction with the academic staff and it results in more substantial direct effects on the students' outcomes than almost any other environmental variable. For example, it has a positive effect on self-esteem, self-reported growth in writing skills, critical thinking abilities, overall academic development, and also an indirect positive effect on degree aspirations and college GPA. Based on the above, Astin suggests that there is a significant price to be paid, in terms of student development, in a faculty where most academic staff are research oriented (Astin, 1993).

Self-evaluations and their connection to academic achievement

Among the psychological factors relating to the learning process there are several factors that can be brought together under the umbrella concept of self-evaluation, among them, the students' academic self-efficacy. Self-efficacy is defined as one's belief in one's ability to succeed in specific situations (Bandura, 1977). The academic aspect of this concept is called academic self-efficacy and is described as an individual's belief that they can successfully achieve at a designated level on an academic task (Bandura, 1977). Robbins et al. (2004) have stated that academic goals, academic self-efficacy and academic skills were shown to be the strongest predictors of college retention. Academic self-efficacy is found to be related to academic expectations and academic performance (Chemers, Hu and Garcia, 2001). Phan (2010) finds that self-efficacy has an influence on cognitive engagement. Individuals with a high sense of perceived competence are more likely to pursue challenging personal goals and spend time and effort realizing them and persisting in the face of difficulties. Therefore, self-efficacy has a positive effect on deep cognitive learning. A study conducted by Prat-Sala and Redford (2010) also suggests that students with a high level of self-efficacy are more likely to adopt a deep or strategic approach to studying, while students classified as low in self-efficacy are likely to adopt a surface approach. Another factor important in the learning process is academic motivation. The Self-Determination Theory states that motivation is divided to intrinsic motivation, which refers to doing something because it is inherently interesting or enjoyable, and extrinsic motivation, which refers to doing something because it leads to a distinguishable outcome (Deci and Ryan, 2000). Intrinsic motivation is associated with deep cognitive information processing – the more intrinsically motivated students are, the deeper their information processing, which in turn is associated with higher academic achievement (Deci and Ryan, 2000). It appears that intrinsic motivation tends to be positively related to future orientation as students who perceived a course to be valuable for their future work showed greater motivation and had better examination results than those who perceived the focus to be on immediate training (Simons et al., 2004). Barber et al. (2009) stated that future-oriented students are more likely to have higher college GPAs than students who are oriented to the present. Also, academic motivation is believed to increase as students believe they are making progress in learning (Schunk, 1991).

In addition to self-efficacy beliefs and academic motivation, self-esteem is also found to affect performance and achievement. Self-esteem is the overall appraisal of one's self-worth (Rosenberg, 1965) whereas academic self-esteem has been described as self-evaluations in school performance (Rosenberg et al., 1995). Individuals who feel good about themselves are more likely to succeed in learning and will pursue performance-related goals (Phan, 2010). Optimism and positive expectations are related to higher expectations for success in academic pursuits. Students who enter college with confidence in their ability to perform well academically do perform significantly better than less confident students (Chemers et al., 2001).

The Estonian case

So, there is a lot of evidence that the students' self-evaluations (SEs) are important in the learning process, but the BFLPE indicates that the élitism of educational institutions is also involved in this process in an unexpected way. The prerequisite for discovering and understanding the BFLPE is that besides the individual differences between students, the differences between educational institutions must also be considered.

Although the BFLPE is shown to be robust in different samples, Estonian undergraduates have not yet been studied. In Estonia there are not many universities and only a few of them have a strong emphasis on research. So, it is important to find out if the shortage of choices is related to the manifestation of the BFLPE. The previous studies reviewed above have been conducted in larger countries, for example the USA, Australia and Japan, where they have many research oriented universities, but these studies would suggest that the BFLPE would also manifest itself in Estonia.

On the other hand, it could be argued that with fewer choices Estonian students are more aware of the prestige of schools and thus are less influenced by a selective environment. As Estonia is a small country, the students' choices regarding universities are limited and therefore they are presumably aware of the possible consequences of choosing one university rather than another. It could be speculated that students selecting a relatively more prestigious academic university are ready for its high standards and perceive this as a motivating challenge. They may acknowledge the fact that it is not easy to be the best in a demanding academic environment. Therefore, there is a possibility that the BFLPE does not manifest itself in the Estonian undergraduates' sample. However, Estonian data does show that the dropout rates of undergraduates from academically oriented study programmes (bachelor studies) are higher than the dropout rates from practically oriented programmes (Tõnisson, 2011). This evidence is surprising so explanations should be sought.

The current study

Based on the studies mentioned above, we propose the following two independent hypotheses in our study: first, we suggest that the BFLPE does manifest itself in the sample of Estonian undergraduates. More precisely, undergraduates' SE levels are lower in research-oriented institutions compared to other institutions of higher education. Second, for students in a research-oriented university (ROU), compared to other indicators of academic achievement and cognitive ability, we suggest the GPA in the university is more closely related with students' SE.

The first hypothesis is largely based on Astin (1993) whose research shows ROUs have a negative effect on students' cognitive and affective development. Astin also finds that an institution's level of research orientation is correlated with its size and selectivity. In other words, universities that emphasise research are usually more selective. In addition to the above, Marsh (1987; Marsh and Hau, 2003; Marsh et al., 2007) has shown with colleagues that a school's average achievement and school selectivity is negatively correlated with the students' SE (i.e. BFLPE). The second hypothesis is based on the studies (Marsh, 1990; Marsh, Hau and Kong, 2002) that show GPA to be more strongly correlated with self-concept when comparing it with standardized tests of achievement.

It is important to point out that in order to test the first hypothesis we will compare the results of national examinations and the SEs of students from different institutions of higher education. For the second hypothesis we will study the relations between SEs and indicators of academic achievement in a research oriented university.

Specifically, we take into account the following SE indicators: motivation and interest to learn, general self-efficacy, academic self-efficacy, self-esteem and academic self-esteem. Previous research has shown different aspects of SE to be closely related to each other as well as to the students′ academic performance. Our purpose is not to investigate the complex relations between different SEs, but to use different scales in order to describe the BFLPE in Estonian institutions of higher education.

Data and Method

Sample

The sample consisted of 366 undergraduates from two different academic environments who had participated in an optional psychology course; one requirement on the course was filling in the SE questionnaires. The two different academic environments were a research-oriented university (ROU) and institutions of professional higher education (IPHEs). The profiles of the IPHEs were agriculture and business. The sample was not split equally between these two academic contexts: the sample from the ROU consisted of 233 students (177 women, 47 men, 9 did not give the information about their gender); whereas the sample from the IPHEs consisted of 133 students (113 women, 15 men, 5 did not give the information about their gender). As can be seen, the gender distribution was not equal either: there were 290 women and 62 men in the total sample. In Estonian higher education, approximately 60 per cent of admitted students are women (Tõnisson, 2011), so our sample was significantly biased towards women students. The number of men in the samples of both institutions was too small to give stable estimates of parameters. Therefore, we decided to research only the samples of women. The average ages for the sample from the ROU was 20.82 years and 23.79 years for the IPHEs. These correspond to the modal age range of 20–24 years of Estonian undergraduate students (Tõnisson, 2011). The cumulative average of participants' academic credit points was 80 at the end of the testing year. As the expected nominal number of credit points per year is 60, the average of 80 means that some of the participants' were second or third year students.

Measures

Five different self-report scales (Table 1) were used in order to measure students' self-evaluations. All scales consisted of several attitudinal statements. Statements were rated on a 5-point scale, ranging from 1 *(strongly disagree)* to 5 *(strongly agree)*. The scale score was calculated as the total sum of the item values.

Table 1. Description of self-evaluative measures

Scale	Acronym	Items in scale	Cronbach's alpha
General self-efficacy [1)]	GEFF	5	.87
Academic self-efficacy [2)]	AEFF	16	.89
General self-esteem [3)]	GEST	10	.85
Academic self-esteem [4)]	AEST	8	.81
Motivation and interest to learn [5)]	MIL	12	.80

1) 5 items from the Estonian version of Schwarzer and Jerusalem Scale of General Self-Efficacy (Rimm and Jerusalem, 1999).
2) 16 items from the Estonian Scale of Academic Self-Efficacy (Üpraus, 2009).
3) The Estonian version of the Rosenberg Self-Esteem Scale (Rosenberg, 1965; Pullmann and Allik, 2000).
4) Academic self-esteem was measured by the 8-item scale developed by Pullmann and Allik (2008) as an analogy to the Marsh (1992) scale for assessment perception of self-competence in the academic domain.
5) 12-item scale developed by Täht and Must (unpublished) on the basis of the PISA 2006 attitudinal questionnaire.

Educational achievement was estimated by the index derived from the results of the national examinations taken when graduating from high school (NER) and the GPA at university. The respondents self-reported their NER grades which are expressed by a 100 point system. The index of NER ranked grades was on a 10 point scale *(1 – all grades are lower than 50 ..... 10 – all grades are higher than 90)*. The values of GPA in university were taken from the official learning-information database of the university.

General cognitive ability (GCA) was estimated from the results of the admission test of the University of Tartu (Must and Allik, 2001). The test consists of 7 sections (vocabulary, tables-diagrams-maps, data sufficiency, text comprehension, mathematics, spatial reasoning and foreign language comprehension). The total test score is the sum of the standardized scores of the subtests with a mean of 50 and a standard deviation of 16 (on the sample of applicants). The GCA test was only administered for students' in the ROU. We combined the measures obtained at different time points. The national examinations and admission test were passed by students before their admission into the university. Part of our sample contained first year students and they did not have university grades before testing their self-evaluations.

We used correlation analysis (Pearson correlations), reliability analysis, Student t-test and regression analysis with SPSS 17.0.

Results

In Table 2, the averages and standard deviations of all measures used in the study are displayed. The t-test (Table 2) was conducted in order to check if there were mean differences in the self-evaluations (SE) scales and the national exam results (NER) in the two different samples. As mentioned before, we admitted only female students into the analyses.

Table 2. Female students' self-evaluations and national examination results. Differences between the standardized scores of students in the Research-Oriented University (ROU) and the Institutions of Professional Higher Education (IPHE)

	IPHEs		ROU		Results of t-test			Effect size
	Average	St. dev.	Average	St. dev.	t-value	df	p-value*	Cohen's d
General self-efficacy	0.38	0.73	-0.29	1.13	5.49	267	<.001	0.71
Academic self-efficacy	0.51	0.75	-0.21	1.03	6.21	267	<.001	0.8
General self-esteem	0.25	0.76	-0.04	1.07	2.37	267	0.009	0.31
Academic self esteem	0.2	0.95	-0.04	1	1.91	267	0.029	0.25
Motivation and interest	0.46	0.59	-0.2	1.06	5.78	266	<.001	0.77
Results of national exams	-.78	.95	.51	0.59	-14.25	288	<.001	-1.63

**for one-tail hypothesis*

There are statistically significant differences in the mean scores of students' self-evaluations and school grades between the two types of institutions of higher education (Table 2). Students' levels of SE indicators are higher in the IPHEs and lower in the ROU. The effect sizes are high (d > .7) for three scales of SE: general self-efficacy, academic self-efficacy and motivation and interest for learning. The effect sizes for general self esteem and academic self esteem are lower, indicating that when considering these scales, the mean values in the ROU are approximately 25 per cent of a standard deviation lower than in the IPHEs, but these differences are still statistically significant. In contrast, the NER levels are higher in the ROU and lower in the IPHEs. The effect size shows large difference (standard deviation of 1.63). Figure 1 helps to develop a visual understanding of this main finding. The levels of NER are statistically different the two academic environments: in IPHE the standardized NER index is -.78 and .51 in the ROU (Table 2). This means that students in the ROU have significantly better educational backgrounds than students in the IPHEs, but the differences on the bases of student self-evaluations are the opposite – students in the IPHEs evaluate themselves in more positive terms than students in the ROU. Variances of indicators of SE were greater for students in the ROU compared with students in the IPHEs. This difference can be explained by the heterogeneity of study profiles of the ROU and the IPHEs. The ROU in our research was an academic university with numerous study fields, programmes and learning requirements. The IPHEs in our research are more homogeneous in the sense that their profiles are narrower (agriculture or business).

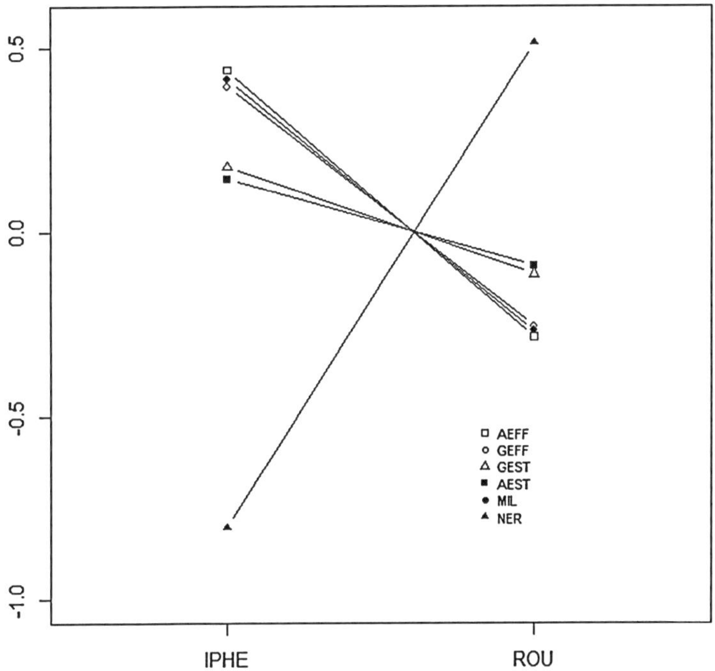

Figure 1. *Students' self-evaluations and national examination results. Differences between standardized scores of students in the Research-Oriented University (ROU) and the Institutions of Professional Higher Education (IPHE). GEFF – General self-efficacy, AEFF – Academic self-efficacy, GEST – General self-esteem, AEST – Academic self-esteem, MIL – Motivation and interest to learn, NER – Results of national exams.*

Students in the ROU

As we had more information about the students from the ROU, we looked more precisely at this sample. One claim of researchers of the pond effect is that the actual GPA in school is most highly related to the students' self-evaluations if compared with other indicators of achievement and cognitive ability (our second hypothesis). Therefore, we investigated which indicator of the intellectual level of students (educational achievements or cognitive ability) is the strongest independent correlate of students' different self-evaluations. We ran five multiple regression analyses where each indicator of SE was associated with GPA, NER,

GCA and age. The purpose of these regression analyses was to estimate which indicator of the students' intellectual level has the highest correlation with indicators of self-evaluations when controlling other indicators of intellectual level. The results of the regression analyses are given in Table 3. Except for GEFF, the other four student self-evaluations are most strongly associated with the GPA at the university. In other words, students' self-evaluations are more highly correlated with GPA when controlling other indicators of intellectual ability and age. The general pattern of associations demonstrates that the GPA at university correlates more strongly with student self-evaluations than their previous grades in high school or their cognitive ability. The independent variables are correlated and this may influence the interpretation of estimates. The inspection of the statistics of multi-collinearity showed that the effect of university GPA on the SE is in small part explained by GCA and NER: tolerance= .84. A tolerance of less than .20 indicates a serious multi-collinearity problem (O'Brian, 2007).

Table 3. *Regression of the Research-Oriented University's female students' self-evaluations on the indicators of educational achievement, cognitive ability and age (standardized regression weights)*

	GPA	NER	GCA	Age	R^2
Academic self-efficacy (AEFF)	.32*	-.04	.00	-.04	.10
General self-efficacy (GEFF)	.04	-.12	.05	-.03	.01
General self-esteem (GEST)	.25*	.02	.13	.00	.11
Academic self-esteem (AEST)	.35*	-.04	.39*	.11	.29
Motivation and interest (MIL)	.29*	-.07	-.00	-.03	.08

** $p<.01$*

GPA – grade point average at university, NER – Results of national exams,

GCA – general cognitive ability.

Discussion

The BFLPE on the sample of Estonian undergraduates

We showed empirically that the BFLPE is demonstrated in the Estonian female undergraduates. Our results showed that students' general and academic SEs are lower in a ROU when comparing with the IPHEs. In the study we used self-reported questionnaires measuring general and academic self-efficacy, general and academic self-esteem, and learning interest and motivation. Previous studies on the BFLPE have shown that the effect occurs on the example of self-concept

(Marsh, 1987; Marsh, Kong and Hau, 2000; Marsh et al., 2007); our study shows the effect to be even more robust. In our sample, a university's selectivity had a negative effect on all of the five scales of self-evaluations that we observed.

Our explanation is that high learning requirements and learning experiences in an ROU are responsible for this unexpected negative association. At the same time we recognize the alternative explanations. It is probable that the differences described in the students' self-evaluations existed before university studies. It is also plausible that the optional psychology course, that was the basis for our samples and data collection, was more attractive for students with critical self-evaluations, at least in the ROU. Differences in the variances of SE scales support the hypotheses that students in the IPHEs are rather similar, but students in the ROU are heterogeneous, and therefore the selection of the optional course has a specific influence in pre-selecting students.

Our result about the BFLPE manifestation in the sample of Estonian undergraduates is quite important because the system of Estonian higher education is unique in terms of its small size and limited number of universities. As noted previously, most of the research on the BFLPE has been done in the USA, Australia, Japan and other countries that have many universities; therefore it is difficult to generalize these results to Estonian studies. However, we can still find similar tendencies in the Estonian sample. Earlier in this chapter we suggested that the shortage of choice, when it comes to selecting a university, may limit the manifestation of the BFLPE, but, our results show that students' levels of SEs are lower in the ROU compared to students in the IPHEs.

Different explanations for the BFLPE have been proposed by researchers. Most influential among them is probably the theory of social comparison (Festinger, 1954) where the students' SEs are influenced by their comparison with other students' achievements. Also, higher expectations in an academic environment could make students more critical of themselves and so, high academic expectations may have a negative impact on the students' SEs. In higher education, one of the explanations is that more selective institutions are more research-oriented and so the students might feel more pressure about their results from academic staff (Astin, 1993).

In contrast to these explanations, the theory of stability of self-esteem claims that self-esteem does not change substantially during a life time. More precisely, most self-esteem stability over time is claimed to be accounted for by genetic factors (Neiss, Sedikides and Stevenson, 2002). This hints at the possibility that the observed differences in the measured variables between the students from different types of higher education institutions had been in place before enrolment. That is, the observed differences might have been driven by self-selection into different types of institutions.

GPA in the university is more important than other indicators of achievement and ability

Previous studies have shown that scores on general cognitive tests and scholastic assessment tests (SATs) are positively related to other indices of academic achievement and different forms of SE (Mattern and Shaw, 2010). A meta-analysis showed that school performance indicators, like GPAs, are more strongly correlated with SE than standardized measures of Intellectual Quotient (IQ) (Hansford and Hattie, 1982). As proposed in the second hypothesis, the tendency found by Marsh and colleagues (Marsh 1990; Marsh et al., 2002) was supported in our study – GPA at university was strongly related to SE. In our data, the results of the GCA tests were only significantly related to academic self-esteem; the results of national exams (NER) had no significant correlation to any SE indicator, when controlling for GCA and GPA. These results could be explained by the fact that the GCA and the NER were taken some time before students reported their SEs. It could be argued that the high or low scores on the GCA and the NER are forgotten during university studies and that comparison with fellow students is more important. The implicit comparison with fellow students is the fact to stress in our study. Students filled in the psychological questionnaires before they knew their GPA.

As the levels of students' SEs in the two types of institutions were different, some implicit influence of comparison with fellow students had to take place. This can be explained by the fact that the exam grades are determined over the course of the university terms, and during this time comparisons can be made via the grades of essays and tests. This means that the identification of ranking with peers could easily be a prolonged process. Mutual comparisons between students start from the application process, continuing in everyday learning activities and they are, of course, significantly influenced by final grades at the end of courses.

Recently Zell and Alicke (2010) suggested the local dominance hypothesis for explaining the BFLPE, claiming that the same objective performance will lead to relatively positive academic self-concepts when the performance ranks favourably in the immediate environment (i.e. the class or school) and relatively negative academic self-concepts when the performance ranks unfavourably. Grades in university are ranking-signs from the immediate environment and this can be why they are more powerful in explaining SEs than previous grades or test scores. In summary, a student's GPA at the university was the only indicator (from three indicators of achievement and cognitive ability) that independently and implicitly related to the student's levels of self-reported SEs.

The importance of our findings

The finding that students who study in the institutions, which are more selective or place more emphasis on research have lower self-evaluations should not be taken lightly. These results are especially important in the light of different studies which have shown that self-concept, self-esteem and self-efficacy beliefs have influence on academic achievement (Schunk, 1991; Chemers et al., 2001; Pullmann and Allik, 2008; Phan, 2010; Prat-Sala and Redford, 2010). In other words, individuals who feel good and value themselves are more likely to achieve and learn successfully whereas individuals who have low self-worth tend to avoid learning (Phan, 2010). Diseth (2011) showed that SE can affect the difference between mediate the effects between previous and subsequent achievement. Lower achievement can lead to lower SEs which in turn can influence subsequent performance. So external influence, like the selective environment described in relation to the BFLPE, can cause a vicious circle.

The BFLPE means that students in the ROU, although having high intellectual potential, are less likely to perceive themselves in a positive manner in the academic context compared to the IPHEs students. This controversy could be explained by the theory of relative deprivation (Davis, 1966): students seem to have lost their feelings of high competence. This feeling of deprivation may lead to low future aspirations and to a bigger risk of dropping out. Both are the kind of problems which institutions of higher education should avoid.

Based on the above, it is important that the teachers as well as the students are aware of the negative effect of selective environments on SEs and the fact that different aspects of SEs are strongly associated with diverse aspects of achievement emphasizes the importance of awareness when it comes to the BFLPE.

In conclusion we think it is important for further studies to focus on the fact that the selectivity of schools and universities and the emphasis on research may have unexpected effects on students′ aspirations and academic achievements, as well as on their overall development. We believe that acknowledging the BFLPE can, in the long run, help to prevent the possible negative effects that the transition from high school to university can have on students.

Our suggestion for lecturers in more research-oriented institutions of higher education is to be aware of the vulnerability of students' self-evaluations. As the BFLPE has been shown to be quite robust, manifesting itself at different levels of the education system, in different nations and on students of different ages (Davis, 1966; Marsh, 1987; Marsh et al., 2007). It could be that the effect is caused by the education system itself, or, to quote Deci and Ryan (2002:61): the harder you push, the worse it gets. As the pressure on students tends to be greater in research-oriented universities one could suggest that these institutions may have forgotten the emotional and psychological well-being of their students.

Limitations of our study and further research

Possibly the biggest limitation of our study is the size of the sample. There were more students from the ROU and female students were more willing to complete the questionnaire. It was difficult to generalize the results to both genders because the proportion of male students in the study was less than 20 per cent. As it was not possible to give reliable estimates for parameters, we decided to exclude men. Therefore, the results hold for female students only. It should be noted that the BFLPE has been found to be greater amongst women than men (Preckel et al., 2008). So, the results of a similar analysis could be different for men. Also it should be noted that the index of NER was self-reported by the respondents so we cannot be sure that they are correct. In terms of self-reported scores it should be taken into account that there is a tendency for overestimation (Mayer et al., 2007).

Our study refers to the mutual relationships rather than influences of some variables to others. We saw that in the ROU students have high NER marks and low levels of SE indicators. As our respondents were mainly first and second year students, the time in that learning environment could be too short to reach conclusions about causal influences. We could not consider the potential impact from the high-schools that the students attended before as we had no information about their previous levels of SEs. Based on this, we believe it is important to conduct a longitudinal study so that the impact of the previous school can be taken into account. A longitudinal study is also likely to give a better overview of the long term impact of the BFLPE on the SEs of individuals.

Acknowledgement

The preparation of this article was supported by a Primus grant (3-8.2/60) from the European Social Fund and by a targeted funding grant from the Estonian Ministry of Education and Research (SF0140094s08).

References

Alexander, K. L. and Eckland, B. K. (1977). High school context and college selectivity: institutional constraints in educational stratification. *Social Forces*, 56, 166–188.

Alwin, D. F. and Otto, L. B. (1977). High school context on aspirations. *Sociology of Education*, 50, 259–273.

Astin, (1968). Undergraduate achievement and institutional "excellence". *Science*, 161, 661–668.

Astin, A. (1993). *What Matters in College? Four Critical Years Revisited.* San Francisco: Jossey-Bass.

Attawell, P. (2001). The winner-take-all high school: Organizational adaptations to educational stratification. *Sociology of Education*, 74, 267–295.

Bandura, A. (1977). Self-efficacy: Toward a unifying theory of behavioral change. *Psychological Review*, 84, 191–215.

Barber, L. K., Munz, D. C., Bagsby, P. G. and Grawitch, M. J. (2009). When does time perspective matter? Self-control as a moderator between time perspective and academic achievement. *Personality and Individual Differences*, 46, 250–253.

Chemers, M. M., Hu, L. and Garcia, B. (2001). Academic self-efficacy and first-year college student performance and adjustment. *Journal of Educational Psychology*, 93, 55–64.

Davis, J. A. (1966). The campus as a Frog Pond: An application of the Theory of Relative Deprivation to career decisions of collage men. *American Journal of Sociology*, 72, 17–31.

Deci, E. L., and Ryan, R. M. (2002). The paradox of achievement: The harder you push, the worse it gets. In Aronson, J. (Ed.), *Improving academic achievement: Contributions of social psychology*. New York: Academic Press, 59–85.

Deci, E. L. and Ryan, M. R. (2000). Intrinsic and extrinsic motivations: Classic definitions and new directions. Contemporary *Educational Psychology*, 25, 54–67.

Diseth, A. (2011). Self-efficacy, goal orientations and learning strategies as mediators between preceding and subsequent academic achievement. *Learning and Individual Differences*, 21, 191–195.

Drew, D. E. and Astin, A. W. (1972). Undergraduate aspirations: A test of several theories. *American Journal of Sociology*, 77, 1151–1164.

Festinger, L. (1954). A theory of social comparison processes. *Human Relations*, 7, 117–140.

Hansford, B. C. and Hattie, J. A. (1982). The relationship between self and achievement/performance measures. *Review of Educational Research*, 52, 123–142.

Marsh, H. W. (1990). Causal ordening of academic self-concept and academic achievement: A multiwave, longitudinal panel analysis. *Journal of Educational Psychology*, 82, 646–656.

Marsh, H. W., Hau, K.-T. and Kong, C.-K. (2002). Multilevel causal ordering of academic self-concept and achievement: Influence of language of instruction (English compared with Chinese) for Hong Kong students. *American Educational Research Journal*, 39, 727–763.

Marsh, H. W. (1992). Content specificity of relations between academic achievement and academic self-concept. *Journal of Educational Psychology*, 84, 35–42.

Marsh, H. W. (1987). The Big-Fish-Little-Pond Effect on academic self-concept. *Journal of Educational Psychology*, 79, 280–295.

Marsh, H. W. and Hau, K.-T. (2003). Big-Fish-Little-Pond Effect on academic self-concept: A cross-cultural (26-country) test of the negative effects of academically selective schools. *American Psychologist*, 58, 364–376.

Marsh, H. W. and Parker, J. W. (1984). Determinants of student self-concept: Is it better to be a relatively large fish in a small pond even if you don't learn to swim as well? *Journal of Personality and Social Psychology*, 41, 213–231.

Marsh, H. W., Kong, C.-K. and Hau, K.-T. (2000). Longitudinal multilevel models of the Big-Fish-Little-Pond Effect on academic self-concept: Counterbalancing contrast and reflected-glory effects in Hong Kong schools. *Journal of Personality and Social Psychology*, 78, 337–349.

Marsh, H. W., Trautwein, U., Lüdtke, O., Baumert, J. and Köller, O. (2007). The Big-Fish-Little-Pond Effect: Persistent negative effects of selective high schools on self-concept after graduation. *American Educational Research Journal*, 44, 631–669.

Mattern, K. D. and Shaw, E. J. (2010). A look beyond cognitive predictors of academic success: understanding the relationship between academic self-beliefs and outcomes. *Journal of College Student Development*, 51, 665–678.

Mayer, R. E., Stull, A. T., Campbell, J., Almeroth, K., Bimber, B., Chun, D. and Knight, A. (2007). Overestimation bias on self-reported SAT scores. *Educational Psychology Review*, 19, 443–454.

McFarland, C. and Buehler, R. (1995). Collective self-esteem as a moderator of the Frog-Pond effect in reactions to performance feedback. *Journal of Personality and Social Psychology*, 68, 1055–1070.

Must, O. and Allik, J. (2001). *Tunne oma võimeid. Abivahend eneseanalüüsiks* [Know your abilities. A tool for self-analysis]. Tartu: Tartu Ülikooli Kirjastus.

Neiss, M., Sedikides, C. and Stevenson, J. (2002). Self-esteem: A behavioral genetic perspective. *European Journal of Personality*, 16, 351–367.

O'Brian, R. (2007). A Caution Regarding Rules of Thumb for Variance Inflation Factors. *Quality and Quantity*, 41, 673–690.

Pascarella, E. and Terenzini, P. (2005). *How college affects students: A third decade of research*. San Francisco: Jossey-Bass.

Phan, H. P. (2010). Students' academic performance and various cognitive processes of learning: An integrative framework and empirical analysis. Educational Psychology, 30, 297–322.

Prat-Sala, M. and Redford, P. (2010). The interplay between motivation, self-efficacy, and approaches to studying. *British Journal of Educational Psychology*, 80, 283–305.

Preckel, F., Zeidner, M., Goetz, T. and Schleyer E. J. (2008). Female 'big fish' swimming against the tide: The 'big-fish-little-pond effect' and gender-ratio in special gifted classes. *Contemporary Educational Psychology*, 33, 78–96.

Pullmann, H. and Allik, J. (2008). Relations of academic general self-esteem to school achievement. *Personality and Individual Difference*, 45, 559–564.

Pullmann, H. and Allik, J. (2000). The Rosenberg Self-Esteem Scale: its dimensionality, stability and personality correlates in Estonian. *Personality and Individual Differences*, 28, 701–715.

Rimm, H., Jerusalem, M. (1999). Adaptation and validation of an Estonian version of the general self-efficacy scale. *Anxiety, Stress and Coping*, 12, 329–345.

Robbins, S., Lauver, K., Le, H., Davis, D., Langley, R. and Carlstrom, A. (2004). Do psychosocial and study skill factors predict college outcomes? A meta-analysis. *Psychological Bulletin*, 130, 261–288.

Rosenberg, M. (1965). *Society and the adolescent self-image*. Princeton, NJ: Princeton University Press.

Rosenberg, M., Schooler, C., Schoenbach, C. and Rosenberg, F. (1995). Global self-esteem and specific self-esteem: Different concepts, different outcomes. *American Sociological Review*, 60, 141–156.

Schunk, D. H. (1991). Self-efficacy and academic motivation. *Educational Psychologist*, 26, 207–231.

Seaton, M., Marsh, H. M. and Craven, R. G. (2009). Earning its place as a pan-human theory: Universality of the Big-Fish-Little-Pond Effect across 41 culturally and economically diverse countries. *Journal of Educational Psychology*, 101, 403–419.

Simons, J., Vansteenkiste, M., Lens, W. and Lacante, M. (2004). Placing motivation and future time perspective theory in a temporal perspective. *Educational Psychology Review*, 16, 121–139.

Zell, E. and Alicke, M. (2010). The Local Dominance Effect in Self-Evaluation: Evidence and Explanations. *Personality and Social Psychology Review*, 14, 368–384.

Zhang, L. (2003). *How college affects students: toward the reconciliation of theory with empirical evidence.* A Dissertation submitted to the faculty of the centre for the study of higher education. The University of Arizona.

Zhang, L. (2005). Do measures of college quality matter? The effect of college quality on graduates' earnings. *The Review of Higher Education*, 28, 571–596.

Thistlethwaite, D. L. and Wheeler, N. (1966). Effects of teacher and peer subcultures upon student aspirations. *Journal of Educational Psychology*, 57, 36–47.

Tõnisson, E. (2011). *Kõrghariduse valdkonna statistiline ülevaade 2011* [Statistical overview of higher education 2011]. Tartu: Estonian Ministry of Education and Research. Available online and only in Estonian: http://www.hm.ee/index.php?048183

Werts, C. E. and Watley, D. J. (1969). A student's dilemma: Big fish – little pond or little fish – big pond. *Journal of Counseling Psychology*, 16, 14–19.

Üpraus, R. (2009). Akadeemiline edukus: Akadeemilise enese-tõhususe mõõtmine. [Academic achievement. Measurement of academic self-efficacy]. Seminaritöö Tartu Ülikool [Seminar paper. University of Tartu].

Chapter 4.
Fatigue does not predict academic performance among university students

Helle Pullmann, Anu Realo, Kairi Kreegipuu, Jüri Allik, René Mõttus

Introduction

'Nothing is so fatiguing as the eternal hanging on of an uncompleted task'.
James (1926)

Subjective fatigue, which is very common in everyday modern life, is described as a perceived state of a pervasive sense of tiredness or lack of energy that is not related exclusively to exertion (Brown and Schutte, 2006), an aversion to continue with the present activity, and a decrease in the level of commitment to the task in hand (Holding, 1983). Mental fatigue is a feeling that people may experience during or after prolonged periods of cognitive activity (Boksem and Tops, 2008), for example during university studies. Mental fatigue has been associated with impaired cognitive and behavioural performance and also with difficulties in focusing attention and planning (e.g. Boksem, Meijman and Lorist, 2005; Lorist, Boksem and Ridderinkhof, 2005; van der Linden and Eling, 2006). However, prolonged intensive effort will not always result in pervasive fatigue but its effect will depend on the outcomes achieved – successful performance or better pay can effectively reduce perceived fatigue (Boksem and Tops, 2008). Moreover, fatigue has a potential negative impact, not only on a student's state of health (Laberge et al., 2011), but also on curricular attendance, pleasure in learning and understanding lectures (Tanaka et al., 2008).

So, clarifying the role of subjective fatigue in academic achievement is potentially very important for reducing the dropout rate and improving success in universities. However, only a few studies (e.g. Lee, Chien and Chen, 2007) have examined the possible lifestyle risk factors associated with fatigue among university students and, surprisingly, the effect of fatigue on post-secondary academic performance is still unclear. The current study provided a comprehensive approach to the fatigue-performance interplay by including various psychological and demographic variables as co-variates. In particular, we proposed and tested a theoretical fatigue-oriented model focussing on academic performance, which incorporated probable antecedents as predictors, as well as possible mediators and some important co-variates.

Theoretical background

Fatigue

Fatigue is a subjective symptom of malaise and aversion to activity or objectively impaired performance (Sharpe and Wilks, 2002) and is a common problem seen in community samples (Chen, 1986; Loge, Ekeberg and Kaasa, 1998). Subjective fatigue is normally distributed in the population and, therefore, can best be understood as a continuum (Lewis and Wessely, 1992), ranging from mild complaints to persistent and severe fatigue, such as chronic fatigue syndrome (CFS), which is a medically unexplained illness with a diversity of phenotypes. Surveys suggest that up to 20 per cent or more of the general population suffer from troublesome and persistent fatigue (Sharpe and Wilks, 2002; Ranjith, 2005; Kocalevent et al., 2011). In a recent survey by the European Commission, about 17 per cent of the Estonian respondents aged 15 years and over felt tired most of the time (Eurobarometer, 2010). Oginska and Pokorski (2006) find fatigue symptoms are as frequent amongst university students as they are amongst hard-working adults.

Fatigue is a complex condition associated with many physiological, psychological and pathological processes and, as a result, possible causal pathways leading to fatigue have rarely been demonstrated (Sharpe and Wilks, 2002). Existing literature indicates that fatigue is a multicausal, multidimensional, non-specific and subjective phenomenon, which results from prolonged activity, health-related, psychological, socioeconomic or environmental factors that affect both the mind and the body (Lewis and Wessely, 1992; Tiesinga, Dassen and Halfens, 1996). As a gradual and cumulative process, fatigue is a general psychophysiological phenomenon that reduces the ability of an individual to perform a particular task, by altering alertness and vigilance and the motivational and subjective states that occur during this transition (Thiffault and Bergeron, 2003). It has even been proposed as a kind of self-fulfilling process: perceived fatigue can be higher after poor performance than after success (Boksem and Tops, 2008). Cognitive tests of CFS patients have revealed disturbances of memory, attention and information processing, altered short-term memory (DeLuca et al., 1997; Wearden and Appleby, 1997; Michiels and Cluydts, 2001; Capuron et al., 2006; Michiels et al., 1996), and a reduction in the ability to plan ahead (van der Linden, Frese and Meijman, 2003). Severe fatigue is associated with impairment of cognitive function and academic performance among students (Mizuno et al., 2011). Research also shows that persistent fatigue has a negative impact on education and career plans, particularly through the failure to attend school (Patel et al., 2003; Sankey et al., 2006; Bakker et al., 2009).

Although fatigue among students may most commonly be due to atypical lifestyle habits, such as irregular meals (Tanaka et al., 2008), insufficient sleep (Lavidor, Weller and Babkoff, 2003) or insufficient physical activity (Viner et al., 2008), there may be other risk factors that are still poorly understood (Lee et al., 2007). When moving to university, students must learn to cope with a new set of intellectual, social and financial demands, while often also living on their own for the first time in their lives. Both fatigue and academic performance at university may be affected by other factors, such as undertaking employment whilst being a student, personality traits, self-concept and motivation.

The role of employment status

A substantial proportion of European university students take jobs while they are at university (Häkkinen, 2006). The Eurostudent survey (2010) found that employment rates for students in Europe ranged from 48 per cent in France to 77 per cent in The Netherlands. On average, 54 per cent of Estonian university students spend at least 5 hours per week in paid employment; however, the rate of employment during studies is much higher for part-time students (75 per cent) and students over 30 years old (89 per cent) (Eurostudent IV, 2010).

While student employment has positive consequences (e.g. becoming independent, learning to manage money, building self-confidence and acquiring job skills) Bradley (2006) reports there is also a range of negative consequences. Research on fatigue's adverse effects have focussed on an increased risk of cumulative sleep deprivation, stress and daytime sleepiness (e.g. Mortimer et al., 1996; Salamonson and Andrew, 2006; Teixeira, Fischer and Lowden, 2006; Laberge et al., 2011). Research also notes a clear correlation between adverse effects and the number of hours worked (Miller, Danner and Staten, 2008; Wang et al., 2010).

So, the employment status (i.e. full-time, part-time, unemployed) of students may be an important factor in the relationship between fatigue and university success measured in grade point averages (GPA). Astin (1993) as well as Tinto (1993) and Salamanson and Andrew (2006) suggest that employment has a negative effect on GPA by limiting the time that a student has for academic studies. This could be confirmed by finding a direct association between employment status and GPA.

The role of personality traits

Although the causes of chronic fatigue syndrome (CFS) are not yet fully understood, many researchers have turned to psychological explanations, including aspects of personality, to examine whether basic personality traits could influence, cause or maintain persistent feelings of fatigue (Abdel-Khalek, 2009). Although several studies suggest that increased post morbid neuroticism and introversion in CFS may have changed as a result of the illness (Buckley et al., 1999), we are using the theoretical framework of the five-factor model of personality (McCrae and Costa, 1996), which suggests that certain personality traits may put a person at a higher risk of developing sub-clinical levels of fatigue. Indeed, research shows that personality traits account for a significant proportion of variance in fatigue (De Vries and Van Heck, 2002).

We expect that neuroticism, that is, a tendency to worry and experience distressing emotions, may predispose people to subjective fatigue. Previous studies show that individuals with high levels of neuroticism feel more fatigued at all points during the day (Matthews and Desmond, 1998; Bolger and Schilling, 1991; Calderwood and Ackerman, 2011). There is some consistent evidence to suggest that patients with CFS score higher on neuroticism scales when compared with the general population (Johnson, DeLuca and Natelson, 1996; Buckley et al., 1999; Taillefer et al., 2003; van Geelen et al., 2007; Deary and Chalder, 2010; Nater et al., 2010). Moreover, in a prospective population-based study, neuroticism predicted chronic fatigue 25 years later (Kato et al., 2006). These studies clearly highlight the important relationship between neuroticism and persistent fatigue, therefore, we expect that neuroticism may also be significant in fatigue amongst university students.

As well as high levels of neuroticism, low levels of extraversion have been identified as a risk factor in the development of CFS (Prins, van der Meer and Bleijenberg, 2006). Based on previous studies demonstrating that low levels of extraversion are associated with increased levels of sub-clinical fatigue (Buckley et al., 1999; De Vries and Van Heck, 2002; Taillefer et al., 2003; Nater et al., 2010), which has also been found in the student population (Abdel-Khalek, 2009), we expect that fatigue is negatively related to extraversion.

Only a few studies examining fatigue have incorporated the personality traits of being agreeable, conscientious and open to new experiences (De Vries and Van Heck, 2002). However, there are some studies that have demonstrated a negative relationship between being conscientious and fatigue (Mills and Huebner, 1998; De Vries and Van Heck, 2002), but inconsistent results have also been reported (Besharat et al., 2011). Since CFS patients report being less conscientious than healthy individuals (Nater et al., 2010), we expect being conscientious to be negatively associated with fatigue.

Personality traits have also been extensively linked with academic performance amongst university students. Meta-analyses confirm that being conscientious is the most consistent predictor of post-secondary academic achievement, whereas neuroticism, being an extrovert, being open to new experiences, and being agreeable have no significant impact on academic success, as measured by university grades (O'Connor and Paunonen, 2007; Trapmann et al., 2007). Being conscientious encompasses many characteristics that are important for college success, including the drive to accomplish, being organised, efficient, systematic, orderly, and steady (Trapmann et al., 2007).

Based on the links between personality traits and fatigue described above, the associations between personality traits and academic performance may be mediated by fatigue. Our study therefore proposed that personality traits are both possible antecedents of fatigue and direct contributors to academic performance.

However, the situation may be even more complicated. First, being conscientious is shown to affect academic performance indirectly through academic motivation (Richardson and Abraham, 2009; De Feyter et al., 2012; Hazrati-Viari, Rad and Torabi, 2012), which suggests the need to include academic motivation as another possible factor (in addition to fatigue) in the personality trait-academic performance association. Second, the predictive validity of being conscientious for academic performance at university may substantially overlap with that of prior school performance (Trapmann et al., 2007). To account for this possibility, we included an indicator of prior school performance as a co-variate in the prediction of academic performance.

In summary we expect that being conscientious is significantly positively related to university grades for Estonian students and has some incremental validity over prior high school performance. We also expect fatigue and academic motivation to be subsequent mediators in the associations between academic performance and personality traits (especially being conscientious). These factors and relationships are graphically presented in Figure 1.

The role of self-esteem

The cognitive behavioural model of CFS (Sharpe, 1997) suggests that core beliefs reflecting low self-esteem lead to the development of rigidly held beliefs that predispose a person to develop a chronic illness when confronted by a stressful trigger. Reduced self-worth is a common complaint among individuals with CFS (Garralda et al., 1999), who report lower general self-esteem than the healthy control group (White and Schweitzer, 2000; Creswell and Chalder, 2002). In addition, a significant positive correlation between fatigue and low self-esteem has been found (Fragoso, Silva and Finkelsztejn, 2009), indicating that general self-esteem may have an effect on an individual's susceptibility to feelings of fatigue. Research has demonstrated that individuals with higher self-esteem are persistent in the face of failure and have greater aspirations than those with lower self-esteem (Baumeister et al., 2003). Individuals with a predisposition to CFS may assume that, in order to be acceptable to themselves and others, they must set and meet high standards of performance (White and Schweitzer, 2000). If these standards are not met, the individual may believe that they have failed as a person, resulting in reduced self-esteem which may in turn induce feelings of fatigue.

Self-esteem is one of the most widely studied personality concepts in psychology (Judge et al., 2002) and its relationship with academic achievement remains an intensively researched topic (Huang, 2011). However, general and academic self-esteem are two distinguishable components with dissimilar functions. Research has shown that general self-esteem is more strongly related to overall psychological well-being and life-satisfaction (see Baumeister et al., 2003, for an overview), whereas academic self-esteem is a good predictor of school performance (Rosenbert et al., 1995; Pullmann and Allik, 2008). Academic self-esteem is a self-perception that is formed through the student's personal experience and interpretation of the school environment (Marsh and Craven, 1997), while general self-esteem is a more stable personal characteristic that is strongly related to personality traits (Pullmann and Allik, 2000) and it may have an effect on perceived fatigue.

Based on the findings described above, we consider general self-esteem to be a trait-like construct and expect it to predict academic performance directly and indirectly via its possible contribution to fatigue. Following Eccles and Wigfield (2002), we consider academic self-esteem to be a motivational construct because of its close links with academic attributions and the evaluation of academic success amongst students. Therefore, like academic motivation, we consider academic self-esteem to be a more down-stream mediator, which may also be affected by fatigue. In addition, we propose academic self-esteem as a possible mediator in the association between general self-esteem and academic performance.

The aims of the study

Our study examined the impact of everyday-fatigue on academic performance (measured in terms of grade point average; GPA) in universities, particularly examining the potential antecedents and mediators of this relationship. Based on the theoretical framework described, we proposed a structural model (presented in Figure 1) that specifies the direct as well as the indirect effects of fatigue, and a number of other variables, on university grades.

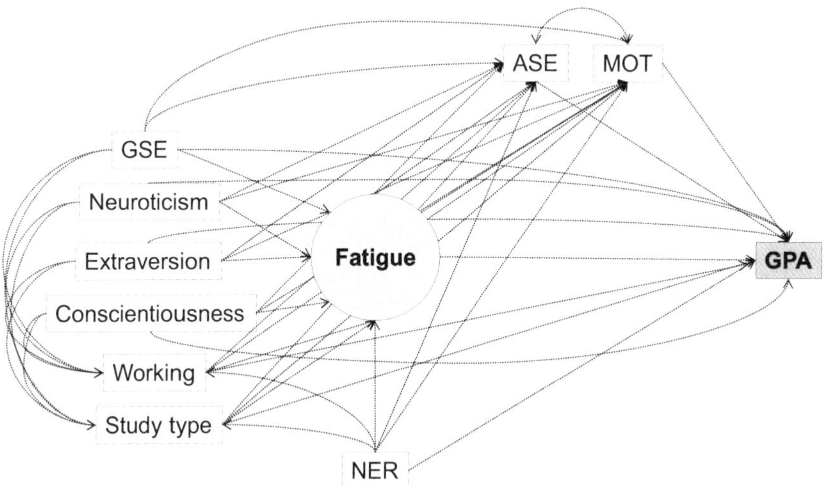

Figure 1. *Hypothesised structural model examining the impact of fatigue on academic performance at university.*

Notes. GSE = general self-esteem, ASE = academic self-esteem, MOT = academic motivation, NER = prior school performance, GPA = weighted grade point average. The latent variable 'Fatigue' (defined by the subscales of the Multidimensional Fatigue Inventory, MFI) is represented by the circle and observed variables are represented by squares; GPA is regarded as an outcome. Single-headed arrows represent regression paths, whereas double-headed arrows represent correlations. Gender and age are included as background variables but not shown in the figure.

In particular, academic performance was linked to a set of increasingly distant predictors. We considered academic self-esteem and motivation as most proximal predictors of university grades, then fatigue and, finally, stable individual differences, such as personality traits and general self-esteem, as the most upstream predictors. Because they were measured before other variables, the results of the national examinations were also seen as distant predictors. We also hypothesised that the students' employment status and whether or not they are part-time or distance learning students may increase the level of fatigue and predict academic performance directly, or via fatigue, academic self-esteem or motivation.

Method

Participants

Cross-sectional data used in this study were collected from 2009 to 2011 from an on-going longitudinal survey *'Factors predicting academic performance in university students'*. During the course *'Know Thyself: A Practical Introduction to the Psychology of Individual Differences'* at the University of Tartu, students completed a large number of self-administered questionnaires and received individual online feedback on their test results. The course was designed especially for the survey referred to above, its aim being to teach the main psychological concepts and methods to students in order to improve their ability to analyse and evaluate their psychological qualities. The majority of the participants were first-year students and on completion of the course the students are followed up for five years until they graduate from university. The project was approved by the Ethics Committee of the University of Tartu and subjects provided their informed consent before participating.

This study was based on data from 232 students from the University of Tartu with a mean age of 28.4 (SD = 8.01) years, ranging from 19 to 53 years. The sample consisted of: psychology students – 41 per cent (n = 94); 'non-psychology students' from other institutes of the Faculty of Social Sciences and Education – 25 per cent (n = 59) and students from a mix of other faculties of the University of Tartu – 34 per cent (n = 79). The sample consisted of 196 women (84 per cent) and 36 men (16 per cent), which is a much higher proportion of women than in social sciences and Estonian higher education in general (Tõnisson, 2011). About 66 per cent (n = 152) of the participants were enrolled for part-time or distance learning studies and about a third were regular students enrolled for non-distance studies (n = 80). Part-time or distance learning students were much more likely to have full-time jobs and family responsibilities, being significantly older than the regular students (m = 31.7 and 22.2 years, respectively, t = 10.3, $p < .001$). About 73 per cent of the part-time or distance learning students were employed during their studies compared to 21 per cent of the non-distance learning students in this sample. Therefore, gender, age, enrolment type, and self-reported employment status (*'Are you currently employed?'*) were included in the analyses as control variables.

Measures

Fatigue

The Estonian version of the Multidimensional Fatigue Inventory (MFI) (Smets et al., 1995; Oberg, 2007) was used to assess the level of self-reported general fatigue. The questionnaire consists of five subscales of fatigue: general fatigue, physical fatigue, mental fatigue, reduced activity, and reduced motivation. *General fatigue* includes general statements about fatigue and decreased functioning and encompasses both physical and psychological aspects of fatigue. *Physical fatigue* concerns physical sensations related to fatigue. *Mental fatigue* refers to cognitive functioning, including difficulty concentrating. *Reduced activity* refers to the influence of physical and psychological factors on the level of activity. *Reduced motivation* relates to lack of motivation for starting any activity. Each subscale included four items that were answered on a 5-point scale (1 – *not true* ... 5 – *true*), with higher scores indicating a higher level of general fatigue. The internal consistency coefficient (Cronbach α) of the total scale was .88. In this sample, the total score of the MFI was strongly correlated ($r = .80$, $p < .001$) with another measure of perceived overall fatigue, the Estonian version of the Fatigue Assessment Scale (Michielsen et al., 2004; Oberg, 2005), confirming the content validity of the questionnaire.

Academic performance

Academic success at university was measured using students' weighted GPAs obtained from the institutional records of the University of Tartu. The GPA consisted of students' average grades (A=5, B=4, C=3, D=2, E=1, F=0) that were weighted by the subjects' credit point value attained in all courses completed during the testing semester. In this sample the mean value of the weighted GPA was $m = 2.88$ ($SD = 1.01$).

Personality traits. The EPIP-NEO (Mõttus, Pullmann and Allik, 2006) measures five personality domains – Neuroticism (N), Extraversion (E), Openness (O), Agreeableness (A), and Conscientiousness (C) – that are each described by six facet scales. The structure of the test is similar to the NEO-PI-R (Costa and McCrae, 1992) but the EPIP-NEO is designed to be linguistically simpler, containing shorter and less grammatically complex phrases (for more detailed information see Mõttus et al., 2006).

General self-esteem. Overall attitude toward oneself or general self-esteem (GSE) was measured by the Estonian version of the Rosenberg Self-Esteem Scale (Pullmann and Allik, 2000). Participants indicated their extent of agreement or disagreement with 10 statements such as '*On the whole, I am satisfied with myself*' on a 5-point scale ranging from 1 (*strongly disagree*) to 5 (*strongly agree*). The internal consistency coefficient (Cronbach α) of the scale was .84.

Academic self-esteem. Perception of academic self-competence or academic self-esteem (ASE) was measured on the 8-item Academic Self-Esteem Scale (Pullmann and Allik, 2008). Typical items include '*I am one of the best students on my course*' and '*I do well in most subjects*'. Agreement with each item was rated on a 5-point scale, ranging from 1 *(strongly disagree)* to 5 *(strongly agree)*. The internal consistency coefficient (Cronbach α) of the scale was .78.

Academic motivation. The 12-item scale to measure academic motivation and interest to learn (MOT) was developed by Karin Täht and Olev Must on the basis of the PISA 2006 attitudinal questionnaire. Agreement with each item was rated on a 5-point scale, ranging from 1 *(strongly disagree)* to 5 *(strongly agree)*. The internal consistency coefficient of the measure was $\alpha = .80$.

Prior school performance. Prior academic performance was estimated by the index based on the results of the national examinations (NER) taken when graduating from high school or before applying to university. The participants were asked to report their NER results (0…100 points) on a 5-point scale (1 – *grades lower than 30* ….. 5 – *grades higher than 90*), with higher values indicating a higher level of school achievement. Research suggests that self-reported grades are reasonably good reflections of actual grades for students with high ability and good GPAs (Kuncel, Credé and Thomas, 2005).

Data Analysis

The initial analyses involved an examination of zero-order correlations of predictor variables with fatigue and GPA. Next, structural equation modelling (SEM) was used to test the theoretical multivariate path model shown in Figure 1; note that the measurement part of the model (i.e., the observed indicators defining the latent fatigue factor) is not shown. A latent fatigue factor was defined by the subscales of the MFI in order to produce a well-defined model of subjective everyday-fatigue (represented by the circle in Figures 1 and 2). The loadings of the MFI subscales on the latent factor varied between 0.60 and 0.91 (not shown in Figure 2). Since fatigue is more prevalent in women than in men, and younger participants report significantly higher fatigue ratings (Junghaenel et al., 2011), all variables in the model were controlled for gender and age (for simplicity these were not presented in Figure 1). Personality traits and general self-esteem were allowed to be correlated (again, for simplicity these were not shown in Figure 1). Other paths can be seen in Figure 1. Statistical analyses were performed using SPSS version 19.0 for Windows (SPSS, Inc.) and the path model was implemented in Mplus 6.12 (Muthén and Muthén, 2011).

Results

Descriptive statistics of the measured variables (including gender differences) are presented in Table 1.

The comparison of the MFI scores did not confirm our hypothesis that students on part-time or distance learning courses have a higher level of fatigue than regular students. On the contrary, the analysis revealed that regular students reported significantly higher levels of general fatigue than part-time or distance learning students, $F(230) = 13.6$, $p < .001$, partial eta squared (η^2) = 0.06. Also, perceived fatigue was significantly lower amongst working students compared to those who were not employed during their university studies, $F(216) = 17.6$, $p < .001$, partial $\eta^2 = 0.07$. As for the university grades, there were no significant differences between employed and non-working students [$F(216) = 0.07$, *ns*, partial $\eta^2 = 0.01$], or for the part-time or distance learning and regular students [$F(230) = 1.53$, *ns*, partial $\eta^2 = 0.01$]. There was no significant interaction between students' employment status (yes vs. no) and enrolment type (regular vs. part-time or distance learning) in predicting their university grades, [$F(212) = 0.20$, *ns*, partial $\eta^2 = 0.01$] or fatigue [$F(212) = 0.76$, *ns*, partial $\eta^2 = 0.03$] with gender and age used as co-variates.

Zero-order correlations between GPA, MFI scores and the other variables are presented in Table 1. The total score of the MFI had a weak but significant negative association with academic success at university, indicating that, on average, academically less successful students report higher levels of perceived fatigue. However, more detailed analyses revealed that only mental aspects of fatigue (including difficulties in concentrating) predicted significantly lower grades in university, whereas physical sensations relating to fatigue, reduced activity and lack of motivation for starting any activity, were not associated with academic performance. Different aspects of fatigue revealed a more consistent pattern of relationships with personality traits, indicating that less neurotic and more extrovert and conscientious students reported lower levels of multiple fatigue. In addition, fatigue was significantly associated with lower levels of self-esteem and academic motivation.

Mean grades in university (as indicated by GPA) were significantly positively correlated with prior school performance (as measured by the results of national examinations), academic motivation, and both self-esteem measures. With respect to personality traits, only being conscientious was significantly related to university grades. The traits of being open and agreeable were empirically unrelated to both fatigue and GPA (ie: academic performance) and this was consistent with the hypothesised model (Figure 1).

The results of the structural modelling revealed that extraversion and conscientiousness were significantly linked to fatigue, albeit with reduced effect sizes (β = -0.26 and -0.31, $p < .001$, respectively) compared to the zero-order correlations presented in Table 1. However, the initial significant relationship between neuroticism and fatigue, as measured by the MFI scale, reduced to β = 0.02, *ns*, indicating that the association was confounded by other personal disposition variables, including general self-esteem, which correlated at β = -0.60 ($p < .001$) with neuroticism and was also the strongest predictor of fatigue (β = -0.37, $p < .001$). No other variable (working, part-time or distance learning studies or national examinations results) was significantly linked to fatigue in the multivariate model.

GPA was significantly predicted by academic self-esteem (β = 0.29, $p <$ .001), results in the national examinations (β = 0.24, $p < .01$) and being conscientious (β = 0.19, $p < .05$). In the multivariate model, the association between the fatigue scale and GPA was not significant, with the standardized parameter estimate of general fatigue on academic performance being β = -0.02 (*ns*). Thus, fatigue did not have an increasing effect on reducing university grades and the significant zero-order correlation (Table 1) was confounded by other variables in the model. There were no indirect associations between fatigue and GPA either; fatigue significantly predicted motivation (MOT), which was not associated with GPA over and above the contributions from other variables, and fatigue was not significantly associated with academic self-esteem (ASE). There was, however, an indirect contribution from general self-esteem (GSE) to GPA (β = 0.14, $p < .05$), primarily via academic self-esteem. Prior school performance (NER) was another significant indirect contributor to GPA (β = 0.09, $p < .05$), primarily via academic self-esteem. The indirect associations are not presented in Figure 1. Overall, the model explained 25 per cent of the variance in GPA.

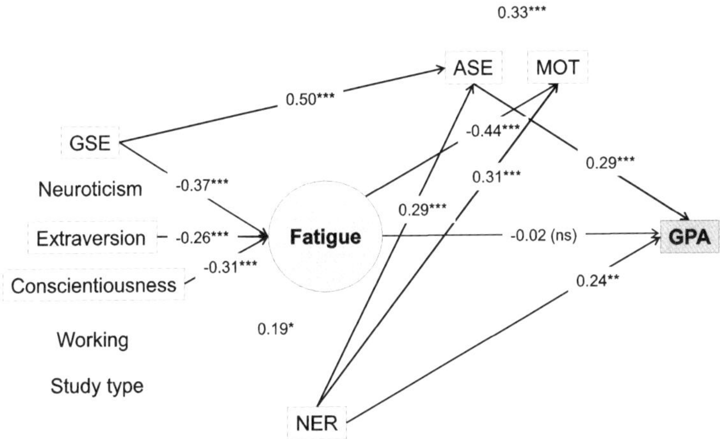

Figure 2. *Standardized parameter estimates of the final structural model examining the impact of fatigue on academic performance in university*

Notes. *** $p < .001$; ** $p < .01$; * $p < .05$; ns = non-significant ($p \geq .05$). GSE = general self-esteem, ASE = academic self-esteem, MOT = academic motivation, NER = prior school performance, GPA = weighted grade point average. Latent variable 'Fatigue' (defined by the subscales of the MFI) is represented by the circle and observed variables are represented by rectangles; GPA is regarded as an outcome. Single-headed arrows represent regression paths, whereas double-headed arrows represent correlations. Gender and age are included as background variables but not shown in the figure.

Table 1. Descriptive statistics, gender differences and bivariate relations of university grades, fatigue and other variables

	Descriptive statistics		*Gender differences*		*Bivariate correlations*						
	Mean	(SD)	*t*	Partial η^2	University GPA	Total fatigue	General fatigue	Physical fatigue	Mental fatigue	Reduced motivation	Reduced activity
Total fatigue	46.6	(15.7)	-0.9	0.00	-.13*						
General fatigue	10.7	(4.0)	0.2	0.00	-.08	.83***					
Physical fatigue	10.1	(4.7)	0.8	0.00	-.05	.78***	.59***				
Mental fatigue	9.1	(3.7)	-1.0	0.00	-.20**	.78***	.56***	.45***			
Reduced motivation	6.9	(2.8)	-2.5*	0.03	-.08	.73***	.49***	.39***	.51***		
Reduced activity	9.8	(4.2)	-2.0	0.02	-.12	.89***	.66***	.56***	.66***	.68***	
Age	28.4	(8.0)	-1.5	0.01	-.01	-.19**	-.15*	-.11	-.24***	-.14*	-.15*
Neuroticism	124.4	(27.8)	1.2	0.01	-.11	.56***	.47***	.43***	.44***	.42***	.47***
Extraversion	162.7	(25.5)	1.6	0.01	.01	-.48***	-.36***	-.37***	-.23***	-.45***	-.52***
Openness	183.8	(16.9)	0.8	0.00	.05	-.12	-.10	-.06	-.06	-.18**	-.12
Agreeableness	173.6	(19.6)	2.6*	0.03	.10	-.13	-.06	-.15*	-.02	-.17*	-.12
Conscientiousness	173.9	(23.3)	3.1**	0.04	.23**	-.55***	-.33***	-.38***	-.51***	-.49***	-.53***
General self-esteem	38.8	(7.0)	0.9	0.00	.18*	-.64***	-.59***	-.38***	-.49***	-.54***	-.60***
Academic self-esteem	24.7	(5.6)	0.8	0.00	.38***	-.36***	-.33***	-.21**	-.36***	-.20**	-.32***
Academic motivation	49.0	(5.1)	2.5*	0.03	.24***	-.47***	-.32	-.26***	-.48***	-.38***	-.45***
National examinations	3.6	(0.7)	0.8	0.00	.27***	.09	.13	.01	.04	.13	.07

Note: *$p < .05$, **$p < .01$, ***$p < .001$. SD = Standard deviation, University GPA = weighted grade point average, Total fatigue = the total score of the Multidimensional Fatigue Inventory (MFI), Partial η^2 = Partial eta-squared. Higher *t*-statistic refers to higher scores in women.

Discussion

In the field of psychological research there has been interest in the predictors of academic performance for over a century, as the accurate prediction of individual differences in academic performance has important implications for education also at the post-secondary level (O'Connor and Paunonen, 2007). Fatigue has been suggested as one of the factors that is supposed to counteract to school success and career plans (Tanaka et al., 2008) but for some reason only a few studies have examined this effect in university students. Furthermore, there is a general problem that conclusions regarding the relationships between psychological variables and academic performance are often drawn exclusively on the basis of zero-order predictor-criterion correlations (O'Connor and Paunonen, 2007).

The present study examined the association between university students' self-reported fatigue and their academic performance. The study took a comprehensive approach to the potential association by embedding it in a set of variables including age, sex, working status, form of enrolment, prior high-school performance, the Big Five personality traits, and general self-esteem. The hypothesized moderators were academic self-esteem and motivation. Although there appeared to be a bivariate association between the level of general fatigue and academic performance, in that students with higher self-reported (especially mental) fatigue, tended to have lower grades, this link virtually vanished in the multivariate model. This means that after controlling for a number of other variables that were associated with both students' self-reported fatigue levels and their university grades, academic performance was independent of fatigue. This empirical finding contradicts our hypothesis. In what follows, we describe the associations that survived in the multivariate model and their possible implications.

We expected high levels of fatigue to be linked to employment status and part-time or distance learning studies, high neuroticism, low extraversion, being conscientious, and general self-esteem. The predictions concerning personality traits were partially confirmed, indicating that the more extrovert and conscientious students reported less fatigue. However, neuroticism was not associated with fatigue in the multivariate model, although previous studies have clearly and consistently highlighted the important role of neuroticism in developing feelings of fatigue (e.g. Johnson et al., 1996; Kato et al., 2006; Nater et al., 2010). This finding can be explained by neuroticism being highly negatively correlated with general self-esteem, a low level of which appeared to correlate most strongly with fatigue. As a result, self-esteem mediated (Sobel test $z = 6.01$, $p < .001$) and absorbed the predictive value of neuroticism on fatigue. Such a 're-allocation' of the predictive value may not be of particular importance since, at a more general level, both neuroticism and self-esteem exploit negative emotions. It remains the case that people who experience negative emotions tend to report themselves as having higher levels of fatigue. Our hypothesis which considered the link between the students' employment status and heightened levels of fatigue was not supported either: everything else being equal, working students tended to report similar levels of fatigue to those students who did not work.

From among the variables considered in this study, academic self-esteem appeared to be the strongest direct predictor ($\beta = 0.29$) of the academic performance of students. A growing body of educational research shows that general self-esteem is only very weakly related to academic outcomes, while academic self-esteem is a good predictor of school grades (Marsh and Craven, 2006). Also, there is convincing evidence for the consistent positive effects of academic self-concept on subsequent achievement, after controlling not only for the effects of prior achievement, but also for other factors that could be confounded with self-beliefs (e.g. Valentine, DuBois and Cooper, 2004). Research has established that increases in academic self-esteem lead to increases in subsequent academic achievement and other desirable educational outcomes; moreover, academic self-esteem also plays a central role in mediating the effects of other desirable educational outcomes (Marsh and Martin, 2011). So, with respect to implications for achievement in school, students with more positive views of themselves and their abilities may engage in achievement-related behaviours, such as studying for tests and completing homework, because these help to confirm their self-perceptions (e.g. Pajares, Britner and Valiante, 2000). These processes may be most relevant specifically in relation to a positive academic self-concept, as opposed to a more general positive self-concept and the results of this study support this general pattern.

The second strongest predictor ($\beta = 0.24$) of academic performance at university was academic performance prior to university (measured in terms of national examination results). However, since prior school performance was significantly linked to academic self-esteem, it also made an indirect contribution to GPA ($\beta = 0.09$) and therefore was the predictor most strongly correlated with academic performance ($\beta = 0.24 + 0.09 = 0.33$). This suggests continuity in the tendency to be a successful learner: those factors that make people successful learners in high-school (and probably even at earlier stages of their studies) continue to contribute to their academic success. Some of these factors, such as personality traits and self-esteem, were considered in the multivariate model. As the association between prior school performance and performance at university persisted despite the inclusion of personality traits and self-esteem, other factors, unobserved in the current study, may be needed to explain the continuity in academic success. One of these unobserved factors may be individual differences in cognitive abilities. It has been extensively documented that general cognitive ability is one of the strongest predictors of academic performance at all levels of education (Kuncel, Hezlett and Ones, 2004). However, we included information about the students' prior academic achievements and this could be regarded as a proxy for intelligence.

The third and the weakest significant predictor of academic performance at university was being conscientious ($\beta = 0.19$). This result was expected as it has been well documented that people who are more conscientious do better at university (O'Connor and Paunonen, 2007; Trapmann et al., 2007) and in life in general (Judge et al., 1999). Although previous studies have suggested that the contribution of being conscientious to academic performance may be mediated by motivation, this did not appear to be the case in the present study because academic motivation was not significantly associated with being conscientious.

Interestingly, and contrary to our predictions, academic performance was independent of whether or not students worked during their university studies. Although previous studies have demonstrated that term-time employment tends to have negative consequences on academic progress, Beerkens, Mägi and Lill (2010) find that, at worst, employment only has a marginal effect on academic progress in Estonia, even though a large proportion of students work, some full-time. So, although it seems straightforward to expect that working limits the time and effort that students can devote to their studies, this does not appear to be the case in Estonia. An explanation might be the compensatory effect of self-selection. More precisely, it is possible that only students who are capable of successfully studying in the face of limited resources (time and or/energy) – or who are more able students to start with – take up a job while they are studying. Bradley (2006) demonstrates that these students, who work long hours and still achieve relatively high grades, are effective time and resource managers. In contrast, students who realise their limited ability to continue to study successfully whilst working may refrain from taking up a job. If so, the self-selection would over-ride or cancel the resource-limiting effect of employment on academic success.

Overall, the variables and associations included in the multivariate model explained approximately a quarter of the variance in university grades. Considering that there are probably many (often idiosyncratic) reasons for individual differences in university grades, the amount of the variance explained can probably be seen as a success. If individual differences in general cognitive ability were measured, the amount of the variance explained would probably have been even larger. This suggestion is based on the well-documented associations between general cognitive ability and academic performance (Jensen, 1998; Kuncel et al., 2004). Therefore, it is probably fair to say that relatively easily measurable psychological and demographic characteristics can predict a substantial proportion of variability in academic performance at university. Only the role of self-reported fatigue tends to be minor, everything else being equal. Those students who report more fatigue tend to be the students who are less likely to be academically successful in the first place, due to their personality characteristics and academic potential which can be observed prior to their entry into university. Likewise, those students who are likely to obtain good grades at university do so even if these are accompanied by high levels of fatigue.

Several limitations of the present study must be acknowledged. First, the sample consisted only of students enrolled in the introductory psychology course at the University of Tartu. Although the participants came from a variety of academic disciplines within the institution, which suggests that there was diversity within the sample, self-selection (indicated by the over-representation of women) might have biased the findings in unknown ways. As for being able to generalise, the use of a larger sample of students would strengthen the findings. In addition, although we used structural modelling, the cross-sectional design limited our ability to draw causal conclusions and alternative interpretations from the observed associations. However, results of this study provide an important impetus for further research and the predictive power of fatigue with regard to university success should be examined in longitudinal studies.

So, despite these limitations, to our knowledge this is the first study demonstrating that self-reported fatigue does not have an independent effect on university grades when various other factors (both antecedents and mediators) are controlled for. Therefore, the results of this study still have important theoretical implications and pose interesting questions for further studies exploring the role of fatigue in predicting academic success. Researchers are encouraged to include prior school performance, personality and self-esteem measures in models in which individual differences are expected to impact on academic achievement, as this may lead to a more thorough understanding of academic performance at university.

Acknowledgments

The current project and preparation of this article was supported by a Primus grant (3-8.2/60) from the European Social Fund to Anu Realo. This project was also supported by the Estonian Ministry of Science and Education (SF0180029s08) to Jüri Allik. René Mõttus was supported by the European Social Fund (via the Estonian Science Foundation Mobilitas grant MJD44).

References

Abdel-Khalek, A. M. (2009). The relationship between fatigue and personality in a student population. *Social Behavior and Personality: An international journal*, 37, 1357–1368.

Astin, A. (1993). *What matters in college? Four critical years revisited.* San Francisco, CA: Jossey-Bass.

Bakker, R. J., van de Putte, E. M., Kuis, W. and Sinnema, G. (2009). Risk factors for persistent fatigue with significant school absence in children and adolescents. *Pediatrics*, 124, 89–95.

Baumeister, R. F., Campbell, J. D., Krueger, J. I. and Vohs, K. D. (2003). Does high self-esteem cause better performance, interpersonal success, happiness, or healthier lifestyles? *Psychological Science*, 4, 1–44.

Beerkens, M., Mägi, E. and Lill, L. (2010). University studies as a side job: causes and consequences of massive student employment in Estonia. *Higher Education*, 61, 679–692.

Besharat, M. A., Behpajooh, A., Poursharifi, H. and Zarani, F. (2011). Personality and chronic fatigue syndrome: The role of the five-factor model. *Asian Journal of Psychiatry*, 4, 55–59.

Boksem, M. A. S. and Tops, M. (2008). Mental fatigue: Costs and benefits. *Brain Research Reviews*, 59, 125–139.

Boksem, M. A. S., Meijman, T. F. and Lorist, M. M. (2005). Effects of mental fatigue on attention: An ERP study. *Cognitive Brain Research*, 25, 107–116.

Bolger, N. and Schilling, E. (1991). Personality and the problems of everyday life: The role of neuroticism in exposure and reactivity to daily stressors. *Journal of Personality*, 59, 355–386.

Bradley, G. (2006). Work participation and academic performance: a test of alternative propositions. *Journal of Education and Work*, 19, 481–501.

Brown, R. F. and Schutte, N. S. (2006). Direct and indirect relationships between emotional intelligence and subjective fatigue in university students. *Journal of Psychosomatic Research*, 60, 585–593.

Buckley, L., MacHale, S. M., Cavanagh, J. T. O., Sharpe, M., Deary, I. J. and Lawrie, S. M. (1999). Personality dimensions in chronic fatigue syndrome and depression. *Journal of Psychosomatic Research*, 46, 395–400.

Calderwood, C. and Ackerman, P. L. (2011). The relative impact of trait and temporal determinants of subjective fatigue. *Personality and Individual Differences*, 50, 441–445.

Capuron, L., Welberg, L., Heim, C., Wagner, D., Solomon, L., Papanicolaou, D. A., Craddock, R. C., Miller, A. H. and Reeves, W. C. (2006). Cognitive dysfunction relates to subjective report of mental fatigue in patients with chronic fatigue syndrome. *Neuropsychopharmacology*, 31, 1777–1784.

Chen, M. K. (1986). The epidemiology of self-perceived fatigue among adults. *Preventive Medicine*, 15, 74–81.

Costa, P. and McCrae, R. (1992). *Revised NEO personality and NEO five factor personality inventory professional manual.*

Creswell, C. and Chalder, T. (2002). Underlying self-esteem in chronic fatigue syndrome. *Journal of Psychosomatic Research*, 53, 755–761.

De Feyter, T., Caers, R., Vigna, C. and Berings, D. (2012). Unraveling the impact of the Big Five personality traits on academic performance: The moderating and mediating effects of self-efficacy and academic motivation. *Learning and Individual Differences*, 22, 439–448.

De Vries, J. and Van Heck, G. L. (2002). Fatigue: relationships with basic personality and temperament dimensions. *Personality and Individual Differences*, 33, 1311–1324.

Deary, V. and Chalder, T. (2010). Personality and perfectionism in chronic fatigue syndrome: A closer look. *Psychology and Health*, 25, 465–475.

DeLuca, J., Johnson, S. K., Ellis, S. P. and Natelson, B. H. (1997). Cognitive functioning is impaired in patients with chronic fatigue syndrome devoid of psychiatric disease. *Journal of Neurology Neurosurgery and Psychiatry*, 62, 151–155.

Eccles, J. S. and Wigfield, A. (2002). Motivational beliefs, values, and goals. *Annual Review of Psychology*, 53, 109–132.

Eurobarometer, 73. (2010). *Mental Health* (Special Eurobarometer 345, TNS Opinion and Social No. Part 1). European Commission.

Eurostudent IV. (2010). *Social and economic conditions of student life in Europe: National profile of Estonia*. PRAXIS Center for Policy Studies.

Fragoso, Y. D., da Silva, É. O. and Finkelsztejn, A. (2009). Correlation between fatigue and self-esteem in patients with multiple sclerosis. *Arquivos de Neuro-Psiquiatria*, 67, 818–821.

Garralda, E., Rangel, L., Levin, M., Roberts, H. and Ukoumunne, O. (1999). Psychiatric adjustment in adolescents with a history of chronic fatigue syndrome. *Journal of the American Academy of Child and Adolescent Psychiatry*, 38, 1515–1521.

Häkkinen, I. (2006). Working while enrolled in a university: Does it pay? *Labour Economics*, 13(2), 167–189.

Hazrati-Viari, A., Rad, A. T. and Torabi, S. S. (2012). The effect of personality traits on academic performance: The mediating role of academic motivation. *Procedia – Social and Behavioral Sciences*, 32, 367–371.

Holding, D. (1983). Fatigue. In Holding, D (Ed.) *Stress and fatigue in human performance*. John Wiley and Sons.

Huang, C. (2011). Self-concept and academic achievement: A meta-analysis of longitudinal relations. *Journal of School Psychology*, 49, 505–528.

James, W. (1926). William James in an 1886 letter to Carl Stumpf. In James, H. (Ed.) *The letters of William James*. Boston: Little, Brown, and Company, 249.

Jensen, A. R. (1998). *The g factor: the science of mental ability*. Praeger.

Johnson, S. K., DeLuca, J. and Natelson, B. H. (1996). Personality dimensions in the chronic fatigue syndrome: A comparison with multiple sclerosis and depression. *Journal of Psychiatric Research*, 30, 9–20.

Judge, T. A., Higgins, C. A., Thoresen, C. J. and Barrick, M. R. (1999). The Big Five personality traits, general mental ability, and career success across the life span. *Personnel Psychology*, 52, 621–652.

Judge, T. A., Erez, A., Bono, J. E. and Thoresen, C. J. (2002). Are measures of self-esteem, neuroticism, locus of control, and generalized self-efficacy indicators of a common core construct? *Journal of Personality and Social Psychology*, 83, 693–710.

Junghaenel, D. U., Christodoulou, C., Lai, J. S. and Stone, A. A. (2011). Demographic correlates of fatigue in the US general population: Results from the patient-reported outcomes measurement information system (PROMIS) initiative. *Journal of Psychosomatic Research*, 71, 117–123.

Kato, K., Sullivan, P. F., Evengard, B. and Pedersen, N. L. (2006). Premorbid predictors of chronic fatigue. *Archives of General Psychiatry*, 63, 1267–1272.

Kocalevent, R. D., Hinz, A., Brahler, E. and Klapp, B. F. (2011). Determinants of fatigue and stress. *BMC research notes*, 4, 238.

Kuncel, N. R., Hezlett, S. A. and Ones, D. S. (2004). Academic performance, career potential, creativity, and job performance: Can one construct predict them all? *Journal of Personality and Social Psychology*, 86, 148–161.

Kuncel, Nathan R., Credé, M. and Thomas, L. L. (2005). The validity of self-reported grade point averages, class ranks, and test scores: A meta-analysis and review of the literature. *Review of Educational Research*, 75, 63–82.

Laberge, L., Ledoux, É., Auclair, J., Thuilier, C., Gaudreault, M., Gaudreault, M., Veillette, S. and Perron, M. (2011). Risk factors for work-related fatigue in students with school-year employment. *Journal of Adolescent Health*, 48, 289–294.

Lavidor, M., Weller, A. and Babkoff, H. (2003). How sleep is related to fatigue. *British Journal of Health Psychology*, 8, 95–105.

Lee, Y.-C., Chien, K.-L. and Chen, H.-H. (2007). Lifestyle risk factors associated with fatigue in graduate students. *Journal of the Formosan Medical Association*, 106, 565–572.

Lewis, G. and Wessely, S. (1992). The epidemiology of fatigue – more questions than answers. *Journal of Epidemiology and Community Health*, 46, 92–97.

Loge, J. H., Ekeberg, O. and Kaasa, S. (1998). Fatigue in the general Norwegian population: Normative data and associations. *Journal of Psychosomatic Research*, 45, 53–65.

Lorist, M. M., Boksem, M. A. S. and Ridderinkhof, K. R. (2005). Impaired cognitive control and reduced cingulate activity during mental fatigue. *Cognitive Brain Research*, 24, 199–205.

Marsh, H. W. and Craven, R. (1997). Academic self-concept: Beyond the dustbowl. *Handbook of classroom assessment: Learning, achievement, and adjustment*, Educational psychology series. San Diego, CA, US: Academic Press, pp. 131–198.

Marsh, H. W. and Craven, R. G. (2006). Reciprocal effects of self-concept and performance from a multidimensional perspective beyond seductive pleasure and unidimensional perspectives. *Perspectives on Psychological Science*, 1, 133–163.

Marsh, H. W. and Martin, A. J. (2011). Academic self-concept and academic achievement: Relations and causal ordering. *British Journal of Educational Psychology*, 81, 59–77.

Matthews, G. and Desmond, P. A. (1998). Personality and multiple dimensions of task-induced fatigue: a study of simulated driving. *Personality and Individual Differences*, 25, 443–458.

McCrae, R. R. and Costa, P. T. (1996). Toward a new generation of personality theories: Theoretical contexts for the Five-Factor Model. In Wiggins, J.S. (Ed.), *The Five-Factor Model of Personality: Theoretical Perspectives*. Guilford Press, 51–87.

Michiels, V. and Cluydts, R. (2001). Neuropsychological functioning in chronic fatigue syndrome: a review. *Acta Psychiatrica Scandinavica*, 103, 84–93.

Michiels, V., Cluydts, R., Fischler, B., Hoffmann, G., LeBon, O. and DeMeirleir, K. (1996). Cognitive functioning in patients with Chronic Fatigue Syndrome. *Journal of Clinical and Experimental Neuropsychology*, 18, 666–677.

Michielsen, H. J., De Vries, J., Van Heck, G. L., Van de Vijver, F. J. R. and Sijtsma, K. (2004). Examination of the dimensionality of fatigue. *European Journal of Psychological Assessment*, 20, 39–48.

Miller, K., Danner, F. and Staten, R. (2008). Relationship of work hours with selected health behaviors and academic progress among a college student cohort. *Journal of American College Health*, 56, 675–679.

Mills, L. B. and Huebner, E. S. (1998). A prospective study of personality characteristics, occupational stressors, and burnout among school psychology practitioners. *Journal of School Psychology*, 36, 103–120.

Mizuno, K., Tanaka, M., Fukuda, S., Yamano, E., Shigihara, Y., Imai-Matsumura, K. and Watanabe, Y. (2011). Low visual information-processing speed and attention are predictors of fatigue in elementary and junior high school students. *Behavioral and Brain Functions*, 7, 1–7.

Mortimer, J. T., Finch, M. D., Ryu, S., Shanahan, M. J. and Call, K. T. (1996). The effects of work intensity on adolescent mental health, achievement, and behavioral adjustment: New evidence from a prospective study. *Child Development*, 67, 1243–1261.

Mõttus, R., Pullmann, H. and Allik, J. (2006). Toward more readable Big Five personality inventories. *European Journal of Psychological Assessment*, 22, 149–157.

Muthén, L. K. and Muthén, B. O. (2011). *Mplus User's Guide (6th)*. Los Angeles, CA: Muthén and Muthén.

Nater, U. M., Jones, J. F., Lin, J.-M. S., Maloney, E., Reeves, W. C. and Heim, C. (2010). Personality features and personality disorders in chronic fatigue syndrome: A population-based study. *Psychotherapy and Psychosomatics*, 79, 312–318.

O'Connor, M. C. and Paunonen, S. V. (2007). Big five personality predictors of post-secondary academic performance. *Personality and Individual Differences*, 43, 971–990.

Oberg, A. (2005). *Eestikeelse väsimuse hindamise skaala (VHS) konstrueerimine* [Construction of Estonian Fatigue Assessment Scale] (Unpublished Seminar Thesis). University of Tartu, Department of Psychology.

Oberg, A. (2007). *Eestikeelse mitmemõõtmelise väsimuse hindamise küsimustiku (MFI-ET) konstrueerimine* [Construction of Estonian Multidimensional Fatigue Inventory (MFI-ET)] (Unpublished Bachelor Thesis). University of Tartu, Department of Psychology.

Oginska, H. and Pokorski, J. (2006). Fatigue and mood correlates of sleep length in three age-social groups: School children, students, and employees. *Chronobiology International*, 23, 1317–1328.

Pajares, F., Britner, S. L. and Valiante, G. (2000). Relation between achievement goals and self-beliefs of middle school students in writing and science. *Contemporary Educational Psychology*, 25, 406–422.

Patel, M. X., Smith, D. G., Chalder, T. and Wessely, S. (2003). Chronic fatigue syndrome in children: a cross sectional survey. *Archives of Disease in Childhood*, 88, 894–898.

Prins, J. B., van der Meer, J. W. M. and Bleijenberg, G. (2006). Chronic fatigue syndrome. *Lancet*, 367, 346–355.

Pullmann, H. and Allik, J. (2000). The Rosenberg Self-Esteem Scale: its dimensionality, stability and personality correlates in Estonian. *Personality and Individual Differences*, 28, 701–715.

Pullmann, H. and Allik, J. (2008). Relations of academic and general self-esteem to school achievement. *Personality and Individual Differences*, 45(6), 559–564.

Ranjith, G. (2005). Epidemiology of chronic fatigue syndrome. *Occupational Medicine*, 55, 13–19.

Richardson, M. and Abraham, C. (2009). Conscientiousness and achievement motivation predict performance. *European Journal of Personality*, 23, 589–605.

Rosenberg, M., Schooler, C., Schoenbach, C. and Rosenberg, F. (1995). Global self-esteem and specific self-esteem: Different concepts, different outcomes. *American Sociological Review*, 60, 141–156.

Salamonson, Y. and Andrew, S. (2006). Academic performance in nursing students: influence of part-time employment, age and ethnicity. *Journal of Advanced Nursing*, 55, 342–349.

Sankey, A., Hill, C. M., Brown, J., Quinn, L. and Fletcher, A. (2006). A follow-up study of Chronic Fatigue Syndrome in children and adolescents: Symptom persistence and school absenteeism. *Clinical Child Psychology and Psychiatry*, 11, 126–138.

Sharpe, M. (1997). Cognitive behavior therapy for functional somatic complaints – The example of chronic fatigue syndrome. *Psychosomatics*, 38, 356–362.

Sharpe, M. and Wilks, D. (2002). Fatigue. *BMJ*, 325, 480–483.

Smets, E. M. A., Garssen, B., Bonke, B. and De Haes, J. C. J. M. (1995). The multidimensional Fatigue Inventory (MFI) psychometric qualities of an instrument to assess fatigue. *Journal of Psychosomatic Research*, 39, 315–325.

Taillefer, S. S., Kirmayer, L. J., Robbins, J. M. and Lasry, J. C. (2003). Correlates of illness worry in chronic fatigue syndrome. *Journal of Psychosomatic Research*, 54, 331–337.

Tanaka, M., Mizuno, K., Fukuda, S., Shigihara, Y. and Watanabe, Y. (2008). Relationships between dietary habits and the prevalence of fatigue in medical students. *Nutrition*, 24, 985–989.

Teixeira, L. R., Fischer, F. M. and Lowden, A. (2006). Sleep deprivation of working adolescents – a hidden work hazard. *Scandinavian Journal of Work Environment and Health*, 32, 328–330.

Thiffault, P. and Bergeron, J. (2003). Fatigue and individual differences in monotonous simulated driving. *Personality and Individual Differences*, 34, 159–176.

Tiesinga, L. J., Dassen, T. W. and Halfens, R. J. (1996). Fatigue: a summary of the definitions, dimensions, and indicators. *Nursing diagnosis: ND: the official journal of the North American Nursing Diagnosis Association*, 7, 51–62.

Tinto, V. (1993). *Leaving college. Rethinking the causes and cures of student attrition.* Chicago and London: The University of Chicago Press.

Tõnisson, E. (2011). *Kõrghariduse valdkonna statistiline ülevaade 2011* [Statistical overview of higher education 2011]. Tartu: Estonian Ministry of Education and Research. Available online and only in Estonian: http://www.hm.ee/index.php?048183

Trapmann, S., Hell, B., Hirn, J. O. W. and Schuler, H. (2007). Meta-analysis of the relationship between the Big Five and academic success at university. *Zeitschrift für Psychologie / Journal of Psychology*, 215, 132–151.

Valentine, J. C., DuBois, D. L. and Cooper, H. (2004). The relation between self-beliefs and academic achievement: A meta-analytic review. *Educational Psychologist*, 39, 111–133.

van der Linden, D. and Eling, P. (2006). Mental fatigue disturbs local processing more than global processing. *Psychological Research-Psychologische Forschung*, 70, 395–402.

van der Linden, D., Frese, M. and Meijman, T. F. (2003). Mental fatigue and the control of cognitive processes: Effects on perseveration and planning. *Acta Psychologica*, 113, 45–65.

van Geelen, S. M., Sinnema, G., Hermans, H. J. M. and Kuis, W. (2007). Personality and chronic fatigue syndrome: Methodological and conceptual issues. *Clinical Psychology Review*, 27, 885–903.

Viner, R. M., Clark, C., Taylor, S. J. C., Bhui, K., Klineberg, E., Head, J., Booy, R., Stansfeld, S. A. (2008). Longitudinal risk factors for persistent fatigue in adolescents. *Archives of Pediatrics and Adolescent Medicine*, 162, 469–475.

Wang, H., Kong, M., Shan, W. and Vong, S. K. (2010). The effects of doing part-time jobs on college student academic performance and social life in a Chinese society. *Journal of Education and Work*, 23, 79–94.

Wearden, A. and Appleby, L. (1997). Cognitive performance and complaints of cognitive impairment in chronic fatigue syndrome (CFS). *Psychological Medicine*, 27, 81–90.

White, C. and Schweitzer, R. (2000). The role of personality in the development and perpetuation of chronic fatigue syndrome. *Journal of Psychosomatic Research*, 48, 515–524.

Chapter 5.
Experiencing learning at university: making the best of lifelong learning?

Larissa Jõgi, Katrin Karu, Kristiina Krabi

Introduction

Our view is that not only does learning take place during the university study process, but it also takes place in different situations and life areas (contexts) which are cross-boundary (life-wide) (Niemi, 2004) and which affect the learning experiences of students. University gives one opportunity for learning, where students learn, grow and develop and learning at university is part of social and continuous (lifelong) learning. University is also a place for active, participative relations for students as adult learners.

The many opinions, theories and studies relating to learning at university indicate that learning is gradually more valued over time and needs to be conceptualised from the perspective of adult and social-constructivist learning theories (Prescill and Brookfield, 2009). The social-constructivist approach and adult learning theories suggest that learning has cognitive as well as social and personal dimensions. The social dimension of learning is influenced by social environment, cultural background, previous life experiences, life knowledge and changes in personal and social life (Jarvis, 1992; Bennington and Derrida, 1993; Alheit, 1995; Heidegger, 2000; Illeris, 2002; Alheit and Dausien, 2002; Alheit, 2004; Jarvis, 2011).

The development visions of universities, increasing heterogeneity of students (age, experience, maturity, background, student status) at all levels, the variety of study modes and changes in the wider learning culture, have increased the expectations of learning and teaching practice at university. Studies and surveys of academics, students and university alumni in Estonia (Valk et al., 2006; Vaade and Tamm, 2007; Remmik, 2008) have shown the need to understand and analyse students' learning experiences, teaching practices, approaches to teaching and their impact on learning at university. Teaching practice in Estonian universities is predominantly teacher centred, demonstrated by the academics' choices of approaches to teaching, assessment, feedback and guidance, their understanding of teaching and learning, and their own and their students' roles (Õppejõudude õpetamisoskuste…, 2006: 8) as well as the students' expectations of teachers and their experiences of learning (Vaade and Tamm, 2007, Valk et al., 2006; Remmik, 2008).

We, the authors, are involved in teaching students at Tallinn University and in researching adult learning and teaching. We also develop and teach professional development programmes for academics. Our experience has shown us the importance of understanding teaching practice as a high-level social practice, based on adult learning principles, valuing discussion, construction and reconstruction and conceptualising the meaning and possibilities of learning at university. Through our experience we sensed a problem in this area and we decided to research students' experiences in order to better understand learning and teaching practices in universities.

It is essential to know about and analyse the learning experiences of students in order to understand how students learn and, as a result, where appropriate, to change and develop teaching practices in universities. Students' experiences impact on how they learn and understand themselves as learners and these factors are affected by teaching practices. Learning and teaching practices at universities influence future choices and support students' continued learning.

Earlier studies on learning from the perspective of students have focused on students' experiences of, conceptions of, and their approaches to learning and learning orientations (Entwistle, 1991; Marton and Booth, 1997; Biggs, 2003; Ramsden, 2003; Honkimäki, Tynjälä and Valkonen, 2004; Kuurme, 2004). Fewer studies have analysed students' perceptions and experiences based on the relationship between learning and teaching. Several extensive studies conducted at the University of Helsinki indicate that teaching practices impact on students' conceptions of learning, their expectations of teaching and their views of themselves as learners. Learning affects the adjustment to university, student academic achievement and teaching practices (Postareff, 2007; Repo, 2010; Haarala-Muhonen, 2011). The more we understand about the learning experiences of university students the better we will be able to support student learning and the development of teaching practice in universities.

Our assumption was that there is a student learning problem, perhaps as a result of the lack of social and personal dimensions in teaching practices in universities (Barnett, 2000; Halpern and Hakel, 2002; Jarvis, 2011), and that there is also a lack of understanding of student learning and learning experiences (Postareff, 2007; Prescill and Brookfield, 2009; Thunborg, Bron and Edström, 2011). Our research question was: what are the experiences of students of learning and teaching practices at university? The focus of the study was on learning at university as a personal, social, relational and experiential process, in which it is important to analyse the experiences of students as adult learner and the meanings ascribed to those experiences. Our aim in this article was to present the findings of an empirical explorative study of university students' experiences of learning and teaching practices and to use the research findings to formulate improved principles of teaching practice at university.

Students' experiences of learning and teaching practices at university

To understand how students experienced learning and teaching practices at university we used the following theoretical principles as our starting point (Mezirow, 1996; Bloomer and Hodkinson, 2000; Brookfield, 2006; Jarvis, 2011):

- Learning at university is part of social and continuous learning throughout life (lifelong and life wide).
- Learning at university is a cognitive, personally transformative, social and inter-relational process.
- Learning is enhanced in contexts where students have supportive relationships and have a sense of ownership and control over the learning process.
- Learning builds on existing perceptions and frameworks of understanding and previous experience.
- Experiences of learning at university involve student-student and student-academic interactions, communication, relationships, reflection and teaching-learning activities.
- Students' experiences affect how students learn, understand themselves as learners and they also affect teaching practices.
- Learning and teaching practices at university affect students' learning experiences, influence future choices and support students' continuing learning.

Teaching practices in universities are based on the concept of adult learning and on the social constructivist approach – this means supporting students' learning through complex, social situations, based on openness, trust, learning from experience, and providing opportunities for relationships and interaction (Brookfield, 2006). The social-constructive approach emphasises the learner-centred perspective at university, which focuses on the students' experiences – this is what the whole study process is supposed to be about and is the *raison d'être* of both academics and universities (Haselgrove, 1994).

Learner-centred education emphasises non-linear, recursive, continuous, complex relational learning. Learning is enhanced in contexts where students have supportive relationships, have a sense of ownership and control over the learning process, and can learn with and from each other in safe and trusting learning environments. In learning-centred education the emphasis is on high quality academic-student relationships. These relational practices include academics' honouring students' voices, adapting to individual and cultural differences, encouraging learning and thinking, and having learner-centred beliefs (Cornelius-White, 2007).

Students' experiences of teaching practices are always interpretations and these interpretations trigger both the engagement of students in learning and the effects of the teaching or learning (Entwistle, 1991; Elen and Lowyck 2000). Students have a range of self understanding as learners, motives for learning and prior experiences about what learning and teaching are and mean. Experience means making sense of, giving meaning to and interpreting what and how something is perceived (Jarvis, 2004). A way of experiencing something depends on what aspects one is aware of and what can be described through these aspects (Marton and Booth, 1997; Roisko, 2007). Individuals act according to the meanings which they attribute to their experiences (Bloomer and Hodkinson, 2000), and these meanings are continually created and recreated through interaction with the social context, and the 'meaning', at any moment in time, is unique to each individual (Haggis, 2002:210).

A student's experience of learning at university has a cognitive dimension, and also social and personal dimensions. The personal dimension in the experience of learning involves changes in meanings, conceptions and values, where the focus is on development as a whole – the development of self as a transformative process (Mezirow, 1996). The personal dimension also means connecting with students' previous experiences (Fink, 2003; Jarvis, 2011; Thunborg, Bron and Edström, 2011) and their lifelong and life wide context (Bruner, 1996; Marton and Booth, 1997; Bourdieu, 1998; Ramsden, 2003; Postareff, 2007; Prosser, Martin and Trigwell, 2007). The social dimension refers to student-student and student-academic interactions, the process of communicating, relationships, reflection and teaching-learning activities (Brookfield, 2006). Therefore, it is important for students to experience the full range of cognitive, social and personal learning and teaching practices.

Method

Sampling. Non-probable, purposeful sampling of 235 students was drawn from three disciplines within Tallinn University: 22.6 per cent (n=53) from educational sciences and teacher education; 23.4 per cent (n=55) from mathematics and natural sciences, and 54.1 per cent (n=127) from social sciences. The sample was 80.9 per cent women (n=190) and 19.1 per cent men (n=45). The age range of the students within the sample was 21 to 50 years (M=25.15); the majority of students were between 22 and 25 years old (81.1 per cent) and 18.9 per cent were over 25 years of age. Sixty three per cent of the students in the sample were undergraduates (n=149) and 37 per cent were Master's students (n=86).

Data collection. Data was collected using the *ÕPPE-questionnaire*, which was developed and officially approved by the Department of Adult Education at Tallinn University from *ePalo 2011 opiskelijakysely [student survey eFeedback 2011]* of Helsinki University (Repo, 2010). The aim of the survey was to collect data about students' learning and study experiences (including teaching practices) at university. As learning experience is a complex phenomenon, it is necessary to research the subject qualitatively and quantitatively (Mackeracher, 2004) and thus we chose the survey method and questionnaire to allow both qualitative and quantitative data to be collected. We also collected qualitative and quantitative data to highlight the links between students' experiences and factors affecting their experiences in order to formulate and conceptualise the study's research problem. Data triangulation was used to give a more detailed and balanced picture and to further develop our understanding of the students' learning experiences.

The survey was carried out during the autumn term of the academic year 2011/2012. Students were asked to complete the questionnaires on paper in the lecture hall in order to ensure higher participation. Participation in the survey was based on informed consent, and the survey results were used anonymously.

The ÕPPE-questionnaire contains eight sections and consists of five blocks of general statements, two blocks of statements for evaluation, and closed, multiple-choice and open-ended questions. By eliciting more information, the combination of open-ended and multiple-choice questions should increase the validity of the results. The statements were evaluated on a pre-defined scale, and some questions also had multiple-choice answers.

Data analysis. We used both statistical and qualitative analysis as we had collected both quantitative and qualitative data.

The units of analysis were:

- Experience of learning at university;
- Experience of teaching and teaching practice at university.

The data from the multiple-choice questions were analysed statistically using SPSS in order to analyse students' learning experiences. The initial stages of the analysis process consisted of screening of the data and then examining the distributions and ranges. The qualitative data analysis was based on a qualitative content analysis (Flick, 2002) and the aim of using a phenomenographic approach (Marton and Booth, 1997) was to find variations in experiences.

The qualitative analysis consisted of four phases. Phase I consisted of the initial screening of the data, then the data was coded structurally. In phase II, researchers read and analysed the structurally coded data independently in order to determine the initial codes of students' experiences of learning and teaching at university. Then, based on the codes, the subcategories were formed and ordered hierarchically. In phase III, the text search query was used in the NVivo programme in order to structure the data by categories. In phase IV the variation in understandings was formed and checked.

Extracts from the data were selected to illustrate how a particular category had been established.

Findings and discussion

The analysis of empirical data allowed us to present and discuss experiences of learning and teaching practice at university.

Student experiences of learning at university

Based on the qualitative, phenomenographic approach we found five sub-categories describing **qualitatively different ways of experiencing learning** at university (Table 1). Each sub-category is described in more detail below, connecting experiences of learning, with citations and the number of respondent students as illustrations.

Table 1. *Students' experiences of learning at university*

Learning is acquiring.
Learning is knowledge and meaning construction.
Learning is study activities.
Learning is communication.
Learning is self-development.

Half of the students stated that *learning is acquiring*, but there was significant variation within the sub-category. Learning is to acquire:

a) Knowledge, information, skills and experience.

> Complementing my knowledge base and getting new knowledge. (Student 147)
>
> For me, learning at university means gaining theoretical and practical experience. (Student 182)
>
> Acquisition of a certain discipline. (Student 208)
>
> I pay for, and receive, knowledge. (Student 164)

b) Competency, profession. Learning is becoming a specialist in a certain field.

> To become a specialist in the field. (Student 10)

c) Wider worldview, wisdom of life; gaining the capability to analyse and interpret.

> [Learning at university means] embedding and illustrating knowledge. Acquisition of analytical capabilities. (Student 207)
>
> To broaden the mind. (Student 203)

d) Education, degree. Learning at university is acquiring a diploma, degree or completing studies.

> I need to obtain the degree. (Student 223)

e) To cope – managing future life and work; to acquire new aims – evolving interests and new aims, to prepare for life.

> Learning at university is a preparation for life. (Student 14)

In the experience of students *learning is construction* – connecting, generating new, and their own, ideas, developing their worldview and constructing personal meanings. Students emphasised that learning is understanding and complementing knowledge.

> Learning is understanding what is learned and creating associations. (Student 152)
>
> Learning at university is creating me opportunities to cope with life and changes my world of thinking. (Student 125)
>
> Learning is understanding how world functions. (Student 160)

In the students' experience *learning is study activities*: taking part in lectures – listening, taking notes, thinking with others, discussing, doing homework, preparing for seminars, active participation, working through scientific literature and materials, finding information and evaluating it critically, understanding, researching, communicating and doing group-work, listening in elective courses, planning time and investing in the future.

> Working with literature. (Student 7)
>
> Learning is more likely receiving information and listening. (Student 37)
>
> A lot of independent learning. (Student 239)
>
> To think along at lectures and participate actively in seminars. (Student 91)

In the students' experiences *learning is communication*: what is understood as communication with specialists, field specialists, academics and researchers and as establishing new contacts, communicating with other students and cooperation.

> [Learning is] communicating with educated people, opportunity for self-expression. (Student 175)
>
> To acquaint yourself with new and interesting people. (Student 75)

In the students' experience *learning is self-development:* learning is for them and for their future; to grow as a person, to feel development, to widen one's worldview and increasing diversity. Learning is one's own responsibility.

> Learning at the university is a developmental process, self-development. (Student 178)
>
> [Learning] develops me as a person. (Student 201)
>
> Development in many ways, including as the human being. (Student 109)
>
> Learning at university is a responsibility and privilege, which one takes. (Student 198)

This kind of learning is an experience, although students experience few variations. These findings overlap with similar research undertaken by Kuurme in 1997 and 1998 at Tallinn University (Kuurme, 2004). Both findings indicate that learning experiences at university are similar to learning experiences at school.

Student experiences of teaching at university

The qualitative analysis revealed that **teaching at university is experienced** through what teaching is not, through expectations of what teaching should be, and through the teaching that is actually encountered by students (Table 2). Three different sub-categories describing the students' experiences of teaching are presented.

Table 2. Students' experiences of teaching at university

Teaching IS NOT saying what is right, enforcing understanding or where academics are active and learners are passive.
Teaching SHOULD BE cooperative, interactive, directed toward students' reflection and development.
Teaching IS creative and involves a learning process to develop opportunities to understand, cooperate, connect and interact critically. Teaching is inspiring and creates new values.

Teaching at university is experienced by what teaching is not, by saying what is right, enforcing understanding or where academics are active and learners are passive.

> Teaching at university should not be so called 'project of the academics', who give orders, and 'hang' [students] if needed. Also not willing to compromise, and not to take into account the students' proposals. (Student 160)

> Teaching is definitely something more than just reading the slides. (Student 68)

> Teaching is not a lecture where the lecturer speaks and seminar where the lecturer asks. (Student 8)

> Teaching at university should not be a textbook countdown or enforcement of understandings. (Student 88)

Teaching at university is experienced through the expectation of what teaching should be. Teaching should be cooperative, participative, interactive, discussion-based, and directed toward students' reflection and development. Students expect to be regarded as adult learners and to have their suggestions taken into account.

> The university should provide an opportunity to understand and form their conceptions, become more aware and more professional in the field. (Student 121)

> Teaching should be a mutual cooperation, which both parties know their responsibilities, tasks and goals. (Student 134)

> Teaching should be practical and provide the prerequisites for independent thinking and logical / analytical conclusions. (Student 139)

Teaching at university is experienced through the teaching that is actually encountered by students. Teaching is creative and a learning process for developing opportunities for cooperation, connections, clarification, illustrations, and critical interactions. Teaching is inspiring, and creates new values.

> University teaching is a process where students need to acquire knowledge of something to accomplish in life. (Student 124)

> For me, the most important has been that I have been taught to think more broadly, to consider various parties, to be tolerant, open and well-educated. (Student 157)
>
> Teaching – moderation, discussion, new ideas, different approaches, widening, understanding. (Student 204)
>
> Teaching at university is an activity through which worldviews are formed, all of which are very closely related, but also one must be critical towards all. (Student 230)
>
> Teaching is creating new values and contributing to the development of society. (Student 73)

Understanding teaching through identifying what teaching should not be and expectations of what teaching should be may indicate the need for students to find more diverse and complex meanings for learning and teaching at university.

The meanings of the students' learning experiences are complex, including attitudes, and sense needs to be made of them as they are very diverse. In the students' experience of teaching there is little variation – meanings connected to teaching are unilateral and repetitive. Further research is needed to understand students' experiences of learning, for example, by conducting in-depth interviews.

Student experiences of teaching practices at university

In the experiences of the study process we discussed factors which were connected to teaching practices. The factors in teaching practices were chosen based on a theoretical framework about adult learning and the social and personal dimensions of learning: 1) understanding and supporting the students' experiences, 2) communication and active involvement. The statistical analysis of the categorized frequency data (see Figure 1) showed that, with reference to communication in a typical study situation, students are more satisfied with communication between students than with academics.

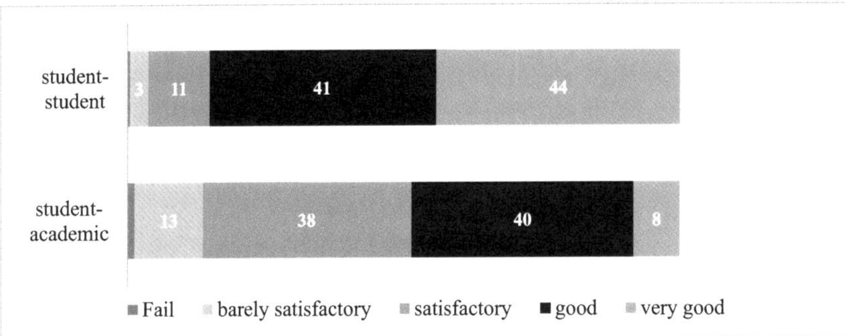

Figure 1. *Evaluative experiences of communication opportunities in a typical study situation (per cent)*

As can be seen in Figure 2 there were differences in communication and relationships:

- With academics, students experienced listening, enquiring and receiving information as the main activities.
- With other students, students experienced discussion, information provision and establishing contact.

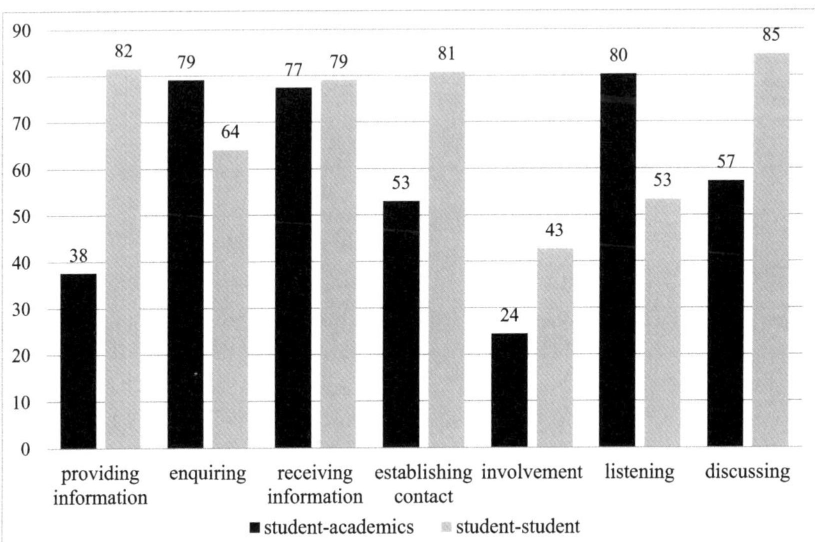

Figure 2. *Communication in a typical study situation (per cent)*

So, communication between academics and students in the experience of students was academics giving information. However, for relational, holistic, social and experiential learning it is crucial that communication between academics and students is interactive.

Our analysis showed that students like to be actively involved in the study process (96 per cent agree or strongly agree), but only a quarter of the students have experienced the active involvement of students by academics. Discussions with other students during the study process (87 per cent agree or strongly agree) helped them to understand better, and 90 per cent agreed or strongly agreed about the importance of students supporting and helping each other. The students' involvement, active participation and interactive discussion in the study process are prerequisites for higher level learning.

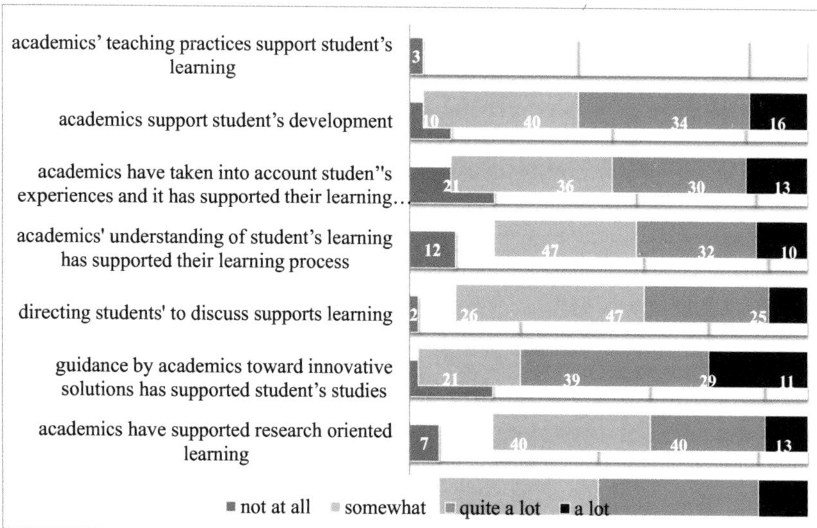

Figure 3. Evaluative experiences of factors supporting students' study process (per cent)

As can be seen in Figure 3 teaching practices that support the students' learning and development processes – understanding students' learning, taking account of students' experiences, interaction-discussion and research oriented learning – were evaluated significantly more as 'somewhat' or 'not at all' in the student experiences.

We argued that the main aim of teaching at universities in the lifelong learning context is to create a social and interactive context that supports a student's capacity for social, contextual, complex, multifaceted, self-regulative and reflexive learning in a super-complex world (Barnett, 2000). The aim is also to create the capacity for knowledge construction, deep and critical thinking and reflection, and develop intrapersonal (self-awareness, autonomy, responsibility and self-regulation) and interpersonal processes (the capacity for dialogue and social communication). However, there were some complex issues and problems brought to light by the research results.

Learning is primarily experienced in situations where knowledge is imparted, which results in passive learning, or acquiring. Disregarding the experiences of students does not generate development prospects for them, nor does it support higher level learning. Being acquirers rather than responsive learners is a disengaged position and for students as adult learners it is important to be honest about the limitation of their experience.

Learning at university does not seem to be a constructive, meaningful or personally transformational experience for students nor do they experience it in a wider and inter-relational social context. The lack of interaction, communication and the active involvement of students are key problems in the study process. Experiences of teaching indicate that students need to come into contact with a greater variety of teaching practices. The results confirmed that the teaching-centred approach to teaching and the learning context were not creating opportunities for inter-relational learning. The empirical results also indicated the limitations of teaching practices at universities.

Conclusive reflections

What are the educational implications of these findings?

First, in the students' experiences learning and teaching at university have different and varying meanings. However, there were strong messages that learning is mostly experienced as acquiring, which indicate that the learning process is mostly experienced as a cognitive activity but not a personally transformative, social or relational one.

Second, the clearest message was that students experience a lack of social dimensions in teaching practice at university. They experience a low level of involvement and few opportunities for communication in the study process, and, in a typical study situation, a lack of support by academics for their development and learning.

Third, students need more interactive opportunities and a variety of supportive possibilities in order to learn and express themselves, and, as adult learners, they need educational opportunities where they can be listened to, heard and understood.

Fourth, there are strong tensions between the theoretical understanding of learning at universities and the empirical results from this study. The personal and social dimensions in learning from experience do not appear nor does the continuity of the lifelong learning dimension.

Why we should be concerned about these findings?

Education at university is still dominated by teaching practices where little consideration is given to the learning experiences of students and where the understanding that students are adult learners is not common. The more that this type of teaching practice tries to dominate university education, the more it determines the forms of learning that can occur (Jarvis, 1992:131). The paradox is that this type of learning and education at universities results in lower rather than higher level learning. Changes have occurred which have resulted in teaching-focused teaching practices losing their position and value as relevant social practice models. Listening, as the main practice of the learning and study process at university, creates normative, universal, common and familiar understandings for academics and students. Abandoning the old ideas of learning at university requires that both academics and students acknowledge and change their understanding of learning, behaviour patterns, choices, ways of communicating, and teaching practices.

From the students' point of view our results showed that they feel mutual support places a high value on communication amongst students, and that they believe that this supports their learning. Students also believe that encouragement from academics to discuss, not merely to share knowledge, supports learning.

Our research was based on the principles of an exploratory study, where theoretical assumptions were used to understand the problem and formulate principles of teaching practice.

The phenomenographic focus in our analysis showed that there is no good or bad learning. However, how learning is experienced depends on how it takes place and how it is supported by teaching. Our analysis suggested that academics should the opportunity to engage with students and their learning experiences. Based on our findings and theoretical assumptions *the starting point for improving teaching practice at university can be summarised in the following principles:*

- Learning and teaching at university is based on lifelong, life wide, holistic, personal, social, relational, experiential learning, on the academics' awareness of students' learning and their capability to support it.
- The study process, learning environment and teaching practices are learning and interaction orientated in order that students, as adult learners, can participate, learn, and change their understanding of learning.
- Students as adult learners are aware of themselves as learners and are aware of the learning process, as well as of their responsibilities, participation, autonomy and reflexive and cognitive capabilities in the inter-relational continuous learning process.

The students' current experience of learning suggests that the quality of the learning experience at university needs to be thought about. Based on the analysis we argue that the students' experiences of learning and teaching not only need to be considered, but also need to be understood.

The results of our analysis suggest questions for future research:

- What are the disciplinary differences in the experiences of learning and teaching practices?
- Why are students' experiences of learning and teaching dominated by acquiring and listening to?
- How are we as academics going to make appropriate improvements?
- How do the results help to understand learning at university as a high-level social practice?

Acknowledgement

The translation of this article supported by the European Social Fund (grant nr. 1.2.0401.09-0070).

The study is based on 'Perceptions of students on changes in learning experience and teaching practice of university teachers' (PRIMUS research grant 30.3-10/479).

References

Alheit, P. (1995). Changing basic rules of biographical constructions and professional attitudes – study motivations of adult education students. In Alheit, P., Bron, A., Brugger, E. and Dominicé, P. (Eds.), *The biographical approach in European adult education*. Vienna: Edition Volkshochschule, 212–231.

Alheit, P. (2004). Challenges of the post-modern learning society: A critical approach. In Bron, A., Kurantowicz, E., Olesen, H. S. and West, L. (Eds.), *'Old' and 'new' worlds of adult learning.* Wroclaw: ESREA & Wydawnictwo Naukowe DSWE TWP, 389–407.

Alheit, P. and Dausien, B. (2002). The double face of lifelong learning: Two analytical perspectives on a silent revolution. *Studies in the Education of Adults*, 34, 3–22.

Barnett, R. (2000). *Realizing the university in an age of supercomplexity*. Buckingham: Open University Press.

Bennington, G. and Derrida, J. (1993). *Jacques Derrida*. Chicago: The University of Chicago Press.

Biggs, J. (2003). *Teaching for Quality Learning at University*. Buckingham: Open University Press.

Bloomer, M. and Hodkinson, P. (2000). Learning Careers: Continuity and Change in Young People's Dispositions to Learning, *British Educational Research Journal*, 26, 583–598.

Bourdieu, P. (1998). *Practical Reason: On the Theory of Action*. Stanford: Stanford University Press.

Brookfield, S. (2006). *The Skillful Teacher: On Trust, Technique and Responsiveness in the Classroom*. San Francisco: Jossey-Bass.

Bruner, J. (1996). *The Culture of Education*. Cambridge, MA: Harvard University Press.

Cornelius-White, J. (2007). Learner-Centered Teacher-Student Relationships Are Effective: A Meta-Analysis. *Review of Educational Research*, 77, 113–143.

Elen, J. and Lowyck, J. (2000). Instructional metacognitive knowledge: A qualitative study on conceptions of freshmen about instruction. *Journal of Curriculum Studies*, 32, 421–444.

Entwistle, N. J. (1991). Approaches to learning and perceptions of the learning environment. *Higher Education*, 22, 201–204.

Fink, L. D. (2003). *Creating significant learning experiences: an integrated approach to designing college courses*. San Francisco: Jossey-Bass.

Flick, U. (2002). *An introduction to Qualitative Research*. 2nd edition. London: Sage Publications.

Haarala-Muhonen, A. (2011). Oikeustieteen ensimmäisen vuoden opiskelijoiden haasteet opiskelussa. *Kasvatusttieteellisiä tutkimuksia 237*. [First-year law students' challenges in studying, Studies in Educational Sciences 237]. University of Helsinki: Institute of Behavioural Sciences.

Haggis, T. (2002). Exploring the "Black Box" of Process: a comparison of theoretical notions of the "adult learner" with account of postgraduate learning experience. *Studies in Higher Education*, 27, 207–220.

Halpern, D. and Hakel, M. D. (2002). Learning that Lasts a Lifetime: Teaching for Long-term Retention and Transfer. *New Directions for Teaching and Learning*, 89, 3–9.

Haselgrove, S. (1994). Why students experience matters. In Haselgrove, S. (Ed.), *The student experience.* London: The Society for Research into Higher Education & Open University Press, 3–8.

Heidegger, M. (2000). *Oleminen ja aika* [Being and time]. Tampere: Vastapaino.

Honkimäki, S., Tynjälä, P. and Valkonen, S. (2004). University students' study orientations, learning experiences and study success in innovative courses. *Studies in Higher Education*, 29, 431–449.

Illeris, K. (2002). *The three dimensions of learning*. Roskilde: Roskilde University.

Jarvis, P. (1992). *Paradoxes of learning: On becoming an individual in society.* San-Francisco: Jossey-Bass.

Jarvis, P. (2004). *Adult Education and Lifelong Learning: Theory and Practice.* London and New York: Routledge.

Jarvis, P. (2011). Learning: the experience of a lifetime! In Jõgi, L. and Krabi, K. (Eds.), *Raamat õppimisest: õppides täiskasvanuks – õppimine erinevates perspektiivides* [The Book of Learning: learning to be an adult – learning in different perspectives]. Tallinn: Andragoogika osakond, 28–47.

Kuurme, T. (2004). Õppimine kui kogemus [Learning as experience]. In Liimets, A., Ruus, V.-R. (Eds.), *Õppimine mitmest vaatenurgast* [Learning from different perspectives]. Tallinn: Tallinna Pedagoogikaülikooli toimetised, 60–71.

Mackeracher, D. (2004). *Making the sense of adult learning.* Toronto-Buffalo-London: University of Toronto Press.

Marton, F. and Booth, S. (1997). *Learning and awareness.* Mahwah: Lawrence Erlbaum Associates Publishers.

Mezirow, J. (1996). *Uudistava oppiminen. Kriittinen reflektio aikuiskoulutuksessa* [Transformative learning. Critical reflection in adult education]. Helsinki: Helsingin Yliopiston Lahden tutkimus- ja koulutuskeskus.

Niemi, H. (2004). Learning towards empowerment in the Future Europe. *Lifelong Learning in Europe*, 9, 10–18.

Postareff, L. (2007). *Teaching in higher education. From content-focused to learning-focused approaches to teaching.* Helsinki: Helsingin yliopisto, Kasvatustieteen laitos, tutkimuksia 214. [Academic dissertation.]

Prescill, S. and Brookfield, S. D. (2009). *Learning as a way of leading: Lessons for the struggle for Social Justice.* Chester: Widener University.

Prosser, M., Martin, E. and Trigwell, K. (2007). Academics' experience of teaching and subject matter understanding: a phenomenographic analysis of their inter-relations. In Entwistle, N. and Tomlinson, P. (Eds.), *Student Learning and University Teaching* (British Journal of Educational Psychology Monograph Series II). British Journal of Educational Psychology, 49–59.

Ramsden, P. (2003). *Learning to teach in higher education.* London: Routledge-Falmer.

Remmik, M. (2008). Õpetamisest õppimise juhtimiseni. [From teaching to learning direction]. In Pilli, E. and Valk, A. (Eds.), *Quo vadis, Eesti kõrgharidus? Uuringud 2005–2007* [Quo vadis, Estonian higher education? Studies in 2005–2007]. Tartu: Tartu Ülikooli Kirjastus, 134–153.

Repo, S. (2010). *Yhteisöllisyys voimavaarana yliopisto-opetuksen ja -opiskelun kehittämisessä.* Kasvatustieteellisiätutkimuksia 228 [A sense of community as a resource for developing university teaching and learning. Studies in Educational Sciences 238]. University of Helsinki, Institute of Behavioural Sciences.

Roisko, H. (2007). Adult Learners' Learning in University Settings. A Phenomenographic Study. *Acta universitatis Tamperensis 1226.* [Academic dissertation.] Tampere: University of Tampere.

Thunborg, C., Bron, A. and Edström, E. (2011). Forming and transforming learning identities in higher education. In Jõgi, L. and Krabi, K. (Eds.), *Raamat õppimisest: õppides täiskasvanuks – õppimine erinevates perspektiivides* [The Book of Learning: learning to be an adult – learning in different perspectives]. Tallinn: Andragoogika osakond (Department of Adult Education), 86–107.

Vaade, V. and Tamm, A. (2007). *Kõrgkoolide vilistlaste uuring (LÜKKA projekt)* [Institutions of higher education alumni survey (LÜKKA project)]. *Tallinn: Klaris.*
Available online and only in Estonian:
www.ut.ee/lykka/orb.aw/class=file/action=preview/id=240992/Vilistlane_L%F5plik.pdf

Valk, A., Marandi, T., Pilt, L., Villems, A. and Ruul, K. (2006). *Kuidas toetada sügavat õppimist ülikoolis?* [How to support deep learning in university?]. Tartu: Tartu Ülikool.

Õppejõudude õpetamisoskuste koolitusvajaduse uuring [Academics teaching skills training needs survey]. (2006). Turu Uuringute AS. Available online and only in Estonian:
http://www.ut.ee/lykka/orb.aw/class=file/action=preview/id=232727/%D5ppej%F5udude+%F5petamisoskuste+koolitusvajaduse+uuring.pdf

Chapter 6.
Adult learners' perceptions of the classroom environment in Estonia and other European countries: the effects on learning confidence and satisfaction

Eve-Liis Roosmaa, Auni Tamm

Introduction

Individual educational paths and educational attainment depend largely on differences in cognitive ability (Strenze, 2007) and socioeconomic and socio-cultural backgrounds (Coleman et al., 1966), but aspects relating to the educational institutions, that is, the schools, also play a significant role (Mortimore et al., 1988). To better understand the motivation for continuing with education as an adult, it is also necessary to consider the psychological aspects of learning and classroom environments. The theoretical concepts and models forming the basis for classroom environment and learning atmosphere studies derive from social psychology and sociology, where individual perceptions and needs are viewed in relation to social structures and processes (O'Fathaigh, 1997). Research has shown that the more academically and socially involved adult students are, the more they feel connected to fellow learners and faculty, and the more likely they are to persist and continue with their studies (Tinto, 1998; Tobias, 1998; *New England Adult Research Network*, 1999; English, 2005). A positive perception of the classroom environment or learning context leads to more wellbeing and enjoyment of learning, better understanding of the learning content and to better performance (Darkenwald and Valentine, 1986; Keller, 1987, 1999).

Most studies on the learning or classroom environment focus on traditional learners, not on non-traditional or adult learners. However, supportive learning environments are important for all learners, so in this study we concentrate on adult learners' perception of the learning process. Adult learners enrich the classroom with their unique learning interests and educational objectives and these bring about the need for certain approaches and methods of teaching and instructing (Miglietti and Strange, 1998).

The aim of our study was to examine how learners who have (re-)entered higher education view the classroom environment; which classroom environment indicators are most important; what the adult learners' expectations of the classroom environment are; and how the classroom environment influences their confidence in completing their studies and their satisfaction with their studies. We focus on Estonia, but also provide comparisons with other European countries.

For the analysis we used questionnaire based data collected in 2007 from actual adult learners in 12 European countries (6th Framework Programme project). In addition we illustrated the Estonian results with qualitative data on learning environments using interviews with active adult learners in formal education who were employed in small and medium sized enterprises at the same time.

Theoretical approaches and previous studies on classroom environment

Andragogy is one of the most commonly applied theories of adult learning and is often contrasted with pedagogy, the teaching and socialising of children and young people. Pedagogy can be characterised as teacher-centred, while andragogy is a learner-centred teaching style, indicating where the initiative for learning action lies. Andragogy suggests that adults prefer self-direction in determining their objectives and outcomes of learning, that they learn via direct experience and that they experience a need to know and thus to learn (Knowles and Associates, 1984). As they sense the need for learning in their lives, it is assumed that adult learners prefer a task- or problem-centred orientation to learning rather than the subject-centred pedagogy approach. Hence, a suitable learning environment for adults could be described as one offering mutual respect, collaboration, support, openness and fun (Knowles and Associates, 1984).

Classroom learning and environment research dates back to social psychology studies of the late 1920s and 1930s (Thomas, 1929; Lewin, Lippitt and White, 1939). These studies included observing children in nursery schools, recording their overt recurrent social behaviour patterns and placing them in psychological test situations. Kurt Lewin and colleagues examined the effect of different leadership roles and the associated group feelings among 10-11-year-old boys. In the second half of the 1940s researchers investigated the effects of teachers' personalities on students' behaviour in the classroom and on their mutual relations (Anderson and Brewer, 1945, 1946). These studies found that different teacher and student behaviour categories developed, those which were socially integrative (promoting differences, flexible, adaptive, objective, scientific, cooperative) and those which were dominative (suppressing differences, resisting changes, autocratic).

In the 1950s classroom environment research became more theoretically and empirically orientated. For example, researchers proceeded with Lewin's (1936) field theory, Murray's (1938) need-press-model, Thelen's (1950) educational dynamics model, and others. Hypotheses were based on the analysis of time-lapse pictures, various recording methods and classroom observations carried out by trained educators. In the following decades numerous classroom environment measures and indexes were developed, but all of them were intended for the study of traditional learners and focused on learning progress and occasionally on improving the curriculum. For further detail please see the review by Cháves (1984).

By and large, classroom environment studies can be divided according to their application and instruments of either high or low-inference measures (Rosenshine, 1970), in which inference refers to the process that intermediates the objective data collected and the coding of those data. In low-inference measures, directly observed classroom behaviour is rated by counting the frequency of certain phrases, sentences and terms used by teachers and also recording the students' replies and reactions – i.e. compiling objective information on relatively objective behaviour. The studies described above used low-inference measures and played an important role in the development of a conceptual framework of classroom environment and learning environment research (Cháves, 1987). Since the mid-1960s, high-inference measures have become prevalent and aim to ascertain perceptions of the classroom environment via specific constructs, such as satisfaction, cohesiveness, relationships between the students and teacher and between students, etc. in order to capture the meaning of classroom events for learners (O'Fathaigh, 1997). High-inference measures require observations from a series of events over a longer period (for example, a whole academic year and thus using a variety of sources before making judgments), while low-inference measures mostly cover shorter periods (Fraser and Walberg, 1981). In addition, the learners' behaviour is often determined by their view of the classroom environment (high-inference measure), rather than by the 'actual' situation recorded by the researcher (low-inference measure).

Adult learners and the classroom environment

Next we will describe some results from studies analysing adult learners' perceptions of classroom environments. In general these studies define adult learners as 25 years and older, and start from the learners own classroom views and interpretations (high-inference measures).

Migletti and Strange (1998) find that adult learners express a greater sense of accomplishment and a more positive total experience with learner-centred instruction. The learner-centred approach is characterised by personalised instruction, relating course materials to student life or work experience, assessing student needs, active participation in the learning process and flexibility for personal development. However, their analysis showed that the age of the student had little effect on classroom expectations and learning style preferences (Migletti and Strange, 1998). Thus, the emphasis is on learner activity and dialogue based learning/teaching.

Studies also show the adult learners' need for a more traditional or teacher-centred approach, placing emphasis on the active role of the teacher. Hence, Ross-Gordon (1991) finds that adult learners perceive effective teaching as that offering availability and helpfulness, concern and respect for students, encouragement for discussion, and flexibility, but accompanied by a more traditional teaching style. Clear presentation of the material, well organised lectures and knowledgeable teachers were also mentioned. Donaldson, Flannery and Ross-Gordon (1993) reach similar conclusions by reanalysing three qualitative studies. Adult students associated effective teaching with a teacher's ability to motivate and encourage participation, the relevance and clear presentation of materials and the knowledge of the teacher. These results are not entirely in accordance with adult learning and teaching theory (andragogy), especially with respect to clarity of material presentation, the knowledge of the instructor and dedication to teaching (Ross-Gordon, 2003). In part these results could be explained by the desire of adult learners to engage less in learning activities because of the different competing roles in their lives: learner, employee, parent, partner, member of the community, etc. (*ibid.*). On the other hand these results might be viewed in line with those that indicate adults face difficulties in connecting 'common knowledge' obtained in everyday life, family, work and community with 'college/university' or academic knowledge (Graham et al., 2000; Murphy and Fleming, 2000).

A study of faculty members (including instructors) concluded that adult learners were seen as more goal oriented, responsible and self-directed (Raven and Jimmerson, 1992), which confirms adult learning theory. In addition, adult learners were also perceived as more competitive.

There are several studies which refer to aspects of adult learners that are not stressed by adult learning theory. These studies suggest that adult learners have problems with confidence, because they do not feel as prepared for studying as fellow learners who have not left the formal adult education system (Lynch and Bishop-Clark, 1994; MacDonald and Stratta, 1998; Ross-Gordon and Brown-Haywood, 2000). This means that when re-entering formal education (for example, during the first semester) adult learners might need more supportive, traditional teaching with the learner-centred approach being applied gradually in the later stages of the learning process as the adult learners gain confidence through successful participation.

In a study examining the learning motivation, views and perspectives of adults with little or no experience of formal post-compulsory education it was shown that 'non-participants' were very interested in learning throughout their lives (Tobias, 1998). They read books, journals, learn from community members, friends and family, attend courses, learn at work, etc. Often these people do not return to formal education due to previous negative experiences. Interviews revealed that learning in large groups did not suit them as they felt uncomfortable and sometimes experienced that they were being judged by fellow learners. They felt that they did not get enough attention from the instructor and that the content of the courses did not always correspond to things they wanted to do in life. So, an unsuitable learning environment is one significant aspect which explains why not everybody wishes to participate in adult formal education.

Methodology

Data

For the quantitative analysis we used data collected under the European Commission 6th Framework Programme project 'Towards a Lifelong Learning Society in Europe: The contribution of the Education System' (LLL2010). In 2007 project partners in 13 European regions[1] conducted an adult learner survey – Adult Learners in Formal Education (ALiFE, 2007). For data collection each country applied layered or quota sampling. First, at the level of higher education all the schools offering adult education were selected. As a second step, in each school certain subject areas were chosen and from those subject areas adult learners who had interrupted their studies in formal education for at least two years (i.e. re-entering adult formal education after completing or dropping out of previous studies) were selected. Thus the definition of 'adult learner' in this survey did not include an upper or lower age limit. In each country or region about 250 questionnaires were collected at the higher education level. In total, the database consisted of 3943 individuals, including 244 adult learners in Estonia[2].

---

1 ALiFE 2007 was conducted in: Austria, Belgium (Flanders), Bulgaria, the Czech Republic, England, Estonia, Hungary, Ireland, Lithuania, Norway, Scotland, Slovenia and Russian Federation (St. Petersburg region).

2 In each country data was also gathered from lower levels of education, but they are not analysed here.

The ALiFE (2007) survey covered the following topics: an overview of previous learning paths, reasons for re-entering adult formal education, factors encouraging and hindering participation, perception of the learning process, learning costs and facilities, other activities alongside learning and learner background information (age, sex, employment status, etc.).

To get a more complete picture of adult learners' perceptions of classroom environments and their expectations in Estonia we also analysed data from qualitative interviews. During 2007–2008, the LLL2010 project consortium conducted in-depth interviews in small and medium sized enterprises (50–249 employees) with employees who were active adult learners in formal education. In Estonia the survey covered seven production and service sector enterprises and in this study we used data from interviews with 12 adult learners. All 12 interviewees were studying for a higher education obtaining professional higher education diploma, baccalaureate or master's degree. We concentrated on adult learners' expectations of classroom environments, as this aspect of the data has only been briefly considered to date.

Measurements

To analyse classroom environment perceptions of adults who had returned to formal education we used the Adult Classroom Environment Scale (ACES) developed by Darkenwald and Valentine (1986). This scale is unique as it is the first one intended to precisely measure the perceptions of adult learners. The ACES measures the relationship between students and teachers, and between students. From the initial scale we distinguished seven learning process indicators based on the research of O'Fathaigh (1997):

- *affiliation* – the extent to which students like each other and interact positively;
- *teacher support* – the extent of help, encouragement, concern and friendship teachers direct towards students;
- *task orientation* – the extent to which students and teachers maintain focus on task and value achievement;
- *personal goal attainment* – the extent to which the teacher is flexible, providing opportunities for adults to pursue their individual interests;
- *organisation and clarity* – the extent to which activities are clear and well organised;
- *student influence* – the extent to which the teaching is learner-centred and allows for student influence in course planning decisions;
- *student involvement* – the extent to which students are satisfied with the class and participate actively and attentively.

In the questionnaire the respondents were presented with two statements for each learning process indicator on a five-point Likert scale (strongly agree – strongly disagree). In addition to the ACES statements we asked the adult learners to consider whether participants discussed real-life examples based on their personal experiences (for more detail, see Table 1a, Appendix). The seven classroom indicators were the main variables in the analysis. We also composed an index variable of the classroom environment consisting of all seven components and we treated it as an independent variable in order to analyse the effect that the classroom environment has on adult learners' confidence and satisfaction.

Our second reference point in this study was Keller's (1987) learning motivation model, which assumes that for successful learning the adult learner must achieve attention, relevance, confidence and satisfaction (ARCS). These criteria are derived from the synthesis of psychological and educational research (English, 2005). Ideally, the ARCS model is sequential, meaning that the four motivational aspects need to be achieved one after the other. First, the attention of the adult learners must be gained and access to learning must be granted, otherwise the adults will not even consider the learning possibilities. Second, adult learners should see that learning is relevant for their own lives and for the wider community or society as a whole. In other words, they need to understand the reasons for learning. Third, the learner must gain confidence in their ability to successfully complete the studies. A sense of accomplishment will give an incentive to continue studying and participate in lifelong learning. Finally, it is important that adult learners are satisfied with their learning outcomes and the learning process, which is a significant indicator of education quality. In addition, it is assumed that the more satisfied learners are also more likely to continue their studies and not drop out.

Because the education system and institutions of higher education are primarily able to shape the confidence and satisfaction of adult learners, in this study we analysed the extent to which the classroom environment affects their confidence to complete their studies, satisfaction with their studies overall, and the knowledge and skills gained through the learning process.

Confidence was measured on a five-point Likert scale where adult learners were asked to agree or disagree with the statement 'I am confident that I will be able to complete the study programme'. The measure of satisfaction with their studies consisted of five statements also based on a five-point Likert scale. Adult learners were asked whether they were extremely satisfied or dissatisfied with the following: the general progress of the entire study programme, the general learning climate in the educational institution, the general practical organisation of the educational institution, what they had learned so far as a result of the course and what they could go on to do after completion of the course.

Our previous analysis, carried out with the same data set (ALiFE, 2007), indicated that adult learners in European countries differ significantly in their views of classroom environment (Roosmaa et al., 2011). However, in this study the classroom environment was analysed more generally and focus was not on all seven ACES aspects (Darkenwald and Valentine, 1986) in particular. In addition, our aim in this study was to look at Estonia in more detail and compare it to other countries, as it is likely that classroom environment reflects differences in the educational systems, organisation of adult formal education and learning/teaching cultures. So, we compared Estonia to four country groups or clusters: Anglo-Celtic countries (England, Scotland and Ireland), continental European countries (Austria and Belgium), former socialist Central and Eastern European countries (Bulgaria, the Czech Republic, Hungary and Slovenia) and former Soviet Union countries (Lithuania and the Russian Federation).

Method

The descriptive results of the quantitative data are presented in contingency tables, and by giving means and standard deviations. We used a linear regression model to study classroom indicators (ACES) by country groups and to examine how the adult learners' confidence and satisfaction is affected by classroom environment and the adult learners' socio-demographic characteristics. In the final steps of the analysis the scale measuring the classroom environment was reduced to one component. This dimension had a Cronbach's Alpha score of .828, which means that the component had a reasonable level of internal consistency. From the socio-demographic characteristics we included in the analysis the variables that appeared, in our previous study, to have a significant effect on confidence and satisfaction (Roosmaa et al., 2011), that is: gender, age (up to 25 years, 25–40 years and over 41 years) and employment status (employed, unemployed, inactive). We introduced a classroom environment summary/index variable and socio-demographic variables into the regression as the separate steps and analysed R-square to detect how much of the variation in the dependent variable (confidence and satisfaction respectively) was explained by these two sets of independent variables.

Results

We start by presenting how adult learners in Estonian higher education perceived classroom environment during their studies. In Table 1 all statements included in the Adult Classroom Environment Scale (ACES) are ranked by the level of agreement respondents gave to them. The majority of adult learners in Estonia agreed that the study programme provided opportunities to make new friends and that getting work done was very important (about 90 per cent). Hence, two very different aspects of classroom environment – affiliation and task orientation – had the highest endorsement. Around 80 per cent of the adult learners felt that the study programme had a clear sense of direction, that teachers respected students as individuals, and that students often asked questions during lectures. Even though the results presented here only refer to adult learners in higher education, this last aspect is particularly encouraging, because wider society often criticises the Estonian education system for not promoting discussions in classes. Most adult learners also agreed that they discussed real-life examples, based on their personal experiences, in class, and that the teacher made every effort to help students succeed. In addition, about 70 per cent felt that they enjoyed the study programme and working together. They agreed to a lesser extent (around 60 per cent) with statements saying that students achieve their personal learning goals, that the study programme was well organised, that activities not related to the study programme objectives are kept to a minimum, and that students felt free to question the study programme requirements. So, although adult learners in higher education ask questions during lectures and discuss real-life examples based on personal experiences, they feel relatively less engaged in shaping study programmes to meet their own visions or needs. The results also show that only a third of adult learners agreed that they were able to select assignments that were of personal interest to them and 10 per cent disagreed that the teacher or instructor insisted on things being done their way.

Table 1. Agreement with classroom environment statements among adult learners in higher education in Estonia (per cent)

Statements regarding classroom environment	Total	Total N
The study programme provides opportunities for making new friends	90	243
Getting work done is very important in the study programme	89	243
The study programme has a clear sense of direction	78	242
The teacher respects students as individuals	78	243

Statements regarding classroom environment	Total	Total N
Students often ask the teacher questions	76	242
Participants in the training discuss real-life examples based on their personal experience	74	243
The teacher makes every effort to help students succeed	73	242
Most students enjoy the study programme	71	242

Table 1. Continued

Statements regarding classroom environment	Total	Total N
The students in the study programme enjoy working together	70	243
Most students in the study programme achieve their personal learning goals	62	242
The study programme is well organised	61	243
Activities not related to study programme objectives are kept to a minimum	61	242
Students feel free to question study programme requirements	60	242
Students can select assignments that are of personal interest to them	32	243
The teacher insists that you do things his or her way *	10	243

* *Agreement with this statement means a negative assessment of an involving classroom environment, thus here we present the percentage of those disagreeing with the statement.*

Source: ALiFE, 2007

Thus, on the whole, the adult learners viewed the learning environment positively, as more than half of the respondents agreed with most of the statements presented. As the next step we analysed the adult learners' answers by the seven indicators of classroom environment (ACES), therefore the statements presented in Table 1 are now merged into respective pairs (for more detail see Table 1a, Appendix).

The results show that during their studies the adult learners rated *affiliation* among fellow students most highly (Table 2) and they were positive in their assessments regarding *task orientation* in the study programme, *support* received from the teacher and *student involvement* in the learning process almost to the same extent. However, it should be noted that two statements under affiliation and task orientation were perceived rather differently (Table 1): agreement was stronger with finding new friends and getting work done and lower with enjoyment of working together and keeping activities not related to study objectives to a minimum.

Table 2. *Perception of classroom environment using ACES indicators, mean values on a five-point scale and standard deviations*

Classroom environment (ACES) indicators	**Mean (std. deviation)**	**Confidence intervals**
Affiliation	4.1 (.6)	4.1 ... 4.2
Task orientation	4.0 (.6)	3.9 ... 4.1
Teacher support	3.9 (.7)	3.8 ... 4.1
Student involvement	3.9 (.6)	3.9 ... 4.0
Organisation and clarity	3.8 (.6)	3.8 ... 3.9
Student influence	3.3 (.6)	3.2 ... 3.4
Personal goal attainment	3.3 (.7)	3.2 ... 3.4
Total N	243	

Source: ALiFE, 2007

The mean results in Table 2 show that the adult learners gave a somewhat less positive reaction to how *well organised* and *clear* the study programme was. In the case of this indicator the adult learners agreed more with programmes having a clear sense of direction and less with programmes being well organised. The adult learners were more critical with regard to *student influence* and as the previous table indicated, especially to the fact that the teacher insisted on things being done their way. Still, the majority of the adult learners agreed with being able to discuss real-life examples based on their personal experiences. Some previous studies (for example Migletti and Strange, 1998) find that student influence (part of a learner-centred approach to teaching) particularly has the most significant impact on adult learners' satisfaction and sense of accomplishment. Finally, the adult learners gave a rather low assessment also to *personal goal attainment*. About one third of the respondents reported neither agreeing nor disagreeing with the personal goal attainment statements. One of the statements asked the adult learners to consider whether most of the students in their group achieved their personal learning goals. This might have been too difficult to assess as adult learners probably spend less time together than learners in initial education do.

Adult learners' expectations of learning environment

The aim of the quantitative questionnaire based survey was to study the classroom perceptions of adult learners, whereas the in-depth interviews conducted with adult learners who were working in small or medium sized enterprises while studying, aimed to identify the factors influencing the adult learners' expectations of the classroom environment and, in the wider sense, the learning environment. We were particularly interested to discover whether adult learners with different characteristics differed in their expectations or opinions of the learning environment, and if there were types of adult learners who could be considered as a group with similar expectations. A typology of working adult learners was developed in the LLL2010 project (Hefler and Markowitsch, 2010), and here we focused on relations between types of learners and learning/classroom environment.

The interviews revealed the significance of the connection between job and field of study. We observed that the adult learners whose subject of study was connected with the content of their job were more similar in their expectations of the learning environment than the adult learners where there was no such connection. Thus, in general, the former tend to be more demanding of the curriculum, subject-matter and the teachers. They expressed the wish to get the maximum return for their money. Their jobs and their studies were connected for nine of the twelve interviewees; of the nine, five interviewees were studying at professional higher education institutions and four were studying at public universities.

We start by presenting the results for the adult learners whose field of study and job are connected. We refer to this type of adult learner as 'specialising learners' and they can be characterised by reinforcing their current position, by seeking to secure a higher qualification in their field/sector of work. These adult learners attempt to secure or develop their occupational or professional competences and integrate their learning experience with on the job learning. For example, an adult learner who had a higher education qualification that is not related to the current job felt that their current studies gave them confidence in their competitive ability, helped to widen their network of contacts and increased their options in their current job and beyond. 'Specialising learners' are of a different age and background, they have basic knowledge in their field of study, either via previous education, work experience and training, or as a result of being sure of what they need to learn, and why, in order to be active in their particular field of interest. As a result, these learners make more informed decisions in school, they know what they want to achieve, what knowledge they already possess and what they need to acquire. Thus they are also ready to make more 'difficult' choices.

> I don't take easier subjects, like organisational management, etc., I already got that in America. I go to the first lecture and see what could be useful... (Public university)

In comparison to those who have just finished high school or work in a different field, 'specialising learners' position themselves as more informed, aware and competent.

> Those coming straight from school have no idea why they're here and why they are studying. Those who have had a job have already developed some sort of worldview. (Private professional higher education institution)

Even within the same subject area it is not always possible to integrate studies and job content. Adult learners see this as positive in terms of obtaining wider knowledge but they tend to be concerned by curricula that are too broad and disperse.

> It doesn't help much. Study programmes are not designed so that you are ready to work in a company afterwards. They are too broad, not focused. A little bit of everything. (...) no subject is taught from the beginning to the extent that is necessary, teaching starts from the middle. Only about 10 per cent of it is related to actual work. (Public professional higher education institution)

In the interviews the 'specialising learners' commented on their satisfaction with their schools and teachers, especially on the ability of the teachers to connect what they teach with practice, to advise learners on solving practical problems and give advice about theses.

> I'm rather satisfied with my school. All teachers are working in the same field too. For secretarial course we had teachers from our own school, but now many are from companies – from Kalev [the biggest and oldest confectionery company in Estonia]; some teachers of more important subjects from the Bank of Estonia. They have so much experience; they don't talk of just dull theory. They talk about their experience so that it is interesting, makes you listen. Otherwise nobody would bother to listen, especially if people have been working since nine o'clock in the morning and then drove to lectures. They don't read out monotonously their materials. Our civil law teacher is so cool – 'so, you didn't understand?' and right away gives an example from real life, which makes everything clear. (Public professional higher education institution)

So, adult learners value supportive teachers, but they also expect teachers to keep up to date and to update their material.

> Some teachers were lousy. Some still teach. Their heyday was during the Soviet time. Talked about management in a loud, bellowing voice. Completely disregarded women, had kind of chauvinistic attitude. What a pity, waste of time. (Public university)

In line with the classroom environment scale developed by Darkenwald and Valentine the interviews referred to the topic of asking questions in lectures or seminars, that is learner and teacher contributions to and involvement in the learning process. The 'specialising learners' found that discussion and asking questions depended on both the teachers and learners. On the one hand, learners should take an active role and ask, and on the other hand teachers have to allow time and give encouragement for questions. Some of these adult learners are not in a hurry to complete their studies (they just put off completion) and thus they are able to choose courses where teachers promote discussions and are flexible in their ways of teaching (for example, they are willing to discuss topics not covered in the material they have prepared for a particular lecture).

Not all students were convinced about the advantages of discussion and active teaching methods. Some public university students mentioned that working in groups gives rather artificial results, which are not applicable to real life. Others said that seminars drift away from the topic and become just a 'jabber', leading to no significant increase in knowledge. However, many of these adult learners did not have professional work experience.

In summary, if studies and work are connected then adult learners tend to say that they had a more positive learning experience: good relations with teachers, teacher support, discussions in lectures, and linking (work) experience to the learning process. Most of these adult learners were undertaking higher education in professional higher education institutions. Adult learners in academic higher education institutions conveyed a somewhat less positive learning experience and, at least in part, this was due to a mismatch between fields of study and work.

Among the interviewees there were only three adult learners for whom work and studies were not at all or only weakly connected; two of them studied in public universities and one in a professional higher education institution. For these adult learners their first priority was learning, with work coming second; this might be because they regard higher education as very important in one's life ('be it good or bad, but higher education I must have'), because after studying they hope to get a job that interests them or because their current job is too routine. The choices of their current study programmes were rather accidental; the adult learners did not possess any previous experience of this field or their experiences were mostly related to learning and not work. They generally found that studies in academically oriented universities offer learning and analytical skills. We refer to this type of adult learner as 'graduating'.

> In the learning environment 'graduating learners' most appreciate flexibility and the freedom to choose the time for learning. Depending on the school, this might be facilitated by the accessibility of learning materials or by a flexible schedule allowing reconciliation between studies and work.
>
> The school has adapted to the needs of learners who work. They can study independently, using study materials provided by teachers, and then sit the exams. Many have lecture materials available in the Internet too; some teachers have the complete course online. You can read them in the evening at home. I am actually satisfied with most of my teachers. (Public university)

Two of the three interviewees stated that managing work and studies simultaneously was essential for maintaining their livelihood. On the other hand, flexibility with good study outcomes made some adult learners doubt the quality of education they had received.

> Let's put it like that... if a person has three jobs and is studying at the same time and almost manages to graduate with red diploma [honours], then it is very likely that the quality of their education has suffered in some way... On the other hand, I have no complaints because our teachers know that absolutely all Master's students are working and they don't have time to attend lectures. We are met halfway. (Public university)

In the cases where work and study field were not connected, the expectations of the curriculum and teachers resemble those of the so called traditional learners – they are mostly willing to receive what the higher education institution has to offer. They had no basis for explicit criticism, and discontent or uncertainties were limited to rather general opinions about higher education and schools. Concrete needs and expectations were not stated.

Based on the interviews we could conclude that the responsibility for the classroom or learning environment was entirely with the teacher – they shape the learning climate and connect everyday life experiences and knowledge with more theoretical, academic knowledge. The role of the students was only mentioned in the context of discussions during the learning process; discussions between fellow students or mutual learning were not emphasised. This is partly due to the fact that the main objective of the interviews was to study employer attitudes towards participation in formal adult education; the learning climate was not the focus. However, when adult learners were presented with an option in the questionnaire to assess the role of fellow students in the learning process, the majority felt that affiliation between students in higher education was strong.

Country comparisons of perceptions of classroom environment

From the questionnaire based survey (ALiFE, 2007), the perceptions of classroom environment, compared with the views from twelve other European countries, were encouraging, as adult learners in Estonia were generally most positive about classroom environment[3]. Figure 1 shows that only with regard to student influence and personal goal attainment were the mean values given by adult learners in Estonia somewhat lower than in other countries. However, the mean of the assessment of student influence and the attainment of personal learning goals was the lowest in Estonia of all of the countries analysed (on average 3.4 on a five-point scale). Thus, compared to the twelve other survey countries, Estonian adult learners were the least likely to agree that they were able to influence the study programme, select assignments that are of interest to them and that most students achieve their personal learning goals. On the other hand, adult learners in Estonia acknowledged, more than learners in other countries, that task orientation and affiliation between students was good.

Although differences in means are not substantial, we still found all those differences in classroom environment indicators in Estonia and other European countries to be statistically significant with the exception of personal goal attainment (the effect is significant at the level 0.1) and teacher support.

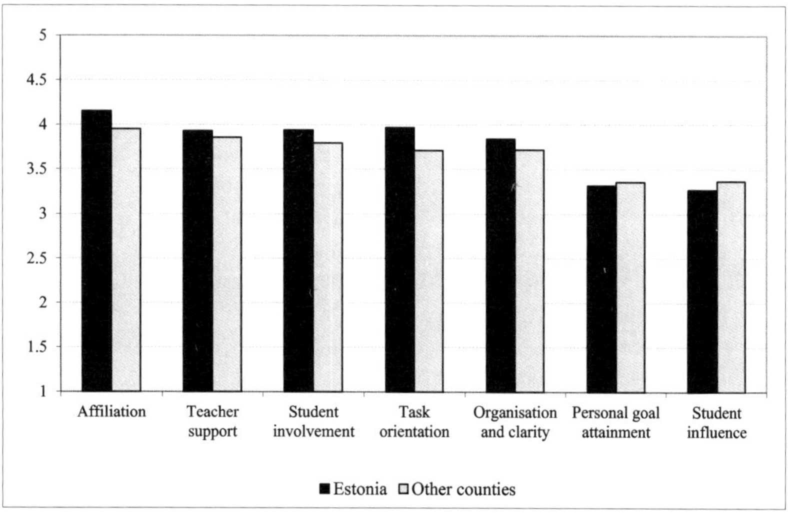

Figure 1. Perceptions of classroom environment using the seven ACES indicators, Estonia in comparison with other countries, mean values on a five-point scale
Source: ALiFE, 2007

3 If we compare results by the level of education, then adult learners obtaining basic or secondary education in Estonia are less positive about the classroom environment than their counterparts in other European countries, but these differences are not statistically significant. At the vocational education level, the assessment of classroom environment was about the same as in higher education.

Adult learners in England, and to a slightly lesser extent in Scotland, were more positive about some of the classroom environment aspects (teacher support and student involvement) than learners in Estonia (for further detail, see Table 2a, Appendix). Adult learners in Norway also viewed their classroom environment very positively. However, the comparison with Norway is partial, because several classroom environment statements were not included in their national questionnaire (usually one out of two paired statements). Nevertheless, agreement with the statements included was always higher than in other countries (mean value 4 and higher). In Norway adult learners agreed the most with the following statements: students enjoy working together, enjoy the study programme, students often ask the teacher questions and teachers respect students as individuals. Adult learners in Hungary, the Czech Republic, Slovenia, Bulgaria and Belgium were less positive about the classroom environment than Estonian adult learners.

Perceptions of classroom environment in relation to confidence and satisfaction

As the final step of the analysis we examined the extent to which adult learners' perceptions of classroom environment in higher education were related to confidence in completing their current studies and to satisfaction with learning process and outcomes – indicators of the ARCS model of motivation (Keller, 1987). Country comparisons were provided in more detail by comparing the results of different country groups with those of Estonia.

In general, nearly all higher education adult learners were confident about their ability to complete their study programme (90 per cent). The majority of adult learners were satisfied with what they had learned, with what they could go on to do after completing the course, and with the overall learning climate in the educational institution (about 75 per cent). They were also quite satisfied with the general progress of the entire study programme (70 per cent), but less satisfied with the general practical organisation of the educational institution (60 per cent). These results were to be expected as the study was conducted among adult learners who had decided to continue their studies and thus they had more positive attitudes towards adult formal education.

The results presented in Table 3 show the ACES indicators impact on confidence in completing studies in Estonia compared to different country groups: Anglo-Celtic (England, Ireland and Scotland), continental (Austria and Belgium), post-socialist (Bulgaria, the Czech Republic, Hungary and Slovenia) and post-soviet (Lithuania and Russia). Here we observed that affiliation between students had a significant positive effect on confidence in all countries with the exception of the post-soviet ones. Thus, adult learners who experience affiliation are more likely to be confident about completing their study programme. Teacher support had a positive effect on confidence only in the continental and post-socialist countries, while task orientation had a positive impact on confidence in the Anglo-Celtic and post-soviet countries and a negative impact in the post-socialist countries. In the post-soviet and post-socialist models we found a negative association between confidence and personal goal attainment. However, when adult learners perceived studies to be well organised, with a clear sense of direction, then, in these countries and in Estonia, confidence tended to be higher, although in Estonia the association was weaker (the effect is significant at the level 0.1). In continental European countries the effect of organisation and clarity was opposite, albeit weak. Student influence had a significant effect in almost all country groups – positive in Anglo-Celtic, post-soviet countries and Estonia; negative in continental countries. For post-soviet countries the association between student influence and confidence was strongest, yet country group differences were small (see Table 3a, Appendix). Student involvement showed a weak effect on confidence only in the post-socialist and post-soviet countries, while for Estonia we found that this effect was not significant. Thus, with respect to confidence in completing one's studies, Estonia does not resemble other post-soviet countries, even though in the past they had similar institutional settings of adult education systems.

Table 3. The probability of being confident about completing studies, single effect of ACES indicators in country groups, standardised coefficients of linear regression

	Anglo-Celtic model	**Continental model**	**Post-socialist model**	**Post-soviet model**	**Estonian model**
Affiliation	.079**	.174***	.110***	.052	.227***
Teacher support	.013	.137**	.139***	.047	.023
Task orientation	.141***	-.028	-.059**	.085**	-.001
Personal goal attainment	-.003	.076	-.049*	-.162***	.049
Organisation and clarity	.053	-.100*	.116***	.125***	.144*
Student influence	.063*	-.125**	.002	.277***	.111*
Student involvement	.067	.030	.054*	.086*	-.040
Adjusted R^2	.067	.049	.071	.180	.116
N	872	391	1463	625	242

*Effect significant at: *** $p < 0.01$; ** $p < 0.05$; * $p < 0.10$*

Source: ALiFE, 2007

Satisfaction with studies is an integral part of the quality of an education system. When compared to confidence in completing studies we saw that satisfaction with the learning process and outcomes was explained more by the ACES indicators (about 40 per cent of the variation was explained) (Table 4). In a similar way to the results about confidence, adult learners experiencing affiliation between students were more prone to show satisfaction with different aspects of their studies. The effect of affiliation was somewhat weaker in the case of Estonia and absent in the continental countries. All in all country groups do not differ significantly in regard to affiliation (see Table 3a, Appendix). Teacher support, and organisation and clarity of studies, had the strongest positive effect on the probability of being satisfied in all country groups. Student involvement was also an important indicator of satisfaction with studies in the Anglo-Celtic, post-social and post-soviet countries, but the effect is nearly non-existent in continental European countries and Estonia. Personal goal attainment had some positive effect on satisfaction in Estonia, and task orientation in Anglo-Celtic countries. Thus, it can be seen that Estonia shows some similarities to other countries, especially the post-soviet and other post-socialist countries. However, if only the ACES aspects having the strongest impact on satisfaction (teacher support and organisation and clarity of studies) are taken into account, then Estonia most resembles the pattern of continental European countries.

Table 4. *The probability of being satisfied with the study process and study outcomes, single effect of the ACES indicators in country groups, standardised coefficients of linear regression*

	Anglo-Celtic model	**Continental model**	**Post-socialist model**	**Post-soviet model**	**Estonian model**
Affiliation	.106***	.065	.055**	.079**	.093*
Teacher support	.149***	.207***	.220***	.212***	.147**
Task orientation	.060**	.056	.011	.028	-.019
Personal goal attainment	.039	.023	.037	-.011	.094*
Organisation and clarity	.407***	.398***	.357***	.354***	.466***
Student influence	-.003	-.039	.017	.039	.067
Student involvement	.100***	.090*	.114***	.165***	.032
Adjusted R^2	.424	.338	.397	.442	.449
N	866	387	1444	623	242

*Effect significant at: *** $p < 0.01$; ** $p < 0.05$; * $p < 0.10$*

Source: ALiFE, 2007

We were also interested in examining how much of the confidence in completing studies and satisfaction with studies could be explained by the classroom environment indicators in total and the socio-demographic characteristics of the adult learners. On the whole, confidence was explained less by classroom environment and by socio-demographic characteristics than satisfaction (Figures 2 and 3). Hence, confidence in completing studies was influenced by some other factors that we have not identified in this study (possibly academic progress, etc.). Having said that, as can be seen in Figure 2, the impact of classroom environment on confidence appeared to be strongest in Estonia. While the impact of socio-demographic indicators on confidence was considerably lower, it was more pronounced in Estonia (one's age and employment status showed significant effects) than in other countries.

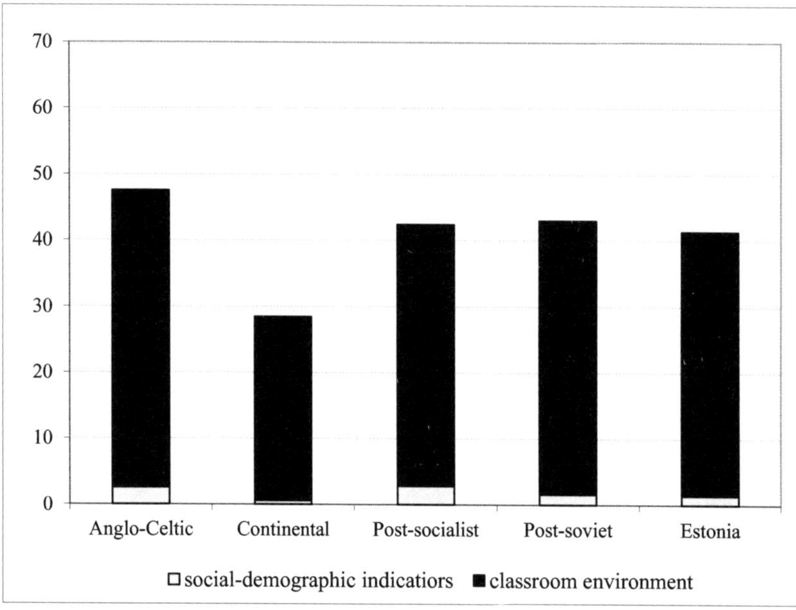

Figure 2. Variation in confidence by country groups, R-square

Source: ALiFE, 2007

As can be seen in Figure 3, classroom environment influences learning satisfaction considerably more, but here Estonia stands out less. Variation in satisfaction was more explained in the Anglo-Celtic countries and less in the countries of continental Europe. Socio-demographic indicators had little influence on the level of satisfaction (still, in post-socialist countries gender and age have significant effect on satisfaction with studies).

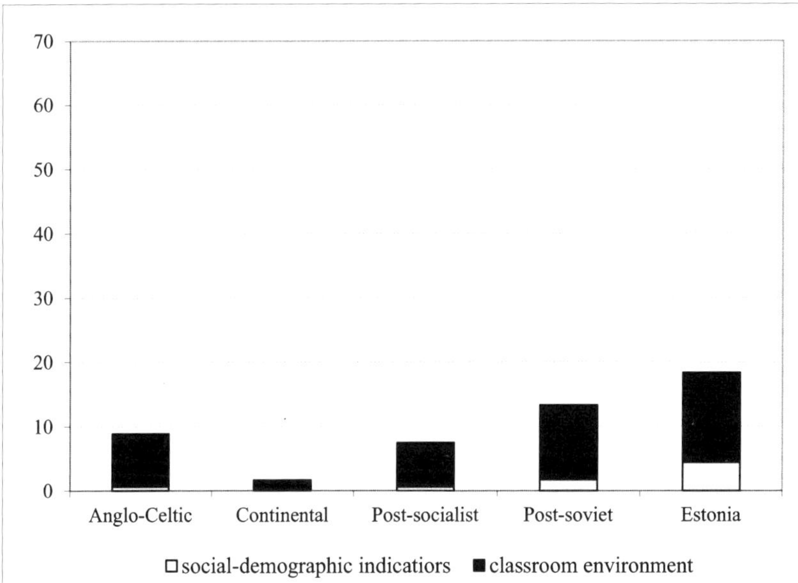

Figure 3. Variation in satisfaction by country groups, R-square

Source: ALiFE, 2007

Similar results with regard to learning environments have been found in research on the learning experiences of adult learners from working class backgrounds (Tobias, 1998). In this study the following learning environment indicators were emphasised: social relations between students, relevance of the learning to the learner's other life spheres (work, family, wider community), respect from teachers and other staff, and in some cases, a particularly supportive key person.

Conclusion

In this chapter we set out to study differences in perceptions of classroom environments in Estonia compared with other European countries. We were interested to show which aspects of classroom environment were seen most positively by adult learners in higher education and which of those aspects related to confidence in completing studies and to learning satisfaction. Most classroom environment studies focus on traditional learners; our study showed the importance of supportive learning environments for adult (non-traditional) learners. It has previously been found that classroom perception was one of the most significant factors influencing the adult learning experience and this was also confirmed by our analysis. The results indicated that, in comparison with other countries, adult learners in Estonia expressed very positive opinions about classroom environments. Estonian adult learners experienced affiliation with fellow learners, they saw teachers as supportive, they felt involved in the learning process and they agreed that their studies were task oriented. However, adult learners did not recognise the possibilities for the attainment of personal learning goals and for influencing the learning process or programme requirements. In these respects Estonian adult students were somewhat more critical than learners in other countries. In higher education teaching often takes place in large groups (lectures); one way to improve this situation would be to divide learners according to their study interests and allow them to undertake different assignments.

Where the field of study and work were connected, the learners tended to get more from the courses, and they also had a better understanding of why they were learning and how they might make use of the knowledge gained. Hence detachment of studies and work makes it difficult to identify with the profession or study subject. Another issue is the extent to which employers are prepared to put the knowledge and skills obtained via adult formal education into practice. Yet this was not in the focus of our chapter.

The results also showed that in Estonia and other former Soviet Union countries the classroom environment has a great influence on how confident adult learners feel about completing their studies. In Estonia confidence was largely shaped by affiliation between students, whereas in other post-socialist and post-soviet countries other indicators had a significant influence. Classroom environment had a greater impact on learning satisfaction than on confidence about completing studies, and here Estonia is more similar to other European countries. The aspects of classroom environment that have the strongest effect on satisfaction are teacher support and organisation and clarity of studies. It is interesting that in Estonia student involvement had no effect on satisfaction, while the relationship was strong for other country groups.

Adult learners should not be considered as a homogenous group in respect of their learning environment needs. They might expect a more supportive and thus, teacher-centred, learning environment at the beginning of their studies (especially after a long break from formal education) and a more independent, learner-centred environment during the later stages of study. In addition, the needs of adult learners according to their socio-demographic and socio-economic backgrounds should be considered in the learning environment. Although this was not the object of the current study, previous research (Tobias, 1998) has indicated that learners from lower social backgrounds might feel uncomfortable because they sense a 'top-down' attitude from fellow students and teachers, they do not receive enough support and attention, they find learning in large groups uninviting and they also find that study materials/subjects are not relevant to their life objectives (including work). Hence, adult learning environments should offer flexible ways of teaching and learning in order to meet the different needs of different adult learners. An inviting, supportive learning environment which allows varied development could be one mechanism to increase the accessibility of adult learning.

Aknowlegement

The preparation of this article was supported by the Archimedes Foundation's Primus programme grant No. 30.3 – 10/296, under the auspices of European Social Fund.

References

Anderson, H. H. and Brewer, H. M. (1945). Studies of teachers' classroom personalities, I Dominative and socially integrative behavior of kindergarten teachers. *Applied Psychology Monographs*, No 6.

Anderson, H. H. and Brewer, H. M. (1946). Studies of teachers' classroom personalities, II Effects of teachers' dominative and integrative contacts on children's classroom behavior. *Applied Psychology Monographs*, No 8.

Cháves, R. Ch. (1984). The Use of High-Inference Measures to Study Classroom Climate: A Review. *Review of Educational Research*, 54, 237–261.

Coleman, J. S., Campbell, E., Hobson, C., McPartland, J., Mood, A., Weinefeld, F. and York, R. (1966). *Equality of educational opportunity*. Washington D.C.: Government Printing Office.

Darkenwald, G. G. and Valentine, T. (1986). *Measuring the social environment of adult education classrooms*. Paper presented at the Adult Education Research Conference, Syracuse, NY.

Donaldson, J. F., Flannery, D. and Ross-Gordon, J. M. (1993). A Triangulated Study Comparing Adult College Students' Perceptions of Effective Teaching with Those of Traditional Students. *Continuing Higher Education Review*, 1993, 57, 147–163.

English, L. M. (2005). *International encyclopedia of adult education*. New York: Palgrave Macmillan.

Fraser, B. J. and Walberg, H. J. (1981). Psychological learning environment in science classrooms: A review of research. *Studies in Science Education*, 8, 67–92.

Graham, S. W., Donaldson, J. F., Kasworm, C., and Dirkx, J. (2000). *The Experiences of Adult Undergraduate Students: What Shapes Their Learning?* Paper presented at the American Educational Research Association National Conference, New Orleans, Apr. 2000.

Hefler, G. and Markowitsch, J. (2010). Formal adult learning and working in Europe: a new typology of participation patterns. *Journal of Workplace Learning*, 22, 79–93.

Keller, J. M. (1987). Strategies for stimulating the motivation to learn. *Performance and instruction*, 26, 1–7.

Keller, J. M. (1999). Using the ARCS motivational process in computer-based instruction and distance education. In Theall, M. (Ed.), *Motivation from within. Approaches for encouraging faculty and students to excel. New directions for teaching and learning*. San Fransisco: Jossey-Bass, 39–47.

Knowles, M. S. and Associates (1984). *Andragogy in Action: Applying Modern Principles of Adult Learning*. San Francisco: Jossey-Bass.

Lewin, K. (1936). *The dynamic theory of personality* (D. K. Adams & K. E. Tener, Trans.). New York: McGraw-Hill.

Lewin, K., Lippitt, R., and White, R. (1939). Patterns of Behaviour in Experimentally Created Social Climates. *Journal of Social Psychology*, 10, 271–299.

Lynch, J., and Bishop-Clark, C. (1994). The Influence of Age in College Classrooms: Some New Evidence. *Community College Review*, 22, 3–12.

MacDonald, C., and Stratta, E. (1998). Academic Work, Gender, and Subjectivity: Mature Non-Standard Entrants in Higher Education. *Studies in the Education of Adults*, 30, 67–79.

Miglietti, C., and Strange, C. C. (1998). Learning styles, classroom preferences, teaching styles and remedial course outcomes. *Community College Review*, 26, 1–19.

Mortimore, P., Sammons, P., Stoll, L., Lewis, D. and Ecob, R. (1988). *School Matters: The Junior Years*. London: Open Books.

Murphy, M. and Fleming, T. (2000). Between Common and College Knowledge: Exploring the Boundaries between Adult and Higher Education. *Studies in Continuing Education*, 22, 77–93.

Murray, H.A. (1938). *Explorations in personality*. New York: Oxford University Press.

New England Adult Research Network (1999). *Factors influencing adult student persistence in undergraduate degree programs*. Amherst, MA: University of Massachusetts.

O'Fathaigh, M. (1997). Irish Adult Learners' Perceptions of Classroom Environment: Some Empirical Findings. *International Journal of University Adult Education*, 36, 9–22.

Thelen, H. A. (1950). Educational dynamics: Theory and research. *Journal of Social Issues*, 6, 5–95.

Thomas, D. S., (1929). *Some New Techniques for Studying Social Behaviour*. New York: Teachers College.

Tinto, V. (1998). Colleges as communities: taking research on student persistence seriously. *The Review of Higher Education*, 21, 167–177.

Tobias, R. (1998). Who needs education or training? The learning experiences and perspectives of adults from working class backgrounds. *Studies in the Education of Adults*, 30, 120–142.

Raven, M. F. and Jimmerson, R. M. (1992). Perceptions of Nontraditional Students, Teaching and Learning Held by Faculty and Students. *Continuing Higher Education Review*, 56, 137–154.

Roosmaa, E.-L., Boeren, E., Saar, E. and Nicaise, I. (2011). Adult learners in formal adult education: experiences and perceptions from thirteen European countries. *LLL2010 SP3 Comparative Report*. Working Paper No 46.

Rosenshine, B. (1970). Evaluation of Classroom Instruction. *Review of Educational Research*, 40, 279–300.

Ross-Gordon, J. M. (1991). Critical Incidents in the College Classroom. *Continuing Higher Education Review*, 55, 14–29.

Ross-Gordon, J. M. (2003). Adult Learners in the Classroom. *New Directions for Student Services*, 102, 43–52.

Ross-Gordon, J., and Brown-Haywood, F. (2000). Keys to College Success as Seen Through the Eyes of African American Adult Students. *Journal of Continuing Higher Education*, 48, 14–23.

Strenze, T. (2007). Intelligence and socioeconomic success: A meta-analytic review of longitudinal research. *Intelligence*, 35, 401–426.

Appendix

Table 1a. Classroom environment scale statements posed in the questionnaire

Classroom environment (ACES) indicators	**Statements posed in the questionnaire**
Affiliation	The study programme provides opportunities for making new friends The students in the study programme enjoy working together
Teacher support	The teacher makes every effort to help students succeed The teacher respects students as individuals
Task orientation	Activities not related to study programme objectives are kept to a minimum Getting work done is very important in the study programme
Personal goal attainment	Students can select assignments that are of personal interest to them Most students in the study programme achieve their personal learning goals
Organisation and clarity	The study programme is well organised The study programme has a clear sense of direction
Student influence	The teacher insists that you do things his or her way Students feel free to question study programme requirements Participants in the training discuss real-life examples based on their personal experience *
Student involvement	Students often ask the teacher questions Most students enjoy the study programme

Note: marked with star (*) is the statement added by the LLL2010 project team.

Table 2a. Perception of classroom environments using the seven ACES indicators in European countries, mean values on a 5-point scale and standard deviations

	Affiliation	**Teacher support**	**Task orientation**	**Personal goal attainment**	**Organisation and clarity**	**Student influence**	**Student involvevolvement**
Austria	4.2 (.5)	3.9 (.8)	3.9 (.6)	3.2 (.8)	3.7 (.9)	3.6 (.6)	4.0 (.5)
Belgium (Flanders)	3.7 (.6)	3.8 (.6)	3.8 (.6)	3.3 (.7)	3.7 (.7)	3.3 (.6)	3.7 (.6)
Bulgaria	4.1 (.6)	3.8 (.8)	3.7 (.6)	3.4 (.7)	3.4 (.8)	3.6 (.6)	3.8 (.6)
Czech Rep	3.8 (.7)	3.4 (.7)	3.4 (.7)	3.1 (.7)	3.6 (.8)	3.7 (.6)	3.3 (.7)
England	4.1 (.6)	4.4 (.6)	4.0 (.5)	3.5 (.8)	4.1 (.7)	3.5 (.5)	4.2 (.5)
Estonia	*4.2 (.6)*	*3.9 (.7)*	*4.0 (.6)*	*3.3 (.7)*	*3.8 (.7)*	*3.7 (.6)*	*3.9 (.6)*
Hungary	3.8 (.6)	3.3 (.8)	3.4 (.5)	3.4 (.7)	3.4 (.9)	3.4 (.4)	3.4 (.7)
Ireland	3.8 (.7)	4.1 (.7)	4.0 (.6)	3.2 (.8)	3.8 (.8)	3.3 (.6)	3.9 (.6)
Lithuania	4.0 (.5)	3.9 (.7)	3.8 (.6)	3.5 (.7)	3.8 (.6)	3.7 (.5)	3.8 (.5)
Norway	4.4 (.9)	4.5 (.7)	–	3.9 (1.1)	4.2 (1.0)	4.2 (1.2)	4.5 (.7)
Russia	4.2 (.6)	3.9 (.7)	3.8 (.7)	3.4 (.7)	3.8 (.8)	3.4 (.6)	3.9 (.7)
Scotland	4.0 (.6)	4.2 (.7)	4.0 (.5)	3.4 (.7)	3.8 (.8)	3.6 (.5)	4.0 (.6)
Slovenia	3.8 (.6)	3.7 (.7)	3.4 (.6)	3.3 (.6)	3.7 (.6)	3.5 (.5)	3.6 (.6)

Note: In the Norwegian questionnaire only one statement per ACES indicator was presented, with the exception of teacher support, where agreement with both statements was asked for and both task orientation statements were excluded.

Source: ALiFE, 2007

Table 3a. The effect of ACES indicators on confidence and satisfaction, linear regression models with country group interactions, R-square

	Confidence		Satisfaction	
	Adjusted R^2	**R^2 change**	**Adjusted R^2**	**R^2 change**
Affiliation				
Model 1	.074		.436	
Model 2	.075	.002	.436	.001
Teacher support				
Model 1	.074		.436	
Model 2	.075	.002	.437	.001*
Task orientation				
Model 1	.074		.436	
Model 2	.080	.006***	.435	.000
Personal goal attainment				
Model 1	.074		.436	
Model 2	.075	.002	.436	.000
Organisation and clarity				
Model 1	.074		.436	
Model 2	.081	.008***	.436	.001
Student influence				
Model 1	.074		.436	
Model 2	.075	.002*	.436	.001
Student involvement				
Model 1	.074		.436	
Model 2	.077	.004***	.437	.002**

*Effect significant at: *** $p < 0.01$; ** $p < 0.05$; * $p < 0.10$*

Note: Model 1 independent variables: seven ACES indicators and country groups (ref. Anglo-Celtic countries, because classroom environment was perceived most positive in those countries). Model 2 independent variables: seven ACES indicators, country groups (ref. Anglo-Celtic countries) and interactions (seven ACES indicators by country groups, ref. interactions with Anglo-Celtic countries).

Source: ALiFE, 2007

Chapter 7.
How non-native speaker students cope in higher education: a case study of ethnic minority students in Estonia

Helena Metslang, Anastassia Šmõreitšik

Introduction

In contemporary higher education the number of university programmes taught in a non-native language is increasing rapidly (e.g. Wilkinson, 2004; Spencer, 2008). Although this is largely due to the expansion of the use of English, university programmes in other languages also receive significant numbers of international and non-native speaker minority students. Higher education in minority languages is protected by state and regional programmes such as the EU (European Charter for Regional or Minority Languages, 1992; Lehtikoinen, 2004).

Studying courses that are not in the student's mother tongue has many advantages: mastering a new language, increasing intercultural understanding, integration and cooperation, but as Hellekjaer (2004) contends a negative aspect is that it can also produce disparities in the quality of received education that cause problems to students, instructors and universities. For example,when studying in a second language (L2)[1], the students have less understanding of the subject matter and they lose their ability to perform at their best (Smith, 2004). Language barriers may affect whether non-native speaker (NNS) students complete their courses on time and may also limit the students' choice of courses and subjects (Vetik et al., 2008) and NNS students are often more passive in courses than their native speaker peers. They are sometimes characterised by shyness about speaking up in class and communicating with native speaker students, by learning style inhibitions ('memorization', i.e. rote learning; Ferris and Tagg, 1996b), by weak academic reading and writing skills (e.g. Hellekjaer, 2004:156–157) and by higher stress levels (Burdakova, Raud and Džalalova, 2011).

Universities in many European countries commonly face two issues that sometimes conflict with each other. On the one hand, in ageing societies universities need to make an *effort to attract and keep as many students as possible* in order to maintain existing volumes of teaching and courses. This often includes enrolling NNS students from within the country as well as from

1 The abbreviations are presented at the end of the paper.

abroad. On the other hand, higher education *curricula are very demanding in terms of the students' language skills*: the NNS students need a very good command of the language in order to thoroughly understand the courses and complete the assignments. Hence, when deciding whether or not to accept students with poorer skills in the language of study, universities face a choice between keeping student numbers high or providing high quality education to everyone.

This article presents the results of the research project 'Development needs for academic language teaching'. **The purpose of the study** was to describe how Estonian NNS students coped in different educational situations and what the instructors' and students' attitudes and strategies were in dealing with the language difficulties in the study process. The study sought to identify:

a) the extent to which the NNS students are perceived to have difficulties when studying in Estonian;
b) what the main difficulties are and what the more problematic student groups and study situations are;
c) whether language support is regarded as necessary and what the possible expectations of language support are;
d) what kind of language support the NNS students receive.

Drawing on the data collected from student and instructor questionnaires from several Estonian universities, and focus groups held at Tallinn University, this study gave a picture of the aspects of this complex set of problems that are directly related to course-setting. The authors hope that the study contributes to a better understanding of the education quality issues of NNS students.

Background

Despite what the language of instruction at a university is – be it a *lingua franca* like English or some other regional or local language – many of the major concerns in ensuring high quality education for NNS students are the same. This section outlines some of the main issues concerning teaching NNS students at universities in any language.

A large part of **NNS students' educational success** is determined by several characteristics of the students. Smith (2004) finds that university language teaching and support systems should be based on these characteristics: NNS students form different groups on the basis of the language they plan to use in their future careers. This can determine their general study motivation, language learning motivation, and the teaching approaches that work the best for them, etc. (pp. 88–91).

The main support measures provided by universities to NNS students are usually **language courses**, often academic language or subject specific language courses (in the context of teaching English, usually called English for academic purposes (EAP) and English for specific (academic) purposes (ESP). In order to avoid any confusion EstSP in this article, is the acronym for *Estonian for specific (academic) purposes*).

As several studies have found, almost all parties involved downplay, or even ignore, the impact of using a foreign language as a means of instruction and learning. Students do have challenges with understanding and performing in an L2 and they need support in this activity (Tella, Räsänen and Vähäpassi, 1999; Räsänen, 2000). The internationally shared challenges in developing the L2 students' academic language skills are the following.

- The **student groups have very different speciality subject and target language needs**. It is not efficient to provide separate language courses for all speciality subjects, therefore language instruction is complicated by the need to teach students from different academic fields together (cf. Hall and Bankowska, 1994).
- To prepare the students for the tasks required of them in subject-matter courses, language instructors have to be aware of the nature of those tasks (e.g. Ferris and Tagg, 1996a:32). However, often the **language teachers lack knowledge of the specific disciplines**.
- The range of student needs, including the **amount of task types that are required from them in the courses is vast,** and it is difficult for the language instructors to make well-informed choices for them. This can also depend on the discipline, for example Ferris and Tagg (1996a:48) show that on average business classes are more interactive than engineering and science classes.
- At universities, **language teaching is usually isolated** from subject teaching. It is expected that language problems will be solved in the language classroom and that students will acquire language knowledge and skills from just being in the language environment (cf. Tella et al., 1999; Snelgrove, 2004:429–430). However, mere contact with the language environment is not an effective development factor if it is not accompanied by language support, obligatory study goals and feedback on correct language use (Milton, 2009:234; Storch and Tapper, 2009:218).

Offering programmes through the means of a foreign language, without setting performance targets for NNS students in the use of the content-related language, puts the quality and the reputation of both the programme and the institution at risk (cf. Wilkinson, 2004:10). Therefore, in recent decades the research and practice of preparing NNS students linguistically for academic situations has greatly improved in many countries. The research field of *language for academic purposes* has developed into a multifaceted and rich discipline in terms of both the language variety description and methodology development. Content and language integrated learning (CLIL) methodology has expanded from secondary to tertiary education (e.g. Dafouz Milne and Llinares García, 2008; Airey, 2009). Content subject instructors – that is instructors in medicine, history, etc. and not language – have been involved in language teaching, and team-teaching methodology is expanding (e.g. Snelgrove, 2004; Kunschak, 2011). The varied nature of language use in academic situations has been addressed by the development of needs analysis techniques for different kinds of language learners (e.g. Dudley-Evans and St. John, 1998; al-Husseini, 2004; Huhta, 2010; Huhta et al., 2012).

The methodology of CLIL integrates several contemporary educational practices some of which are also common in other paradigms and non-CLIL practice. Mehisto, Marsh and Frigols Martín (2010) find that CLIL incorporates the following principles: the content courses also contain L2 teaching, L2 courses directly support learning of the content subjects, the content subjects and language teachers work together, the new material is taught in a way that supports understanding, and learning skills are developed. Although applying CLIL principles in the content courses makes them more manageable for the NNS students, their application is often hindered by the content subject instructors' lack of awareness, will, skills and emphasis. The application of CLIL depends on the mix of NNS students and native speakers, class size, delivery style and type of institution (Ferris and Tagg, 1996a:50).

The Estonian case

There are two types of secondary schools in Estonia: those where the teaching is in Estonian and those where it is largely in Russian (about 17 per cent of secondary schools)[2]. As a result of the Russian language schools' 2007–2012 reform, in the upper secondary levels (years 10-12), 60 percent of the subjects are taught in Estonian. In the lower levels (years 1–9) the lessons mostly take place in Russian and there is no requirement to teach in Estonian. At public universities the majority of courses are in Estonian (teaching in the Estonian-language in higher education is a national priority), however, about 6 per cent of

2 Source: Ministry of Education and Science web page, www.hm.ee, 06.02.2012.

the students are from Russian language secondary schools[3]. Also the number of foreign students in Estonian universities is rising[4]. Table 1 gives an overview of the numbers of minority students at Estonian universities.

Table 1. Russian-language school students entering Estonia's universities

Students	**2009/10**	**2010/11**
Number of Russian language secondary school graduates	1,924	1,805
Of these university entrants	1035 (53.6%)	863 (47.8%)
to Estonian language courses	59.6%	61.9%
to Russian language courses	39.6%	37.5%
to English language courses	0.8%	0.6%

Source: Data Analysis Department of the Ministry of Education and Science (pc, 25.04.2012)

The total of 19,167 students entered Estonian universities in 2009/2010, 18,404 in 2010/2011 and 17,233 in 2011/2012[5]. In the same way as foreign universities, Estonian higher education institutions encounter the conflicting issues of struggling for student numbers while at the same time needing to provide high quality education despite the students' varied language skills. For example at Tallinn University, new students are allocated to Estonian courses at all language levels, from complete beginner to advanced level[6]. While trying to preserve high student numbers, Estonian universities also have to deal with the competition from universities in Russia and in other countries in the world where the Estonian minority students are highly competitive (cf. What are the students of Estonian universities like, 2010). To support minority students, for example, two major public universities provide some curricula in Russian in the first years of study. Tallinn Technical University and Catherine's College of Tallinn University provide partly Russian curricula[7]. Tallinn Technical University also provides five programmes taught entirely in Russian[8]. By contrast Tartu University, the oldest state university, does not deliver courses

3 Data Analysis Department of the Ministry of Education and Science (pc, 25.04.2012).
4 Between 1993 and 2012 it has risen 10 times. Source: Ministry of Education and Science web page, www.hm.ee, 06.02.2012.
5 Source: Ministry of Education and Science web page, www.hm.ee, 06.02.2012.
6 Source: Tallinn University Study info system ÕIS www.tlu.ee, 13.05.2012.
7 2 curricula at Tallinn University (http://www.tlu.ee/?LangID=1&CatID=2673, 07.12.2012), 21 curricula at Tallinn Technical University (http://www.ttu.ee/sisseastujale/abituriendile/venekeelne-ope/, 07.12.2012).
8 Source: http://www.ttu.ee/sisseastujale/abituriendile/venekeelne-ope/, 07.12.2012.

taught in Russian at all[9]. Several private universities teach higher education courses in Russian.

Data and method

In the university context, the instructors and students can be viewed as an internally hierarchical speech community. In this paper we studied a phenomenon in this community that is personal and subjective in nature: it describes the network of stakeholder opinions and actions concerning non-native studies in higher education and in this case it is appropriate to employ an interpretative approach (cf. Bruce, 2011:25–29). This qualitative method is also good for 'better understanding complex interactions, tacit processes and often hidden beliefs and values in an organization' (Marshall and Rossmann, 2006:15, 53). An efficient mainstream qualitative method for documenting the phenomena that are less well identified by observational methods – people's attitudes and experiences, group meanings, behaviours and norms that are also subject to various influences – is the focus group (Bloor et al., 2001:17; Barbour, 2007:36). Therefore, the study uses both quantitative and qualitative approaches and is based on both instructor and student questionnaires and focus groups.

In the research process, two pilot questionnaires and four focus groups were initially carried out. They helped to get an insight into the circumstances of NNS students. The pilot questionnaires consider the research topic thoroughly; they consisted of a large number of questions and were answered by a small group of respondents[10]. To find out how wide-spread the identified recurring themes, dominating and more exceptional attitudes and behaviours were, two final questionnaires were constructed on the basis of the pilot questionnaires and focus groups. The full list of data collection activities were as follows:

The first stage of the study (carried out at Tallinn University) consisted of:

- a pilot questionnaire for content subject instructors (n=23);
- a pilot questionnaire for NNS students (n=19);
- two content subject instructor focus groups (n=11 and n=5);
- two NNS student focus groups (n=3 and n=8).

The second stage of the study (carried out at different higher education institutions in Estonia) consisted of:

9 Source: University of Tartu Office of Academic Affairs.

10 The instructor questionnaire contains 18 closed-ended questions and 20 open-ended questions, the student questionnaire has 65 closed-ended questions and 8 open-ended questions.

1) a short questionnaire for content subject instructors (n=191);
2) as hort questionnaire for NNS students (n=887).

The instructor focus groups were made up of staff from different specialities (humanities, education, social sciences and natural sciences) and the Students' Union.Most of the instructors who took part taught in Estonian, however, in each focus group there were some lecturers who taught in Russian (see Appendix 1 for information on the instructors' focus groups). The participants in the student focus groups were from a variety of specialities: humanities, teacher education, sciences, natural sciences and social sciences and consisted of both men and women of two distinct age groups (See Appendix 2 for the overview of the students' focus groups).

The main questionnaires for the instructors and students contained eight questions each. They were filled out both electronically and on paper (see Appendix 3 for the details of the main questionnaires). In the student questionnaire, the questions dealing with the content of the L2 courses looked at a balanced set of 16 language use skills:

1) 4 oral communication skills (participating in seminar discussions, expressing one's opinion, asking and answering questions, making a presentation);
2) 1 listening skill (listening to lectures);
3) 2 reading skills (effective reading and use of texts, finding information, e.g. searching the internet);
4) 6 writing skills (good written expression, expressing one's opinion, writing summaries, writing short texts (0.5–2 pages), writing a research paper, and providing written answers, as in an exam);
5) 3 general skills (EstSP, learning grammar, coping with an internship)[11].

The remainder of this section outlines the respondent profiles for the main questionnaires. The invitation to fill in the questionnaire was sent to the major universities in Estonia. Most of the instructor and student responses came from three largest universities (i.e., the public universities: Tallinn Technical University, the University of Tartu and Tallinn University which together have 63 per cent of the students in Estonia; see Table 2)[12].

---

11 The skill of expressing one's opinion can manifest itself in both oral and written forms, therefore they are presented under both. EstSP, command of grammar and coping with an internship are also general skills that can manifest themselves indifferent modes of language use.

12 Source: Ministry of Education and Science web page, www.hm.ee, 06.02.2012.

Table 2. The respondents' universities (per cent)

University	**Instructors**	**Students**
Tallinn Technical University	45	60
Tallinn University	30	9
University of Tartu	12	17
Estonian University of Life Sciences	10	3
Estonian Academy of Arts	3	2
Euroacademy	0	3
University of Applied Sciences	0	2
Tallinn School of Economics	0	1
Estonian Academy of Music and Theatre	0	1
Estonian Business School	0	1
Other	0	1
Total	**100**	**100**

The gender ratio among the student respondents was men at 36 per cent and women at 64 per cent. The group mainly consisted of students who were less than 25 years old (see Table 3).

Table 3. Age of the Non-Native Speaker student questionnaire respondents (per cent)

Age group	**Respondents**
18–21	30
22–24	33
25–30	27
31–35	6
36–45	3
46–62	1
Total	**100**

The majority of responses to both the student and instructor questionnaires came from four subject areas: engineering and construction, sciences and natural sciences, social sciences, and humanities (see Table 4). Two common subject areas amongst the students were also information technology (most likely also common among the instructors' responses but classified under engineering and construction) and economics and business (most likely classified under social sciences in the instructors' responses). The student questionnaire was more specific in asking about the specialities because it also contained an open-ended question about them.

Table 4. Specialities of the instructor and the student questionnaire respondent, (per cent)

Field of study	**Students**	**Instructors**
engineering and construction	16	29
sciences and natural sciences	30	26
Social sciences and business	22	18
humanities and languages	8	10
education	5	7
Arts	5	4
Medicine	3	2
Law	2	2
Other	5	2
unspecified	4	0
Total	**100**	**100**

The majority of the students were from the first three years of undergraduate studies or undertaking Masters degrees. There were fewer responses from doctoral and other students, see Table 5.

Table 5. Year of study of the Non-Native Speaking student questionnaire respondents (per cent)

Year of study	**Respondents**
Masters	29
Undergraduate, 3rd year	25
Undergraduate, 1st year	17
Undergraduate, 2nd year	16
Doctoral	6
Undergraduate, 4th year and older	4
Undergraduate, year unspecified	1
Graduated	1
Unspecified	1
Total	**100**

Some students left some questions unanswered (for example, because they had not participated in a language course), therefore, the number of respondents to each question is shown when displaying the results. In three questions in the NNS student questionnaire, one of the 16 language skills under scrutiny –

knowledge of general language (as opposed to EstSP) – has been excluded from the study results as we believe the respondents' understanding of the term was in consistent.

Results

This section summarises the results of the main questionnaires and focus groups. Some results are illustrated with quotes from the pilot questionnaires. The section first outlines the results concerning the NNS students' ability to cope with language problems in their academic studies, and then the language support that they wish to get and are receiving in both the subject courses and the language courses. The final part of this section discusses the content subject instructors' opinions on providing language support within their courses. In this study we distinguished two main strategies for providing language-related support to NNS students: the more established system of language courses (the second and third subsections of Results) and the naturally developed and more spontaneous support and adaptations taking place in subject courses (the fourth and the fifth subsections).

How NNS students cope with different course types

In general, NNS students reported that they were managing well with their studies in Estonian. Seventy nine per cent of the NNS students coped satisfactorily, well or excellently with all the course types they participated in. More specifically, they were asked about four course types:

1) lectures (primarily in the form of a talk delivered before a student audience for instruction);
2) seminars (the instructor and the students meeting regularly to exchange information and hold discussions);
3) tutorials (intensive instruction in a small group);
4) writing research papers (term papers, theses).

Figure 1 outlines the opinions of the students who claim to have participated in the respective course types (874 in lectures, 844 in tutorials, 843 in seminars and 772 in writing research papers).

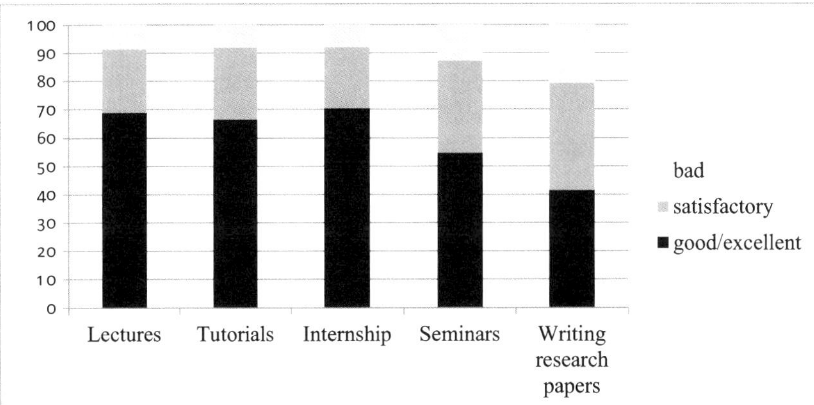

Figure 1. *Non-Native Speaking student questionnaire respondents' evaluation on how they manage in different course types in Estonian (n=887)*

Among the instructors there was a great difference in how they reported the ability of NNS students to manage linguistically. Forty seven per cent of the instructors said that only a few NNS students had difficulty completing course work. At the same time over half reported a significant proportion (ranging from one-third to virtually all) of NNS students having problems. A quarter of the instructors claimed that two-thirds or more of the NNS students had language difficulties (Table 6).

It is less evident that studying in an L2 has a direct influence on the ability to keep to deadlines. Over half of the instructors found that in only a few exceptional cases did the students' language barrier cause delays. Twenty eight per cent reported that language caused delays for a significant proportion of the NNS students (1/3 of NNS students to almost every NNS student). It is often hard for the instructors to know the exact reason for delays, and some reported that they did not know whether the NNS students' delays were caused by language difficulties or something else.

Table 6. *The impact of studying in an L2 on students' academic success. Instructors' views, per cent (n=191)*

Question	**Only few exceptions**	**1/3 of NNS students**	**2/3 of NNS students**	**Almost everyone**	**Hard to say**
What proportion of your NNS students have problems with understanding the content of your courses and fulfilling the course requirements?	47	27	15	9	2
What proportion of your NNS students fail to meet deadlines because of inadequate language skills?	55	17	8	3	17

The instructors suggested that the NNS students' language problems appear in the different lecture types and class sizes, and in students in all years (Table 7). In the views of the instructors the problem was especially noticeable in tutorials and amongst first year students.

Table 7. *The courses and student categories where studying in an L2 causes most problems. Instructors views, per cent (n=191)*

Characteristics	**Responses**
tutorials	44
lectures	40
undergraduate, 1st year students	40
seminars	36
students of different years	24
courses with over 30 students	22
undergraduate, 2nd year students	22
undergraduate, 3rd year students	19
Masters students	17
courses with 16–30 students	15
courses with 8–16 students	11
courses with fewer than 8 students	4

To conclude, the NNS students largely had a higher opinion about how they coped with their studies in their L2 than the instructors did. This discrepancy may come from different ways of looking at what coping well is. The students were more likely to judge it on the basis of the marks they got and their ability to pass a course. However, the instructors were likely to have higher expectations of the students' output. Some instructor focus group participants reported that they let the NNS student pass if they demonstrated sufficient subject knowledge, even if there were many grammatical errors in their presentations or if their papers did not show mature and smooth academic expression skills. Nevertheless, they did report that such students had problems. In some cases the instructors seemed to lack an overview of how the NNS students were doing in their courses, for example: '*It was only when the series of lectures was followed by tutorials that I noticed that this NNS student had not understood anything.*'(Instructor, Focus Group).

Students' expectations of L2 courses

The students reported being especially interested in acquiring Estonian language skills to help them to be more expressive and communicate their ideas better in both oral and written forms (the choices *expressing one's opinion, participating in discussions* and *good written expression*). The students also wished to deal with perfecting their grammar and subject specific Estonian (EstSP; e.g. Estonian for historians), see Table 9. Among the more specific skills mentioned the most common were writing research papers, asking and answering questions, and making presentations.

The results showed that the more general skills were selected more often than the specific skills (*writing short texts (0.5–2 pages), coping with an internship, writing answers in exam*s and *writing summaries*). This may be because the students regard the more general skills involving the narrower (smaller) ones or that they are not used to thinking of language learning as a focused activity consisting of small individual steps.

Table 8. *Most frequent skills in Non-Native Speaking students' responses to the question* Please choose three most important skills that should be taught in Estonian L2 courses, *per cent (n=887)*

Language use skills	Responses
expressing one's opinion	60
participating in discussions	39
good written expression	37
learning grammar	26
ESP	26
effective reading and use of texts	16
writing research papers	14
asking and answering questions	11
making presentations	10
listening to lectures	8
finding information	7
writing short texts (0.5–2 A4)	6
coping with internships	6
writing answers (exams)	3
writing summaries	3

Recurring worries concerning language skills reported at the student focus groups included, for example: 'Due to limited knowledge of vocabulary I am only able to express my thoughts in an overly simplistic way. I avoid getting into discussions with my Estonian peers because I am afraid of making language mistakes'. (Student, Focus Group).

Among the three most important language skills that the NNS students wished to develop, the most frequently occurring combinations can roughly be divided in two on the basis of either prioritizing oral or written communication (Table 9). All the most frequent triples involved the skill of expressing one's opinion in an L2.

Table 9. The most frequent triples in NNS students' responses to the question Please choose the three most important skills that should be taught in Estonian L2 courses *(occurring over 20 times, n=687)*

Triple No	Skills		
1	expressing one's opinion	participating in discussions	good written expression
2	expressing one's opinion	participating in discussions	EstSP
3	expressing one's opinion	participating in discussions	asking and answering questions
4	expressing one's opinion	good written expression	learning grammar
5	expressing one's opinion	good written expression	EstSP
6	expressing one's opinion	good written expression	effective reading and use of texts

It turns out that it was difficult for the NNS students to prioritize the language skills they needed at university. When they were asked about the necessity of teaching each separate language use sub-skill they rated their importance almost equally, the most common answer being *I totally agree* (that this skill should be taught). The NNS students actually regarded all of the skills as necessary and did not have very strong specific preferences. The results confirmed that the students felt they did need a broad range of different skills to cope in all higher education situations.

Current language support for the Non-Native Speaking students: language courses

This section looks at how the NNS students evaluated the language courses that they participated in. Those NNS students who reported having participated in an Estonian course at university (320) were asked to evaluate whether the course helped them progress in several language use activities[13]. The students reported that grammar skills were among the five most common skills that the Estonian courses helped to develop, three were written communication skills (*good written expression, writing short texts, effective reading and use of texts*) and one was a skill that occurs in both written and oral communication (*expressing one's opinion*). Among the five skills least developed in the Estonian courses were EstSP, two oral communication skills (*participating in seminar discussions, making presentations*), one written communication skill (*writing research papers*) and one skill that can be both written and oral (*coping with an*

13 As filling in this question was only optional, the actual proportion of NNS students having participated in an Estonian course is probably larger.

internship). The results suggest that the L2 courses at Estonian universities tend to be oriented more towards writing rather than oral skills.

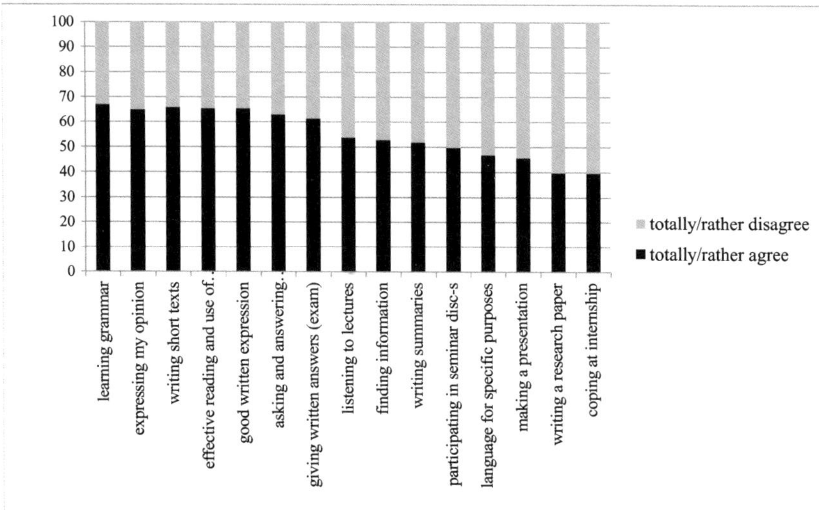

Figure 2. *Do you notice progress in the following areas thanks to Estonian language courses? (n=320)(per cent)*

At a standard 95 per cent confidence interval, the proportion of NNS students who responded positively to the second question in the survey (*What skills should Estonian courses focus on?*) was significantly different to the proportion who responded positively to the third question (*Can you notice progress in the following areas thanks to Estonian courses?*) for all the skills. The students uniformly expressed the need to acquire an array of language skills but they reported that the Estonian courses that they participated in were not very successful in providing them with these skills. When looking at the wide range of expectations that NNS students have of language courses, it is understandable that it is not realistic to ensure progress in all of these areas. The language instructors had prioritised focusing on some skills over others.

The skills that the students wished to acquire and the skills that they saw that the L2 courses helped them to develop partially overlap. Among the five skills that the students thought most important, two skills were not developed very much in the language courses:

- *participating in seminar discussions* (second in the ranking of the preferred skills but only eleventh in the ranking of skills that progressed thanks to language courses);
- *learning EstSP* (fifth in the ranking of the preferred skills but only twelfth in the ranking of skills that progressed thanks to language courses).

The remaining three preferred skills were ranked highly in terms of real progress (*expressing one's opinion, good written expression, asking and answering questions*). Of the five skills where the students saw most progress as a result of the Estonian courses, they only marked three as very important (*expressing one's opinion, effective reading and good written expression*) and they marked the other two skills that they acquired as lower priority:

- *learning grammar* (first in the ranking of skills that progressed due to language courses but only seventh in the ranking of the preferred skills that the students wished to develop);
- *writing short texts* (third in the ranking of skills that progressed due to language courses but only eighth in the ranking of preferred skills).

To conclude, the L2 courses partly met the students' expectations. However, in addition to students' expectations there were, of course, other factors that language instructors needed to take into account: e.g. the subject matter instructors' expectations, teaching conditions and possibilities, including the capacity for teaching specific academic languages for all NNS students and the lengths of the courses.

Current language support for the Non-Native Speaking students: content courses

There are many support measures that the instructor survey respondents need to use to help the NNS students cope linguistically. These measures shed light on the extent of the NNS students' language difficulties and, thus, on which language use areas may require more attention in the language courses. This section summarizes the question in the focus group and staff questionnaire results on whether, how and to what extent the instructors supported the NNS students in coping with content courses.

In discussing the extent to which instructors adapted their courses to the NNS students' language needs, **two distinct course types** need to be considered separately. First – the majority of the educational situations discussed in this study – are the predominantly Estonian student groups.. Second, a less common case, was when lecturers were teaching mostly NNS groups (e.g. Catherine's College at Tallinn University).

When **the group was predominantly Estonian** and there were between 0 and 50 per cent NNS students (but more often just a few) then the students' linguistic problems only affected the lecturer in minor ways. The study showed that the lecturers' approaches during these courses ranged from ignoring the potential language problem completely to making some adjustments to the teaching process, study materials and/or assessment. In the focus groups, two lecturers who give lectures to large groups (humanities and informatics) reported that sometimes they had not been aware at all that some course participants were failing to understand a significant part of the course.

More extensive adjustments were reported to take place in courses where the NNS students dominated. There were two lecturers in the focus groups who gave **courses to entirely NNS groups** studying bilingual programmes. One was expected to give the course in Russian (humanities) and the other in Estonian (social sciences). The humanities course was all in Russian – that is the lectures, study materials and assessments – and the students' Estonian skills were not developed at all. The social sciences' lecturer reported that the Estonian skills of the whole group were poor and therefore found it necessary to give part of the course in Russian. However, in order to develop the students' Estonian skills the lecturer included some Estonian components in the course and the assessment. The language knowledge of such groups would benefit immensely from the adoption of CLIL methodology. However, the instructors who participated in this survey did not show awareness of the existence of methodological frameworks that help to systematically develop both the NNS students' content and language skills. The instructors seemed to lack help in making informed language-related decisions about their subject.

The content subject instructors reported using a variety of ways of addressing the poor Estonian skills of their NNS students. Broadly, they took two kinds of approaches to providing support. The instructors who took the **'mere development of subject knowledge'** approach were not actively striving towards the students achieving good written and oral expression in Estonian. They tended to address the NNS students' linguistic problems by translating, by providing Russian or English study materials and by allowing papers to be submitted in the NNS students' mother tongue or English. The instructors who took the **'development of subject and language knowledge'** approach tried to ensure that the NNS students improved their academic Estonian skills. The support measures used in this approach take advantage of good contemporary teaching methods to develop the students' language knowledge (e.g. providing the students with lecture materials in advance, giving group work tasks, using peer support). The amount of effort required varied between the two approaches; and also, of course, there are intermediate and mixed ways of dealing with these situations. The data suggested that the instructors had many options to choose from and that all of these could be helpful in different situations. Some staff reported that they made allowances for the NNS students (e.g. they were less strict in assessing their exam papers) but, in most cases, these allowances only took account of the linguistic correctness of the student output, not its content. Other instructors were strongly against making allowances, stating that it is their responsibility to ensure that all university graduates have a very good command of Estonian and they saw assessment as one of the main tools for ensuring this.

As mentioned above, the **teaching process related NNS student support and adjustments** occurred in the interactive seminar-like courses rather than in the large audience lectures. To varying degrees all of the participants in the focus groups adapted their teaching, ranging from just encouraging the NNS students to ask questions during the study process, to specially prepared thesis defence rehearsals between the student and the supervisor. One focus group participant (natural sciences) said she started to give special attention to the NNS students from the very beginning of the course: *In the beginning of the course I ask the students: who is from a Russian-medium secondary school? Throughout the course I pay attention to whether they understand everything, especially if they are first year students*.

In the case of **study materials**, one of the support measures used requiring most effort was the provision of the whole set of lecture videos and course slides on the internet (this was a participant from teacher education). Instructors often made suggestions on literature for the students to read in Russian or English. The drawback of this approach is that the students do not learn the Estonian subject terminology properly (questionnaire: informatics, social sciences). Table 10 presents the questionnaire and focus group responses categorized according to the problematic language skill areas of NNS students and the amount and type of special effort put into language support adaptations[14].

14 To highlight the option of peer support as an effective support opportunity, it is presented separately in the Table, although peer support activities may often be categoized under contemporary engaging teaching methods.

Table 10. *Language support provided to Non-Native Speaking (NNS) students by content subject instructors (from the instructors' responses in focus groups and an open-ended question in the questionnaire)*

Support measures / Addressed difficulty in Estonian	**Listening**	**Discussion, speaking**	**Reading**	**Writing**	**Estonian for Specific (Academic) Purposes, vocabulary**	**Grammar, correctness of language use**
Contemporary engaging teaching methods	providing information orally and simultaneously on the blackboard /presentation slides encouraging asking questions clearly explaining target learning outcomes	group work in mixed language groups discussion topics on the projector screen encouraging asking questions clearly explaining target learning outcomes ensuring warm supportive atmosphere for presentations, accepting that NNS students make mistakes	new (e-learning) materials available before lecture encouraging asking questions clearly explaining target learning outcomes	clearly explaining target learning outcomes encouraging asking questions	clearly explaining target learning outcomes encouraging asking questions	clearly explaining target learning outcomes encouraging asking questions

Table 10. Continued

Support measures / Addressed difficulty in Estonian	**Listening**	**Discussion, speaking**	**Reading**	**Writing**	**Estonian for Specific (Academic) Purposes, vocabulary**	**Grammar, correctness of language use**
Significant support measures in classroom	speaking more slowly explaining individually longer translations into the students' mother tongue translating task instructions questioning to ensure that the NNS students have understood the essentials assigning individual tasks	allowing to speak/respond in the mother tongue correcting mistakes during presentations assigning individual tasks	explaining individually questioning to ensure that the NNS students have understood the essentials assigning individual tasks	assigning individual tasks	providing translations of key terms assigning individual tasks	assigning individual tasks
Minor support measures in classroom	shorter translations into the students' mother tongue repetitions	encouragement of presenting in Estonian			occasional translation of words	

Table 10. Continued

Support measures / Addressed difficulty in Estonian	**Listening**	**Discussion, speaking**	**Reading**	**Writing**	**Estonian for Specific (Academic) Purposes, vocabulary**	**Grammar, correctness of language use**
Study materials	lecture videos and course slides on the internet		providing partly multilingual study materials providing study materials both in Estonian and Russian providing study materials only in Russian or English		providing partly multilingual study materials	
Peer support	peers giving explanations peers whispering translations	pair work with native-speaker students peers giving explanations	peers giving explanations peers whispering translations	Estonian peers proofreading NNS students' papers	peers translating difficult words	

Table 10. Continued

Support measures / Addressed difficulty in Estonian	Listening	Discussion, speaking	Reading	Writing	Estonian for Specific (Academic) Purposes, vocabulary	Grammar, correctness of language use
Support-related activities outside classroom	individual meetings with NNS students explanations via personal emails giving a supportive course	giving a supportive course bachelor thesis defence simulations	individual meetings with NNS students explanatio ns via personal emails giving a supportiv e course	Accepting and correcting student papers, including exam papers in Russian or English individual meetings with NNS students proofreading the students' work translating student texts giving a supportive course	providing terminology in 2 or 3 languages individual meetings with NNS students giving a supportive course	individual meetings with NNS students individual feedback on recurring grammar mistakes, suggesting the right grammar rule to use
Assessment		not assessing NNS students' language use giving NNS students more time at exams translating exam questions	giving NNS students more time at exams	giving NNS students more time at exams requiring part of learning portfolio in a second language (L2) requiring expression of the student's own opinion (not just reproducing learned items) requiring having course papers proofread not assessing NNS students' language use accepting course papers in Russian	allowing the use of dictionaries at exams not assessing NNS students' language use giving NNS students more time at exams allowing the use of English or Russian terminology	not assessing NNS students' language use giving NNS students more time at exams

A number of respondents to the questionnaire also reported that they did **not provide language support** to the NNS students. In this case it was unclear whether or not they used contemporary methodologies that support both native speakers and NNS students. Table 11 summarises the responses evaluated according to the criteria presented in Table 10. As some respondents used several kinds of measures in their courses the results overlap.

Table 11. Language support measures that instructors use with NNS students (n=191)

Support measures	**Per cent**
Teaching methods	
contemporary engaging teaching methods	30
significant support measures in classroom	40
minor support measures in classroom	30
peer support	3
support-related activities outside classroom	10
Study materials	11
Exceptions in assessment	5
Not providing support	12

To conclude, the content subject instructors reported extensive use of language support techniques to help the NNS students understand and pass the content requirements of the course. However, conscious activities to help the NNS students develop their Estonian were rare. For example, the following CLIL methods were not mentioned: setting special language learning goals for NNS students, teaching the discipline's specific textual and linguistic patterns to the students and co-operating with language instructors to support the students' EstSP development. Such deep integration of language learning and speciality subject courses depends above all on the instructor's recognition of its necessity. The following section looks at this issue more closely.

Instructors' attitudes towards giving special support to NNS students

In order to cope with the particular subject vocabularies the NNS students need more specific language skills than it is usually possible to provide in general language courses; this is due to the very varied student needs and the financial costs of meeting these. In the survey this question considered the instructors' attitudes towards helping the students with poor Estonian skills. They were asked whether the content subject instructors should use special support methods (like checking NNS students' understanding, uploading lecture recordings to an online learning environment, etc.). The answer options were elaborated with statements reflecting some recurring views from the pilot questionnaire and focus groups (regarding concerns about instructors' time constraints, education quality and NNS students' own responsibilities), see Table 12.

Table 12. Content subject instructors' attitudes to whether or not academic staff should provide language support to the NNS students on their courses, per cent (n=191)

Statements	**Responses**
Strongly agree. It is important that all students get quality education despite their language problems. Also content subjects' instructors should devote a little time to language support preparation and participate in methodology training.	13
Rather agree. It is important that all students get quality education despite their language problems. Although the student himself should undertake the main role in coping linguistically, the instructor should also use some support measures that do not take additional time.	51
Rather disagree. Supporting NNS students would be good but it is not a priority.	20
Strongly disagree. Motivated NNS students cope with L2 studies by themselves. It is the students' own fault if they do not cope linguistically.	6
Hard to say.	10

The results indicated that the instructors tended to consider putting effort into NNS students' language suppor as necessary and worthwhile. The results suggested that they did see themselves having a role in this (and, in this way, complementing the work of the language instructors) but they were worried about the extra time that it might take and sometimes about the NNS students' study motivation. Most of the instructors did not have strong opinions about the question (responding *rather agree* or *rather disagree*), however 19 per cent reported that they either strongly agreed or strongly disagreed with the need to offer support. A comment by an instructor from the pilot questionnaire illustrated a contrasting view: '*Coping in the necessary languages should be a precondition of getting enrolled at a university. No-one else should need to worry about whether the student manages or not*'. A respondent from the instructor focus groups expressed an opposite approach: '*At my seminars the whole group ensures the NNS students a warm and supportive atmosphere and ample opportunities to practice presenting in Estonian. The content instructors should also carefully adapt their exam tests, so that poor language skills would not cause lower results*'. In the comments section an opinion was also stated that language support should be organized centrally.

The student questionnaires and focus groups revealed that they preferred and appreciated it if the instructors make adjustments (e.g. provide them with the terminology in advance, both in their mother tongue and L2; provide literature in their mother tongue, repeat in Estonian and in their mother tongue, answer questions and speak clearly).

Conclusion

In this study we investigated non-native speaker students studying Estonian-language courses at Estonian universities. The students and their instructors were questioned about how the students coped studying in a second language, what their main challenges were and what the support strategies of the content subject instructors were.

Most NNS students studying in an L2 at Estonian universities coped quite well. Only a quarter of instructors and less than 13 per cent of the students considered the situation to be problematic in some course types (lectures, seminars and tutorials). Writing research papers posed the greatest problem for the students: 21 per cent of those who had experience of this form of study reported having difficulties with it. However, the fact that NNS students were successful at passing most of their courses does not mean that there is no room for improvement. Coping does not mean that the students have high level academic expression skills. As the NNS students' views of language courses reflected, the challenges are in the areas of participating in discussions and expressing one's opinion, and in smooth written expression (especially in writing research papers). Further analysis needs to be done looking more specifically at the challenges and expectations of the different respondent groups to the student questionnaire.

Supporting the NNS students' ability to cope linguistically was a controversial issue among instructors. A number of staff had strong and differing opinions about this and 26 per cent were against it for a variety of reasons. However, the majority of instructors had a positive attitude towards giving support and were using a range of strategies to achieve this. Even so, their support was limited to helping the students fulfil the course content requirements and only a few active steps were deliberately taken to improve the NNS students' target language skills (like setting special language learning goals, teaching the discipline's specific textual and linguistic patterns and co-operating with language instructors). The instructors lacked awareness of the existing methodological approaches to supporting NNS students' language development and they were concerned that introducing them would mean a considerable amount of extra work. Also, most of them had no help with the NNS students' language problems and systematic support and training may be needed to implement content and language integrated learning principles effectively.

There are a number of potential solutions to the linguistic challenges of NNS students. It was not the purpose of this paper to discuss policy solutions in detail but we are proposing a few early thoughts. The ability of content subject instructors to provide language support could be improved by increasing their awareness of the existing methodological systems of enhancing NNS students' language skills, and importantly, by addressing content subject instructors'direct concerns and prejudices about implementation. As a further step practice-based training could be provided for interested instructors. Second language courses at universities could benefit from this study by shifting the focus more towards the skills the students expect from them.

Acknowledgement

The preparation of this article was supported by a Primus grant (No. 30.3 – 10/569) from the European Social Fund. We thank Ingrid Krall, Olga Pastuhhova, Jelena Helemäe, Peeter Mehisto, and Jean-Marc Dewaele for advice and support. We are responsible for any errors and misconceptualizations.

Abbreviations

CLIL	content and language integrated learning
EAP	English for academic purposes
ESP	English for specific purposes
EstSP	Estonian for specific purposes
L2	second language
NNS students	non-native speaker students

References

Airey, J. (2009). Estimating Undergraduate Bilingual Scientific Literacy in Sweden. CLIL Journal, 1, 26–35. Available online: http://www.icrj.eu/12/article3.html (1.03.2012).

Al-Husseini, S. S. N. (2004). An Analysis of the English Needs of Omani Students on Vocational and Technical Courses with Implications for the Design of Foundation Year English Language Programmes. Doctoral dissertation. University of Leeds.

Barbour, R. (2007). Doing Focus Groups. London: Sage.

Bloor, M., Frankland, J. Thomas, M. and Robson, K. (2001). Focus Groups in Social Research. London: Sage.

Bruce, I. (2011). Theory and Concept of English for Academic Purposes. Basingstoke / New York: Palgrave Macmillan.

Burdakova, O., Raud, N. and Džalalova, A. (2011). *Методика интегрированново обученияпредмету и языку в учебномпроцессе Нарвсково колледжа* [Conent and Language Integrated Learning Methodology at Narva College]. Narva: University of Tartu Narva College.

Dafouz Milne, E. and Llinares García A. (2008). The Role of Repetition in CLIL Teacher Discourse: A Comparative Study at Secondary and Tertiary Levels. *CLIL Journal*, 1, 50–59. Available online: http://www.icrj.eu/11/article4.html (1.03.2012)

Data Analysis Department of the Ministry of Education and Science (pc, 25.04.2012).

Dudley-Evans, T. and St. John, M. (1998). *Developments in English for Specific Purposes: A Multi-Disciplinary Approach.* Cambridge: Cambridge University Press.

European Charter for Regional or Minority Languages. Strasbourg, 5.XI.1992. http://conventions.coe.int/treaty/en/Treaties/Html/148.htm, accessed 21.02.12.

Ferris, D. and Tagg, T. (1996a). Academic oral communication needs: What subject-matter instructors actually require. *TESOL Quarterly*, 30, 31–58.

Ferris, D. and Tagg, T. (1996b). Academic listening/speaking tasks for ESL students: Problems, suggestions, and implication. *TESOL Quarterly*, 30, 297–320.

Hall, J. and Bankowska, A. (1994). *Foreign languages for vocational purposes in further and higher education.* Interchange. Scottish Office Education Department Research and Intelligence Unit, 25.

Hellekjaer, G. O. (2004). Unprepared for English-medium instruction: A critical look at beginner students. In Wilkinson, R. (Ed.), Maastricht: Universiteit Maastricht, 147–161.

Huhta, M, Vogt, K., Johnson, E. and Tulkki, H. (2012). *Needs Analysis for Language Course Design: A holistic approach to ESP*. Cambridge: CUP.

Huhta, M. (2010). *Language and Communication for Professional Purposes – Needs Analysis Methods in Industry and Business and Their Yield to Stakeholders.*Doctoral dissertation. Helsinki University of Technology.

Kunschak, C. (2011). Team Teaching Project at Shantou University Language Centre. Presentation at IATEFL Annual Conference. Brighton, UK (16th April 2011).

Lehtikoinen, A. (2004). Foreign language medium education as a national strategy. In Wilkinson, R. (Ed.). *Integrating content and language: meeting the challenge of multilingual higher education.* Maastricht: Universiteit Maastricht, 41–48.

Marshall, C. and Rossmann, G. B. (2006). *Designing qualitative research.* London: Sage Publications. 4th Edition.

Mehisto, P., Marsh, D. and Frigols Martín, M. J. (2010). *Lõimitud aine- ja keeleõpe* [Content and Language Integrated Learning]. Tallinn: Integration and Migration Foundation Our People.

Milton, J. (2009). *Measuring Second Language Vocabulary Acquisition.* – Second Language Acquisition, 45. Bristol: Multilingual Matters.

Ministry of Education and Science web page, www.hm.ee, 06.02.2012.

Räsänen, A. (2000). *Learning and Teaching through English at the University of Jyväskylä.* Project Report from Jyväskylä University Language Centre, 4. Jyväskylä: Jyväskylä University Language Centre.

Smith, K. (2004). Studying in an additional language. What is gained, what is lost, what is assessed. In Wilkinson, R. (Ed.). *Integrating content and language: meeting the challenge of multilingual higher education.* Maastricht: Universiteit Maastricht, 78–93.

Snelgrove, H. (2004). Developing assessment grids for language and content in a multidisciplinary Medical course. In Wilkinson, R. (Ed.). Maastricht: Universiteit Maastricht, 147–161.

Spencer, D. (2008). EUROPE: Huge increase in English-medium courses. University World News, 22 (April 6). Available online: http://www.universityworldnews.com (11.04.2012).

Storch, N. and Tapper, J. (2009). The impact of an EAP course on postgraduate writing. *Journal of English for Academic Purposes,* 8, 207–223.

Tella, S., Räsänen, A. and Vähäpassi, A. (Eds.) (1999). *Teaching through a Foreign Langauage: From Tool to Empowering Mediator. An Evaluation of 15 Finnish Polytechnic and University Level Programmes, with a Special View to Language and Communication.* Publications of Higher Education Evaluation Council, 5. Helsinki: Edita.

Vetik, R., Lauristin, M., Helemäe, J., Korts, K., Kruusvall, J., Nimmerfeldt, G., Saar, E., Trumm, A., Vihalemm, P. and Vihalemm, T. (2008). *Eesti ühiskonna integratsiooni monitooring* [Integration Monitoring of Estonian Society]. Tallinn: Integratsiooni Sihtasutus ja Rahvastikuministri Büroo.

Missugune on Eesti üliõpilaskond? Uuringu „Õiglane ligipääs kõrgharidusele Eestis“ lõppraport [What are the students of Estonian universities like? Report of the study 'Fair Access to Higher Education in Estonia']. (2010). Federation of Estonian Student Unions.

Wilkinson, R. (2004). Introduction. In Wilkinson, R. (Ed.). *Integrating content and language: meeting the challenge of multilingual higher education.* Maastricht: Universiteit Maastricht.

Appendix 1. Content subject instructor focus groups at Tallinn University

	Focus group 1	**Focus group 2**
Purpose	Understanding the study context and NNS students' and instructors' problems and behaviours	Finding out what strategies work best in giving language support to NNS students and whether organizational support measures are needed.
Duration	70 min	90 min
Number of participants	11	5
Men/women	2 men, 9 women	2 men, 3 women
Specialty fields of participants	Humanities (3), IT (2), sociology (1), biology (2), teacher education (2), advertising (1)	Humanities (2), IT (1), biology (1), Students' Union (1)
Moderator	Experienced instructor and researcher, same age or older than the participants, did not know most of the participants	Young language instructor, younger than most of the participants, did not know most of the participants
Instructors' characteristics		
Teaching in Estonian (predominantly Estonian groups)	3	1
Teaching in Estonian (groups with a considerable number of NNS students)	6	2
Teaching in Russian	2	1
Mainly giving lectures (30-300 students)	4	2
Mainly giving interactive seminars	7	2

Appendix 2. Student focus groups at Tallinn University

	Focus group 1	**Focus group 2**
Purpose	Finding out about the NNS students language-related problems and coping strategies at the university, about the language support they are currently getting and wish to receive.	
Duration	60 min	90 min
Number of participants	3	8
Men/women	3 women	2 men, 6 women
Specialty fields of participants	Social studies (Catherine's College, 1), teacher education (1), Slavonic philology (1)	Humanities (Catherine's College, 2), social studies (Catherine's College, 1), Slavonic philology (2), mathematics (1), German philology (2)
Moderator	Experienced instructor and researcher, older than the participants, does not know the participants	Young instructor, the participants' language teacher (special effort was made to ensure trustful atmosphere)
Participant characteristics	Over 30 years old, working, low language learning motivation, knowing each other	Advanced Estonian course students who know each other, not working, 18+ years old, high language learning and academic motivation

Appendix 3. Instructor and student main questionnaires

	Instructor questionnaire	**Student questionnaire**
Purpose	Finding out about the extent and specifics of NNS students' language problems in content courses, instructors attitudes towards and strategies in supporting the students	Finding out about the NNS students' perceptions of how they cope with different types of courses and what language use skills they got and expect to get at university's language courses
Form of the questionnaire	Electronic, advertised at universities general lists, at institutes' and general lists, personal emails. The same questionnaire was also filled in on paper.	Electronic, advertised at the universities' student lists. The same questionnaire was also filled in on paper.
Question types	6 closed-ended questions and 2 open-ended questions	8 closed-ended questions

PART 2

TEACHING AT HIGHER EDUCATION INSTITUTIONS

Chapter 8.
From teaching to guiding learning: novice university teachers' conceptions of teaching

Marvi Remmik, Mari Karm

Introduction

At research universities, academics are expected to produce and disseminate knowledge. Therefore, academics trained as researchers are often well prepared for this role but have had little or no formal teacher training to prepare them for their teaching role. In order to develop academics into 'excellent teachers', the academic community needs to understand how teachers' current belief systems developed and what factors or events could influence beliefs and teacher actions (Kane, Sandretto and Heath, 2002).

Analysing university teachers' concepts of teaching and learning can be confusing as researchers tend to use inconsistent terminology. The most commonly used terms are teaching conceptions and teaching beliefs. Kember (1997) indicates that researchers usually leave the term undefined, but by analysing various studies, he takes the position that these terms are largely synonymous. We follow Kember's (1997) model of conceptions of teaching and therefore also use the teaching conceptions and beliefs as synonyms.

Research has demonstrated that university teachers' teaching conceptions have an impact on their teaching practice (Trigwell and Prosser, 1996). These conceptions are formed partly by the communities that teachers act within and partly by previous experience of teaching and learning contexts (Sugrue, 1997). Teaching beliefs are important conceptions when attempting to understand teachers' thinking, thought processes and teaching practices (Taylor, 2002; Samuelowicz and Bain, 2001). Taylor (2003) argues that beliefs play a significant role in determining how we organise knowledge and information, and are essential in helping individuals adapt, understand, and make sense of themselves and their worlds.

Our research aimed to develop the understanding of Estonian novice university teachers' beliefs and conceptions of learning and teaching, and identified factors that have enabled or prevented them from acting according to their beliefs and conceptions. This article focused on the following questions:

(1) How do novice university teachers describe their teaching practice and their aims in teaching?

(2) How do novice university teachers interpret their own and their students' roles during the teaching-learning process?

(3) What has shaped novice university teachers' understanding of teaching and learning?

University teachers' teaching conceptions and influencing factors

Kane, Sandretto and Heath (2002) argue that the understanding of university teaching is incomplete without considering teachers' beliefs about teaching and a systematic examination of the relationship between those beliefs and teaching practices. Based on their research, Samuelowicz and Bain (1992) identified five conceptions of teaching that range from 'teaching as supporting student learning' to 'teaching as imparting information', with the other three conceptions placed in between these two extremes. By analysing different studies about university teachers' teaching conceptions Kember (1997) finds that generally the conceptions are placed under two broad orientations: *teacher-centred,* those that focus on communication of defined bodies of content or knowledge, and *student-centred* that focus on students' learning. Van Driel et al. (1997) agree with Kember (1997), though they also introduce an intermediate conception called *student-directing*. Student-directing is characterised by intensive interaction between teachers and their students. However, it is still the university teacher who leads the study process, while simultaneously supporting student learning by offering opportunities for individual consultations outside their studies and providing learning feedback (Van Driel et al., 1997).

Subsequent studies of teaching conceptions also support Kember's (1997) conceptualization. For instance, Postareff and Lindblom-Ylänne (2008) analyse university teachers' descriptions of teaching and find that most of the university teachers' descriptions of teaching are divided between the content-centred and learning-centred conceptions. They also find that the teaching conceptions based on aspects of the teaching process (including planning of teaching, teaching and assessment practices), learning environment (roles of teachers and students, interaction, atmosphere), conception of learning and pedagogical development (personal teaching development, pedagogical awareness).

Kember and Kwan (2000) demonstrate that teachers' conceptions of teaching influence their approach to teaching, which is also influenced by curriculum design, departmental and institutional pressures and the nature of the students. It appears from their research that university teachers who conceived good teaching as transmitting knowledge were more likely to use content-centred approaches to teaching. Teachers who conceived of good teaching as facilitative learning tended to use learning-centred approaches (Kember and Kwan, 2000).

Studies about teaching conceptions have also brought out several contradictions. Parpala and Lindblom-Ylänne (2007), for example, find that descriptions by teachers of their own teaching and their vision of ideal teaching may differ significantly. For example, when teachers were describing what is important in their own teaching, none of them mentioned the student's role, their motivation or the physical environment, whereas these dimensions were of significant importance in the descriptions about ideal teaching.

Some studies have found a link between conceptions of teaching and aspects of student learning (Kember and Gow, 1994; Prosser and Trigwell, 1999). The quality of teaching is related to the students' learning outcomes. Ramsden (2003) claims that good teaching definitely supports and aids students in achieving high-quality learning. Entwistle et al. (2000) suggest that good teaching can be defined as extended awareness of the relationship between learning and teaching.

Although the conception of good teaching is multifaceted, there seems to be agreement among researchers that good teaching encourages deep learning (Prosser and Trigwell, 1999; Ramsden, 2003).

Several studies show that pedagogical courses have a positive impact on university teachers' comprehension of teaching and on the development of their teaching skills (Gibbs and Coffey, 2004; Postareff, Lindblom-Ylänne and Nevgi, 2007; Remmik and Karm, 2009). Also, participation in pedagogical courses might motivate the university teacher to transform their teaching conceptions and teaching practice (Remmik et al., 2011). However, values emphasised in pedagogical courses might conflict with those of the department, and therefore, after the course, a lecturer might be under pressure to re-adopt the department's teaching practices (Lindblom-Ylänne et al., 2006; Remmik et al., 2011). Gibbs and Coffey (2004) find that in departments that do not value teaching there is pressure to conform to largely teacher-focused teaching conventions. Richardson (2005) notes that research on teaching in US higher education institutions found that beliefs about teaching vary markedly across different disciplines and that these variations are related to the teachers' beliefs about the nature of the discipline in which they teach.

The aim of this study was to analyse novice university teachers' conceptions of what they consider important in their teaching and their conceptions of good teaching.

Method

Participants. Forty-one novice university teachers were interviewed during the study. The interviewees were from five Estonian research-intensive universities (the University of Tartu, the Tallinn University, the University of Life Sciences, Tallinn University of Technology and the Estonian Academy of Arts) and five applied higher education institutions (Tartu Health Care College, the Estonian Academy of Security Sciences, the Estonian Maritime Academy, the University of Applied Sciences and the Estonian National Defence College). Contact was made with the novice lecturers through the human resource departments of their respective institutions. Interviewees were contacted by e-mail and they were invited to participate in the study. The interviewees' specialities were distributed across four subject areas as follows: humanities (6), social sciences (14), exact and natural sciences (16), and medicine (5). The academic posts of the interviewees varied from assistant teachers, lecturers, and researchers to administrative posts with some teaching responsibilities, such as project management, etc. All participants had teaching experience of 1–6 semesters. The age range of the interviewees ranged was 22–61 years.

Interviews and analyses. The interviews were semi-structured, focusing on the teachers' descriptions of their teaching practice (including planning, teaching, assessment, teacher and students roles), the teaching traditions of their discipline and the impact of their previous experience as a student to their teaching practice. It was also important to find out about novice university teachers' aims in teaching and what they consider important in teaching. These questions preceded the questions about how they would teach in an ideal situation and what their conceptions of good teaching were.

An interview method was chosen because it 'attempts to understand the world from the subjects' points of view, to unfold the meaning of their experiences, to uncover their lived world prior to scientific explanations' (Kvale and Brinkmann, 2009:1). At the same time the interviews provided the interviewees with the opportunity for self-reflection, where they describe their teaching practice and open their teaching conceptions and beliefs. Interviews lasted from 40 to 90 minutes, they were conducted in Estonian and the extracts of the transcripts were translated into English. Participants' responses have been coded to protect their anonymity.

The interviews were analysed using qualitative content analysis and both authors conducted the analysis of the interview transcripts. First, thematic excerpts that reflected novice university teachers' teaching conceptions were extracted. Then these thematic excerpts were thoroughly analysed in the framework of content-centred and learning-centred teaching conceptions. The analysis identified the following sub-categories in the novice teachers' teaching conceptions' descriptions: the study process (including planning, teaching and assessment), attitude and relationships with students, the background of the formation of the teaching conception, emotions during planning and teaching practice, professional development and learning as a university teacher.

Results

It became evident from the analysis of the research results that novice university teachers are only just beginning to define and seek their teaching conception and try these out in their teaching practice. Though the novice university teachers' conceptions of teaching may be viewed on a content-centred – learning-centred axis, the university teacher's position on this axis is not fixed but changes. University teachers' teaching conceptions became clear from the descriptions of their teaching practices, where the main aspects of teaching (selection of subject's content, teaching and assessment) and attitude towards the students were brought out most often.

The content-centred teaching conception

Selection of subject's content, teaching and assessment

University teachers who believe the content-centred teaching conception say that the main aim of their teaching is transferring knowledge. They use traditional lectures as the main teaching method, illustrate their lecture material with relevant pictures and examples, and provide explanations. For them teaching often equates to performing. From the descriptions of teaching we also find examples how the novice university teachers with content-centred teaching conception sees their and students' roles in the study process.

> Let's talk more about this first course. did I understand correctly that it was mainly in the format of traditional lectures?
>
> Yes. I talk, show pretty pictures, give my comments on them, in theory, the students are supposed to listen and write all this knowledge down, but of course, this didn't happen much there.
>
> They didn't take notes?
>
> Well, only very few of them. Most of them were sitting behind their computers and were probably chatting online with each other. (Exact and natural sciences, F35)
>
> I'm more of a performer. I like to talk myself. I'm not very skilful at making people work. The lecturer has the upper hand, you know that you are the boss and he (the

> student) has to make the grade and he tries hard to contact you… (Social sciences, M21)

In planning the teaching, attention is paid to the selection of the material and the novice university teacher often worries whether there is enough material and whether they will know how to answer the students' questions. At the same time, several admit that their performance remains very theoretical because they do not have much experience of how the theory works in practice. In fact, the weakness that the novice teachers mention most often is their limited ability to make connections with other subjects in the curricula and the difficulty of finding real life examples.

Biggs and Tang (2007) find that good teaching is based on constructive alignment, that is, teacher support of a student's deep approach to learning by aligning the teaching method and assessment to the learning activities stated in the objectives. Teaching, learning and assessment are strongly related and their alignment has always been crucial for achieving the goals of education. Assessment serves an important role in determining what and how students learn.

Research reveals that for the novice university teachers who share the content-centred teaching approach assessment is not acknowledged as an aspect that supports student learning. Assessment focuses on checking factual knowledge, tests and written exams. In most cases in content-centred instruction, assessment does not serve the aim of supporting learning, but it is used as a regulating tool, with tests being given during lectures to give points that contribute to final grades. These tests ensure attendance at lectures.

Biggs and Tang (2007) suggest that for the university teacher on the first level of teaching the biggest factor influencing teaching success are the abilities of the learners. Similar traits emerged from the interviews with the novice teachers who support the content-centred teaching conception. If the students' test and exam results do not meet the university teacher's expectations, it is not because there is something wrong with the teaching, but because the students are not intelligent or motivated enough, or the lectures take place at a bad time, or there are too many students and so there is no another way of teaching them. Biggs and Tang (2007) call this the *blame-the-student* theory of teaching.

> I haven't experienced any surprising wow-moment yet. Never felt that wow, my students are so smart and marvellous. It might be that I'm too pessimistic myself or it seems to me that they are not even slightly interested in what I'm saying there. They listen to me with dull faces. Any questions? Sometimes I get some out of politeness. Sometimes the lot is so passive, unhappy eyes… I can't make the content simplistic, it shouldn't be real easy. People should work more. Somehow I have sensed recently that students do not try hard enough anymore. It could be just my perception. I've heard it from others, experienced teachers, what is happening.

> It's not possible to change anything as the audience is big. Seminars do not work and you can't really change much. (Exact and natural sciences, F35)

The background of the formation of the content-centred teaching conception

Thomas and Pedersen (2010) claim that teachers' beliefs, attitudes and practices may be linked to previous experiences. Novice teachers use their teachers as models for developing themselves as teachers. It became apparent from the interviews that models and discipline-specific teaching traditions are often followed when novice teachers do not know how to teach in any other way.

When seeking interpretations of novice teachers' teaching practice, one of the reasons for methods used might be that the previous lecturer, who passed on their lecture notes, slides, photo materials, indirectly passes on the teaching methods as well. The same seems to apply on assessing. Often the previously used tests are taken over.

> Oh, I have been doing a lot of thinking about the way how to teach well and what I should take as a basis for my lectures. I've discovered that I can't manage to come up with anything new. I teach the way I was taught, the way lectures were at my time. I copy my own university teachers a bit. I don't think I have a specific role model... (Exact and natural sciences, F35)

Confusion and the need for change

As they gain more experience, university teachers reflect more on their teaching styles. The university teacher notices the students and students' activity in the auditorium more. Experience might create doubts and motivate the teacher to question if their existing conceptions about teaching are reasonable.

By reflecting upon their teaching, problems are noticed, tendencies that the teacher does not like, but does not always know how to change. For example, students seem to be bored and there are fewer and fewer students from lecture to lecture.

> Well, I do see that. Last year my first lectures were exactly like I had read...I tried to read it to them in four hours...And then I noticed that in the first row...and I thought how terrible and I didn't know how to react at the time when someone is sitting next to you and is saying that they're bored to death. And I was thinking, it's too bad I can't tell you that I'm also. I'm also bored to death... (Social sciences, F41)

> And there are fewer and fewer of them with each lecture, don't know why... [uneasy laughter] (Exact and natural sciences, F2)

Some changes towards the learning-centred concept may mention that when novice university teachers' teaching experience increases, they will increase their consideration of the prior knowledge of the students. They will also be more flexible in designing the course, and use more participatory teaching methods.

> At first there were only lectures. Then I started to think that I should motivate them to talk more and then last year I tried to conduct seminars, so that they would have a chance to talk, it was a short presentation, about 5-10 minutes on some general topics. (Exact and natural sciences, F35)

They will make changes to the grading system as well. For example if written, test based exam results do not meet the university teacher's expectations, then they will analyse the teaching as well as the assessment methods used and will plan modifications. Several interviewees had replaced the multiple choice and other tests they originally used with oral examinations that make the importance of the immediate contact and communication with the student obvious.

Doubts about the efficacy of their teaching strategies might motivate novice teachers to attend pedagogical courses. Several of the novice university teachers interviewed had decided to participate in various pedagogical courses and it came out from the interviews that such courses had motivated them to think about the roles of students and university teachers and active participation in the study process.

> Perhaps I am a bit too enthusiastic in the sense that I try to transmit really a lot to the students. Maybe I should let them do more work themselves. I just recently attended a problem-centred learning and teaching training course and realized that maybe I should step back a bit and let the students do more. (Medicine, F20)

From these pedagogical courses novice teachers had gained ideas that had extended their teaching and assessment repertoire and added to their ways of giving feedback. As teachers attend pedagogical courses for a number of reasons (e.g. doctoral students have a course on university pedagogy as a compulsory subject in their curriculum) and their motivation for developing their teachings skills differs significantly, it could be that one training event is not sufficient. Some previous studies have shown that implementing new ideas and strategies needs more support and time (Postareff et al., 2007).

Among the interviewees there were those who did not see any benefit in the pedagogical courses for developing their teaching practice. This might be because they do not know how to put the things suggested during the course into practice. Also the university teachers might not be ready for change, especially if the ideas and tips taken from the pedagogical courses are significantly different from their existing teaching conception and practice or different from their disciplinary teaching traditions

> There were many little things that could be tried out. Specifically these small interactive exercises or for testing or some little exercises to apply. But most of the topics were some bigger things that require some digesting in order to apply them. For example the topic of reflection, I didn't manage to take anything concrete from there that I'd really know how to apply... (Humanities, M38)

Implementation of new teaching strategies is also hindered when novice teachers fail to put the training ideas into practice at their first attempt. More experienced colleagues who share the content-centred conception of teaching, and who do not support changes in teaching, can further impede the novice teacher's attempts to implement new teaching strategies.

The interviews do not provide grounds for the prediction of what is going to happen to the teacher in the future: whether they stick to their teaching conception or change their perceptions depends on many factors, such as subsequent personal experience, the attitudes of colleagues, training, the existence of support systems, student feedback, etc.

The learning-centred conception of teaching

Selection of subject's content, teaching and assessment

Kember (1997) and Kember and Kwan (2000) describe the learning-centred conception of teaching as teaching in which the aim is to facilitate students' learning processes. Some studies (Coffey and Gibbs, 2000; Postareff et al., 2008) demonstrate that teachers who approach teaching in a learning-centred way have been found to use a wider repertoire of teaching methods than teachers who adopt a content-centred approach to teaching. This was also confirmed by the present study. It becomes apparent from the interviews that university teachers with a learning-centred teaching conception pay much more attention to teaching methods and plan various activities including lectures, seminars, independent reading, and group work, peer-discussions, discussions and debate. University teachers with a learning-centred teaching conception realise that learning requires time and effort and that implementing different strategies is also more time consuming than lecturing. If a university teacher values student learning and deeper understanding, they will be willing to spend time on discussion, debate and answering questions rather than just lecturing.

Novice university teachers with learning-centred approach formulate the aims of the tasks they give. It is not the activity itself, but the aim of the activity that is important. Students' learning and their comprehension of the material is important to the university teacher.

> ...the set-up of the tasks should broaden students' thinking, so that they would understand these things correctly. (Exact and natural sciences, M37)

> It's important that the students would understand, the material should be simplified if needed, adjusted suitable for the students, so that they would really understand. (Exact and natural sciences, F29)

The background of the formation of the teaching-centred teaching conception

It emerged from the interviews that a pre-requisite for the development of a learning-centred university teacher has often been the university teacher's own negative learning experience. Now that they are teachers themselves they have reflected their own experiences as a student and taken the new role they want to teach differently. The teaching conception may also have been positively influenced by pedagogical courses and knowledgeable and experienced colleagues.

University teachers with a learning-centred teaching conception are characterised by a positive attitude towards their professional development, acknowledging the need to learn and develop. There were university teachers among the interviewees who had participated in pedagogical courses before entering teaching; after entering teaching they wanted to try what they had learned to see if it worked in practice (they used group work, mutual teaching and others). Teaching practice confirmed the efficiency of the learner engaging methods of teaching.

Previous work as a practitioner also gives an advantage in developing into a learning-centred university teacher. While novice university teachers are often concerned about their competence in the subject field, university teachers who have previously worked in practice emphasise that they feel relaxed in the auditorium as they have real examples to provide from their experiences. As they do not have to worry so much about the subject's content, they have more time to think about other aspects of teaching. They also point out that the university teacher is not the sole source of knowledge, but that while teaching they learn from the students.

> Open University students bringing in their own experience....This is also something I've realized that since they are in a real work life and they have the experience, then it is possible for me to really learn a lot from their experiences and to also use these experiences next year. Also the notion that I am not the only source of knowledge, that very much (knowledge) also comes from them as well. (Social sciences, 40)

Assessment and feedback

The form and content of learning is greatly influenced by how assessment appears to a university student. Biggs and Tang (2007) find that assessments should give a clear message to the student about what and how to study. Novice university teachers with a learning-centred teaching conception see a clear connection between assessment and students' learning, and therefore they thoroughly describe their assessment practice and bring out a number of doubts and problems related to this topic.

University teachers try to formulate the aims of their assessment tasks and whether it would be reasonable to assess the outcome only or take other factors into account as well. It is difficult to assess how many points one assignment deserves over another, and also, the question of balance raises questions: they would like to receive the assignments on time, at the same time they wish to be accommodating. Which is more important – promptly handing in the assignment or the outcome/content? How should they react in situations where a student actively and comprehensively participates in seminars, but disappoints in assignments? What is the allowed rate of subjectivity in assessments? University teachers with a learning-centred teaching conception value mid-term evaluations. They note that although they involve a lot of additional work, they enable them to advise the students on the topics that they should learn more about in a timely way.

Teaching is also affected by the broader context. It was obvious from the interviews that even though novice university teachers had only worked at a university for a short time, they had already sensed changes that required them to adapt to new situations and that did not always allow them to follow their own teaching principles and beliefs. For example, university teachers had experienced teaching situations, where the previously used assessment method was no longer suitable because group sizes had increased and these increases also obstructed the implementation of creative assessment tasks.

University teachers with a learning-centred approach value two-way feedback. On the one hand, university teachers found that giving feedback was important in supporting students' learning, on the other, they valued students' feedback to their own teaching, understanding that feedback is important to their professional development.

Confusion, obstacles and setbacks

For university teachers who intend to be learning-centred, there may be situations where they feel that they did not have sufficient skill or expertise to put learning-centred teaching into practice. Åkerlind (2007) emphasises that professional teaching requires the mastery of various teaching methods, but if learning does not take place, the teaching methods do not have any significance. From several interviews it was clear that novice teachers could not always say why they used particular teaching methods.

> The main thing I want is that they (students) would be interested. That I could spark an interest in them. Because I remember when I used to be a student myself, then every school day was just so interesting. (Medicine, F20)

University teachers with a learning-centred teaching approach also described the obstacles and setbacks they experienced when they tried to implement the learning-centred conception. For example, directing students towards more independent work and seeing that they do not immediately engage in that way of working can be disappointing and cause the teacher to reconsider.

> Yes, exactly. I expected it to work, but it didn't. Well, one of the ideas is that next semester I should take into account that it takes a bit of time for them to get used to the new system. Maybe it scared me off a bit when I tried the first group work with them and no one had prepared, and while it wasn't a complete failure, then it was still clear that it wasn't what I had planned. And after that I was afraid to try this again, so maybe it's good to give them some time to get used to everything and then do these traditional group works. (Exact and natural sciences, M31)

University teachers have also found that the preparation for learning-centred teaching is very time-consuming. In addition, there might be conflicts with the university system. For example, the university teacher would like to give a student a chance to retake an exam, in order to give the student the opportunity to study more, but the university system does not allow that. University teachers stated that as teaching is a process, they should be able to make changes during the course of the process, and have the opportunity to make mistakes and then to improve in a flexible manner. Current university systems require detailed planning that does not leave room for changes and unexpected outcomes.

> In this sense there should be a bit of flexibility at the university, so that when you teach the subject for the first time, you are teaching all alone, then some room should be given, because it's the middle of the semester when you realize that your course plan has been constructed wrongly. And then there's nothing you can do anymore because a student comes and says (knocks on the table). Shows the study regulations and shows the course plan... (Social sciences, F17)

Common characteristics of university teachers with different teaching conceptions

As in Postareff's and Lindblom-Ylänne's (2008) study, similar features appeared in the novice teachers' learning conceptions, irrespective of whether their conceptions were learning-centred or content-centred. This became most evident in the theme about communicating with the students and relationships, which was brought out by university teachers with both teaching conceptions. Kember's (1997) model of teaching conceptions, places the interaction between the two conceptions of teaching as if there is a transition from one conception to another. By contrast, Postareff and Lindblom-Ylänne (2008) find that interaction and engagement are important for teachers with all teaching conceptions and it is necessary to examine the purpose of the interaction in the university teacher's opinion.

It emerged from the interviews that all participants in the study had acknowledged the need for the students' engagement, but there are differences in what is meant by engagement, and what the aims of engagement are. University teachers with a content-centred teaching conception also found that lectures should include some degree of communication with the students, but the reasons for this communication and things to be done to make it successful are not described much. The one explanation here might be that novice university teachers do not see yet links between engagement and student learning.

> And another thing maybe is to engage the students more, because they were all quite reserved, so having a kind of communication happening there during the lecture was quite difficult. I'm sure that in the most part it's the lecturer's own fault or well, my fault, that I cannot engage the students, so yeah, I'll probably have to come up with something more. (Exact and natural sciences, F30)

Some university teachers commented that they had tried asking questions to encourage student engagement, but only very few students were willing to answer them.

University teachers with a learning-centred teaching conception see that in the two-way communication there is an opportunity to learn and develop. Interaction in the study process offers different challenges for the students: it gives the opportunity to fail, doubt and discover new knowledge.

> I try to make it in a way that it wouldn't be only me speaking in the lectures. I have, for example, given them some scientific article to read beforehand, so that they could form better connections. And then we discuss it together at class. I have noticed that their answers are much more thorough and argumented at the exams if they have played it out or discussed it amongst themselves... (Social Sciences, R32)

University teachers with a learning-centred teaching-conception admitted that through communication with the students, they also learn themselves. For instance, examples are given about positive experiences with Open University students, who have wide practical experience and through whom a university teacher can supplement their teaching practice with relevant practical examples.

Relationships and communication are also essential preconditions for the success of the study process. Here, a common concern for many novice teachers emerged – will the students accept me, and will they take me seriously as a university teacher? The age gap between novice teachers and the university students is often very small, with the exception of Open University students who may be as much as a couple of decades older than novices. So the university teachers' teaching practice can sometimes be influenced by their age. Lecturing feels safer than a seminar, which is open to more informal communication. The awe, that the novice teachers have of the Open University students, is increased by knowing that they are practitioners operating in their subject area.

> I was really scared, I felt a huge awe towards the Open University, because the people there have worked in this domain longer than I have.
>
> What were you scared of?
>
> I guess I was scared that someone's going to say that listen, you don't actually know anything about this. Even now I'm sometimes scared of this.
>
> That someone's going to say this?
>
> Yes, or it's more that they think that. If they'd said it out then, but they are thinking it… (Social sciences, F17)

Also there was no clear differentiation between learning- and content-centred conceptions in the descriptions of the ideals. In the descriptions about real teaching practice, the theme of relationships between the university teacher and the students stood out, but only one interviewee said that the key to good teaching lay in university teacher-student communication.

> Basically I think that... the most important thing is what the communication with the students is like. For example, you can be very smart, but it's not enough when no-one could follow you or no-one has the courage to approach you or whatever. So, the kind of university teacher who is willing to communicate with the students, let's say on a quite equal level, and the kind who's a rather a bit more relaxed than very conservative. I think that in universities there's no need for as much hierarchy of this kind as there is in lower education levels. (Exact and natural sciences, F30)

When characterising good teaching identifying the needs of the students is most important.

> I think when talking about goodness, we have to look at this from someone's point of view, and I believe it should be from the listener's one. So when teaching meets the students' expectations, then I believe it's good teaching. For me it seems that the really essential things are understandability, explaining and illustrating, not just lecturing the numerous facts, so yeah, good teaching is explaining. I don't know... (Medical Sciences, F22)

A common theme that the interviewees emphasised, irrespective of their teaching conception, is that the most time consuming and complicated thing for novice teachers is planning the whole process, starting with creating the syllabus, and especially with matters regarding the selection of material.

> I still put a huge amount of time into the preparation of these lectures. I don't know where's the line, that I could stop reading the material, because I can not transmit it all to them, there's simply too much of it, but still, maybe there's still things I don't know. Well, a kind of a dumb feeling that I should know everything, but it is completely unrealistic in reality. So I'm starting to acknowledge it to myself that it's not realistic. (Social sciences, 41)

Reflection is another common theme that emerges from the interviews with university teachers of both teaching conceptions. The differences that arose from the interviews were the depth of reflection and what was being reflected upon.

> Now once you're teaching, how much do you afterwards think back of the day. I probably have a bit, but not a lot, it's not like I sit down and spend the whole evening pondering over it. But lightly I have yeah. And about some things I have thought about later, after some time. I have been thinking and then just some things have come back to me. Primarily when preparing the next lecture I think back on how the previous ones have gone and what else could be done. (Humanities, M38)

While university teachers with a content-centred teaching conception mostly reflect upon their own activities, university teachers with a learning-centred teaching approach reflect considerably more deeply, analysing their own activities as a university teacher and planning changes. They also consider the students – thinking about and analysing the students' activities in the lecture and how well the students learned.

Conclusions

As staff developers we are concerned with supporting new academics on their journey to becoming excellent academics and university teachers. This study demonstrated that novice university teachers' conceptions of teaching can be viewed on a content-centred – learning-centred axis. However, the university teacher's position on this axis is not fixed but changes, because the novice teacher is trying out and searching for the most suitable position for them. In the process of searching, everyday practice is reflected upon and changes are planned as a result. Teachers implement their beliefs and conceptions of teaching in their classrooms by constructing learning environments, which promote or discourage learning by all students. The study process as a whole provides challenges and food for thought for a university teacher. So, for example, university teachers with a learning-centred conception may question whether using a range of different methods does actually lead to student learning. It may also turn out that teaching according to certain conceptions does not work in practice. For example, if the university teacher has not explained the reason for a sudden change of practice sufficiently and the students are not engaging with it.

If the teaching conception matches the university teacher's perception of their own competence, then they feel confident, but if not they question whether they are good enough. Virtanen and Lindblom-Ylänne (2010) emphasise the university teacher's role as the key role in designing the study environment. At the same time they find that university teachers must raise their pedagogical awareness to identify the factors that have an effect on the teaching-learning environment, the conceptions of learning and teaching and they must learn methods to integrate deep learning in their discipline. Here, pedagogical courses and other supporting activities, such as mentoring and community of practice etc. are a great help (Remmik et al., 2011; Virtanen et al., 2010).

As with previous research (Gibbsi et al., 2004; Postareff et al., 2007, 2008) we found that participation in pedagogical courses might motivate the novice university teacher to change their teaching practice, and give support to their ideas about changing their practice. The research also revealed that when a university teacher is not ready for change or when discipline specific teaching traditions do not support change, then there is a danger that the novice teacher will turn back to the content-centred teaching conception. Even though some of the earlier studies show that university teachers' teaching is influenced by disciplinary teaching traditions, this research showed that there were university teachers with both conceptions in every subject area. Only in two interviews, with university teachers from the exact and natural sciences, were some serious doubts expressed about the efficiency of applying group work and other student engagement methods, for example, in their speciality. At the same time, among the interviewees there were several university teachers from the exact and natural sciences, who applied what they had learned at the training course to their teaching practice and had experienced positive changes in student feedback and teaching effectiveness.

References

Åkerlind, G. (2007). Constraints on academics' potential for developing as a teacher. Studies *in Higher Education*, 32, 21–37.

Biggs, J. and Tang, C. (2007). *Teaching for Quality Learning at University.* Buckingham: SRHE and Open University Press.

Coffey, M. and Gibbs, G. (2002). Measuring teachers' repertoire of teaching methods. *Assessment and Evaluation in Higher Education,* 27, 383–390.

Entwistle, N., Skinner, D., Entwistle, D. and Orr, S. (2000). Conceptions and beliefs about "Good teaching": An integration of contrasting research areas. *Higher Education Research and Development*, 19, 5–26.

Gibbs, G. and Coffey, M. (2004). The impact of training of university teachers on their teaching skills, their approach to teaching and the approach to learning of their students. *Active Learning in Higher Education*, 5, 87–100.

Kane, R., Sandretto, S. and Heath, C. (2002). Telling Half the Story: A Critical Review of Research on the Teaching Beliefs and Practices of University Academics. *Review of Educational Research*, 72, 177–228.

Kember, D. (1997). A reconceptualization of the research into university academics' conceptions of teaching. *Learning and Instruction*, 7, 255–275.

Kember, D. and Gow (1994). Orientations to teaching and their effect on the quality of student learning. *Journal of Higher Education*, 65, 58–73.

Kember, D. and Kwan, K. (2000). Lecturers' approaches to teaching and their relationship to conceptions of good teaching. *Instructional Science*, 28, 469–490.

Kvale, S. and Brinkmann, S. (2009). *Interviews. Learning the Craft of Qualitative Research Interviewing.* SAGE Publications.

Lindblom-Ylänne, S., Trigwell, K., Nevgi, A. and Ashwin, P. (2006). How approaches to teaching are affected by discipline and teaching context. *Studies in Higher Education*, 31, 285–298.

Parpala, A. and Lindblom-Ylänne, S. (2007). University teacher' conceptions of good teaching in the units of high-quality education. *Studies in Educational Evaluation*, 33, 355–370.

Postareff, L. and Lindblom-Ylänne, S. (2008). Variation in teachers' descriptions of teaching: Broadening the understanding of teaching in higher education. *Learning and Instruction*, 18, 109–120.

Postareff, L., Lindblom-Ylänne, S. and Nevgi, A. (2007). The effect of pedagogical training on teaching in higher education. *Teaching and Teacher Education*, 23, 557–571.

Prosser, M. and Trigwell, K. (1999). *Understanding learning and teaching: The experience in higher education.* Buckingham: SRHE and Open University Press.

Ramsden, P. (2003). *Learning to teach in Higher Education* (2nd ed.). London: Routledge.

Remmik, M. and Karm, M. (2009). Koolituse mõju õppejõudude õpetamisoskustele – väljakutsed ja võimalused [Impact of training on teaching skills of university lecturers – challenges and opportunities]. *Haridus*, 11–12, 20–26.

Remmik, M., Karm, M., Haamer, A. and Lepp, L. (2011). Early-career academics' learning in academic communities. *International Journal for Academic Development*, 16, 187–199.

Richardson, J. T. E. (2005). Students' approaches to learning and teachers' approaches to teaching in higher education. *Educational Psychology*, 25, 673–680.

Samuelowicz, K. and Bain, J. D. (1992). Conceptions of teaching held by academic teachers. *Higher Education*, 24, 93–112.

Samuelowicz, K. and Bain, J. D. (2001). Revisiting academics' beliefs about teaching and learning. *Higher Education*, 41, 299–325.

Sugrue, C. (1997). Student Teachers' Lay Theories and Teaching Identities: their implications for professional development. *European Journal of Teacher education,* 20, 213–225.

Taylor, E. (2002). Using still photography in making meaning of adult educators' teaching beliefs. *Studies In The Education Of Adults,* 34, 123.

Taylor, E. W. (2003). Attending Graduate School in Adult Education and the Impact on Teaching Beliefs: A Longitudinal Study. *Journal of Transformative Education*, 1, 349–367.

Thomas, J. A. and Pedersen, J. E. (2010). Reforming Elementary Science Teacher Preparation: What about Extant Teaching Beliefs? *School Science and Mathematics,* 103, 319–330.

Trigwell, K. and Prosser, M. (1996). Congruence between intention and strategy in university science teachers' approaches to teaching. *Higher Education*, 32, 77–87.

Van Driel, J. H., Verloop, N., van Werven, H. I. and Dekkers, H. (1997). Teachers' craft knowledge and curriculum innovation in higher engineering education. *Higher Education*, 34, 105–122.

Virtanen, V. and Lindblom-Ylänne, S. (2010). University students' and teachers' conceptions of teaching and learning in the biosciences. *Instructional Sciences*, 38, 355–370.

Chapter 9. The impact of Estonian research, development and education policies on perceived value conflicts in universities

Krista Jaakson, Anne Reino

Introduction

Professional value conflicts probably occur in every area, but in academic work they are particularly common, because this profession consists of contrasting assignments, which need the distribution of limited resources, mainly time and money (Dill, 1982; Scriven 1982). Conflicting values in academic organisations (henceforth: universities) have been thoroughly covered in the literature and the studies show that there are different ways of dealing with these conflicts (Scott, 2003; Berchem, 2006).

The subject of value conflicts has intensified because the idea of the role of universities in society has changed, and stakeholders' expectations of universities have also changed. This can be seen in the funding of universities, which has moved from governments to individuals, either directly or indirectly, i.e. through study loans (McCulloch, 2009; Maringe 2011). Fuller (2003:48) finds that a university as 'a place where practical concerns are not paramount and where learning for its own sake is possible' is now irreversibly in the past. A post-modern university is characterised by concepts like *entrepreneurial university*, *academic capitalism*, and the *student as a client* (Clark, 1998; Palfreyman and Warner 1998; Etzkowitz et al., 2000; Sotirakou, 2004; White, 2007). Hakala (2009) also characterises the modern university as a place where there is competition for external resources, where efficiency is significant, and where the commercialisation of research results are important. In this context, a university employee does not differ from a typical knowledge employee.

It must be emphasised that these changes did not occur at the request of the universities, but because of changes and regulations in the external environment. The changes, which always bring a need for new approaches and new values, have been quite rapid. Jørgensen and Vrangbæk (2011:494) find that introducing new values hastily does not supersede old values, they just 'scratch the surface'. For instance, it has been found that old values are the greatest sources of resistance, when it comes to evolutionary and strategic changes (del Val and Fuentes, 2003). So, in the context of changes, the value conflicts that may occur between old and new values are very topical. In this chapter, these particular value conflicts, which have been caused by the Estonian research, development and education policy, will be analysed (henceforth, the R&D policy). The value conflicts discussed here are those that were raised by participants in this study. The aim of this chapter is to show which goals and methods in the R&D policy create value conflicts among university employees. As perceiving a conflict is subjective, value conflicts cannot always claim to have an objective basis. However, it is still necessary to know which conflicts are caused by distorted perceptions, because these may be as a result of shortcomings in the communication strategy or the execution of the strategy at the organisational level. Our data only comes from the employees of the University of Tartu (UT), so our results are not applicable to the entire Estonian higher education system, but they can be used to generate hypotheses.

The nature and sources of value conflicts

A value conflict can be defined as a situation where an individual senses a contradiction between two or more values which the organisation considers important. The ambiguity of values is behind value conflicts and this has been researched thoroughly on an individual level (for instance, Tetlock, 1986). On an organisational level, a value conflict can be seen as a phenomenon accompanied by 'contradicting values' (Brunsson, 2006; de Chernatory and Cottam, 2008). Different values in universities are especially topical, because employees are expected to perform different roles: traditionally, these were research and teaching, but lately administration and service roles have been added. By service role mean cooperation between enterprises and universities for mutual benefit. Every role is associated with different stakeholders – among them college students, colleagues, the directorate, funders of research and society – and these stakeholders may have expectations and demands that are not compatible with each other (Beauvais et al., 2007). So, value conflicts can take place within a role or between roles.

One of the supporting values of research is academic and intellectual freedom. This means that an organisation does not dictate the content of knowledge, and results of research (De George, 2003). Oakeshott (2003) supports this point of view by saying that the idea of research is not to achieve a certain goal, but, foremost, to apply scientific methods. The second value of research is integrity, which according to some authors is under threat, because questionable contracts are entered into between researchers and enterprises for purely financial reasons (Evans and Packham, 2003). Also, integrity can be compromised by publishing research for pragmatic reasons, for example, to justify prior funding or to fulfill evaluation criteria (Foo and Wilson, 2011). The third traditional value of research is cooperation, because rarely does a single researcher accomplish a spectacular achievement in research. Cooperation in turn relates to employees' professional roles in a university. Clark (1998) and Vadi and Haldma (2010) encourage universities to be more entrepreneurial and to value this kind of cooperation, but the connection of this process with other traditional academic values, like freedom, integrity and objectivity, is sensitive (Dill, 1982). Freedom, responsibility, respect and objectivity towards students are important values in teaching (Kuther, 2003) and as teaching puts students in a position of less power, the responsibility of a lecturer to use that power appropriately is critical (Markie, 1994).

In addition to these traditional academic values (*freedom, responsibility, science-base, cooperation* etc.), UT, as a national, research-intensive university has its own specific values. These include, for instance, *intellectuality*[1], *dignity, excellence in research*, and *continuity*. These can be considered to be the core values of the university, and those which distinguish UT from other institutions in Estonia (Lencioni, 2002; Urde, 2003).

Traditional academic values and the core values of an institution are influenced by a range of stakeholders. In this article, the main focus is on university administrators and policy makers. The aim of the policy makers is to increase the competitiveness of the Estonian economy through up-to-date education and cutting edge research, while using the funds allocated to the university efficiently and wisely. The university's management has to bring together the goals of the policy makers and employees and ensure that standards, like transparency and efficiency (including standardisation, simplicity of measurement, centralisation, and profit orientation) are met. Dolan and Richley (2006) call this value dimension an economic and control dimension, which, as we found in our study, brings out several value conflicts. Value conflicts in universities are analysed in this study in two parts: conflicts caused by the administration and by 'the mass university'[2]. Such a division is somewhat conditional: even though 'the mass university' is a strategic choice of the university management, it is quite unique among value conflicts, so it needed to be addressed separately. Pol-

1 By intellectuality UT employees mean both bohemian attitude and creativity, as wll as wisdom, ethics, tolerance, traditions and openness to new knowledge. Respondents argued that intellectuality is 'something you can perceive more in UT compared to the other universities in Estonia'.

2 'Mass university' is the result of massification of higher education which at university level means broader access to education resulting in 'worsening student/teacher ratios, and a concomitant decline in the quality of student services within increasingly alienating institutional environments'. (Stevenson, 1999:314).

icies and programmes initiated by government have definitely influenced both of these conflict areas.

Methodology and survey sample

In this study, the interview results from 15 focus groups that met in October and November 2011 were analysed. In every focus group there were between two and nine employees from UT, including faculty leaders. The sample was randomly constructed by the personnel department, based on the principle that all faculties, institutions and academic levels should be included. Invitation of participation was sent to 66 professors, heads of subunits and lead research fellows (39 per cent of them refused to participate and 21 per cent did not answer the e-mail); 160 academic personnel (35 per cent refused; 46 per cent did not answer) and to 125 employees who belong to the support personnel (43 per cent refused and 42 per cent did not answer the invitation). Altogether 70 employees (34 men and 36 women) participated in the focus groups. Following table gives an overview of focus groups and their composition[3].

Table 1. Composition of the sample

No of FG	No of participants		Positions of employees	Affiliation
	men	women		
FG1	3	3	Academic employees	Faculty of law; UT units
FG2	0	2	Academic employees	Faculty of Science and Technology; Faculty of Philosophy
FG3	2	4	Academic employees	Faculty of Economics and Business Administration; Faculty of Mathematics and Computer Science; UT colleges
FG4	2	2	Academic employees	Faculty of Exercise and Sport Sciences; Faculty of Social Sciences and Education
FG5	2	1	Academic employees	Faculty of Theology; Faculty of Medicine
FG6	5	1	Foreign professors and academic employees	

3 In further analysis the focus group number is used as a reference in case of quotations from interviews.

Table 1. Continued.

No of FG	No of participants		Positions of employees	Affiliation
	men	women		
FG7	4	0	Professors and heads of subunits	Faculty of law; Faculty of Medicine; colleges; UT units
FG8	4	1	Professors and heads of subunits	Faculty of Science and Technology; Faculty of Social Sciences and Education
FG9	2	4	Professors and heads of subunits	Faculty of Philosophy; Faculty of Exercise and Sport Sciences
FG10	5	4	Professors and heads of subunits	Faculty of Economics and Business Administration; Faculty of Theology; UT units
FG11	3	0	Professors and heads of subunits	Faculty of Mathematics and Computer Science; Faculty of Science and Technology
FG12	1	3	administrative personnel	Faculty of Medicine; Faculty of law; Colleges
FG13	0	6	administrative personnel	Faculty of Economics and Business Administration; Faculty of Theology; UT units
FG14	1	3	administrative personnel	Faculty of Science and Technology; Faculty of Mathematics and Computer Science; UT administration
FG15	0	2	administrative personnel	Faculty of Exercise and Sport Sciences; Faculty of Social Sciences and Education; Faculty of Philosophy

The interviews were undertaken by two moderators with appropriate training, one of them was an observer and the second an active interviewer. In every focus group, from a list of values the participants chose those most important for the UT and they discussed the problems and challenges relating to them. The interviews, which lasted about 90 minutes, were recorded and transcribed. The transcribed interview was analysed using the QSR Nvivo9 software. A data-based inductive approach was used for systematising the information (Hsieh and Shannon, 2005). The units for coding were citations/quotations, which indicated a value conflict stemming from the mass university or managing an academic institution. During the interviews, the conflicts were discussed spontaneously, that is, the participants were not directed towards talking about them. The conflicts coded by one author were double-coded by the other author. When there was no consensus, the interview was analysed again by both authors together until consensus was achieved. Even though placing conflicts under particular values was somewhat questionable in some cases, multiple coding was avoided. In other words, every citation was put into the most suitable conflict category.

Value conflicts caused by leading an academic institution

Values are often not situation-specific and not connected to the roles in organization (Roe and Ester, 1999; Aadland, 2010). This means that one value can be discussed in various contexts and by people in different roles, but here they have not been separated – it is not important, whether the discussants are researchers, teachers or have a support role. In Figure 1, there are values that employees considered to be in danger, because the university management did not support those values. Of course, some values, for example, science-based and excellence, are bound together so closely that achieving one administrative goal could further or inhibit both of them at the same time.

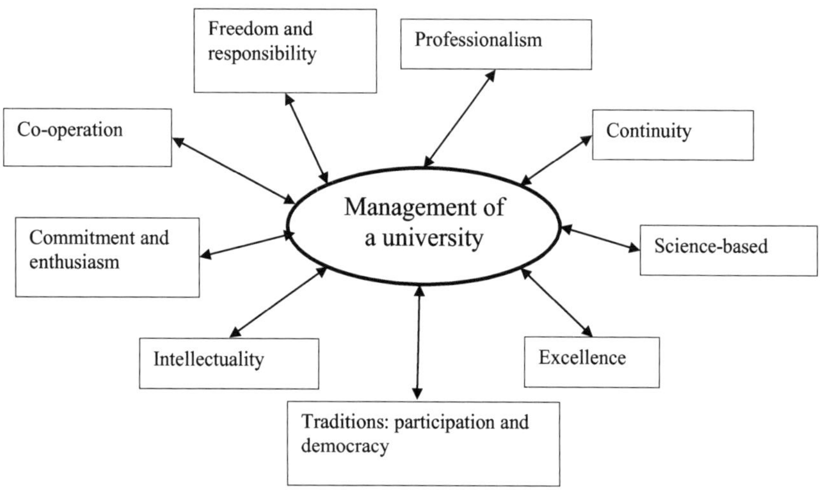

Figure 1. Value conflicts caused by the management of a university

One very clear conflict appeared in the focus groups. This concerned the conflict between scientific publications accounting i.e. measuring success in research, and achieving actual **excellence**. The interviewees reflected that the current system of publications' accounting had got to the point where employees concentrated more on jobs that are short-term and 'prosperous' on a personal level, rather than 'interesting' or necessary. Achieving true excellence is restricted by the need to stay within frameworks and to minimise risks. Research (the entire process from application for funding to publication of research) has changed to be predominantly guideline oriented.

> Chasing after money and the pursuit of excellence makes people not do interesting, but profitable things. [...] There should be less pressure exerted in publishing in specific journals, [...] riskier projects should be allowed as well. (FG5 academic employee[4])

> ...I think you should publish, when you have an idea and you want to write about it, not, when you are told, you have to write three publications. (FG12, administrative employee)

With the general race for publishing, respondents in arts and social sciences feel the most discriminated against, since the evaluation of the quality of their publications is based on the logic of natural sciences. It has been stressed that different disciplines should have different assessments for the quality of research.

> Excellence means concentrating on journals that are read by 1 per cent of the society. But this does not fit with the social sciences, [...] the social scientist is squeezed into ill-suited frames. (FG 5, academic employee)

> There is a mistake in evaluating research here. I discovered [...] that world-famous professors would work as assistants here, maybe as lecturers. But they are world-famous! (FG 1, academic employee)

Also, in *realia,* the authors' collective is common, but in *humaniora,* the practice of publishing and the contribution of a single individual is different:

> When researchers in natural science, five or seven of them, publish an article together then there are no questions asked, because it is seen as a strong article, but when one historian writes a monograph the question arises, whether this monograph is as valuable as one seventh of that article. (FG 1, academic employee)

Interviewees stressed that excellence sometimes conflicts with the aim of the university to advance internationalisation. Even though going in that direction is largely considered to be the right strategy, bureaucracy makes it take strange forms at times:

> When they [students] come [...] to masters and they finally have the only course that they can get about Estonian Church History, and it`s in English because the

---

4 In all block quotes from respondents FG refers to Focus Group.

> university demands a certain amount of courses to be in English, I find it to be completely ridiculous. (FG13, administrative employee)

A second problem is the uncertainty of funding and the constant pressure to acquire extra resources. Being **science-based,** as it is understood traditionally, is constantly under attack, because employees feel that they are being pressurised into thinking in an applied way. They have to think about where to get money and they have to write project applications, where, in an ideal world, they could be writing research articles.

> Yes, this kind of basic science should not disappear. We try to put everything into some sort of manufacturing and try to apply everything, but without basic science we cannot do that. Research takes time and it is more like a process, so it takes time to understand... (FG 1, academic employee)

> ...ultimately, I ask, why do I do all this? I mean, when I write a project application, then I have no time to do research. I just write what has been requested, but I have no time to do the research itself... (FG 1, academic employee)

Employees have to deal with writing project applications and reports as part of their workload and, overall, workloads are felt to be too high. Management roles have been distributed and academic employees are overloaded with them. This is associated with a decrease in **commitment**.

> I think lack of commitment is actually connected with the fact that some people are heavily burdened. They have many different roles... (FG 8, academic employee)

The respondents argued that internationalisation also decreases dedication and enthusiasm, because the conditions for the foreign teachers are significantly better than those for the local teachers:

> The thing that really kills enthusiasm of the local teachers is when foreign teachers get paid more for the same thing, even though, sometimes, the workload of the foreigners is even a lot smaller. (FG 6, academic employee)

> The thing we should thrive for is for our teachers to have the same kind of conditions and demands like they [foreigners] have. (FG 13, administrative employee)

As a result of heavy workloads, the employees are so fully occupied that they have no opportunity for spontaneous, interdisciplinary and mutually interesting **cooperation**.

> Colleagues from other disciplines have at times turned to me. But it [cooperation] is not possible, because my time has already been planned over the following year or two, which I have had to do in order to retain my position...it is not possible to make spontaneous, enjoyable, fun projects. […] something very special could be born

from these kinds of sudden ideas, but there is no possibility for that. (FG 5, academic employee)

Cooperation and, also, individual dedication, is hindered by the general lack of resources and uncertainty about the future and is also limited due to varied financing schemes for different projects. The result is that every department looks after their own interests, not the interests of the students or the university as a whole:

...why would you want to cooperate? You will then lose money. We have the same situation. Why would you want to bring in a lot of experts when we can do it ourselves. We would lose money otherwise. (FG12, administrative employee)

It causes tension when nobody knows what is going to happen next year. [It] does not help along to the general cooperation within the university. (FG4, academic employee)

Freedom, **intellectuality** and **responsibility** are harmed when processes are standardised and procedures created in order to ease the work of the management. Academic employees also find that rules and regulations, as well as affecting freedom, kill off responsibility, both of which go together with research and teaching:

[…] freedom should be used responsibly, it is a little bit too over formalized, so the responsibility... the whole administration and curriculum administration of the university...it should be a bit more supportive, but it just seems to take too much attention to itself. (FG 1, academic employee)

[…] us [teachers], are treated according to […] some kindergarten principles when it comes to responsibility. It is not important that you can do your work well, which you could do alright on your own, with your inner systematization, but apparently, there is someone, somewhere, who knows how to do it better. (FG 1, academic employee)

A standardised and efficiency oriented environment is not attractive for top professionals and it encourages mediocre people to remain at the university.

[…] eventually, only mediocre people remain here. The brighter ones – they won`t like it here. We have to consider that the gifted people are quite moody, […] they know their worth and if they don`t like something, they won`t like it. (FG11, academic employee)

Academic employees who participated in our study were concerned because, in their opinion, the attempt of the administration to organise the university in a rational way solely focused on efficiency threatens to destroy **traditions**:

Is a faculty important in today's university? In my opinion, it should be, but it isn`t really ...An example might be the sad graduation day, where the faculty of law and faculty of economics are put together. (FG 1, academic employee)

> […] this development does bring along abandoning the main building and the disappearance of the old auditoriums. Well, I don`t get it. There is no point of it anymore. […] it is traditional, some things should stay as they were. (FG13, administrative employee)

In a way, **participation** and **democracy** are part of traditional university management. Centralisation and making the management more efficient directly opposes these values:

> […] the other version, which is a more difficult way of management, is to strengthen democracy, so, that there is more decision making within the faculties. And not close down smaller faculties and only stress efficiency of management. (FG11, academic employee)

> I have […] changed my work desk, moved from one floor to the other, by now, from one building […] back to the main building again […], and, […] no one has asked me, whether I would like to do it. (FG14, administrative employee)

Due to the pursuit of efficiency, employees do not perceive the university as having the broad role of carrier and promoter of intellectuality in society anymore; but they see the university as just a provider of particular services.

> Intellectuality is actually the general atmosphere and a certain irrationality belongs to this atmosphere […] in a sense that you don`t always have to make financially and purposefully rational moves, but it`s still part of the intellectuality. (FG11, academic employee)

Intellectuality in itself is long-term, but being project-based is short-term and this does not contribute to creating or upholding intellectuality.

> […] there should be institutions, where there is time to think about things peacefully...that the actual teaching and discussing with the students wouldn`t be oriented to some usefulness […], but to general intellectuality. (FG 4, academic employee)

> Life is getting even more project-based and the intellectuality gets fragmented in those projects... (FG 7, academic employee)

Project-based financing also determines whether a talented person can remain in the university or not, depending on whether or not it is possible to transfer them into existing financial schemes. Hence, **continuity** is in danger.

> The system is built in a way that when there is funding, then you can employ whoever you want and pay them, but if there`s no funding, then there is no money and then you can`t get anyone. (FG 2, academic employee)

As continuity is disrupted, filling positions with eligible candidates becomes difficult.

> It`s a long-term process and if all of a sudden you`re looking for a professor and[they haven't] been developed since [their] doctorate, then where should you get them from? (FG 10, academic employee)

Leading an academic organisation is, in a strange way, in conflict with professionalism: leading positions in universities are mainly given to professionals in research, who, as a rule, are not professional leaders. The respondents felt that regulations in this area should be more flexible – so applicants for top leader positions need not be professors. . Similarly, professional support teams could be led by non-professional leaders.

> We do have technological things and large labs that need to be run...many colleges have a research director, who assists [the leader] with these kinds of matters ... but at this moment, all of these extra functions have been taken [...] to the unified cauldron of the university. (FB 8, academic employee)

> Such an administrator or such a person is needed, […] who would have some authority to verify some things, because deputation is about checking, if the replacement is there, if the curricular work is going smoothly, does the one on business leave has a financier... why should the poor department manager do all that? (FG 14, administrative employee)

> Here, of course, is a contradiction or a paradox. When, usually, professionalism is based on learning and education, then [...] becoming a leader is based on success in research, and they have no understanding of leadership or the people, they will start doing this kind of work without reading even a brochure of management... (FG 8, academic employee)

Within the current systems developing professionalism is particularly difficult among young teachers, because there are insufficient financial resources for self-development. It is only possible to attend conferences (with EU funding) when one has a paper to present:

> […] we still get back to financing. They [the young teachers] don`t always have an opportunity to give their report, an article, or a poster, because they haven`t gotten so far, but information is needed in order to know, what is being done and to really listen, so, it could help along to professionalism. (FG 14, administrative employee)

So, in conclusion, it can be said that the value conflicts attached to leading an academic organisation stem from 'measuring' research (and its results), centralisation, the pursuit of efficiency, financing (applied) project-based research, a general lack of resources and the uncertainty of funding. The extent to which university management has been influenced by government policy is examined below.

The role of R&D policy in value conflicts

The strategy document 'Knowledge-Based Estonia' states that, in Estonia, the assessment of research and development should be based on comparisons with the world-class level in the same area (Teadmistepõhine Eesti:9, 20). The success of research is determined mainly by the number of publications in international peer-reviewed journals. The aim for 2013 is to raise the number of quality publications to 1200 according to the internationally recognised bibliometric database, ISI Web of Science. In the EU, the average annual growth rate of the numbers of publications is 5 per cent, but the Estonian average growth rate is 11 per cent (HTM, 2011:11). Also, the planned number of publications for 2015 has been achieved (RAKE/CDP…: 36). As seen in the report of the National Audit Office, the target financing and the grants from the Estonian Science Foundation are determined mainly by the quality of prior publications not by the socio-economic relevance of the planned research. In this light it is easy to understand the university employees need to publish, as was described above. Even though it is stated in the National Audit Office report that specific quality criteria, depending on the research area, are considered in the grant application (p. 26), the implementation of this has either been slow or the employees have not understood it adequately.

Also, in the strategy, one negative consequence of the pressure to publish in scholarly journals has been realised – the alienation of researchers from the rest of society. This idea was also expressed by Professor Alar Karis, rector of Tartu University when he told a daily newspaper (Koch, 2012): 'We forget why we have universities. They are for serving the public'. In the R&D strategy, this has also been addressed: in order to reduce alienation, specific measures to motivate scientists to present their ideas to the public in clear and interesting ways are introduced (Teadmistepõhine Eesti:30). So, publishing is still of paramount importance, but the range of desirable outputs has been expanded.

Publishing is one of the main criteria for funding research and is undoubtedly a national level matter. In order to achieve the goals of the Lisbon strategy, an aim was set to increase the volume of R&D funding in 2010 to 3 per cent of GDP (the so called Barcelona target), of which two thirds was supposed to come from the private sector. In 2005, core funding of research was introduced, which gives the R&D institution a chance to plan and develop their own activities outside project funding (Teadmistepõhine Eesti:11–12). However, the government's R&D investments have not grown at the planned rate, which has made it impossible to fully achieve the goals set out in the strategy. Since there is no secure funding, the unclear future of the programmes leads scientists to concentrate on scientific publishing. The RAKE/CDP (2011) assessment report shows that in addition to the lack of financing for certain planned activities, many R&D activities, by their nature, only have short-term effects (development of web-pages, researches, expertise, auditing, training, visits by foreign teachers, study trips etc.). This is where extra resources and follow-up activities are needed in order to guarantee continuity and to maximise the effects of the initial investment (p. 64–65). Without these extra resources there is a danger that financed and executed R&D activities will not yield the intended results.

Financial resources are strongly polarised between faculties. Funds are channelled towards those R&D areas, 'which have the potential to achieve results at the frontier of world research, which are important to sustainable economic development, which support important socioeconomic goals, and the maintenance of the nation and the culture' (Teadmistepõhine Eesti:3). For achieving success at an international level it is necessary to concentrate human and material resources to increase specialisation in the research and development facilities. Therefore, key areas have been identified (biotechnology, energy technology, material technology, environmental protection and technology, healthcare, information and communication technology). However, according to the National Audit Office report, these areas have been too loosely specified. In whatever way funds are allocated between these key areas the chances for other areas to secure funding are diminished and their competitiveness decreased (Riigikontrolli audit, 2012:28). At the same time, there are plenty of measures for the key areas (for instance, 40 per cent of the projects with target financing are within the key areas) and compared to labour force much more money has accumulated there. However, this means that scientists in key areas are overloaded with projects. So, the situation is bad on both sides: employees in the key areas are overloaded and those in other areas suffer from under-financing. To mention a positive element, there is a plan to initiate research and development programmes to guarantee and ensure the stability and continuation of Estonian national culture, language, history, and nature (Teadmistepõhine Eesti: 3–4). These are investments, in which the direct socioeconomic effects will only be seen after a long time, but they are important for Estonia to help to develop a national state and culture, and to be part of world development.

Government strategy really does favour applied research and it puts pressure on researchers to acquire projects for themselves. Knowledge-Based Estonia (2011) states: 'Scientific and applied research are closely bound and the overlap of both directions are even wider. That is why it is important to find a suitable balance between the two directions of research' (p. 7). In the same document, it is also stated that in assessing research and development activity applicability is taken into account as a criterion (p. 27).

Financing Estonian research is strongly dependent upon foreign funding. In recent years 13–17 per cent of all R&D investments have been foreign (the average figure in the EU is 7–8 per cent). The success of Estonian researchers in acquiring foreign funding is connected with active and successful participation in EU research, technology development and framework programmes. In the context of the European Commission's 5th Framework Programme (FP) 809 project applications were made, of which 195 (24.2 per cent) were successful and received funding. During the first three years of the 6th FP there have already been 252 successful applications (23.4 per cent of the total applications) (Teadmistepõhine Eesti:11). However, these impressive numbers also have a flip-side: the National Audit Office points out that different funding agencies are funding projects with similar goals (Riigikontrolli audit, 2012). This is unreasonable because it increases, among other things, the resource expenditure of the applicants (separate applications demand separate project accounting). In other words, acquiring and fulfilling (foreign funded) projects has become the main activity of researchers in Estonian R&D institutions and this is to the detriment of values such as science-based, continuity and dedication.

University employees would like more interdisciplinary cooperation. In theory, the R&D policies do not disagree with this, in fact, they seem to encourage it. A leading principle of the R&D strategy is to promote cooperation on a national and international level, between all parties (Teadmistepõhine Eesti:9). Cooperation allows access to knowledge, divides risks, and enables projects with critical mass to be undertaken. The HTM report (2011) also reveals that the Structural Funds measures have problems covering general expenditure and with minimizing risks (p. 4). The employees interviewed also commented that researchers do not like to take on riskier projects because of the pressure to publish. So, we can see that research cooperation and publishing potential may not always go hand in hand, because employees are focused on maximizing the number of their publications, which may be at the expense of cooperation. An interesting distinction can be added, since interdisciplinary research is favoured when it comes to financing; as the large (cooperative) projects get funding more easily, researchers sacrifice the research areas that really interest them, in favour of areas suitable for funding. This kind of behaviour is not in accordance with academic freedom.

Lastly, we focus on internationalisation, as it has conflicted with the value 'commitment'. The aim for 2013 is to increase the number of foreign scientists and students coming to Estonia (Teadmistepõhine Eesti:22). International mobility creates opportunities to hire better employees (Konkurentsivõime kava:13), which, without doubt, supports the value of excellence. However, bringing top foreign scientists and doctorates to Estonia has been more difficult than expected, because of the lack of well-known Estonian academic institutions and the unattractive local conditions. In 2010/11, foreign teachers made up 5.1 per cent of all teachers working in Estonian universities. In 2009, 40 positions for foreign employees were confirmed within the DoRa programme, but by the end of 2011, only 23 of them were filled. Thirteen top scientists have arrived in Estonia through the Mobilitas Program (HTM, 2011:21). The National Audit Office points out that the salaries offered to foreign teachers in Estonia cannot compete internationally, and recommends that the salaries offered are increased and that the financing is made more flexible. It became evident during this research, that when pursuing excellence with measures such as these, the commitment of local teachers is undermined.

In Table 2, the role of the national R&D strategy in the value conflicts discussed above has been summarised. An upward arrow shows that the measure enables employees to stay true to the value and take it into account, but a downward arrow shows that a measure conflicts with a given value.

Table 2. The effect of R&D policy on values

Strategic goal and/or measure	Values connected to goals and the effect on them
Raising the number of quality publications	excellence ↓, cooperation ↓
Specific criteria are taken into consideration when assessing research	(*humaniora*) professionalism ↑
Measures that motivate scientists to publish their results to the public in a clear and interesting way	Professionalism↑, responsibility↑
National R&D investment growth at a planned rate	science-based↑, commitment ↑, cooperation↑
Channelling human and material resources to key areas	commitment↓, science-based ↓, continuity ↓ (not in the key areas)
Applicability as one important criterion, when assessing projects	science-based ↓
Growth of the success in acquiring foreign money	commitment↓ , science-based ↓, continuity ↓
Interdisciplinarity is taken into account when assessing projects; encouraging national and international cooperation	cooperation ↑, excellence ↓, science-based ↓, freedom↓
Increase in the number of foreign scientists and university students coming to Estonia.	excellence ↑, commitment ↓

As can be seen in Table 2, either or both a goal and a measure can have positive and negative influences on the university employees' value conflicts. The only measures that have no negative influence in the context of value conflicts are (unsurprisingly) the growth of national R&D investments and the application of area specific quality criteria when assessing research. Many of the value conflicts can be categorised under the autonomous activity of the university management: for instance, it is difficult to see the influence of the national R&D policy on value conflicts connected with traditions, freedom, intellectuality and responsibility. However, the indirect influence of achieving maximum efficiency by standardisation comes as a result of limited resources, and the state has a role in this.

Value conflicts caused by mass university

Our research showed that academic employees feel the UT to be a mass university. Does this claim have a basis? The phenomenon of a mass university can be understood in different ways: e.g. the percentage of students in the whole population; the average number of students per higher education institution and the number of students per academic employee.

When comparing internationally, Estonia does not stand out as having an exceptionally high proportion of higher education students in its population (see Table 3 for statistics for selected countries). It can be seen that in Finland and Latvia, for instance, the proportion of students is slightly higher than in Estonia. However, compared to other Central and Eastern European countries, like Hungary and the Czech Republic, Estonia educates relatively more students.

Table 3. Number of students per 100 inhabitants in selected countries

Country	2009	2010
Estonia	5.10	5.15
Czech Republic	3.98	4.16
Hungary	3.96	3.88
Latvia	5.55	5.01
Finland	5.57	5.67
Sweden	4.57	4.87

Source: Eurostat, authors' calculation

The notion of mass education is not only about magnitude, it is also about the resources devoted to students. OECD statistics for 2008 (OECD, 2011) show that expenditure per student in tertiary education was rather low in Estonia – USD 6022 – compared to other countries. The closest were the Slovak Republic and Poland with USD 6560 and USD 7089, respectively, whereas, for instance, in Finland, the figure was USD 15402. This poor position has continued despite the fact that higher education expenditure in Estonia has risen by more than 50 per cent since 2000.

This tendency towards mass universities in Estonia can be further understood by looking at the number of higher education institutions in relation to students. As a whole, the number of institutions providing higher education in Estonia has declined in the past 10 years, while the number of students has stayed the same (see Figure 2).

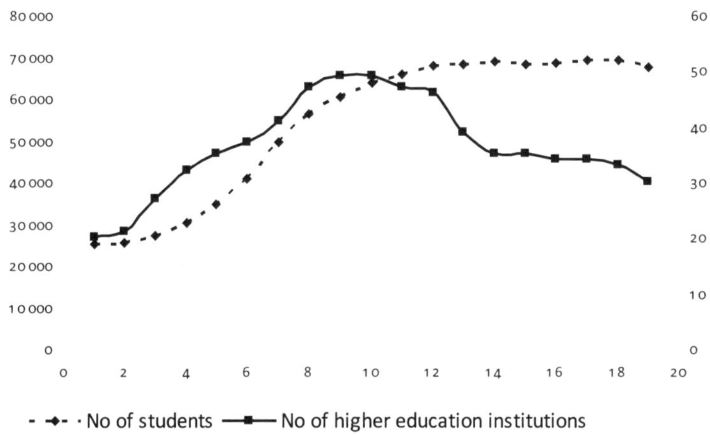

Figure 2. The number of students and higher education institutions in Estonia, 1993/94–2011/12

Source: Haridus- ja Teadusministeerium. Uuringud, statistika,...(2012), authors' calculations

So, it is likely that all of the remaining institutions are on average more 'mass universities' than they were before. However, focusing on the UT situation, by looking at the ratio of students to academic employees, it can be seen that the situation over the last 10 years has marginally improved compared to 2002–2003 (see Table 4). In comparison with some of the top universities the number of students per academic employee at the UT is substantially higher, than, for instance, at the University of Helsinki (7.5 in 2010), the Massachusetts Institute of Technology (6.3 in 2011), or Oxford University (4.2 in 2010. We believe that our respondents' arguments about the UT being a mass university were influenced by these statistics. A large number of students in the classroom have a direct influence on university employee's every-day workload and this embeds a critical attitude towards mass universities.

Table 4. The ratio of students to academic employees in the UT from 2001–2011

Category / year	2001	2002	2003	2004	2005	2006	2007	2008	2009	2010	2011
College students* per academ-ic employee	12.6	13.9	13.2	12.7	12.1	10.9	10.0	10.0	10.1	10.5	10.3
College students per teacher	17.9	20.1	20.0	19.7	19.8	18.6	18.0	18.0	18.4	19.6	18.9

Source: Statistics of personnel and college students of UT 2001–2011

*Note: * except foreign students and trainee doctors*

The value conflicts, caused by the mass university, which are based on the opinions of the university employees in the focus group, are shown in Figure 3, and the conflicts are discussed below with corresponding citations.

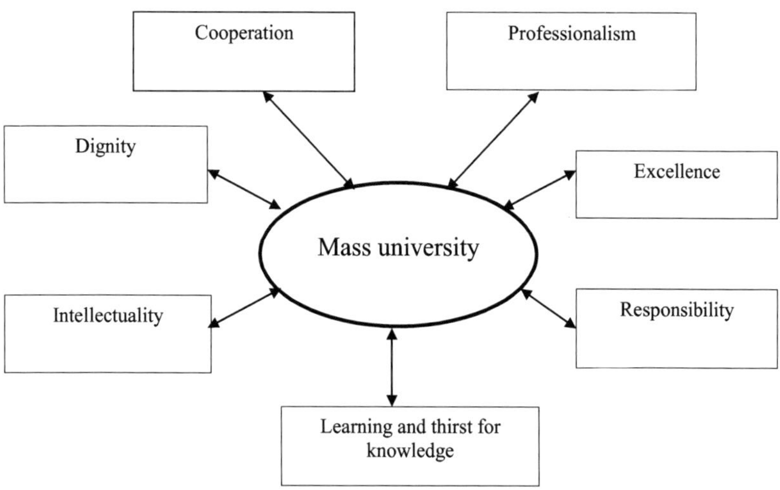

Figure 3. Value conflicts perceived in connection with the mass university

The mass university has clearly challenged values like **responsibility** and **dignity**. Academic employees believed that the mass university can only function in a situation where the responsibility of the teacher has been significantly decreased. One view that came up was the decline of the reputation of higher education in society:

> ...for instance, in my opinion, the students with bachelors aren`t valued. And not just the students, but even the graduates. (FG 2, academic employee)

The reputation of the university and the efforts to improve that reputation were considered very important, but it was thought that the quality of the students had declined and the UT's place in the ranking tables had been damaged by the move towards a mass university. Academic employees consider the position in rating lists to be an inadequate assessment method, because the UT is compared to institutions that are not mass universities.

> Ranking has been taken too far and after a while it causes sort of self-pity [...] And those top universities aren`t mass universities either... (FG 10, academic employee)

Excellence, as a value, was considered to be inappropriate for the mass university model and some doubt was expressed about the minimum accepted quality level in the mass university.

> The university just gives them [credits] out quite easily or pointlessly, so there really is no studying behind it. When we give 2 ECTs for six hours of work and say that the student did something herself, then, how does that show quality? (FG 15, administrative employee)

When the number of students accepted onto university courses is large, it is inevitable that their abilities will vary, so the demands of the courses have to be lowered, rather than raised. Also, meaningful contact with the student, which is considered to be connected with **intellectuality** and **continuity**, disappears. The result is that these developments have also had a negative effect on the **professionalism** of teachers.

> The general level got worse with the principle of benchmark admission [...]. Half the auditorium can`t understand [the lecture] at all, so, the standard of lecture had to be lowered... (FG 2, academic employee)

> Many of my younger [...] colleagues were disappointed, because they had thought that they were the young teachers here, who could pursue their own topic, communicate with intelligent and interesting teachers and students. But now there is a large amount of students here, who shouldn`t be here in the first place, so, a lot of time and energy goes into helping them and dragging them along and giving them chances to do their exams again... (FG 11, academic employee)

> […] let's look back: Ariste[5] used to sit in the university cafeteria, where one student, a second student, and a third student would approach him. He knew them all, and this formed his school. But, if there are 50–60 students, then this school cannot ever form. (FG 12, administrative employee)

It is somewhat paradoxical that the **thirst for knowledge** is under threat in the mass university, even from the students' perspective. Although the mass university is based on the presumption that the thirst for knowledge has grown in society, and the activity of the university has been regulated accordingly, the university employees think that attending a university aimed at the masses has long ignored the inner wish to acquire knowledge. Instead, people 'just work in the name of getting the paper'. The resource limitations and the workloads of the teachers mainly worsen the situation of the small proportion of students who really do want to study.

> Maybe, what is missing, is this thirst for knowledge. Many things are done because of money. Students are accepted because of money, the quality has gone down […] I understand the background of this system, but... (FG 12, administrative employee)

> Why should the better students we have suffer and not get the knowledge or skill they`ve wanted? (FG 11, academic employee)

When it comes to mass higher education, students financing their own studies has also proved to be quite important. On the one hand, it has made the increase in the number of students possible, but on the other hand, it has changed the character of the student-university relationship:

> I see, many of the students presume for that kind of service; they pay the money and just wait for the paper to come to them in three years' time. I think, we should pull on the breaks here, the university shouldn`t stay on this path for a long time. (FG 13, administrative employee)

Of course, the previous statements cannot all be generalized - there may be differences between faculties. For instance, the higher the salaries for particular specialities in the employment market, the greater is the chance that the speciality will be taken for pragmatic reasons, not because of a thirst for knowledge:

> I`m quite sure, people learning physics have a larger interest, unlike the people studying economics, who are oriented for their own welfare later. (FG 13, administrative employee)

University employees value the thirst for knowledge highly, and this is why it is hoped that education reform brings it back to universities:

5 Prof. Paul Ariste (1905–1990) – Estonian linguist in the field of Finno-Ugric languages.

> But I imagine, the coming reforms […] should start selecting the type of young people, who really do have the thirst for knowledge and the desire to study. (FG 13, administrative employee)

Finally, **cooperation** as a value that is not supported in the mass university can be mentioned:

> Maybe I`m very naive by saying that when the university used to be more compact and there were less students, then there was more communication between faculties. Not only among the respectable teachers, but also the students used to communicate with each other a lot more.[…] Now, everything is stuck behind this mass, it`s a big mass, no one can manage it or control it. (FG 12, administrative employee)

So, it can be seen that the model where there are many students on one course and some of them are self-financing, causes a lot of value conflicts – especially from the aspects of responsibility, excellence, intellectuality, professionalism, and even the thirst for knowledge. These values have to be compromised daily, and this is not seen as a pleasant process.

The role of R&D policy in the mass university

When analysing R&D strategy documents from the mass university point of view, it can be seen that the aim of creating a knowledge-based society, and the measure corresponding to it – 'Developing Human Resources', paved the way for the mass university. Developing Human Resources, amongst other things, means training scientists and engineers, and universities are being supported to do this in order to provide society with appropriately skilled people (Teadmistepõhine Eesti: 20). The Estonian competitiveness plan shows that during the past five years there has been a stable growth in the number of people aged 30–34 who have undertaken higher education. From the level of 35.7 per cent in 2009, there was rapid growth to 39.7 per cent in 2010. This shift can be explained by the number of university graduates, which has grown substantially since 2000 (which is when the so called boom in higher education began).

There is no indication in the strategy documents about the further continuing growth of graduates beyond 2015–2020 because the aim is that a stable 40 per cent of people in the given age group will undertake higher education (which means zero growth), Instead, in the longer term, the main aim of the education policy is to raise the quality of higher education and its international competitiveness. However, there is also the aim of doubling the proportion of adults engaged in lifelong-learning by 2020, and decreasing the proportion of adults with no vocational education by 2 per cent (Eesti konkurentsivõime kava:8–9). There can be no guarantee that there will be an alternative to the mass university in the future, because even when the number of Bachelor degree curricula decreases (according to forecasts during the next few years the number of Bachelor degree students will decrease by about 5 per cent a year), lifelong learning will mean that more emphasis will be put on further education and graduate studies (Eesti konkurentsivõime kava:11–12). Neither can the aim of enrolling 2000 foreign students in Estonia by 2015 be overlooked.

It can also be asked, whether the concentration of competencies in universities, which is one of the main aims of the higher education system, will decrease or intensify the perception of university employees about teaching the so called masses? As the aim is to minimise duplication and decrease the total number of courses in Estonian universities, then in future students interested in the same subject area, who have previously been able to attend one of many universities, will have to attend one particular university. This means that the teachers, who have remained in their positions, might feel that the mass university phenomenon has increased, rather than decreased, unless the number of teachers in the subject area grows significantly in the given university. In conclusion, the goals above do not give hope that the total number of students in one university (or total number of students per teacher) will decrease rapidly.

However, there are trends in the opposite direction. Our study showed that many academic employees hope that higher education reform, i.e. the Law of University that will come in effect in 2013, will break the mass university trend. The plans are that the number of State subsidised places will increase by 40 per cent, but it can be assumed that this will only take place within those subject areas where the mass university is most viable as a result of its paying students. A research question which is beyond the scope of this study is whether a sustainable model of operation can be found for those less popular subject areas where funding and workload (as a result of fewer self financing students) are decreasing.

Making Estonian higher education attractive to foreign students can definitely be seen as positive, because in addition to the other measures, improving the quality of higher education is important. Establishing quality assurance systems are part of this, where all universities are required to be involved in institutional accreditation every 7 years, including the assessment of curricula. Improving the quality of higher education also means implementing measures to improve the quality of supervision and the efficiency and the pedagogic competence of teachers.

In Table 5, the presumed influence of R&D policy on the increase or the decrease of the mass university phenomenon, compared to the situation today, is shown. The goals and measures, that, according to the authors, facilitate the mass university phenomenon, are marked with an upward arrow, and those that are assumed to have the opposite effect are marked with a downward arrow.

Table 5. The effect of R&D policy on the mass university

Strategic goal and/or measure	The effect on the mass university
The proportion of 30–35 year olds with higher education is 40%	–
Doubling the proportion of adults in lifelong learning by 2020	↑
Decreasing the proportion of adults without special education and further education by 2%	–/(↑)
To accept 2000 foreign students by the year 2015	↑
Work distribution between universities and concentrating competences	↑
Law of University that will take an effect in the year 2013	↓
Establishing a system of quality assurance for higher education	↓
Developing the supervision system to conduct research	↓

In conclusion, it is difficult to tell which measures will be most significant for the mass university, but it is likely that there will not be any large changes in the total number of students in any one university. However, the proportions of levels of study and the profile of students will change (a decrease in self-financing students, more adult students and more foreign students). From the results of our research we can conclude that the pressure on values such as excellence, intellectuality, the thirst for knowledge and professionalism will decrease, but that these changes will not be drastic.

Conclusions

In this chapter we aimed to demonstrate that state-level R&D policies have played a significant role in the value conflicts perceived by university employees. It is not unique to Estonia that developments in higher education cause tensions among university professionals, as similar trends have been referred to in the literature before. For example, Sotirakou (2004) brings out that overcrowded courses, tight budgets, the constant need to search for alternative financing, performance appraisal criteria and the proliferation of fixed-term contracts, generate value conflicts and consequent stress to employees in universities. In this section, we bring out the main findings of our study.

The study revealed that the management of a university and the pursuit of mass higher education are the reasons for numerous value conflicts for employees in academia – concerning both traditional academic values, such as freedom, responsibility, co-operation etc., and also perceived values specific to the University of Tartu as a traditional national university (intellectuality, dignity, continuity and excellence). In line with the new public management trend, the management structure and ideology of the University of Tartu have moved closer to that of a business enterprise during last ten years. The conflicts that are rooted in these university management practices are, to a large extent, influenced by the general R&D policy, as many administrative decisions are motivated, if not imposed, by state-level regulations. For example, complying with European-wide reforms (the Bologna process) that require universities to do more and to do it differently (Shaw, Chapman and Rumyatseva, 2011) or implementing national policies. With respect to implementing national policies, the structure and resources for departments in the university largely depend on specialisations defined as key areas or priorities by the ministry. In most areas, however, both the internal and external competition for money and students guides administrative decisions. In turn the actions of management shape organisational culture and the employees' understanding of values (Cha and Edmondson, 2006; Buchko, 2007; Jaakson, 2009; Reino, 2009).

The most problematic area is the pressure to publish, which, when linked to budgetary policy, is found to be detrimental to excellence and co-operation. No matter how the value for money of research, as an activity largely supported by tax-payers, is measured, criticism by academics everywhere is guaranteed. For instance, Martin (2011) points out that relatively crude measures are perceived as unfair whereas more complicated ones entail other serious drawbacks. In a similar way to Estonia, the UK measurement systems have been criticised for introducing perverse incentives and unintended consequences including quick publication rather than longer-term research, 'mainstream' research rather than more 'risky' research, and so on (Furedi, 2002; Martin and Whitley, 2010). Our view is that the best way to tackle these problems is yet to be found in Estonia just as is the case elsewhere. We can only note that in our study nobody questioned the relevance of research, as such (see Hacker and Dreifus (2010) for a discussion of such a possibility), only the technicalities of measuring its importance were criticised.

Next, university employees felt that insufficient, and project-based financing favouring applied research, jeopardises various academic values, most notably being science-based, commitment and academic freedom. Again, Estonian scholars are not alone with this concern. Assessing the value of research by its usefulness to industry has become the strategy of most agencies responsible for research funding (Van Looy et al., 2004; Martin, 2011; Sterckx, 2011) and academic employees do not always agree with this (e.g. Furedi, 2002; Hakala, 2009, Philpott et al., 2011). Pressure from universities on their researchers to find possibilities to use new knowledge for commercial uses (Sterckx, 2011) is a widespread practice in modern universities, even though this is often not in accordance with the values held by academic employees. While the debate about the inherent mission of universities shows no sign of fading, it can be said that for the time being there is an enduring view among academics that the usefulness of research to society can only be judged in the long-term and being too attentive to 'customers' needs', as is the case in many applied projects, may in fact hamper genuine knowledge creation and exploratory innovation (Andriopoulus and Lewis, 2009).

Administrative attempts to standardise and centralise processes in universities aimed at promoting academic efficiency are in part related to scarcity of resources and the search for this has spread throughout the western world. However, Barrow (2010), based on examples from the US, refers to the rationality crisis that managers are facing at some points in this process, i.e. administrative apparatus that is charged with resolving the fiscal crisis in higher education is incapable of doing so, because its decision-making process is the problem. However, the perceived administrative solution to this problem is to do more of the same – the very essence of a fetish – a bureaucratic system which culminates with an administration administering an administration (p. 343). In Australia and the UK, the managerial approach has also transformed the higher education systems, and not always for the better (Furedi, 2002; Schapper and Mayson, 2005). On the downside, the authors claim that by centralisation and standardisation the contribution of scholars is devalued and deskilled (they have become 'academic production line' labour), education is infantilised and academic autonomy is threatened. Academic staff have responded by conspiring against, resenting and resisting these developments. The value conflicts triggered by the pursuit of efficiency are recognised internationally and have probably always been present (Hacker and Dreifus, 2010). It is the recent economic crisis coupled with the poor demographic outlook that has intensified these conflicts. In Estonia it is estimated that within next three years the drop in the number of potential university entrants will be at least 30 per cent. When the 'market' shrinks, cost-cutting is inevitable and academic employees certainly do not differ from other employees when opposing these measures. Therefore, efficiency remains important for the future no less than it is important today, but ways of achieving it with better adherence to academic values will be a challenge for every university administration.

The final distinct policy area that has caused much discontent among academic employees is the 'massification' of higher education[6]. Here, country level R&D policy has played a dominant role, and even though some positive developments can be foreseen in the near future, these are probably not big enough to substantially diminish the related value conflicts. Again, value conflicts as a result of the provision of mass education are shared among academics in many other countries as governments all over Europe struggle to fund increasing student numbers and universities must be increasingly financially autonomous (Hüfner, 2003). The role of a university teacher today resembles that of a provider of a service that has been laid out in detail in a contract, i.e. course outline and reading list (Furedi, 2002; McCulloch, 2009) and the student as the 'customer' is always right (White, 2007). In this setting, value conflicts characterise employees working in public research universities that were formerly in monopoly positions (just like the University of Tartu) rather than those working in the more recently established and for-profit teaching oriented universities.

Even if we accept that the developments described above are inevitable, irreversible and internationally recognised, the accompanying negative effects should be acknowledged and both policy measures and institutional support mechanisms to alleviate these should be introduced as soon as possible. No doubt academic employees need to adapt to the changing environment just as employees in other professions do, but a smoother adaptation, with less painful value conflicts, would be in the interest of policy makers, university administrators, academic employees and, last but not least, the students.

Acknowledgements

This publication has been supported by European Social Foundation through the Research and Innovation Policy Monitoring Programme.

6 Although there are positive aspects of a mass university system, the university personnel who participated in this study only commented on the 'dark side' of mass education.

References

Aadland, E. (2010). Values in Professional Practice: Towards a Critical Reflective Methodology. *Journal of Business Ethics,* 97, 461–472.

Andriopoulos, C. and Lewis, M. (2009). Exploitation-exploration tensions and organisational ambidexterity: Managing paradoxes of innovation. *Organisation Science*, 20, 696–717.

Barrow, C. W. (2010). The Rationality Crisis in US Higher Education. *New Political Science*, 32, 317-344.

Beauvais, L. L., Desplaces, D. E., Melchar, D. E. and Bosco, S. M. (2007) Business Faculty Perceptions and Actions Regarding Ethics Education. *Journal of Academic Ethics*, 5, 121–136.

Berchem, T. (2006). The University as an Agora – Based on Cultural and Academic Values. *Higher Education in Europe,* 31, 395–398.

Brunsson, N. (2006). Administrative reforms as routines. *Scandinavian Journal of Management*, 22, 243–252.

Buchko, A. (2007). The effect of leadership on values-based management. *Leadership & Organisation Development Journal*, 28, 36-50.

Cha, S. E. and Edmondson, A. C. (2006). When Values Backfire: Leadership, attribution, and disenchantment in a values-driven organisation. *The Leadership Quarterly*, 17, 57–78.

Clark, B. R. (1998). *Creating Entrepreneurial Universities: Organisational Pathways of Transformation*. Oxford: International Association of Universities and Elsevier Science Ltd.

De George, R. T. (2003). Ethics, Academic Freedom And Academic Tenure. *Journal of Academic Ethics*, 1, 11–25.

de Chernatony, L. and Cottam, S. (2008). Interactions between organisational cultures and corporate brands. *Journal of Product & Brand Management*, 17, 13–24.

del Val, M. P. and Fuentes, C. M. (2003). Resistance to change: a literature review and empirical study. *Management Decision*, 41, 148–155.

Dill, D. D. (1982). The Structure of the Academic Profession: Toward a Definition of Ethical Issues. *The Journal of Higher Education*, 53, 255–267.

Dolan, S. L. and Richley, B. A. (2006). Managing by values (MBV): a new philosophy for new economic order. *Handbook of Business Strategy,* 7, 235–238.

OECD (2011). Education at a Glance 2011: OECD Indicators. Available online: http://www.oecd.org/edu/highereducationandadultlearning/48631582.pdf (03.09.2012).

Evans, G. R. and Packham, D. E. (2003). Ethical Issues at the University-Industry Interface: A Way Forward? *Science and Engineering Ethics, 9,* 3–16.

Etzkowitz H., Webster, A., Gebhardt, C. and Terra, B. R. C. (2000). The future of the university and the university of the future: evolution of ivory tower to entrepreneurial paradigm. *Research Policy*, 29, 313–330.

Foo, J. Y. A. and Wilson, S. J. (2011). An Analysis on the Research Ethics Cases Managed by the Committee on Publication Ethics (COPE) Between 1997 and 2010. *Science and Engineering Ethics*, DOI 10.1007/s11948-011-9273-3

Fuller, T. (2003/2004). The Idea of the University in Newman, Oakeshott, and Strauss. *Academic Questions*, 17, 37–53.

Furedi, F. (2002). The Bureaucratization of the British University. In Hayes, D. and Wynyard, R. (Eds.). *The McDonaldization of Higher Education*. Westport, CT: Bergin and Garvey, 33–42.

Hacker, A. and Dreifus, C. (2010). *Higher Education? How Colleges are Wasting Our Money and Failing Our Kids – and What We Can Do About It.* Times Books. New York.

Hakala, J. (2009). The future of the academic calling? Junior researchers in the entrepreneurial university. *Higher Education*, 57, 173–190.

Haridus- ja Teadusministeerium. Uuringud, statistika, andmebaasid [Estonian Ministry of Education and Research. Research, statistics, databases]. Available online and only in Estonian: http://www.hm.ee/index.php?048055#k6rgharidus (03.12.2012).

Hsieh, H. F. and Shannon, S. E. (2005). Three Approaches to Qualitative Content Analysis. *Qualitative Health Research*, 15, 1277–1288.

Haridus- ja Teadusministeerium (2011). Eesti teadus- ja arendustegevuse ning innovatsiooni strateegia 2007–2013 'Teadmistepõhine Eesti'. Aruanne strateegia eesmärkide ja rakendusplaani täitmisest 2010. ja 2011. aastal. [Estonian Ministry of Education and Research. The Estonian Research, Development and Innovation Strategy 2007–2013, 'Knowledge-based Estonia'. Report on fulfillment of the objectives of the strategy and implementation plan in 2010 and 2011.].

Hüfner, K. (2003). Higher Education as a Public Good. *Higher Education in Europe,* 28, 339–348.

Jaakson, K. (2009). *Management by values: the analysis of influencing aspects and its theoretical and practical implications*. Dissertationes Rerum Oeconomicarum Universitatis Tartuensis, 27. Tartu University Press.

Jørgensen, T. B. and Vrangbæk, K. (2011). Value Dynamics: Towards a Framework for Analyzing Public Value Changes. *International Journal of Public Administration*, 34(8), 486–496.

Koch, T. (2012). Karis: õpetajatega on Eestis kehv seis. *Postimees*, 9.04.2012, 6. [Karis: Teachers are in poor state in Estonia].

Konkurentsivõime kava 'Eesti 2020' [Plan of competitiveness 'Estonia 2020']. Available online: http://ec.europa.eu/europe2020/pdf/nrp/nrp_estonia_et.pdf (3.09.2012).

Kuther, T. L. (2003). A Profile of the Ethical Professor: Student Views. College Teaching, 51, 153–160.

Lencioni, P. M. (2002). Make Your Values Mean Something. *Harvard Business Review,* July, 113–117.

Maringe, F. (2011). The student as consumer: Affordances and constraints in a transforming higher education environment. In Molesworth, M., Scullion, R. and Nixon, E. (Eds.) *The marketisation of higher education and the student as consumer*. New York; Oxon: Routledge, 142–154.

Markie, P. J. (1994). *A professo's duties. Ethical issues in college teaching.* Rowman & Littlefield Publishers, Inc.

Martin, B. R. (2011). The Research Excellence Framework and the 'impact agenda': are we creating a Frankenstein monster? *Research Evaluation*, 20, 247–254.

Martin, B. R. and Whitley, R. (2010). The UK Research Assessment Exercise: a case of regulatory capture? In Whitley, R., Gläser, J. and Engwall, L. (Eds.) *Reconfiguring Knowledge Production: Changing Authority Relationships in the Sciences and their Consequences for Intellectual Innovation.* Oxford: Oxford University Press, 51–80.

McCulloch, A. (2009). The student as co-producer: Learning from public administration about the student-university relationship. *Studies in Higher Education,* 34, 171–83.

Oakeshott, M. (2003/2004). The idea of a Universty. *Academic Questions*, 17, 23–30.

Palfreyman, D. and Warner, D. (1998). *Higher education and the law: A guide for managers.* Buckingham: Open University Press.

Philpott, K., Dooley, L., O'Reilly, C. and Lupton, G. (2011). The entrepreneurial university: Examining the underlying academic tensions. *Technovation*, 31, 161–170.

RAKE / CDP Arenduskeskus (2011). Hindamisaruanne riigihanke „Perioodi 2007–2013 struktuurivahendite vahehindamine“ elluviimiseks. [Mid-term evaluation of structural assistance for 2007–2013]

Reino, A. (2009). *Manifestation of Organisational Culture on an Example of Estonian Organisations.* Dissertationes Rerum Oeconomicarum Universitatis Tartuensis, 26. Tartu University Press.

Riigikontrolli audit (2012). *Riigi tegevus teadus- ja arendustegevuse võtmevaldkondade edendamisel.* Retrieved from: www.hm.ee/index.php?popup=download&id=11653 (03.09.2012). [Activities of the state in developing key areas of research and development].

Roe, R. A. and Ester, P. (1999). Values and Work: Empirical Findings and Theoretical Perspectives. *Applied Psychology: An International Review*, 48, 1–21.

Schapper, J. and Mayson, S. (2005). Managerialism, Internationalization, Taylorization and Deskilling of Academic Work: Evidence from and Australian University. In Ninnes, P. and Hellstén, M. (Eds.) *Internationalizing Higher Education: Critical Explorations of Pedagogy and Policy.* Dordrecht: Springer, 181–197.

Scott, P. (2003). Challenges to Academic Values and the Organisation of Academic Work in a Time of Globalization. *Higher Education in Europe,* 28, 295–306.

Scriven, M. (1982). Ethics and the Academic Profession. *The Journal of Higher Education*, 53, 307–317.

Shaw, M., Chapman, D.W. and Rumyatseva, N. L. (2011). Organisational culture in the adoption of the Bologna process: a study of academic staff at a Ukrainian university. *Studies in Higher Education*, DOI: 10.1080/03075079.2011.614336

Sotirakou, T. (2004). Coping with Conflict within the Entrepreneurial University: Threat or Challenge for Heads of Departments in the UK Higher Education Context. *International Review of Administrative Sciences*, 70, 345–372.

Sterckx, S. (2011). Patenting and Licensing of University Research: Promoting Innovation or Undermining Academic Values? *Science & Engineering Ethics,* 17, 45–64.

Stevenson, M. A. (1999). Flexible education and the discipline of the market. *International Journal of Qualitative Studies in Education*, 12, 311–323.

Teadmistepõhine Eesti. Eesti teadus- ja arendustegevuse ning innovatsiooni strateegia 2007–2013. Retrieved from: www.hm.ee/index.php?popup=download&id=5771. [Knowledge-based Estonia. The Estonian Research, Development and Innovation Strategy 2007–2013].

Tetlock, P. E. (1986). A value pluralism model of ideological reasoning. *Journal of Personality and Social Psychology*, 50, 819–827.

Urde, M. (2003). Core value-based corporate brand building. *European Journal of Marketing,* 37, 1017–1040.

Vadi, M. and Haldma, T. (2010). Knowledge transfer through university-industry relations: some aspects of organisational culture. *Discussion on Estonian Economic Policy,* 490–506. Berlin and Tallinn: Berliner Wissenchafts-Verlag, Mattimar.

Van Looy, B., Ranga, M., Callaert, J., Debackere, K. and Zimmermann, E. (2004). Combining entrepreneurial and scientific performance in academia: towards a compounded and reciprocal Matthew-effect? *Research Policy,* 33, 425–441.

White, N. R. (2007). The customer is always right? Student discourse about higher education in Australia. *Higher Education,* 54, 593–604.

Wilson, E. K. (1982). Power, Pretense, and Piggybacking: Some Ethical Issues in Teaching. *The Journal of Higher Education,* 53, 268–281.

Chapter 10. Supervisors' activities in supporting PhD students in the supervisory process

Liina Lepp, Mari Karm, Marvi Remmik

Introduction

The content of doctoral studies as well as the requirements for doctoral theses have both changed as a result of reforms in higher education over the past few decades. Acker, Hill and Black (1994), Kyvik and Tvede (1998), and Kehm (2007) point out that approaches to supervision are affected by a wide range of factors which may be specific not only to the individual supervisor-supervisee relationship, but also to the context within which the supervision takes place. On the one hand, the institutional requirements and the supervising practice of a specific faculty or speciality are the influencers; while on the other hand, the general requirements of doctoral study and the need for a maximum utilization of resources are important.

The higher education sector in Estonia has experienced major changes over the last 20 years. These changes have led to the need to review supervisory practices, because the changing external factors have led to the need to adapt on an individual level, to fit into the externally influenced activity pattern and into academic life. According to Pearson and Brew (2002) it is important that supervisors expand their repertoire of skills as educators and leaders.

In this article we analysed the supervising practice of supervisors of educational studies' PhD students. This qualitative, interview-based, study maps the supervising practice of thirteen supervisors of educational studies′ doctoral students in the context of the changes taking place in higher education in Estonia and we reviewed how the supervisors interpreted their and their supervisees' roles, duties and responsibilities during the doctoral studies process.

Literature review

Much of the current literature concentrates on identifying the functions that the effective supervisor needs to carry out (e.g. Pearson and Brew, 2002; Wisker, Robinson and Shacham, 2007). The capability of the supervisor is seen as a key factor in the success of candidates (e.g. Park, 2004). Supervisors' activities for supporting PhD students in the supervisory process have been covered less (Lee, 2008). Traditionally, supervising has been viewed on the basis of an apprenticeship model, which means that a faculty member supervises on a face-to-face basis (Walker et al., 2008).

Numerous studies have attempted to explain the supervising activity through supervisors orientations (e.g. Emilsson and Johnsson, 2007; Murphy, Bain and Conrad, 2007); concepts (e.g. Lee, 2008); approaches (e.g. Sinclair, 2004); dimensions (e.g. Vilkinas, 2002, 2008; Dietz, Jansen and Wadee, 2006) and constructs of supervisory practice (e.g. Pearson and Kayrooz, 2004).

Previous studies conceptualising supervising activities have viewed supervision through:

(1) the aim of supervisors' supervising activities where the focus is on the task-to-person continuum (e.g. Vilkinas, 2002, 2008; Murphy et al., 2007) or on teaching *versus* research (e.g. Connell, 1985);
(2) the nature of the supervisor's activity (e.g. Murphy et al., 2007);
(3) the extent of intervention by the supervisor (e.g. Sinclair, 2004).

Murphy et al. (2007) and Vilkinas (2002, 2008) find that supervision orientations can be characterised by two broad distinctions: task-focused or person-focused, and controlling or guiding beliefs. With task-focused beliefs supervision is concentrated on the immediate implementation of research tasks and skill development through those tasks. In the context of person-focused beliefs supervisors concentrate on developing the candidate as a researcher, and are concerned more broadly with the candidate's development as a person. Table 1 shows approaches to supervision in research conceptualising supervision.

Murphy et al. (2007) distinguish four supervision orientations: controlling and task-focused, controlling and person-focused, guiding and task-focused, and guiding and person-focused, and they find that there is a systematic tendency for controlling beliefs to be accompanied by beliefs that are task-focused, and for guiding beliefs to be accompanied by beliefs that are person-focused. Emilsson and Johnsson (2007) distinguish supervision, that also focuses on tasks that are undertaken together with the PhD candidate, comprising identified problems to be solved (problem-oriented supervision), and supervision, where the relationship between the supervisor and the PhD student is central (process-oriented supervision).

In describing supervisors' activities and behaviours Burns, Lamm, and Lewis (1999), Pearson and Kayrooz (2004), and Lee (2008) also view supervision as characterised by task focused distinctions, and also introduce the dimension of becoming a member of the academic community. In terms of focus, divisions may be viewed as functional to relationship development (Lee, 2008), orientations from thesis to person (Burns et al., 1999), and expert coaching to mentoring (Pearson and Kayrooz, 2004), but in additional, supervising activity that focuses on the supervisee adapting to academic life and developing reflective thinking, and facilitating the candidature and supporting reflective practice in general, are also brought forth. In addition, the aspect of sponsoring in supervision is separately introduced.

Burns et al. (1999) argue that supervision orientation is presented as having three strands: focus on thesis, where the focus of the supervisor is on helping students produce their theses in an efficient and scholarly manner; professional orientation, where supervisors see the process as a kind of apprenticeship for induction into academic life; and person orientation, where the supervisors' focus is on the whole person, being sympathetic and supportive of the academic and non-academic aspects of students' lives.

In their studies, Pearson and Kayrooz (2004) and Lee (2008) broaden the meaning of supervision. Five concepts of supervision are identified by Lee (2008) when describing supervisory activities: functional, where the issue is one of project management and the supervisor's activity is to ensure rational progression through tasks in a negotiated order; enculturation, where the student is encouraged to become a member of the academic discipline community and the supervisor's activity is gatekeeping; critical thinking, where the student is encouraged to question and analyse their work and the supervisor's activity is evaluation; emancipation, where the student is encouraged to question and develop themselves and the supervisor's activities are mentoring and supporting; relationship development, where the student is enthused, inspired and cared for, and the supervisor's activities are supervising by experience and developing a relationship. In the view of Pearson and Kayrooz (2004) supervision is seen as: expert coaching (the supervisor provides expertise on the research topic, methodology, and in writing); sponsoring (they assist with access to resources); facilitating the candidature (they provide guidance in negotiating a programme of study); reflective practice (the supervisor models openness to new ideas and encourages critical discussion); mentoring (the supervisor supports the student's development of personal and career goals and links them to research, academic and professional networks).

In addition to these categories, Sinclair (2004) describes PhD supervision in terms of the frequency of supervisory contact on a 'hands off' to 'hands on' intervention continuum. The 'hands off' supervisors intervene minimally, and the 'hands on' supervisors and others regularly intervene. The 'hands on' approach involves strategies to help candidates overcome comparatively common problems through trust, and a consistent and viable relationship between the supervisor and candidate. Table 1 shows approaches to supervision in research conceptualising supervision.

Table 1. Approaches to supervision in research conceptualising supervision

Authors	Approaches to supervision
Murphy et al. (2007)	controlling beliefs / guiding beliefs task-focused beliefs / person-focused beliefs
Emilsson and Johnsson (2007)	problem-oriented supervision / process-oriented supervision focus on task / focus on interpersonal processes and relationship
Burns et al. (1999)	thesis orientation / professional orientation / person orientation
Lee (2008)	functional enculturation critical thinking emancipation relationship development
Pearson and Kayrooz (2004)	expert coaching sponsoring facilitating the candidature mentoring reflective practice
Vilkinas (2002, 2008)	task focus / people focus
Sinclair (2004)	hands on approach / hands off approach

In the light of this range of approaches, this study examined the supervisory process focusing on supervising activities ranging from those with a functional, task oriented focus to relationship development, person- oriented and 'hands on-hands off' approaches. We looked at the strengths and weaknesses of the different approaches based on the data we collected.

The study

Context

Just as there have been dramatic changes in Estonian society since regaining independence in 1991, there have also been changes in the Estonian higher education system, including doctoral studies, which have undergone several reforms. The first Statute of Research Degrees in Estonia was completed in 1990; this gave Estonian universities and research institutes the right to award

PhD degrees. The Candidate of Science degree of the former Soviet Union was equivalent to a PhD.

The system of having three levels of degrees in university education was established in 1999. After the completion of a four-year bachelor's programme and two years at master's level, a doctoral study, lasting four years, would lead to a PhD. The next big change took place in 2002 when Estonia adopted a new system of higher education as a result of the Bologna reform. The new system consisted of 3-year bachelor degrees and 2-year masters degrees. The doctoral level degree remained the only research degree and 4-years of bachelor's level study was equivalent to master's level.

The reforms in higher education created a situation where the level of academic preparation was not the same for all doctoral study entrants. Those who can currently study at the doctoral level are: (1) people who have undertaken a 4-year bachelor and 2-year research master's degree; (2) graduates from 5-year university courses who received a diploma (until 1991); (3) starting from 2002, people with a 3-year bachelor and 2-year master's degree; and (4) people with a 4-year bachelor's degree. Since doctoral students' previous learning and research experiences may vary to a great extent, different amounts of preparation must be taken into account when preparing programmes as well as when supervising the doctoral students. Current doctoral studies in Estonia consist of compulsory and optional subjects (60 ECTS) and research (180 ECTS).

In addition to the changes in the entrants' academic preparation, the small number of doctoral students researching education in Estonia is concentrated in two universities – the University of Tartu and Tallinn University. As the financial remuneration of doctoral fellowships is small and only available to doctoral students studying on state-commissioned student places, many education doctoral students work full time and, as a result, little time is left for their doctoral studies. In the cases of doctoral students working as lecturers at the universities, supervisory relationships often become entwined with colleague and employer-employee relationships.

Although, according to the Statutes of Academic Degrees, in both of the universities offering doctoral studies, a doctoral thesis can be defended as a series of publications or as a monograph, the general tendency in the field of education in recent years has moved from monographs towards writing articles. For example, of the 13 doctoral theses defended at the University of Tartu Institute of Education between 2003 and 2011, the initial four were monographs and nine of the remaining were article-based doctoral theses.

Through this study we analysed the supervising practice of supervisors of educational studies' PhD students in the context of the changes taking place in higher education in Estonia. The reason that the study focused on these supervisors, is that, in Estonia most of the education studies PhD students exceed the nominal period of study and also that the dropout rate is high.

This paper will focus to the following questions:

(1) how do supervisors describe their supervisory process?

(2) during the doctoral studies process how do supervisors interpret their roles, duties and responsibilities and those of their supervisees?

Method

The sample. The participants (henceforth interviewees) in the study were all educational sciences PhD supervisors (n=13), 5 men and 8 women comprising 6 professors, 3 assistant professors and 4 lecturers. The interviewees worked at either University of Tartu (8) or Tallinn University (5), and were supervising a total of 59 doctoral students. Seven of the interviewees had experience of supervising doctoral students with an aggregate of 20 PhD graduates.

Data collection and procedure. Data was collected using semi-structured, in-depth interviews (Kvale, 1996). The interview method was chosen because it is an efficient way of gathering detail rich data and it is flexible, enabling information to be collected on topics that come to the fore during the interviews (Lindlof and Taylor, 2002; Cohen, Manion and Morrison, 2007). Also interviews gave the interviewees the opportunity for self-reflection as they described their actions and beliefs (Murphy et al., 2007), and this opportunity for the participants to reflect added value to the study.

Each interview was conducted in the participant's office or in a place chosen by the interviewee; took an average of 1.5 hours and consisted of three sets of topics: (1) a description of the supervisor's supervision activities; (2) the supervisor's beliefs and notions about doctoral studies and about supervising PhD students; (3) how the supervisor's own experience with PhD studies had influenced their supervisory practices. This article is part of a larger study and it focuses mostly on describing and analysing supervisors' supervision activities. The supervisors were asked to describe their regular supervision activities (e.g. How does contact with the potential supervisee begin?; Please describe your usual supervisory activities?; How does your activity or communication with the supervisee change over the course of the supervisory process?). These initial questions were followed by additional specific questions about the supervisor's role.

The participants and people named in the interviews were given pseudonyms from the beginning of the transcription process, in order to protect their identities. Ethical aspects relating to the study were discussed with the members of our research workgroup. The supervisors participated in the study voluntarily.

Data analysis. The analysis of the data was undertaken using thematic analysis, and consisted of discovering themes and subthemes, deciding which themes were important in this research, and building hierarchies of themes (Huberman and Miles, 2002; Ryan and Bernard, 2003). The analysis took place in several stages, allowing for increasing levels of information extraction.

The process of identifying themes began with transcribing the tapes and continued with proof reading the material several times. Each author identified all the excerpts that related to the identified themes by repeatedly reading the transcriptions and listing the themes and excerpts in a table.Finally, a brief profile was written about each doctoral supervisor based on the information in the table, in order to get complete and compact descriptions and also preserve and highlight the uniqueness of the individual.

For coding, two researchers coded the data manually and one researcher used the computer software program Atlas.ti. We discovered that using different tools did not reveal any significant differences in coding but some of the differences that did occur gave the researchers opportunities for discussion, resulting in more considered thought about the coding principles. The researchers were aware that theme identification and coding does not produce a unique solution; however the collective judgement of the researchers increased the validity of the concepts.

Next, the findings of the study that focused on describing the supervisors' supervising activities and possible interpretations were presented. The findings were grouped by the topics that were based on the themes identified in the data analysis. As far as the results are concerned, it must be pointed out that they are made up of the supervisors' descriptions of current circumstances.

Results

Selecting and allocating supervisors

Supervisors of PhD students participating in the research described the procedure of finding PhD students in three possible ways: (1) the PhD student is allocated to a supervisor by the management; (2) the student comes to the supervisor with a selected topic or because they want that specific person to supervise their work; (3) the supervisor invites the PhD student. At this stage it was not clear that anyone of these three procedures was more common than the other two.

In the selection and allocation of a supervisor to a PhD student by the management the main reasons mentioned were strategic, including that the supervisor's qualifications met the required standard and the limited number of appropriate supervisors with expertise in very specific subject areas. The interviewees pointed out that the PhD student's theme may not necessarily always correspond to the supervisor's research interests.

> It seems that I am the weakest link accepting anyone rejected by others or accepting students who have received the answer that it is not in the corresponding field of expertise. (Vambola)

On the basis of the interviewees' responses, the second option within this theme appeared to be that the potential PhD student comes with their chosen topic to a supervisor or wants a certain supervisor to supervise their work. The interviewees described the process from the point of view of the PhD student, bringing out the following aspects: that they had had personal contact with the student during previous levels of study; via personal acquaintances (in several cases colleagues who were taking up doctoral studies); based on the research published by the supervisor; and/or on the basis of someone's recommendation.

The majority of the interviewees pointed out the relevance of the subject focus of the future doctoral thesis being within the supervisor's overall research area. On the other hand, the interviewees agreed to supervise research themes that were outside their research area because they felt flattered that they were 'selected' or because they were not yet able to assess their supervisory abilities.

In the majority of cases, the interviewees pointed out that being familiar with the supervisee from former studies was regarded a positive factor. If a supervisor receives an application for supervision from a student they do not know, the interviewees said that they researched the person's background.

> I always study the background. It is reasonable to supervise so that the thesis are finished and defended, I always ask if the person speaks English/…/sometimes I want to have a look at the Master's thesis in order to get some idea of the work. The theme should also be interesting to me; I am not interested in being a supervisor just for the sake of it. (Uno)

The third clearly distinguished option was that the supervisor invited the student to undertake doctoral studies. In this case the potential PhD students were invited to work on a certain theme or the student's potential for doctoral studies was noticed and the theme was determined later. One of the advantages of such an invitation was that it was based on earlier personal cooperation with this person, which had led to mutual confidence in each other.

The interviewees appeared to prefer to take doctoral students on to their research projects, and thus into subject areas that they research themselves. This seemed to enable them to meet the expectation to increase the level of doctoral studies accomplished within the nominal time.

> I said that I would not accept anything else at the moment, and would become more modern and take only themes which I research myself. (Lembit)

At the same time some of the interviewees expressed doubts about accepting supervisees on major projects because there are many minor research areas still to investigate. However, the interviewees did point out that several people can write doctoral theses based on one project, ensuring that the area is thoroughly researched, and also guaranteeing the training of 'successors'. One interviewee expressed doubt with regard to taking on supervisees in very closely connected research themes because the supervisees might become competitors in the labour market. Only a few interviewees said that they had recommended a candidate to choose another supervisor or to undertake some more courses before starting their doctoral studies.

In the case of the interviewees, the functional concept of supervision (Lee, 2008) may be observed because the supervisor's goal is the best possible rational progression towards completing the task. Supervisors choose supervisees mainly as a result of the academic match between the PhD student's research topic, the supervisor's research projects, and the supervisor's expertise. Ives and Rowley (2005) report that students who felt involved in supervisory selection and whose topics matched the supervisors' expertise, and who developed good interpersonal working relationships, were more satisfied and more likely to make good progress.

If a supervisee applied to a supervisor or the supervisor was found via personal relations (e.g. experience with earlier supervising), the interviewees explained that they made their supervisory decisions based on the supervisee's research potential and their ability to perform in a functional way. Functional supervising and general focus on task was also apparent in the cases of interviewees who preferred to take on supervisees to certain themes. It is understandable that in the selection phase, the supervisor focuses on the task because doctoral studies involve post-graduate training and have a certain time limit for graduation. However, it is not clear how functional the selection of doctoral candidates is in practice. The interviewees said that they examined the supervisees' backgrounds but they actually made the decision to supervise a candidate before considering, or despite of, the candidate's background. Therefore, finding a supervisor is not only based on functional factors but also on personal approaches. Supervisors performed functionally in theory when considering supervision, but in practice personal contacts, the capabilities and experiences of the supervisor and the supervisee, and the primary assessment of suitability were of most importance. At the same time the supervisor had to be sure of the supervisee's potential and be aware of the expectations of the PhD student.

Summarising the responses of the interviewees, concerning the selection of PhD students, they considered that supervising was more effective when the supervisor knew the student from an earlier period or the supervisor invited the student to undertake doctoral studies.

The beginning of the supervisory process

At the beginning of the supervisory process, supervisors generally assist in the planning phase of the research project and when prepearing the individual study plan. In the planning phase of the research project, the supervisors participating in the survey considered their tasks to be identifying the theme, explaining the general research design and assessing the research methodology.

With this supervisory approach, the beginning of the supervisory process is most clearly described as 'hands on' (Sinclair, 2004). Activities performed at the beginning of this process also most clearly reflect functional supervising (Lee, 2008), that is dealing actively with project management, the choice of the research methodology and guidance on reading. However, there is controversy about the functional approach at the beginning of the supervisory process, when the research project has been identified by the supervisor and the student just has to carry it out. Supervisors who provide students with ready-made methodologies, and supervise in functional ways (without encouraging emancipation, i.e the development of the student as an independent researcher), will be dissatisfied with themselves.

> The methodology and everything was already written and she/he just had to do it, but so-far she/he has not done anything. So she/he kept counting on that [...], that the grant team has to do it anyway and so she/he didn't bother to think what she/he should do, or about the methodology, and well then I found that I don't want to prepare the methodologies anymore, that they should know and understand what they do and how they do it. (Maria)

Developing the PhD student's individual plan includes discussing and recommending subjects, specifying the research methodology, and suggesting reading. There are research supervisors who do not interfere with the supervisee's choice of subjects and their proposed schedule; there are also those who discuss the selection of subjects, and when to undertake them, in detail. Supervisors are able to point out the importance of different subjects and their value in the PhD student's further development. Interviewees also point out that there are subjects that will not help to achieve a doctoral thesis.

The supervisors' teaching activities were discussed less and rather superficially (mainly as feedback to written materials). It was indicated that the role of the supervisor is not to assist the supervisee to interpret the information acquired during the doctoral studies programme or to help them with the implementation of the transferred skills during the development of a doctoral thesis. At the beginning of the supervisory process which topics and when to take them were discussed, but in the later phases, the students had to study and acquire the material on their own. The inadequacy of training in research methods in doctoral studies is discussed by Pearson and Brew (2002), who find that research education has become too narrow and concerned with producing research results at the risk of limiting the educational function.

At the beginning of the supervisory process a general decision is made on whether the PhD student writes the dissertation as a monograph or bases it on articles. The study enabled the differentiation of two distinct groups of supervisors. The first group considered that doctoral theses should be based on articles. Among this group were supervisors who started their supervisory practice by creating an overall picture, comprising certain articles and a survey article, and other supervisors who accepted that the supervisee would write articles, integrating them into one overview article at a later stage in their doctoral studies. The second group were more flexible and accepted both article-based and monograph-based doctoral theses. The representatives of this group included supervisors who had supervised theses of both kinds, but preferred monograph-based scientific work, considering it to give a broader picture of the student's knowledge of the subject area. The interviewees who preferred monographs had recognised the changing circumstances, and allowed the students to write an article-based work. The interviewees pointed out that when selecting either article-based or monograph-based work, they had to take into account the theme of the work, the student's preferences, writing skills and experience. In addition, the internal agreements within departments were relevant in the selection of the type of doctoral thesis as the academic degree statutes of the university may allow both kinds of doctoral thesis. However departmental resolutions may favour article-based theses.

> I have realised that writing a dissertation based on articles is much reasonable perhaps. Well, all our latest dissertations are moving in that direction. I have got a feeling that it has become also a prevailing trend on the international level in recent years [...] On one hand it is the same thing that you get the same publications and it provides confidence that it is accepted also/…/I have got a feeling that when writing a monograph you have to do everything two times. (Kristel)

The interviewees mainly encouraged students to write article-based papers, however, those who were in favour of writing monographs did allow the students to decide whether to write their research as articles or a monograph. The selection of the type of thesis depended largely on the objectives of the supervisory process and the general goals of doctoral study. When supervising article-based theses the focus is particularly on task and the objective is to defend the dissertation as soon as possible (functional supervision). At the same time, article-based dissertations support the process by which the supervisee acquires the traditions of the academic community, by writing and publishing articles in international journals and by becoming a member of the academic community (enculturation). Researchers have to publish articles in peer-reviewed journals and when working on an article-based thesis, this experience is being gained during the course of the doctoral study.

Common supervision process

The interviewees described a common supervision process of PhD students: individual or group meetings or communications by e-mail. Two kinds of supervision practices were described: (1) the supervisor convenes regular seminars or individual meetings, during which time the instruction of the supervisees takes place, feedback on the work they have undertaken is provided and further plans are specified, and (2) meetings initiated by the PhD students.

The majority of the interviewees who regularly met their students described the meetings as regularly convened seminars, taking place once or twice a month. Individual meetings with students were described as meetings generally initiated by the student. However, some interviewees liked to take the initiative and set the dates.

In the seminars the students made presentations based on their doctoral theses, irrespective of the form, and discussed issues relating to their research. Group seminars provide students with the chance to communicate with each other and generate a community of practice.

The interviewees who had regular meetings with students described the work phase that the students had reached more precisely, showing that frequent regular contact provides the supervisors with more information about the progress of the work. The interviewees who did not have regular meetings with their supervisees were vague and could give little information about their students' work and progress. The 'hands on' supervisory approach gives the supervisor the opportunity to be familiar with the research theme and assist and support the student in overcoming critical phases.

The descriptions of meetings initiated by the PhD students included face-to-face meetings and communications via e-mail. The aims of the meetings were mainly to assist the student to execute the current work phase – providing feedback and detailing new plans.

The content of the individual meetings was generally described as relating to the writing process, and the interviewees described their assistance in two different ways: (1) writing as equal partners (the article is divided and both the supervisor and the PhD student are responsible for writing their part, and the supervisor gives feedback and edits; (2) the PhD student writes and the supervisor's role is to give feedback and be the editor.

When analysing the interviews there was a lot of information about how the interviewees helped to compile the individual plans, assisted the students in choosing courses, or, alternatively, how they decided not to interfere in the selection of the courses. What happens later in the supervisory process was discussed much less in the interviews. This showed that students are often left on their own and are expected to take the initiative ('hands off' supervision); or it may be that the supervisors intentionally supported the students' development in becoming independent scholars, or that the supervisors themselves were not yet clear about what is required in supervision and did not want to talk about this. At the beginning of the functional, task-oriented and 'hands on' supervision process, there were numerous descriptions of how 'hands off' supervision takes over, which could explain the small number of thesis submissions. Lovitts (2005) finds that the a critical phase for any student is the transition from dependence to independence, during which PhD students move away from the structure provided by course schedules and enter into a self-directed study, although, according to Egan (1989) PhD students might not be ready for such freedom and independence.

The supervisor as the finder of resources and the supporter of becoming a member of the academic community

From the interviews we found that the general supervisory process consists of different activities, which support PhD students in writing their theses and becoming members of the academic community. Finding resources and becoming a member of the academic community are often described by interviewees as closely related activities.

By 'finding resources', the interviewees meant providing scholarships for the PhD students, resources for doctoral training and funding from different research grants. The interviewees pointed out that due to the relatively small scholarships available, PhD students cannot give up working and, as a result, they do not have enough time to write their doctoral theses. With respect to funding from other sources it was considered important that the supervisor could trust the PhD student and that the student was highly motivated. It was also considered important for PhD students to be able to attend conferences and work in libraries abroad during their studies. This can be achieved by applying for different funding or working on international projects. An ideal situation for a PhD student to achieve this would be as a research fellow working in a university or participating in a project which is directly related to the theme of their doctoral thesis.

> I think finding resources is my main task. One of my principles is that a PhD student must have a wide horizon, I try to find finances in order to be able to take them to conferences abroad, find foreign contacts. (Anne)

Finding resources, called 'sponsoring' by Pearson and Kayrooz (2004) is an area that supervisors consider to be part of their supervisory activity. Providing finances usually means helping to find funding for assignments abroad, although in some cases the description includes the options of finding a research project or job that would support the accomplishment of the PhD student's research work. In some cases the lack of resources (i.e. the amount of the PhD student's scholarship) is used to justify the reduced amount of supervision or the reduction in the number of tasks required of the student. The interviewees said that in these cases their attitude is one of understanding, and putting less pressure on the student to finish their thesis and keeping their distance. So, this dependence on resources was one of the reasons why the interviewees' earlier focus on task was transferred to a focus on the person, or why 'hands on' supervision was replaced by 'hands off' supervision.

> At the same time there's the problem with our young university teachers [...] he/she tells me, that it takes so much time to prepare (the subject) that no time left for doctoral things. I remember it well, when I was a young university teacher myself, it took me 2–3 years before the course more or less [...] started to take shape and during this time I couldn't do anything else. So that's the situation, and there's nothing I can do about it. He/she cannot concentrate on research [...] Tolerant attitude forms – what else can you expect from them. (Vambola)

The interviewees pointed out that among the activities that helped the PhD students to become full members of the academic community, were their contacts and participation in academic events with the PhD students. Conferences and training were attended together, and during these the supervisor introduced the supervisee to the academic community. Finding funding to work abroad for longer periods allows the students to only focus on their doctoral theses, the accomplishment of which would be hindered due to other obligations in Estonia. It was considered especially valuable for supervisors and supervisees to go to libraries and conferences together, because they can then discuss what they have read and heard, and also develop their interpersonal relationships.

In addition to finding resources and supporting the student in becoming a member of the academic community, the interviewees emphasised the necessity of supporting the development of the supervisees' community of practice. The interviewees mainly spoke about supporting students with other supervisees in seminars, which take place within the framework of the curriculum; during these the supervisees can present their research work and get feedback from their fellow students. There were some interviewees who considered it important that PhD students communicate with each other in a non-formal environment and support each other in the management of their academic life.

In Estonia, where the supervision of PhD theses in the area of education is concentrated into two universities, the supervisory process appears to be peculiar due to the fact that people often perform in different roles, and thus, the supervisory process may be complicated. The survey described several respondents-supervisors who regarded the supervisor-supervisee relationship differently (where the supervisee is considered as a colleague or even a friend) whereas for some interviewees the relationship when supervising would be one of teacher-student or employer-employee. In some cases close relationships at work or personal relationships were described as possibly hindering or complicating supervising.

The variety of different relationships may have an impact on the supervisory practice. The interviewees described how they have sometimes seen their PhD students being stressed by their work. In these circumstances they avoided causing additional tension and did not talk with their supervisee about their doctoral thesis, because maintaining the relationship was more important. This results in 'hands off' supervision, which could also be seen as avoiding or escaping supervision.

Preparation for the defence of doctoral theses

The interviewees considered that the final phase of the supervisory process was the preparation for the defence of doctoral theses. Before reaching the defence stage, the interviewees described their task, when in their or their supervisee's opinion the dissertation was ready for defence, as putting a stop to further requests for improvements before defence (from the supervisee), and encouraging the supervisee to submit the work. The interviewees who had previously supervised students until they were ready to defend their theses, summarised their pre-defence supervision as primarily comprising encouragement, providing moral support, discussion of the opponent's questions and questions that might be asked during the defence procedure.

If the interviewee allowed the student to work independently according to their own timetable in the earlier phases of their studies and expected initiative from the supervisee (the 'hands off' approach), then in the final work phase they checked the presentation and slideshow together, prepared possible answers to the opponents' questions, discussed the procedure and supported the PhD student morally. The final phase of a doctoral study consists of certain routines and activities and may be described as 'hands on' functional supervision.

Conclusions

As researchers, we understand that our research had limitations. The research outcomes may be influenced by the researchers' own experiences as PhD students or supervisors. We tried to minimize this during our discussions and to reach an understanding as far as coding and the presentation of results of the work were concerned. Despite these limitations, this research introduced important information about supervising practice in the supervisors of educational studies PhD students in the context of the changes taking place higher education in Estonia.

Overall, the activity of the interviewees (supervisors) was rather varied over the different phases of supervising practice. Both the 'hands on' and 'hands off' (Sinclair, 2004) approaches were used, and different combinations of functional approaches, enculturation, critical thinking, emancipation and relationship development concepts (Lee, 2008) were introduced. Focus on task, interpersonal processes and relationships (Emilsson and Johnsson, 2007) can all be observed.

The functional and focus on task approaches and 'hands on' supervising were mainly applied in the initial phase of the supervisory process. In some cases the interviewees focused on relationships (relational), but after the planning phase, they started to follow the functional style. In many cases, after the initial phase, the supervisory style may be described as avoiding or escaping supervision, when communication occurred only if initiated by the supervisee, irrespective of whether or not a confident relationship with the supervisor was established prior to this. In most cases the functional and 'hands on' approaches were applied again at the end of the supervisory process.

We found it natural that in the initial phase of the supervisory process, the supervisees needed clear instructions and during the process acquired more independence and became independent researchers. The conclusions drawn from the interviews showed that the transition from the functional style and 'hands on' supervision to giving independence to supervisees, happened sharply and without explanation. It is thus understandable that supervisees might have felt that they had been left on their own. Being independent should not mean that the students are left on their own, but it should be that the supervisees feel able to turn to their supervisors if problems occur. They should feel comfortable with the supervisor and that the supervisor is willing to help with the progress of the work at any time.

In the interviews with the supervisors the activities associated with critical thinking and the concept of emancipation were only slightly described. In order to support the supervisee, we propose that more of Lee's (2008) critical thinking and emancipation concepts should be applied, helping the PhD students to become educational scientists with the ability to think critically.

The interviewees expressed discontent at how the supervisees integrated knowledge from PhD courses into their own study. So, we also think it important that the pedagogical component of supervising practice should be considered, where, if necessary, the supervisor can be a teacher and help to transfer the knowledge obtained in different subjects into the context of the student's work.

We found that the supervisors should have more clearly established where the different approaches could have been used, which would have allowed them to analyse the suitability of their chosen approaches in specific contexts. Of course, there is not a single supervisory approach which will guarantee that all PhD students writing their doctoral theses in the area of education will: succeed in their studies within the required time; become independent researchers; acquire the ability to see and set problems; be original, independent, think critically, and develop theoretical concepts.

Further research is needed to study the supervising practice of PhD supervisors in other areas (e.g. science); the role of the supervisor's degree studies and the impact of previous supervision practice on the current supervising practice.

We believe that by undertaking research in the area of supervising, and providing supervisors with the opportunity to discuss their supervising practice, we can assist supervisors to learn lessons from their own supervisory practice and from others.

Acknowledgements

This study was supported by an Eduko grant from the European Union Social Fund.

References

Acker, S., Hill, T. and Black, E. (1994). Thesis supervision in the social sciences: Managed or negotiated? *Higher Education*, 28, 483–498.

Burns, R., Lamm, R. and Lewis, R. (1999). Orientations To Higher Degree Supervision: A Study Of Supervisors And Students In Education. In Holbrook, A. and Johnston, S. (Eds.), *Supervision of Postgraduate Research in Education.* Australia: Aare, 55–74.

Cohen L., Manion, L. and Morrison, K. (2007). *Research Methods in Education* (6. ed.). London: Routledge-Falmer.

Connell, R. W. (1985). How to supervise a PhD, *Vestes*, 2, 38–41.

Deitz, A. J., Jansen, J. D. and Wadee, A. A. (2006). *Effective PhD supervision and mentorship: a workbook based on experiences from South Africa and the Netherlands: South Africa-Netherlands Research Programme on Alternatives in Development (SANPAD).* Amsterdam: Rozenberg Publishers.

Egan, J. M. (1989). Graduate school and the self: A theoretical view of some negative effects of professional socialization. *Teaching Sociology,* 17, 200–208.

Emilsson, U. M. and Johnsson, E. (2007). Supervision of supervisors: on developing supervision in postgraduate education. *Higher Education Research & Development*, 26, 163–179.

Huberman, M. and Miles, M. B. (Eds.). (2002). *The qualitative researcher's companion: Classic and contemporary readings.* Beverly Hills, CA: Sage.

Ives, G. and Rowley, G. (2005). Supervisory selection or allocation or continuity of supervision: PhD students' progress and outcomes. *Studies in Higher Education*, 30, 535–555.

Kehm, B. M. (2007). Quo Vadis Doctoral Education? New European Approaches in the Context of Global Changes. *European Journal of Education*, 42, 307–319.

Kvale, S. (1996). *Interviews: An Introduction to Qualitative Research Interviewing.* London: Sage Publications.

Kyvik, S. and Tvede, O. (1998). The doctorate in Nordic countries. *Comparative Education*, 31, 9–25.

Lee, A. (2008). How are doctoral students supervised? Concepts of doctoral research supervision. *Studies in Higher Education*, 33, 267–281.

Lindlof, T. R. and Taylor, B. C. (2002). *Qualitative Communication Research Methods* (2. ed.). Thousand Oaks, CA: Sage.

Lovitts, B. E. (2005). Being a good course-taker is not enough: A theoretical perspective on the transition to independent research. *Studies in Higher Education*, 30, 137–154.

Murphy, N., Bain, J. B. and Conrad, L. (2007). Orientations to research higher degree supervision. *Higher Education*, 53, 209–234.

Park, C. (2004). The graduate teaching assistant (GTA): lessons from North American experience. *Teaching in Higher Education*, 9, 349–361.

Pearson, M. and Brew, A. (2002). Research Training and Supervision Development. *Studies in Higher Education*, 27, 135–150.

Pearson, M. and Kayrooz, C. (2004). Enabling critical reflection on research supervisory practice. *International Journal for Academic Development*, 9, 99–116.

Ryan, G. and Bernard, H. R. (2003). Techniques to identify themes. *Field Methods*, 15, 85–109.

Sinclair, M. (2004). *The Pedagogy of 'Good' PhD Supervision: A National Cross-Disciplinary Investigation of PhD Supervision*. Australia: Commonwealth of Australia.

Walker, G. E., Golde, C. M., Jones, L., Bueschel, A. C. and Hutchigs, P. (2008). *The formation of scholars: Rethinking doctoral education for the twenty first century.* San Francisco: Jossey-Bass.

Vilkinas, T. (2002). The PhD process: the supervisor as manager. *Education + Training*, 44, 129–137.

Vilkinas, T. (2008). An Exploratory Study of the Supervision of Ph.D./Research Students' Theses. *Innovative Higher Education*, 32, 297–311.

Wisker, G., Robinson, G. and Shacham, M. (2007). Postgraduate research success: communities of practice involving cohorts, guardian supervisors and online communities. *Innovations in Education and Teaching International,* 44, 301–320.

Chapter 11. Defining the determining element of content mastery as the key aspect in congruence between learning outcomes and assessment

Einike Pilli, Kätlin Vanari

Introduction

In recent years European higher education institutions have introduced outcome-based curricula, and the same has happened in Estonia. From the academic year 2008/2009, all higher education curricula have been expressed by the members of higher education institutions and employers on an outcome basis and the students' workload is measured by European Credit and Transfer Points (Standard of Higher Education, 2008). From the academic year 2010/2011, university lecturers have used a new system of assessment (Uniform Marking System on the Level of Higher Education, Complete with the Conditions of Issuing of a Diploma with Honours [Cum laude] 2009), which is also based on learning outcomes that are described in more detail in the assessment methods and criteria.

Every reform risks being perceived as a formality, not as an actual change in the mindset of all parties involved. The change is effective only if the intended learning outcomes and their assignments are aligned. Biggs (2003) and Biggs and Tang (2009) find that assessment has a backwash effect on students' learning and construction of knowledge. In order to determine the extent to which educational reform is successful in producing meaningful change in education practices, we conducted a study in 2010 to analyse the congruence of the assessments with the planned learning outcomes of two curricula of the Estonian Academy of Security Sciences (EASS). The study was carried out as a part of the Primus Programme (2008–2013), which aims to support the development of high quality higher education and increase the competitiveness of Estonian graduates.

Previous studies (Bers, Davis and Taylor, 2002; Prosser et al., 2005) notice some changes in the courses and in the written descriptions of those courses. The aim of this paper was to analyse the changes in the congruence of learning outcomes and assessment. Therefore, we used the congruence model, described in detail below, to analyse the differences in the assessments of the 2009/2010 and 2011/2012 school-year courses. We posed the following research questions:

- What are the changes in learning outcomes between the 2009/2010 and 2011/2012 school-year courses?
- What are the changes in assessments between the 2009/2010 and 2011/2012 school-year courses?
- What are the changes in the congruence of the learning outcomes and assessments with the determining element of content mastery, described in detail below?

The Concept of Constructive Alignment

Learning outcomes and assessment make it possible to design education systems that optimise the conditions for quality learning. A system where all aspects of teaching are tuned to support learning is called constructive alignment by Biggs (2003), who considers that constructive alignment represents a marriage between a constructivist understanding of the nature of learning and an aligned design for teaching. Learning outcomes, particularly the target verbs, are the objectives that students need to display. Therefore, teaching methods need to encourage and assessment tasks need to evaluate, in order to ascertain the extent to which the students have been successful in meeting their objectives.

Constructive alignment consists of two concepts of educational theory – the constructive aspect of learning and the alignment aspect of the educational process. The alignment aspect refers to what a lecturer does to create a learning environment that supports the learning activities appropriate to achieving the desired outcomes (Biggs, 2002). The alignment is based on the behaviourist idea of instructional alignment which ensures the precise match between what is taught, what is measured and what is intended to be learned (Jervis and Jervis, 2005). So, the idea of alignment is older than the Biggs' concept of constructive alignment. One of Tyler's (1949) basic principles of curriculum development was that of instructional alignment, which refers to the degree to which the curriculum across the grades builds and supports what is learned in earlier grades. In the 1960s the concept of alignment was used in several instructional design modules (for example *programmed instruction*, *criterion-referenced instruction*) (Cohen, 1987). The concept of alignment started from the focus on teaching and instruction.

In the 1990s, the concept of curricular alignment took a step further to 'look at the degree to which the expectations and assessments are in agreement and serve in conjunction with one another to guide the system toward students learning what they are expected to know and do' (Webb, 1997:7–25). This corresponded with other shifts towards the learner-centred approach in education.

Often its similarity with the behaviourist learning theory is used as an argument against outcome-based education. We point out and support Biggs' remark that when we refer to constructive alignment, the word 'constructive' refers to the constructive learning theory. Constructive alignment makes the shift from behaviourist pedagogy to constructivist via the statement of learning outcomes, in terms of the level of understanding, required of a student, rather than a list of topics to be covered (Biggs, 2003). The constructive aspect refers to what a learner does to construct meaning through relevant learning activities (Jackson, 2002). An aligned instructional system, resulting in aligned classroom instruction, should not only produce better results on aligned assessment methods, but also knowledge, application and skills that are more meaningful and valuable to society (Porter et al., 2007).

Nowadays alignment has many definitions. It refers to learning outcomes, activities and assessments that are mutually supportive of each other (Martone and Sireci, 2009). Curricular alignment describes a situation where students are assessed according to what is expected of them, as detailed in educational standards, as well as from what is taught. Alignment is a characteristic of the instructional system; it is a consistent message from all of the parts of the educational process (Martone and Sireci, 2009). By focusing on the match between the assessment task and what is intended to be taught, common methods emerge that are used for studying content validity.

Content validity refers to the degree to which a test appropriately represents the content domain it is intended to measure. There are at least four potential aspects of content validity – domain definition, domain representation, domain relevance, and appropriateness of the test construction process (Martone and Sireci, 2009). It is important to understand the fundamental aspects of validity. Validity refers to the appropriateness of the assessment method for a particular purpose. It requires multiple sources of evidence to evaluate the utility and appropriateness of a test for particular purpose. Validity is not a static event; it is a continuous process, to evaluate the validity of the assessment method (Sireci, 2007).

When lecturers implement outcome-based assessment, they have to ask themselves about the alignment of learning outcomes and assessment. The different approaches and aspects of constructive alignment outlined below help us to understand and analyse the educational process.

Methods of evaluating alignment

There are several methods of evaluating alignment (Martone and Sireci, 2009; Porter et al., 2007).

- the Webb (1997) methodology investigates the degree of alignment between assessments and educational standards. Four subcategories have been applied in exploring the objective match between the assessment and learning outcomes in educational standards: (a) categorical concurrence looks at the match between the broad content area in learning outcomes and the assessment method; (b) the depth of knowledge compares the cognitive level to what is expected and what is assessed; (c) the range of knowledge measures the number of learning outcomes that are covered by the assessment method (d) the balance of representation focuses on the learning outcomes assessed and then on the assessment methods compared to the number of learning outcomes.
- the Achieve methodology (Martone and Sireci, 2009) is applied in two stages. First an item-by-item analysis is undertaken to confirm that the assessment method is aligned with learning outcomes. The second stage is a holistic evaluation of the challenge that is described in the learning outcome and in the assessment method.
- the Porter methodology (Porter et al., 2007) consists of two components – a content map and a quantitative index of alignment. The content map is analogous to a topographical map in which the topics refer to north and south and cognitive demand to east and west. The quantitative index of alignment has two dimensions for describing the content: topics and categories of the cognitive demand.

There are a number of issues about alignment methodology. First, the methods described above are too complicated to be used by university lecturers. Most of the methods require experts to use them and involve complicated data analyses (Martone and Sireci, 2009). Second, the traditional methods of evaluating the alignment or content validity focus on knowledge. In knowledge based thinking about teaching and learning the main consideration is 'what kind of knowledge do we want students to acquire?' When we adopt an outcome approach we also have to consider questions like 'what do we want students to be able to do with the knowledge they acquire?' and 'how do we help them to use it?' Third, several methods use the lecturers' self-reports and there might be problems collecting data from them (i.e. the lecturers may not complete the reports) or they might not provide accurate data (Potter et al., 2007).

The Congruence Model of Learning Outcomes and Assessment

In order to better understand the relationship between learning outcomes and assessment we suggested an alternative model, which used a third variable in addition to learning outcomes and assessment, that is, the determining element of content mastery (Pilli and Vanari, 2012). The introduction of such a 'third variable' is also used in other studies (Feldman, 2007). The determining element of content mastery is the most important knowledge, skill or attitude or a combination of these, that effectively summarises the whole content of the learning unit (course, module or curriculum). The determining element is not written down in learning outcomes, but it describes the whole learning unit and it is the main target or goal that the lecturer wants the students to achieve in the subject area. This means that the lecturer has to select particular knowledge or skills without which the students will not pass the course.

Considering assessment as one component of the model, it is important to review the principles that have been agreed in outcome-based assessment in the Estonian university education context. In Estonian university-level curricula learning outcomes are stated at the minimum or threshold level and all of these need to be achieved. The verbs described in learning outcomes need to be assessed via valid assessment methods, which means, for example, that practical skills cannot be assessed only by writing about the skill. It is also important that the assessment criteria fit the level of learning outcomes.

These three variables – learning outcomes, assessment, and the determining element of content mastery – are presented in a triangular model, which we call the Congruence Model of Learning Outcomes and Assessment (Pilli and Vanari, 2012) (Figure 1).

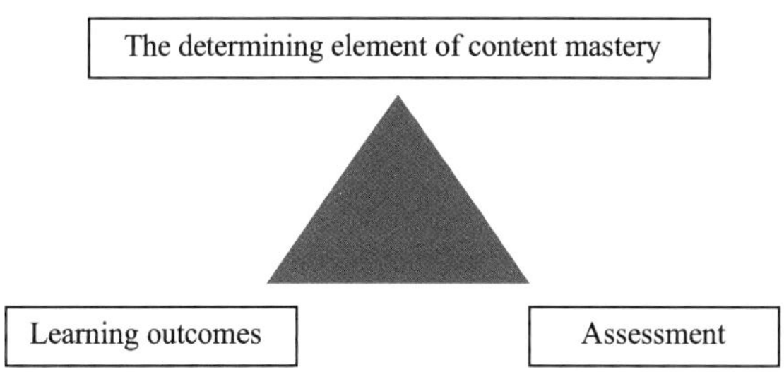

Figure 1. The congruence model of learning outcomes and assessment

Source: Pilli and Vanari, 2012

The basic components of a course are aligned if the determining element of content mastery is well matched with both the learning outcomes and the assessment. In the case of congruent learning outcomes and assessments, the lecturer has clearly stated the determining element of content mastery in the learning outcomes and this is assessed by the lecturer. The lecturer formulates the assessment criteria in such a way that it is not possible for students to pass a course without achieving the determining element of content mastery. Ideally, the assessment of the determining element of content mastery also makes up the highest percentage of the final mark in any course.

Our previous study (Pilli and Vanari, 2012) found signs of partial incongruence between learning outcomes and how lecturers assessed student learning in their courses. However, we also found partial alignment of the determining element of content mastery, learning outcomes and the assessments. Comparing learning outcomes with the determining element of content mastery showed that the learning outcomes in the syllabuses were more idealistic and less focused than the determining element of content mastery that the lecturers identified in their interviews. When comparing assessment with the determining element of content mastery, we discovered a lack of congruence in how lecturers determined students' final grades. Another problem with alignment was that the determining element of content mastery was often mentioned as a practical skill, while the main target of assessment was theoretical knowledge.

Implementing outcome-based curricula is an on-going process. Previous studies show that lecturers' understanding of the course content changes as the courses take place (Prosser et al., 2005) and over the years the lecturers change the syllabuses. Bers, Davis and Taylor (2002) find that when the content of syllabuses was first analysed, there was no clear information about the types of tests, definitions of class participation, the components of final grades or their weights in the final grade calculations. By the second period of content analysis of the syllabuses the lecturers had given more specific information about some aspects of assessment.

Methodology

The study was conducted using case-studies. It is appropriate to use case studies when investigating things that are hard to distinguish from the context and different types of sources are needed to analyse the facts (Laherand, 20008; Punch, 2009). The EASS was used as the case study as it was one of the first Estonian universities to redesign its curricula to an outcome basis. In the first phase of the case study we used two methods: content analysis of syllabuses, and interviews with the lecturers. In 2009/2010, we analysed the course syllabuses and interviewed lecturers from nine courses in the Police and Border Guard Service. During the content analysis, we coded and categorised the learning outcomes, assessment methods and criteria, based on theoretical starting points (Biggs and Tang 2008; Muldoon and Lee, 2007).

The questionnaire we used for the interview consisted of three parts: (a) the lecturer's explanation of the course and its determining element of content mastery, (b) the lecturer's explanation of the course assessment, and (c) the lecturer's general understanding of assessment. Our focus was on how the lecturer talks about their experience during the course. This was the second order analysis of how the lecturers describe their courses (Prosser et al., 2005).

In 2011/2012 we re-analysed four Police and Border Guard Service courses and we added five new courses from the Correction curriculum into the content analysis in order to exclude the possible impact of lecturers who had participated in the first phase interviews. The content analysis of syllabuses used the same codes and categories as before, but the questionnaire was simplified and focused only on the determining element of content mastery and its appearance in the assessment.

The collection and analyses of the data took place during the winter of 2011/2012. The lecturers from the first phase interviews expressed the stability of the idea of the determining element of content mastery. So, if they knew about the determining element of content mastery from the first phase of the research in 2010, we did not ask about it again. However, if the lecturers had not been interviewed before, we asked them three questions. One was about the determining element of content mastery, the second was about how the determining element of content mastery was presented in the assessment, and in the third question we asked if they would change the learning outcomes or assessment of their course, and if so, how. The lecturers answered these questions by e-mail.

For the purposes of the analyses we created spreadsheets with different elements: learning outcomes 2009/2010, learning outcomes 2011/2012, the determining element of content mastery, assessment 2009/2010 and assessment 2011/2012. Each course or case had a separate spreadsheet. On these sheets we wrote down the main aspects of the analyses as follows: alignment of the determining element of content mastery and 2009/2010 learning outcomes, alignment of the determining element of content mastery and 2011/2012 learning outcomes, alignment of 2009/2010 learning outcomes and assessment, alignment of 2011/2012 learning outcomes and assessment, changes in learning outcomes (comparison between 2009/2010 and 2011/2012), and changes in assessment (comparison between 2009/2010 and 2011/2012). Thus our two main focuses of interest were the alignment of the three elements of the congruence theory and how this had changed over the two years studied.

Results and discussion

Changes in the learning outcomes between the 2009/2010 and 2011/2012 school-year courses

There were three different types of changes in the learning outcomes.

- The number of learning outcomes had decreased. This had happened in four of the nine cases. In most cases the change had happened at the expense of generic outcomes and the general overview of the area. In some cases (Police Ethics) there were no longer learning outcomes like '*acknowledges the core values of organization*' or '*is able to communicate ethical values*'.
- The analysis supported the conclusion that changes in learning outcomes had happened as more attention was paid to assessment. For example, in the subject 'Surveillance Activities in Prison' the number of learning outcomes had reduced from nine to five. We compared assessment and learning outcomes in 2009/2010 and there were several learning outcomes, which were not assessed. However, there is almost perfect alignment between assessment in 2009/2010 and the changed learning outcomes in 2011/2012. So, the things which were not assessed have also disappeared from the learning outcomes.
- The level of learning outcomes had become more realistic. In several cases learning outcomes were more realistic in 2011/2012 than in 2009/2010. For example, in the case of 'Surveillance Activities in Prison' '*is able to solve different conflict situations with prisoners*' was no longer a learning outcome because it was too high a level of achievement. In another case 'Introduction to State and Public Administration' the earlier version (2009/2010) required the ability to '*explain and analyse the developmental periods and trends in Estonian public administration*', while the later version (2011/2012) described the expectation '*to explain the principles of how public administration operates, including the main factors and structures of Estonian public administration*'. The change was that the learning outcome had a more specific focus.
- In the case of 'Self defence' the person was expected to use arresting manoeuvres both alone and together with another person in the earlier version of the learning outcomes, while in the later version the learner was only expected to demonstrate different manoeuvres of arresting. The learners were not expected to know how to ensure the safety of them-

selves and a companion in the case of an attack. What is not clear from the syllabus is why this change had taken place and if this aspect had also disappeared from the actual educational process.

- The number of learning outcomes had increased and they had become more detailed. This happened in only one of nine cases, 'Self defence'. In this case learning outcomes had become more like assessment criteria, describing the specific skills and tools that the learner was expected to use well.

In three of the subjects analysed the learning outcomes had stayed the same.

Changes in assessment between the 2009/2010 and 2011/2012 school-year courses

Some aspects had changed in the assessments in each of the subjects analysed. This was expected because the lecturers had had time to get used to the new system of assessment (Uniform Marking System on the Level of Higher Education, Complete with the Conditions of Issuing of a Diploma with Honours [Cum laude] 2009). One of the main changes in this new system was the disappearance of 100 per cent based assessment criteria and the introduction of predominantly qualitative assessment criteria, which were based on the learning outcomes.

Most of the cases showed an understanding of the outcome-based approach, that is, that all learning outcomes need to be achieved at some level. Several lecturers emphasised that all learning outcomes should be achieved. For example, the lecturer of 'Prison Law' wrote in the syllabus: '*In the final test learners must demonstrate that they have acquired all learning outcomes at least on the level of lowest positive mark (E). Even if the person has enough points for the positive summative mark, but lecturer doubts learner's knowledge or skills, this may result in negative result or much lower mark than the points indicate*'. Also, in the e-mail to us, the lecturer of 'Surveillance activities in the prison' wrote: '*Student will most probably not get positive result if she is so uncertain even in one of the themes that she does not demonstrate the activity at all or does it in such a way that it is dangerous to herself or to the jail*'.

There were signs that the lecturers had redesigned their assessment methods in ways that made it possible to assess achieving the learning outcome at the minimum level, as the Standard of Higher Education (2008) claims. The practice of using two parts in the final test – A and B, was interesting. In the subject 'Basics of records management and language of documents' learners have to answer all of the questions correctly in the A-part of the test to guarantee that they have achieved all of the learning outcomes at the basic level. After this basic level is guaranteed in part A, the B-part of the test determines the student's grade.

However, the ways in which the assessment criteria were presented in the syllabuses indicated that the lecturers were in a transitional phase, moving from one system to the other. This could be seen where criteria were presented twice, using qualitative and quantitative versions simultaneously. For example, even though marks were awarded through qualitative descriptions of the subject 'Basics of records management and language of documents', they were duplicated by a system of points – *test can give maximum 50 points, mark 'E' will be between 13–16 points, 'C' between 27–34 points and 'A' 43–50 points*. This seemed like a 'just in case' double system, because these points did not have any specific meaning over and above the qualitative descriptions.

The same double system was used to arrive at the final grade. For example, in the subject 'The use of criminalistic techniques and the conduct of forensic examinations in crime investigation' the final grade was reached via four different tests – the first accounted for 40 per cent of the total marks, the three others accounted for 20 per cent each. Another example was the 'Introduction to State and Public Administration' where six seminars accounted for 10 points of the total marks each and the final test accounted for 40 points. The minimum level for a positive grade in the test was 15 points. In neither of the cases was it explained how the final mark was arrived at from these points and grades, because the old percentage-system was no longer in use. In some cases the specific system of points finished with a general qualitative description from the new law about assessments, as mentioned earlier. In some of the subjects there were only qualitative criteria with no duplicating systems, which meant that new understanding had been gained.

One common change in several cases was that the number of assessment methods had slightly decreased. For example, in the 'Basics of records management and language of documents' there were two tests, while by 2011/2012 there was just one. In 'Surveillance activities in the prison' there used to be three different assessment methods, by 2011/2012 they had one big exam with two parts. In other cases the trend was in the opposite direction – some of the methods, which were described earlier as a precondition for taking the final test, had become assessment methods which influenced the final grade.

Despite the signs of still being in a transitional phase, all of the syllabuses had been improved in terms of their assessment criteria. Most of the criteria were described qualitatively, and they were not always sufficiently specific, and not every activity had its own criteria. For example, in the assessment criteria of the 'Surveillance activities in the prison' a person was expected to '*charge the metal detector*' or '*carry the radio transmitter properly with his uniform*'. In the

'Basics of records management and language of documents' a criterion for 'A' was described as follows '*Examples given are relevant and connected to the theoretical knowledge*'.

At the same time there were difficulties connecting the level of learning outcomes with the two lowest grades, D and E. The descriptions of 'D' and 'E' tended to be quite vague and in some courses did not appear to be at the level required by the learning outcomes. This was not the case with all of the subjects analysed; for example in 'Self defence' a criterion for 'E' was described as '*does manoeuvres of arresting in technically right way, but in slow speed*'. It was interesting that the levels of assessment criteria correlated well with learning outcomes if they were written into the syllabuses at the same time. This variation was caused by the syllabus form, where the assessment section was not very structured.

Most of the changes in assessment had occurred in assessment criteria, where there were improvements in terms of the readability of the descriptions, reflecting the growing ability of the lecturers to understand and use the technique of writing outcome-based syllabuses. This was also an important aspect of the study process and it will improve the transparency and coherence of syllabuses for students. If students understand what is expected of them, they will learn more effectively. The transformation to outcome-based curricula has required changes in assessment methods and in future it will be worth studying what influences lecturers to change their assessment methods.

There are two main conclusions to draw from this consideration of the changes in learning outcomes and assessment between the two periods (2009/2010 and 2011/2012). First, by applying the principles and practices of outcome-based curriculum reform, syllabuses have become increasingly aligned and their components have become more congruent with each other. Second, there were several signs of being in a transitional phase from one system to another, the most noticeable being the double-system assessment criteria, confusion with terminology and with the formulation of the final grade.

Changes in the congruence of learning outcomes and assessment with the determining element of content mastery

The changes in syllabuses have led to greater congruence between learning outcomes and assessment. Analysing the determining element of content mastery and its alignment with the two other components of the congruence model could give ideas for future changes towards a more aligned model.

In most of the cases there was good alignment between the three elements of the congruence model. For example, in the case of 'Introduction to State and Public Administration' the determining element of content mastery was stated as '*knowledge about Estonia as a state, its public administration and Estonian political system'*. Learning outcomes explain it more specifically, requiring that by the end of the course the learner is able to explain how the state, political system and public administration operate, using the example of Estonia.

The assessment consisted of 6 seminars (and the student had to write a report for each seminar) and an exam. The seminar topics covered all learning outcomes and the exam checked these once again. The assessment criteria at the 'E' level corresponded more or less with the learning outcomes. If assessment criteria were more content-oriented, the alignment would have been even more visible. In conclusion, we considered that 'Introduction to State and Public Administration' was a well aligned subject.

In the cases of practical or combined practical-theoretical subjects, the alignment between the three elements of the congruence model was not easy to achieve. The most typical deviation from the alignment between the determining element of content mastery and learning outcomes took place on the practical-theoretical continuum. In most cases lecturers mentioned practical skills as the determining element of content mastery in their subject. However, in several cases learning outcomes involved both practical skills and theoretical knowledge. This was not a very serious deviation as long as theoretical knowledge was considered as a mean to acquiring practical skills and the assessment concentrated mainly on practical skills.

Among the cases analysed practical skills were covered by the assessment methods, but often not as much as expected from the determining element of content mastery. For example in 'The use of criminalistic techniques and the conduct of forensic examinations in crime investigation' the lecturer defined the determining element of content mastery as '*they would use tools and techniques practically*', but the assessment methods were mainly written tests. These tests did involve some practical exercises, but the biggest part of the mark was awarded for theoretical knowledge.

In the case of 'Basics of records management and language of documents' the determining element involved both understanding the origin of the documents and the ability to compile them. However, 90 per cent of the final grade was awarded on theoretical knowledge and 10 per cent on practical skills. During the course there was plenty of practice in compiling documents, but the final grade was awarded mainly on the basis of theoretical knowledge.

The analysis of the alignment between the three elements of the congruence model was based on what was written on syllabuses and on the short questionnaire that the lecturers completed. As these sources were limited in their scope, it is possible that, in practice, there is more alignment than is written in the documents. If this is the case, the challenge is to align the documents and practice with each other.

Conclusions

Outcome-based assessment is an ideal way to ensure a precise match between what is taught, what is measured and what is intended to be learned. Previous attempts to apply an aligned system of outcomes, instruction and assessment contradicted the conventional expectation of a normal distribution of assessment results. That distribution requires either poorly taught content or assessments whose stimulus conditions differ from those taught in the instructional phase (Cohen, 1987). In Estonian higher education, which is outcome-based, assessment is criterion-referenced and therefore finding congruence between the learning outcomes, assessment, and the determining element of content mastery is possible.

In order to better understand the relationship between the learning outcomes and assessment we used the Congruence Model of Learning Outcomes and Assessment. In the model two basic components of the study process – learning outcomes and assessment – were expected to be aligned, if they are to be congruent with the third variable called the determining element of content mastery. The determining element of content mastery refers to the most important knowledge, skill or attitude or a combination of these, which effectively summarises the whole content of the learning unit. In addition, this element of the congruence model helps to ensure that assessment is holistic and that a student would not pass without central competence. In our previous studies (Pilli and Vanari, 2012) it has proved to be an effective model to evaluate the alignment and focus the analysis of the subject.

The analysis of case studies showed changes towards better aligned models, when comparing 2009/2010 and 2011/2012. In the later year, 2011/2012 most of the cases were closer to understanding outcome-based curricula. However, we still found some signs of transition, which included a double system in assessment criteria, limited alignment between the determining element of content mastery and assessment, and unclear expressions about how the final grade was calculated.

As the results of this study showed, there have been several positive changes towards outcome-based education, in learning outcomes, assessment and congruence with the determining element of content mastery, although there are still some signs of transition and confusion. In conclusion we can say that the time period studied was not long enough to observe the complete transformation of teaching and assessment.

Acknowledgements

The program is implemented by Archimedes Foundation and supported by the European Union, European Social Fund (the preparation of this article was supported by a Primus grant nr 30.3 -7.5/364 and co-financed by the European Union, European Social Fund).

References

Bers, T. H., Davis, B. D. and Taylor, B. (2000). The Use of Syllabi in Assessments: Unobstrusive Indicators and Tools for Faculty Development. *Assessment Update*, 12, 4–7.

Biggs, J. (2002). Aligning the curriculum to promote good learning. Paper presented in *Constructive Alignment in Action: Imaginative Curriculum Symposium.* LTSN Generic Centre.

Biggs, J. (2003). Aligning teaching and assessing to course objectives. In *Teaching and Learning in Higher Education: Nwe Trends and Innovations.* University of Aveiro, 1– 9.

Biggs, J. and Tang, C. (2008). *Õppimist väärtustav õpetamine kõrgkoolis*. [Teaching for Quality Learning at University] Tartu: Tartu Ülikooli Kirjastus.

Cohen, A. S. (1987). Instructional Alignment: Searching for a Magic Bullet. *Educational Researcher*, 16, 16–20. Available online: http://er.aera.net

Feldman, K. (2007). Identifying exemplary teachers and teaching: Evidence from student ratings. In Perry, R. P. and Smart, J. C. (Eds.), *The Scholarship of Teaching and Learning in Higher Education: An Evidence-Based Perspective*, Springer, 93–143.

Jackson, N. (2002). QAA: Champion for constructive alignment. In *Constructive Alignment in Action: Imaginative Curriculum Symposium*. Available online: http://www.heacademy.ac.uk/resources/detail/resource_database/id169_QAA_Champion_for_Constructive_Alignment

Jervis, L. M and Jervis, L. (2005). What is the Constructivism in Constructive Alignment. In *Bioscience Education,* 6. Available online: http://www.bioscience.heacademy.ac.uk/journal/vol6/Beej-6-5.aspx

Laherand, M. L. (2008). *Kvalitatiivne uurimisviis.* [The Qualitative Research]. Tallinn: Sulesepp.

Martone, A. and Sireci, S. G. (2009). Evaluating Alignment Between Curriculum, Assessment, and Instruction. *Review of Educational Research*, 79, 1332–1361.

Muldoon, N. and Lee, C. (2005) Formative and summative assessment and the notion of constructive alignment. In Frankland, S. (Ed.), *Enhancing teaching and learning through assessment.* Dordrecht, Netherlands: Springer, 98–108.

Pilli, E. and Vanari, K. (2010). Dokumendist teostuseni: väljundipõhise hindamise rakendumine politsei ja piirivalveteenistuse õppekavadel. [From document to practice: Application of Outcome-Based Assessment in the Curricula of Police and Border Guard Service]. *Sisekaitseakadeemia Toimetised*, 162–176.

Porter, A. C., Smithson, J., Blank, R. and Zeidner, T. (2007). Alignement as a Teacher Variable. *Applied Measurement in Education*, 20, 27–51.

Prosser, M., Martin, E., Trigwell, K., Ramsden, P. and Lueckenhausen, G. (2005). Academics' experience of understanding of their subject matter and the relationship of this to their experience of teaching and learning. *Instructional Science*, 33, 137–157.

Punch, K. F. (2009). Introduction to Research Methods in Education. Sage Publications. 169–209.

Robley, W., Whittle, S. and Murdoch-Eaton, D. (2005). Mapping generic skills curricula: outcomes and discussion. *Journal of Further and Higher Education*, 29, 321–330.

Sireci, S. G. (2007). On Validity Theory and Test Validation. *Educational Researcher*, 36, 477–481.

Tyler, R. W. (1949). *Basic principles of curriculum and instruction.* Chicago: University of Chicago Press.

Vanari, K. and Pilli, E. (2012). From Document to Practice: Application of Outcome-Based Assessment in the Curricula of Police and Border Guard Service. In Groccia, J. E., Alsudari, M. and Buskist, W. (Eds.) *The Handbook of College and University Teaching: Global Perspectives.* Sage Publications, 45–58.

Webb, N. L. (1997). *Criteria for alignment of expectations and assessments in mathematics and science education* (Research Monograph No. 6). Washington, DC: Council of Chief State School Officers.

Chapter 12.
The trends and problems of planning outcome-based courses in e-learning

Kairit Tammets, Kai Pata

Introduction

Recently, the systematic planning of courses with measurable learning outcomes has become the norm in Estonian higher education institutions (Standard of Higher Education, 2008). However, lecturers have faced difficulties in planning the complementary learning outcomes, activities and assessment methods for their courses. This paper analysed e-learning course planning practices, with the aim of identifying the critical issues and trends in Estonia. The goal was to propose course design solutions rooted in the actual e-learning practices of professionals. These designs might provide a framework for the teaching and assessment of all types of learning outcomes in e-courses carried out in personal learning environments as suggested by the Estonian Standard of Higher Education.

Kennedy, Hyland and Ryan (2006) report that, in June 1999, representatives of the Ministers of Education of 29 European countries convened in Bologna, Italy, to formulate the Bologna Declaration, which aimed at establishing a common European Higher Education Area (EHEA). The Bologna process spells out a number of 'action lines' in which learning outcomes should play an important role (Adam, 2006). One of the decisions was that education in higher education institutions throughout the EHEA should be based on the concept of learning outcomes, and that curricula should be redesigned to reflect this. O'Neil (1994) suggests that outcome-based education (OBE) is based on a simple principle which is that decisions about curriculum and instruction should be driven by the outcomes that students should display at the end of their educational experience. These outcomes would become the foundation for decisions about the curriculum, instruction, assessment, staff development and so on. The European Qualifications Framework (EQF) also promotes OBE. The EQF is an important European Union (EU) tool designed to transform higher education in Europe and to increase compatibility between different educational systems, and thus facilitate student and worker mobility across the EU. It is also believed that OBE can support a learner-centred approach to course and curriculum design, as the teacher's role becomes that of a team member who facilitates and instructs, instead of being an autonomous information deliverer in the classroom (Shipley, 1995).

There are a few concerns about OBE. Van der Horst and McDonald (1999) find that one of the problems lies in the teachers' ability to translate the imprecisely worded outcomes into their teaching and learning practice and thus the defined learning outcomes and real practice may be different. Some researchers (Schlafly, 1993; Van der Horst and McDonald, 1999) fear that learning outcomes do not focus sufficiently on knowledge and thus the goals of learning are no longer academic. Rothman (1993) points out that one of the concerns facing OBE is assessment – traditional assessment methods, like testing and quizzes, are no longer valid and new assessment methods need to be developed.

An important trend in higher education is the increasing use of e-learning courses ('The European Commision's Lifelong Learning Programme', 2009, 'National program of ICT in higher education Tiger University+', 2009–2012, 'Estonian strategy for e-learning in vocational and higher education', 2007–2012) with a focus on the application of learner-centred, open and personal learning environments. Personal learning environments are blogs, e-portfolios and other personalised social software that students may use for learning activities on e-courses. Using personal learning environments in formal and informal learning, as well as in their activities outside education, allows students to bring together the different contexts in which learning takes place, at home and in the workplace, as well as in education institutions (Attwell, 2010). Razavi and Iverson (2006) suggest that developing a personal learning environment should incorporate integrating weblogs, e-portfolios and social networking functionality, both for enhanced e-learning and knowledge management, and for developing communities of practice.

Estonian universities have been among the leaders in developing e-learning courses in personal learning environments. Design solutions for various learning environments of a distributed nature have been developed and empirically tested (Pata, 2009; Fiedler and Pata, 2009; Väljataga and Laanpere, 2010). In such learning environments students can participate in course activities with their own set of social media tools, such as blogs, social bookmarking and microblogging tools. Teaching in portfolio-based communities has been tested in higher education as another design solution for e-courses (Tammets, Pata and Laanpere, 2012). There are also lecturers who use personal learning components such as blogs and portfolios that are available in more traditional learning management systems (LMS) (e.g. in Moodle and IVA) for their e-course activities. As yet, little is known about how Estonian lecturers would realise outcome-based e-learning using personal learning environment components for planning the goals, carrying out learning activities and assessment. Also, information about the learning activities and assessment types that might be used for realising certain types of learning outcomes is limited (see Mödritscher, Spiel and García- Barrios, 2006; Conole, 2007).

When planning the learning outcomes for e-learning courses, the recommendations set out by the Standard of Higher Education (2008) should be followed and suitable learning activities and assessment types for these e-learning environments should be identified. In order to create the basis to support the outcome-based planning of e-learning, our qualitative study mapped the actual implementation practices and problems of outcome-based e-learning in Estonian higher education courses conducted in different learning environments. We also discussed how the activities in different personal learning environments could better support the learner-centred approach to learning. This article provided empirical evidence of the simultaneous use by higher education staff of certain Higher Education Standard learning outcomes, learning activities and assessment types on e-learning courses. As a result of this study we proposed design guidelines to better structure the process of planning learning activities and assessments in OBE e-learning courses that aim to support the learner-centred approach.

Theoretical background

Outcome-based education and the learner-centred approach to learning

James Towers (1996) claims that OBE is a learner-centred, results-oriented system founded on the belief that all individuals can learn. In addition, he lists the principles that are necessary for OBE to work. First, what the student has to learn must be clearly identified; second the student's progress is based on demonstrated achievement; third, multiple instruction and assessment strategies need to be available to meet the needs of each student, and finally, adequate time and assistance need to be available so that each student can reach their maximum potential. In addition to this, in 1997 the American Psychological Association (APA) launched Learner-Centred Principles that provide a framework for developing curricula that emphasise active and reflective learning. Amongst other aspects, the Principles emphasise the cognitive and meta-cognitive factors influencing learners, the intrinsic motivation to learn and the social influences on learning. Based on the OBE theoretical approaches and Learner-Centred Principles, learning and teaching should challenge learners, give learners control over the learning process and encourage them to work collaboratively.

However, implementing only OBE and Learner-Centred Principles does not make the learning process learner-centred, as actual learning activities and assessment methods need to be part of the process as well. In recent years there has been a lot of discussion about learner-centred teaching and its importance, but less attention has been paid to the question of which learning activities and assessment types would support learner-centred teaching. Studies such as Duffy and Cunningham (1996), Amin and Khoo (2003), Dupin-Bryant (2004) and Billings and Kowalski (2005) emphasise that a learner-centred approach gives students opportunities to improve their analytical skills, problem solving skills, as well as their deep learning, lifelong learning, self-directed learning and knowledge construction skills, and that collaborative tasks increase the learner-centred approach. However, it is not widely known whether or not academic staff really uses these types of tasks. Liu, Xiaomei and Yingliang (2005) indicate that the dominant teaching style in the university that they studied was teacher-centred. Conti (2004) claims that the teacher-centred style is currently the dominant approach throughout all levels of education in North America. The concern here might be that although educators perceive that they use a learner-centred approach to the learning process, they do not know exactly what it is and which learning activities and assessment methods support it. For example, Pedersen and Liu (2003) indicate that the teachers that they studied did not have a common definition of student-centred learning, although they had previously claimed to be familiar with the term. Some of them thought that any activity in which students are active and work with their classmates was student-centred. In the e-learning context, teachers may not be aware of the possibilities that LMS systems offer, and using a forum in a LMS might be sufficiently learner-centred for them. However, from the learner-centred perspective, e-learning technology can provide useful tools and the capacity for networked learning communities to expand and transform the ideas of learning and schooling in ways that produce healthy and productive lifelong learners (McCombs and Vakili, 2005).

Learning activities and assessment in e-learning courses

Mödritscher et al. (2006) claim that in the course design process the facilitator should first define what competences (or learning outcomes) the students are expected to achieve. In the next phase, it is important to decide to what extent and under what circumstances the students should master these competencies. Therefore, a teacher has to define learning objectives by following some kind of taxonomy, which the Standard of Higher Education in Estonia prescribes. Finally, Mödritscher et al. (2006) add that learning objectives that are defined by a teacher always have to be assessed and evaluated in some way – to grade the students and to improve the quality of the course for future sessions. Overall, they claim that it is recommended to determine the assessment method with respect to the priority of the learning objective.

Few studies have focused on investigating which learning activities and assessment types are efficient to use in the e-learning context, and particularly, what activities should be combined with which assessment types. McCombs and Vakili (2005) propose a learner-centred framework for e-learning. In this framework, they suggest, amongst other things, that providing a context and opportunities for networking and collaboration is important in e-learning, and that visualisation, simulation and modelling should also be part of the e-learning process. Students may globally assess and evaluate class discussions and share feedback with peers and the instructor, and they may create electronic portfolios and other authentic assessments, such as student self-evaluations. However, this framework does not focus on learning activities and assessment types together – how should the teacher assess portfolios, which method is the best for assessing the use of simulations, whether the collaboration should also be assessed, and so on.

For the assessment of learning activities in e-courses, Mödritscher et al. (2006) propose that most e-learning systems offer the possibility to create and administer limited-choice questions. However, it is also necessary to use open-ended questions within e-learning, for instance, by means of tasks such as writing essays or submitting project work, although it is obvious that the evaluation of such tasks is time-consuming for a teacher. Another method is peer assessment which may achieve high-level objectives for all possible subject areas and provide other advantages, such as using natural language processing, reducing the effort for the teacher, etc. Anagnostopoulou et al. (2004) claim that good feedback in the e-learning context should encourage the students to reflect on their own work and work towards managing their own learning, and be motivated but not overwhelmed. Feedback should concentrate on the student's achievements, emphasising their strengths, and how they have improved, and give credit for what the student has learnt.

To fill this gap in knowledge, our study aimed the following:

- to identify the learning outcomes, activities and assessment methods that are commonly used by the lecturers in Estonian education e-learning courses;
- to clarify whether not lecturers plan the learning outcomes, activities and assessment methods in association with each other in e-learning courses;
- to propose, based on literature review and empirical data the combinations of learning outcomes, activities and assessment methods that might best support the development of learner-centred e-learning in personal learning environments.
-

Research methodology

Research design

Our study consisted of four phases: First we identified lecturers in the three largest Estonian universities who used e-learning in their teaching activities and also interviewed two lecturers from applied higher education institutions. In this phase, the e-learning centres of the educational institutions helped us to find lecturers who were giving e-learning courses and to access their course programmes. Secondly, we conducted interviews with the course instructors, to discuss their course programmes. Thirdly, we conducted a word-for-word transcription of the interviews. The fourth and last phase comprised the data analysis a variety of analytical methods. First, content analysis was used to code the written interview transcriptions with the categories of learning activities, assessment types and learning outcomes from the Standard of Higher Education; then Chi-square analysis and cross tabulation was conducted using SPSS.20 in order to find the frequency and co-existence of prescribed learning outcomes, assessment types and learning activities.

Sampling and data collection

We conducted 16 interviews with experienced academic staff from Tallinn University, Tallinn Technical University, the University of Tartu and two applied higher education institutions that actively use e-learning in their courses. Each interview lasted about an hour and was recorded. The interviews focused on the use of learning outcomes, activities and assessment types on the courses. During the interviews, the course programmes of each lecturer were discussed, and we tried to identify how they associated their course outcomes with those of the Standard of Higher Education, and how, and for what purposes, learning activities and assessments were actually conducted. Such an approach gave in-depth information that was not evident from the course programmes.

Out of 16 courses, 6 were conducted in the LMS Moodle, 4 in the LMS IVA, 4 in an open personal learning environment and 2 courses contained web-based tasks in a special learning system designed for practical assignments. The subjects of the courses were: a) politics; b) educational technology; c) educational sciences; d) interactive media; e) philosophy; f) mechanics; g) dentistry; h) languages; i) accountancy, and j) gardening.

Data analysis

Qualitative content analysis of the interviews was undertaken for each e-learning course to find: a) the learning outcome categories according to the Standard of Higher Education, Annex 1 (2008), b) learning activity categories and c) assessment type categories. The Estonian Standard of Higher Education was used in this study because all Estonian higher education curricula follow the principles and learning outcomes formulated in this standard. Generally it is applied in such a way that the curriculum boards develop the learning outcomes of the curricula based on the standard, and lecturers on each course then develop the course learning outcomes based on the curriculum. We wanted to emphasise the importance of using the Estonian Standard of Higher Education in the course design process.

The learning activity categories were based on two systems, defined by Conole (2007), and Laurillard and McAndrew (2003). Although Conole's system is thorough and widely known, it did not identify the learning categories of self-regulative learning, networking, evaluating, and designing one's own personal learning environment. Conole's categories are based on Laurillard's and McAndrew's taxonomy of learning activities, which contains the missing categories; therefore, these two taxonomies of learning activities were combined.

Table 1. *Explanation of categories and examples*

Category	Explanation	Example
Regulative	Designing learning environment, network /groups /communities, learning planning, learning contract, time planning	The student develops a personal learning environment from social software to actively participate in the course activities. The student defines 3-5 learning goals at the beginning of the course
Assimilative	Attending and understanding content, analysing, self-reflection	The student reads theoretical material and reflects in their blog how they understand the material
Information handling	Gathering and classifying resources or manipulating data	The student looks for additional learning material on the web, bookmarks and classifies them with tags
Communicative	Dialogue-related activities, e.g., pair dialogues or group-based discussion in forum, presentations	The students express their opinions about theoretical material in forum The students embed the slides that summarise their projects in their blogs.
Productive	Individual or collaborative construction of a piece of work such as a written essay, new chemical compound, or a sculpture	The student prepares the analysis of an article in the blog. In groups the students prepare reports about theoretical material
Experimental	Practicing skills in a particular context or undertaking an investigation	The student reads theoretical material and performs practical tasks

Table 1. Continued

Category	Explanation	Example
Evaluating	Self-evaluation, peer-evaluation, portfolio evaluation, test, completing exercises, drills, tutorials	The student reads theoretical material and undertakes the test The students evaluate the other students' work using video-clips, write an evaluation and upload it.
Supportive	Including peer-support	The students work in the online environment and support others by suggesting technologies, materials etc.

We used assessment types from Angelo and Cross (1993), because their approach for assessing learners seems to be learner-centred. They claim that teachers need a continuous flow of accurate information on student learning, instead of only the 'terminal' assessment that takes place at the end of the semester, which provides little feedback to assist the student in their learning. Angelo and Cross (1993) identify 50 classroom assessment techniques, and for our study we narrowed them down to four categories that match with the types of learning outcomes: a) content (has the learner acquired the theoretical knowledge?), b) skills (has the learner skills to perform a specific activity?), c) values (has the learner ethical understanding and values related to the subject area?), d) feedback (is the learner capable of providing feedback to peers, to the course and to evaluate himself?).

In the content analysis phase we also aimed to study the gaps in current practices, and therefore, we used the category 'missing' if the teacher did not specify the prescribed learning outcome from the Estonian Standard of Higher Education, or if the learning activity or assessment method was not specified by the teacher in the course programme for a particular outcome.

Two researchers categorised the interview data. Those categories that were categorised differently by the two researchers were discussed to achieve consensus. This kind of activity added to the reliability of the study. The frequency and co-existence of learning outcomes, activities and assessment types was studied using Chi square analysis and cross-tabulation.

Results

Which learning outcomes, learning activities and assessment types prescribed by the Standard of Higher Education are more frequently used on e-learning courses?

Our study indicated that none of the instructors on e-learning courses had used the learning outcomes prescribed by the Standard of Higher Education directly in their course design process. Two teachers said that the learning outcomes from the Standard of Higher Education are usually considered in the curriculum design process by the head of the curriculum. Once a year the curriculum board discusses the learning outcomes at the level of the curriculum, but never at the level of each course. One teacher indicated that the Standard document is too difficult to understand and, for example, in Finland the system is more flexible and outcomes are based on four types of activities: learner knows, learner knows how to do, learner understands, and learner synthesizes. Three teachers said that they had never heard of the Standard of Higher Education document and that they just did not have time to deal with comparing the actual course plans with the formal standard. Our conclusion was that the e-course instructors did not consider the prescribed learning outcomes from the Standard of Higher Education at the course-planning level.

During the interviews, the instructors were asked to map the learning outcomes from their course plans with the ones from the Standard of Higher Education. After mapping it was found that the most frequently used learning outcomes from the Standard of Higher Education focused on acquiring the subject knowledge and knowing (but not using) its application possibilities:

1. Student should have deep knowledge in some domain area – 9 per cent of all the learning outcomes;
2. Student should know the theoretical trends of the domain, actual problems and application possibilities – 8 per cent of all the learning outcomes;

It was found that lecturers do not emphasise developing self-directed learning competences as one of the goals of e-learning. *Self-analysis of learning* and *professional development* was seldom mentioned as a course outcome, although some course activities were supporting the development of such competences:

1. Student should continue learning and be involved in the research activities, act as a specialist of his own domain field (including internationally) – (1 per cent);

2. Student should evaluate himself and others' need for additional learning, professional development and to own needed methods for efficient learning – (1 per cent);

It appeared that 44 per cent of the learning activities and assessment type pairs (N_{total}=191) were not covered by any learning outcomes in the course plan. Many communicative (25 per cent) and evaluative (25 per cent) learning activities described in the course plans were not associated with the learning outcomes of the course. For those activities knowledge-based assessment prevailed. It seemed that when planning the courses, the course activities and assessment were more important to the lecturers than the learning outcomes. It may also be assumed that the lecturers actually had in mind developing the students' knowledge, their communication and evaluation skills, and their skills in using the knowledge in productive activities.

Based on the taxonomy of learning activity category systems defined by Conole (2007) and Laurillard and McAndrew (2003), our study identified the following eight most commonly used categories of learning activities (see Figure 1):

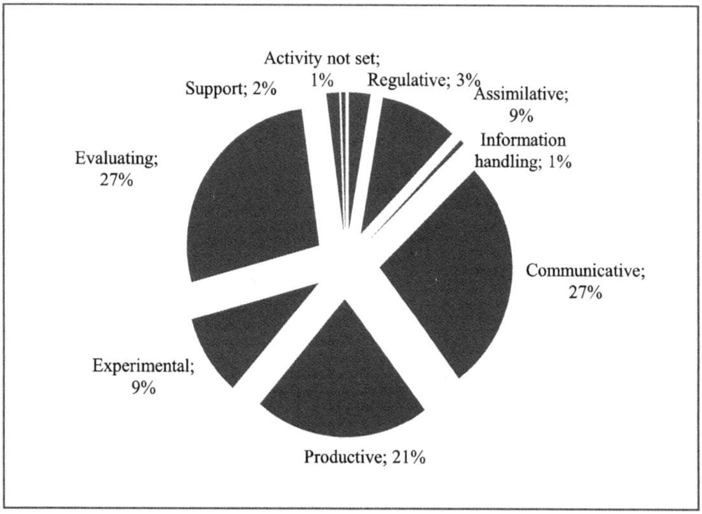

Figure 1. Learning activity categories based on taxonomies defined by Conole (2007) and Laurillard and McAndrew (2003)

- **Communicating** (dialogue-related activities, e.g., pair dialogues or group-based discussion, presentations) – 27 per cent of all the activities belonged to this group. The most frequently used activities in this category were a) forum discussion about the presented learning material, and b) discussing the problem in the forum and responding to the problems of peers. Sometimes the communicating activity included responding to the problems formulated by the teacher, and sometimes the students were supposed to find the problems by themselves. This category also contained discussions in Skype chat rooms about learning materials, problem-solving tasks in Skype chat rooms or in face-to-face meetings, group presentations of the collaborative tasks, seminar discussions and web-based seminars.

- **Evaluating** activity (self-evaluation, peer-evaluation, portfolio evaluation, tests, completing exercises, drills and tutorials) was mentioned almost as frequently as communicating activity – 27 per cent of all the activities belonged to this type. In this activity, in order to achieve the learning outcomes of the course, learners were supposed to perform a test in a LMS, but only in two cases did the learners have to evaluate the work of other students using video-clips, writing an evaluation and uploading it to the LMS. Peer-review or self-evaluation activities were not used.
- **Productive creation** (individual or collaborative construction of a piece of work, such as a written essay, new chemical compound or a sculpture) – 21 per cent of all the learning activities mentioned belonged to this category. Written group-analysis or term papers were mentioned the most frequently in this category (more than 2/3 of the cases). In some cases the learners were supposed to develop pieces of work, such as creating the learning object or learning material and presenting it in the LMS or weblog. Learners were also supposed to write an essay individually or analyse some learning material and upload it to the LMS.

The following learning activity categories were used infrequently:

- **Assimilative** (understanding content by reading and listening) – nine per cent of learning activities. In these activities learners were expected to analyse themselves or reflect about the learning material.
- **Experimental** (practicing skills in a particular context or undertaking an investigation) – nine per cent of learning activities. It was mainly the learners from technical subject areas who had to perform these activities. They were supposed to read the instructions and then perform practical tasks in a web-based learning environment or in a real life situation.
- **Regulative** (designing a learning environment, network/groups/ communities, learning how to plan, learning about contracts, time planning) – only three per cent of learning activities. The learners were supposed to

design their own learning environment, select suitable tools and resources for their learning process, and create groups with some technological tools.

- Note. Few learning activities focused on self-regulation, self-reflection and self-analysis. The teachers who used these elements used an open learning environment as well and expected that the learners would use personal weblogs. This suggested that using a learner-centred approach maybe more common amongst teachers who are comfortable using technology.
- **Support** (including peer-support) – was mentioned in two per cent of learning activities, and only in the context of one course where learners were supposed to support peers in the forum when they presented their individual assignments. The goal was not evaluating and assessing peers, but guiding and facilitating.
- **Information handling** (gathering and classifying resources or manipulating data) – one per cent of learning activities when learners had to find learning materials from the Web related with the subject.

The following learning activity categories were not mentioned in the e-course plans:

- **Adaptive** (use of modelling or simulation software).

For analysing the results of the assessment types, we used the taxonomy proposed by Angelo and Cross (1993) and added the category 'not evaluated' when the learning activity was not evaluated by the teacher. Using such a general category system for identifying assessment types was selected because the lecturers did not use the outcomes from the Standard of Higher Education for describing assessments in their e-courses. Yet, these assessment categories covered most of the learning outcome types. The most frequent assessment types were the following:

- **Content** category (assessing prior knowledge, recall and understanding; assessing skills in analysis and critical thinking; assessing skills in synthesis and creative thinking) – 57 per cent of the assessment types. The teachers assessed if the learners had achieved the theoretical knowledge via the tests or they evaluated the theoretical correctness of the essay.
- **Skills** category (assessing skills in application and performance; assessing course related learning and study skills, strategies and behaviours) – 17 per cent of the assessment types. The teachers assessed, for example, if learners knew how to collaboratively create a learning object. For the assessment it was not important that the learning object was theoretically informative, rather it was important that the learners knew how to create a piece of work collaboratively.

- **Feedback** category (assessing learners' reactions to the teacher and teaching; assessing learner reactions to class activities, assignments and materials) – 3 per cent of the assessment types. The teachers assessed if the learners performed peer-evaluation, self-evaluation, course evaluation and document evaluation.
- **Values** category (assessing students' awareness of their attitudes and values) – 10 per cent of the assessment types. Teachers assessed the learners' values about their own and their peers' projects, in terms of economic value, or the learners had to express their thoughts about the values in a forum. The value assessment did not depend on right or wrong answers, but it was important that the assignment was done.
- **Not evaluated** – 13 per cent of the learning activities were not evaluated by the teacher at all.

These results indicated that the main assessment type used on courses was the assessment of subject knowledge. Students' problem-solving and self-regulation competences were seldom assessed. The assessment of values and the ability to give feedback to the learning process were used even more rarely.

Which types of learning outcomes, activities and assessment types were frequently used together on e-learning courses?

With cross tabulation and Chi square analysis we found no statistically significant relationship between the co-use of certain course outcomes, learning activities and assessment types. Our study indicated that when planning e-courses, the instructors were rather lead by practical learning activities, which they associated with assessment, and the learning outcomes were considered more as formal elements of planning, in separation of activities and assessment (χ^2=68.697; df=56; p<0.114). To some extent, the learning outcomes were associated with particular learning activities (χ^2=140.259; df=112; p<0.036) and the learning activities and assessment types appeared to be significantly related to each other in their e-courses (χ^2=112.010; df=32, p<0.001). It was clear that in planning these e-learning courses, the instructors mainly harmonised activities with assessment.

There were some types of activities and assessment types that appeared together (see Figure 2).

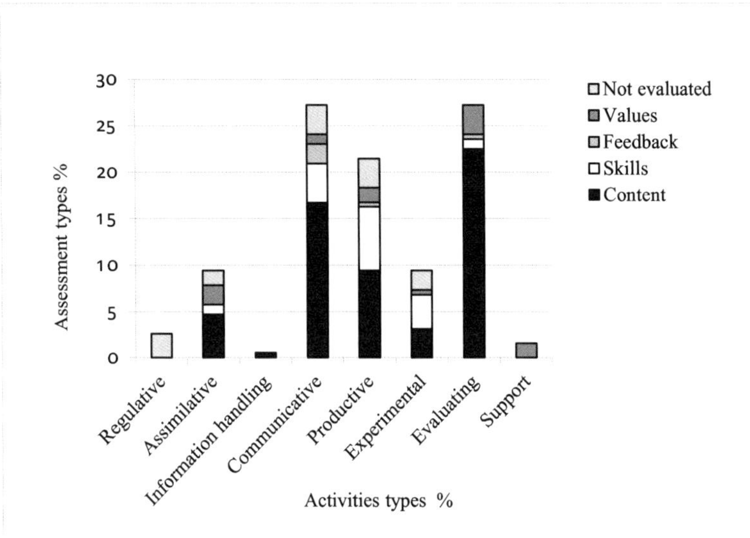

Figure 2. *Activity and assessment types used together on e-courses*

The study found that content assessment was most prevalent in the evaluative learning activities. Sometimes this meant that the learning activity was peer-evaluation, but in most cases it meant that learners were supposed to undertake an electronic test or self-control test in which prior knowledge, and the degree to which the learner had acquired the content of the learning materials, was assessed. Content knowledge was also assessed in the communicative learning activities. In these cases learners had to read the learning material and discuss it in the forum or at the discussion board. Learners could choose whether they set up a problem themselves based on the learning material or responded to some of their peers' problems, commenting on them and discussing them in relation to the theoretical material. The teacher assessed how the theoretical material had been understood based on the discussions. Knowing the content was also assessed in the productive learning activities where learners had individually or collaboratively created written pieces of work (essays, group works, and comparisons of some theoretical approaches).

Our study indicated that 13 per cent of the learning activities that were not evaluated were of a particular assessment type. For example, the information handling learning activity was only once assessed on the basis of knowing the subject. The learners were supposed to look at the Internet learning materials related to the subject and then the teacher assessed whether the learners could identify which were theoretically important. Although the learners were supposed to give feedback and assess each other on many courses, the evaluation activity was assessed only once in the feedback category. This indicated that the teachers did not assess the peer-to-peer feedback in the e-courses.

Regulative learning activities were not evaluated (although the significant relationship appeared between these categories). This indicated that the teachers were not consciously developing self-direction in these learning activities (e.g. learners were supposed to create their own learning environment, plan their learning, form groups and keep to the learning contracts).

Discussion

Based on our findings it is clear that teachers might need help in designing e-learning courses with a learner-centred approach. They need more guidance about the kind of learning activities and assessment types that might be combined to achieve the learning outcome types described in the Estonian Standard of Higher Education. Guidance is also needed on how to achieve and assess more than one learning outcome from the same learning activity. In Table 2 we suggest some example combinations of learning outcomes, activities and assessment types that teachers could use for designing student-centred e-learning courses with personal learning tools.

Table 2. Example combinations of learning outcomes, activities and assessment types for designing student-centred e-learning courses with personal learning tools

Learning activity example and activity type	**Learning outcomes from Estonian Standard of Higher Education**	**Assessment type**
The student (or group of students) solves a problem-based task (real or computer-based) by following the instructions given by the facilitator. The report about the problem-solving process, problem solution and its application possibilities is documented in the personal portfolio. **Assimilative, Experimental, Productive**	The student knows the theoretical trends of the subject area, the actual problems and application possibilities; The student has deep knowledge in some subject areas The student formulates problems related to the subject field and analyses and evaluates different solutions to the problem	The teacher assesses the problem solution (for example with Bloom's taxonomy) and the learner's skills at solving the problem (e.g. with general problem-solving and subject-specific skills). **Content, Skills**

Table 2.Continued

Learning activity example and activity type	Learning outcomes from Estonian Standard of Higher Education	Assessment type
The student reads the theoretical learning material and analyses it, synthesizes different concepts and reflects on the material in their personal portfolio. **Assimilative, productive**	The student has a systematic overview and broad knowledge about the subject area's concepts, theories and research methods The student knows the theoretical trends of the subject area, the actual problems and application possibilities The student recognises and creates interdisciplinary connections	From the portfolio the teacher assesses the level of conceptual knowledge (for example with Bloom's category system) **Content**
The students are responsible for teaching one module (conducting a web-based lecture, preparing learning materials and tasks or other activities). The students write a reflection with a self-evaluation of themselves as a teacher and they assess their peers' as teachers. **Regulative, Evaluation, Experimental, Productive**	The students should evaluate themselves and others' needs for additional learning, professional development and the methods they need for efficient learning The student should be competent in transferring the knowledge through teaching, guiding or in other ways	The teacher assesses how well the student taught others and how the students evaluated their peers as teachers **Skills, Evaluation**
Group work about a problem related to civil society and its values and ethical aspects. Collaboration may take place in a forum, google.docs or Skype and the results should be presented in portfolios. **Communicative, Productive**	The student is able to act in ethically different situations, acknowledge the ethical aspects, possibilities and restrictions of their behaviour and give justified opinions about their specialisation The student is ready to actively participate in civil society and pay respect to the diversity of attitudes and values The student has deep knowledge in some subject areas	The teacher assesses whether more than one subject-related value was covered **Values**

Table 2. Continued

Learning activity example and activity type	Learning outcomes from Estonian Standard of Higher Education	Assessment type
The student composes a concept map of the subject area containing two or three overarching interdisciplinary concepts and a variety of related subordinate elements associated with the larger concepts. **Assimilative**, **Productive**	The student has a systematic overview and broad knowledge about the subject area's concepts, theories and research methods The student recognises and creates interdisciplinary connections The student knows what methodologies and technologies are suitable for solving the problems of the subject area and also student evaluates the possible consequences of the problem	The teacher assesses the concept map for correctness, cross-branch connections and the student's ability to construct the knowledge of the problem subject map using the concept-map method **Content**, **Skills**
The student gathers, classifies (for example by tagging) and evaluates information about some subject area and then presents the results as an annotated collection of data. **Assimilative**, **Information handling**, **Productive**	The student has a deep knowledge in some subject areas The student recognises and creates interdisciplinary connections	The teacher assesses if the learner knows how to find and organise relevant subject area information **Content**, **Skills**

Although a test is an efficient way of measuring knowledge and provides the easiest way for a teacher to assess if a student has acquired the content of theoretical material, we tried to avoid using tests as a learning activity in our study, as Table 2 indicates. Tests and essays can be added to course design at any time, but we focused in this study on collaboration, problem-solving activities, synthesis of materials, self-reflection, evaluation and peer-evaluation activities in order to support a more learner-centred approach. These activities could be performed in closed and institution-centred learning management systems as well as in open learning environments.

Conclusion

The aim of this study was to map the current trends and problems of planning outcome-based courses in e-learning in the Estonian higher education context. We conducted a survey of 16 higher education staff in order to study the practices of designing e-learning in courses – is the Standard of Higher Education taken into account in the design process, what learning activities have been planned and how these activities have been assessed in outcome based courses. In the data analysis phase we focused on studying what learning outcomes, learning activities and assessment methods were mainly used, but we also studied the practice of using different types of learning activities and assessment types together. The main result of our study indicated that lecturers do not take the Standard of Higher Education into account in the course design process, and course planning is activity-assessment centred. This finding indicated that outcome based course planning, as described by Towers (1996), is not carried out in practice. It may be, as Van der Horst and McDonald (1999) find, that teachers cannot relate the too generally worded outcomes of the Standard of Higher Education with their teaching and learning practice. One reason why teachers focused mainly on planning the learning activities might be that the length of the course is too limited to conduct the many activities that meet the variety of learning outcomes. What the teachers did not do in our study, was couple the learning activity with the several learning outcomes that this activity was actually developing. Without clearly defining the different outcome types and taking examples from the Standard, the teachers were not able to design specific assessments. For example, the Standard contains several outcomes related to knowledge and its applications, but, in general, the knowledge was mainly assessed in the studied courses. Suggesting a variety of learning activity types that enable different learning outcomes to develop might help the instructors in planning the e-courses so that different outcomes are achieved.

Surprisingly, we found that in e-learning courses the main learning activity is taking a test in the LMS or communicating in a forum. This does not support a learner-centred approach to learning as proposed, for example, by McCombs and Vakili (2005) who suggest that e-learning should involve networking and collaboration, and also visualisations and simulations. For learner-centred learning it would be good to implement constructivist learning activities, such as essay writing and project work, which enable knowledge to be applied in a meaningful context. Our study also indicated that the main assessment method focused on assessing the acquisition of the content of the learning materials, and mainly using the tests that Mödritscher et al. (2006) describe. Feedback for students should also include more than the grade of the test; good feedback should encourage students to reflect, and evaluate themselves and their peers (Anagnostopoulou et al., 2004).

The results of the study are based on empirical data collected from 16 staff members from different universities, who had experience of using e-learning in their courses. However, this study sample does not allow general conclusions to be made on the whole population of Estonian e-learning teachers. Our study indicated that in order to design e-learning courses based on measurable learning outcomes, the academic staff would need support in order to be aware of and consider the different learning outcome types recommended in the Standard of Higher Education. A more intuitive way of planning a course would seem to be to first select the learning activities (as they may depend on the subject area practices) and next, identify all the outcomes that could be achieved with these activities using the Standard of Higher Education. The final step would be planning specific assessments for each learning outcome in this activity context. In this paper we proposed some examples, suitable for personal learning environments, of how coupling the learning activities with several learning outcomes and their assessment could be done. The results of our study will be used to design a framework system with examples, for teachers, to help them to plan outcome-based e-courses in personal learning environments.

Acknowledgements

This study was conducted in collaboration by MER targeted research 0130159s08 and funded by Primus project.

References

Adam, S. (2006). An introduction to learning outcomes. In Froment, E., Kohler, J., Purser, L. and Wilson, L. (Eds.), *EUA Bologna Handbook – Making Bologna Work*. Berlin: Raabe, 7–8.

American Psychological Association (APA). (1997). Learner-Centered Psychological Principles: A Framework for School Redesign and Reform. Available online: http://www.apa.org/ed/lcp.html

Amin, Z. and Khoo, H. E. (2003). *Basics in medical education.* Singapore: World Scientific Publishing.

Anagnostopoulou, K., Haynes, M., Bakry, W. and Jackson, B. (2004). *e-learning: A Tutor Guide*. London: MUPress.

Angelo, T. A. and Cross, K. P. (1993). *Classroom assessment techniques. A handbook for college teachers* (2nd ed.). San Francisco: Jossey-Bass Publishers.

Attwell, G. (2010). Supporting Personal Learning in the Workplace. The PLE Conference, ISSN 2077–9119. Available online: http://pleconference.citilab.eu

Billings, D. and Kowalski, K. (2005). Teaching for Higher Order Learning, *Journal of Continuing Education in Nursing*, 36, 244-245.

Conole, G. (2007). Describing learning activities: tools and resources to guide practice. In Beetham, H. and Sharpe, R. (Eds.), *Rethinking pedagogy for a digital age*. Oxford: RoutledgeFalmer, 81–91.

Conti, G. J. (2004). Identifying Your Teaching Style. In Galbraith, M. W. (Ed.), *Adult Learning Methods: A Guide for Effective Instruction.* Malabar: Krieger Publishing Company, 75–91.

Duffy, T. M. and Cunningham, D. J. (1996). Constructivism: Implications for the design and delivery of instruction. In Jonassen, D. H. (Ed.), *Handbook of research on educational communications and technology*. New York: Scholastic, 170–198.

Dupin-Bryant, P. A. (2004). Teaching Styles of Interactive Television Instructors: A Descriptive Study. *The American Journal of Distance Education*, 18, 39–50.

Estonian strategy for e-learning in vocational and higher education, 2007–2012.

European Commision's Lifelong Learning Programme, 2009. Available online: http://ec.europa.eu/education/llp/doc/call09/part2_en.pdf

Fiedler, S. and Pata, K. (2009). Distributed learning environments and social software: in search for a framework of design. In Hatzipanagos, S. and Warburton, S. (Eds.), *Handbook of Research on Social Software and Developing Community Ontologies*. Hershey, PA: IGI Global Information Science, 145–158.

Kennedy, D., Hyland, A. and Ryan, N. (2006). Writing and Using Learning Outcomes: A Practical Guide. In Froment, E., Kohler, J., Purser, L. and Wilson, L. (Eds.), *EUA Bologna Handbook – Making Bologna Work*. Berlin: Raabe, article C. 3. 4–1. Available online: http://www.bologna.msmt.cz/files/learning-outcomes.pdf

Laurillard, D. and McAndrew, P. (2003). Reusable educational software: a basis for generic learning activities. In Littlejohn, A. (Ed.), *Reusing Online Resources: A sustainable approach to e-learning*. London: Kogan Page, 81–93.

Liu, R. Xiaomei, Q. and Yingliang, L. (2005). A paradigm shift of learner-centered teaching style: reality or illusion? *Arizona working papers in SLAT*, 13, 77– 91.

McCombs, B. and Vakili, D. (2005). A learner-centered framework for e-learning. *Teachers College Record,* 107, 1582–1609.

Mödritscher, F., Spiel, S. and Garcia-Barrios, V. M. (2006). Assessment in E-Learning Environments: A Comparison of three Methods. In Crawford, C., Carlsen, R., McFerrin, K., Price, J., Weber, R. and Willis, D.A (Eds.), Proceedings of Society for Information Technology & Teacher Education International Conference 2006. Chesapeake, VA: AACE, 108–113.

National program of ICT in higher education Tiger University+, 2009–2012.

O'Neil, J. (1994). Aiming for new outcomes: The promise and the reality. *Educational Leadership*, 51, 6–10.

Pata, K. (2009). Modeling spaces for self-directed learning at university courses. *Journal of Educational Technology & Society*, 12, 23–43.

Pedersen, S. and Liu, M. (2003). Teachers' beliefs about issues in the implementation of a student-centered learning environment. *Educational Technology Research and Development*, 51, 57–76.

Razavi, M. N. and Iverson, L. (2006). Design Guidelines for an Information Privacy Management System for Personal Learning Spaces, In *Proceedings of the eLearn '06 Conference on E-Learning in Corporate, Government, Healthcare, and Higher Education*, Honolulu, Hawaii, USA, October 4–7, 2006

Rothman, R. (1993). Taking Account. *Education Week,* 12, 72–75.

Schlafly, P. (1993). What's Wrong with Outcome-Based Education? *The Phyllis Schlafly Report,* 26, 1–4.

Shipley, D. (1995). Transforming Community Colleges Using a Learning Outcomes Approach. Paper presented at a workshop sponsored by the Advanced Education Council of British Columbia and the Centre for Curriculum and Professional Development, Richmond, British Columbia, Canada. (ED 388 346)

Standard of Higher Education (2008). Available online: https://www.riigiteataja.ee/failid/K%C3%B5rgharidusstandard.pdf

Tammets, K., Pata, K. and Laanpere, M. (2012). Implementing A Technology-Supported Model for Cross-Organisational Learning and Knowledge Building for Teachers. *European Journal of Teacher Education*, 35, 57–75.

Towers, J. (1996). An Elementary School Principal's Experience with Implementing an Outcome-based Curriculum. *Catalyst for Change*, 25, 19–23.

Väljataga, T. and Laanpere, M. (2010). Learner control and personal learning environment: a challenge for instructional design. *Interactive Learning Environments*, 18, 277–291.

Van der Horst, H. and McDonald, R. (1999). *Outcomes Based Education: A teacher's Manual*. Cape Town: Kagiso Education Publishers.

PART 3

FROM HIGHER EDUCATION TO LABOUR MARKET AND BACK

Chapter 13.
From bust to boom and back again: social positions of graduates during the last decade in Estonia

Marge Unt, Kristina Lindemann

Introduction

Previous research has demonstrated that young people's labour market entry chances are disproportionately affected by changes in overall labour market conditions (Gangl, 2003). Young people's employment chances plummet during crises but they benefit more from economic booms (European Commission, 2010). Recently, after the global economic crisis, the vulnerability of young people in the labour market featured strongly on the social agenda, as more than 5 million young people were unemployed in the European Union at the end of 2011 (European Commission, 2011). Faced with rising levels of unemployment, it is becoming harder for young people to find work and many may decide to prolong their studies. This could be an investment for the future provided that they will have the opportunity to make use of their skills. In parallel, there is a growing proportion of young people who are neither in work nor in education or training. This proportion has increased from 10.8 per cent in 2008 to 12.8 per cent in 2010 for the EU as a whole. In Bulgaria, Estonia, Greece, Ireland, Italy, Latvia, Romania, Slovakia and Spain over 14 per cent of the younger generation is neither studying nor in employment. Thus, there are altogether more than 7.5 million young unemployed and inactive people aged 15–24 in the EU. This generation, entering adulthood during the economic crisis, is called 'the lost generation' (European Commission, 2011) as previous research has demonstrated that unemployment at the beginning of a work career has a scarring effect for both future unemployment and future earnings (Bell and Blanchflower, 2010). The European Commission has launched several initiatives since 2008 to combat youth unemployment and precarious employment (European Commission, 2011).

Estonia serves as an excellent case study for analysing the boom and bust effects on youth labour market outcomes. Estonia has experienced exceptional economic boom years from 2000–2007 after the crisis in the late 1990s and it was then hit by the deep recession in Europe which was amplified by the global economic crisis in 2008. In parallel with that, Estonia has kept up with, and even overtaken, the tremendous international growth in tertiary education. In 2011, 39 per cent of Estonia's population aged 25–34 had a university degree, certificate, or diploma, compared to 32.6 per cent in 2005, and 30.2 per cent in 1997 (Statistics Estonia, 2012). At the same time, the organisation of tertiary education has changed due to the process of harmonising higher education throughout Europe.

The aim of this article was to present a picture of the social positions of educational cohorts graduating during different stages of the economic cycle in Estonia. First, we analysed all possible routes together as they might be mutually interdependent. For instance, continuing education might be correlated with the avoidance of risk of unemployment etc. Following that, we include only those who do not continue their educational career to test if our results hold.

We were looking for answers to questions like: are cohorts graduating during a downturn less likely to obtain positions at the top of the occupational ladder? Are the chances of cohorts succeeding deteriorating due to increasing global economic volatility and the expansion of education in Estonia? Does the timing of graduation affect the social position of the young undertaking different types of higher education differently? As educational choices differ according to gender and ethnic background in terms of the field of study and the type of school attended (Tõnisson, 2011), we looked at whether there are gender and ethnic specific pathways after graduation.

Theoretical background

Education is the main resource for labour market entrants with limited or no work experience. Therefore, studies analysing the value of education in the labour market often focus on youth labour market entry (Müller and Gangl, 2003; Shavit, Müller and Tame, 1998). However, other factors may also determine the different pathways that people with the same qualifications take. School leavers engaged in searching for a job may differ according to their abilities, previous labour market contacts and networks, resulting in different job allocation patterns, etc. In addition, characteristics like gender, ethnicity and social origin may influence the labour market success of jobseekers.

If we consider education to be a crucial factor in determining the career chances of the young, how can we explain the observed labour market returns to educational investment? *Human capital theory,* developed in the early 1960s, sheds light on the relationship between an individual's level of schooling and their earning power in the labour market. Education develops skills (human capital) that make graduates more productive in their jobs and this is reflected in higher earnings (Becker, 1964; Mincer, 1974). Human capital theory has also been used to explain other labour market outcomes in addition to earning, including the social positions attained by graduates. People with the most human capital are said to be the most productive, and thus secure the best jobs and the highest salaries (Boudarbat and Chernoff, 2009). At the macro level, this theory paints a positive picture of higher education, portraying it as providing the skills needed to perform complex jobs, making people more productive and thus sustaining economic growth.

On the other hand, *credentialist theory* questions the linear link between productivity and schooling. From the credentialist viewpoint, skills are, by and large, acquired on the job, and employers see credentials as predictors of the future productivity and trainability of employees. Collins (1979) argues that employers use the credentials obtained by graduates as a form of currency, hiring only those who have the highest degree results, but these results have very little actual worth. Credentials become valued in themselves as they are used as a threshold to exclude those not possessing them. Justifications for educational credentialism have been used to explain the non-linear wage returns to schooling. These non-linear returns, often interpreted as 'sheepskin' effects (Habermalz, 2003) or 'rents' (Sørensen, 2000), presumably indicate that given levels of schooling are rewarded beyond their contribution to marginal productivity. That is, people are alleged to be rewarded for holding credentials which are not directly connected to their real productivity, thus, increasing the differences between them and the people who do not have those credentials (Bills and Brown, 2011).

While both the human capital and credentialism theories concentrate on the supply side, matching models are very explicit about the relevance of the demand side of the labour market. The foundation of matching theory lies in queuing theory (Thurow, 1975), which asserts the existence of two kinds of queues, a worker queue and a vacancy queue. The position gained is dependent on the positions available as well as on the other potential candidates. Since the two queues might not necessarily match, people who have undertaken higher education, who are thus ranked higher in the worker hierarchy, will not necessarily get higher status jobs. In cases where there are more applicants with high level qualifications than corresponding jobs available, people with more education might push the less educated down the worker queue, by taking positions previously available to the less educated. This idea is developed by Sattinger (1993) in the job assignment model, which explains the incidence of job mismatches by differences in the numbers of vacant jobs at a given level and available workers with adequate educational qualifications (Kogan and Unt, 2005).

There is a growing consensus that the relationship between education and the labour market is culturally and institutionally embedded, and that the strength and pattern of this relationship differs between contexts and periods (Shavit and Müller, 1998; Müller and Gangl, 2003; Smyth and McCoy, 2011). The consensus refers to the idea that different components of a country-specific institutional structure, like the training system, labour market structure, industrial relations and labour management, are mutually interdependent and reinforcing. The consensus also refers to the idea that labour market behaviour might correspond to different mechanisms in different settings: some systems promote credentialist sorts of behaviour, while in others, human capital processes seem to dominate (Bills, 2003).

Educational opportunities, as the specific structures of educational systems, are as important for mobility in labour markets as are the attributes of the individuals who make careers in those markets (Allmendiger, 1989). As the number of students in higher education has grown, the number of universities and other tertiary education institutions has grown too. They can no longer be considered as a homogeneous group in most countries. Shavit et al. (2007) analyse how the differentiation inside higher education affects social inequality in the access to higher education. They classify higher education systems into three clusters: unified, diversified and binary. In a unified higher education system, there are only universities which provide academic higher education. In a diversified system, higher education institutions differ from each other by their prestige, selectivity and resources. In binary systems, there exists a clear separation between the academic and vocational tracks. Their analyses of 15 countries indicate that both eligibility for entry to higher education and levels of attendance are higher in more diversified systems. Social inequality in entry levels is lower in diversified than in binary systems. However, inequality is greater for 'first tier' enrolment in both diversified and binary systems, and in diversified systems there is greater inequality in entry to first-tier institutions than in unified systems (Shavit et al., 2007).

Obviously, the differences in the structure of higher education affect the labour outcomes of graduates. One can expect that if a higher education system is unified, the graduates enjoy a higher labour market premium due to the high selectivity of higher education. Against this, if the higher education system is more diversified, there is more differentiation in the labour market outcomes of graduates. An analysis of labour market outcomes of graduates in five new Member States showed that although the field of study matters, the degree level is the central determinant of occupational status in the respondents' first job, with university masters graduates reaching the highest occupational positions, followed by university bachelor and vocational college graduates (Noelke, Gebel and Kogan, 2012).

There is a well-established tradition in studies of youth labour market entry to explain the role of educational credentials in job assignments in the context of the segmented labour market (Doeringer and Piore, 1971). The role of educational credentials proved to be much stronger in recruitment decisions made in the occupational labour market (OLM) compared to the internal labour market (ILM). In the OLM, the education system and labour market are closely connected and supported by the standardised occupational norms present in the labour market, while in the ILM, the link between the education system and labour market is loose and training takes place in the workplace. Also, a distinct Southern European labour market entry pattern had been revealed, where both strong qualifications and strong experience effects occur in conjunction with very high unemployment risks at the beginning of work careers (Gangl, 2003). Some attempts have been made to identify the position of single Central and Eastern European (CEE) countries in typologies of labour market entry patterns. Cedefop (2001) finds that the majority of CEE countries have been moving away from the model of regulated inclusion, characteristic of occupational labour markets (e.g. Germany), to the model of competitive regulation, characteristic of the flexible labour markets of the USA. Previous analysis shows that CEE countries are moving in different directions, adopting various employment protection models and welfare systems, and changing their educational systems (Hampalová, 2003; Saar, Unt and Kogan, 2008). All in all, a uniform classification for a post-socialist transition system is not possible.

The economic cycle may also have an impact on job assignment (see Smyth and McCoy, 2011). There are obvious connections between economic cycles and youth unemployment. Employment prospects grow worse for all school leavers in periods of economic crisis, although the relative advantage of those who have undertaken higher education tends to increase (Gangl, 2002). The gap between the most and the least qualified is seen to widen during recessions (Wolbers, De Graaf and Ultee, 2001). However, the link between the occupational positions obtained by labour market entrants and economic recession is not so clear cut. Gangl (2003) points out in his analysis covering 12 European countries from 1988–97, that there is no evidence of substantial cyclical effects on occupational status, either in terms of the main effect or in terms of any interaction effect with the overall unemployment rate. However, Saar and Unt (2012) detect the opposite in analysing 10 new European Union member states from 2000–2007. They find that the probability of obtaining professional employment decreases for tertiary educated people during economic crises, especially for ISCED 5B graduates. The next analysis by Saar and Unt (2011), based on 28 European countries from 2000–2009 reveals opposite trends for the labour market positions for lower and higher tertiary graduates during a recession. For higher tertiary (Bachelor's, Master's and doctoral studies) graduates the likelihood of starting as a manager or professional increases. For lower tertiary (applied or vocational programmes), it decreases dramatically, although graduates from lower tertiary institutions are successful in entering the labour market, but at the cost of job quality.

The Estonian context

The context of labour market entry varies over time as a result of different factors. In the following paragraphs we address three major trends affecting youth starting positions: the economic situation; changes in tertiary education, including educational expansion; and the up-skilling of the occupational structure in Estonia.

The Estonian economy underwent a big recession which started in August 1998. On 13 August 1998, the Russian stock, bond and currency markets collapsed and Estonian exporters lost their competitiveness compared to local Russian manufacturers. This crisis was most painful for manufactures of food products, as foodstuff exports fell by 44 per cent (Rei, 2009). There had been a substantial decrease in employment in the first half of the 1990s, and between 1997 and 2000 a further 44,700 jobs disappeared. From 2000 to 2007, Estonia was amongst the fastest growing emerging market economies. During this period, 77,600 new jobs were created: including 35,700 management and professional jobs and 29,200 blue-collar jobs[7]. Estonian income levels tended to converge with the income levels in the euro area, with living standards exceeding those in most new member states of the European Union. However, growth was unbalanced and driven by overexpansion in the non-tradable sectors, particularly real estate and construction. It was financed by large capital inflows, which led to unsustainable current account deficits and high private debt. External financing became a key source of rapid credit growth, mainly to households for real estate purchases, in the form of variable interest rate and foreign currency loans. Pro-cyclical fiscal policy and wages amplified the cycle (Brixiova, Vartia and Wörgötter, 2010). Exactly ten years after the previous downturn, in September 2008, Estonia entered a new, deep recession, the key issues being the collapse of the real estate market and the global financial crisis. The combination of plummeting real estate prices and a substantial reduction in the number of transactions led to a rapid decline in output and jobs in construction, finance and real estate services. Overall employment dropped by 85,600 between 2008 and 2010; in 2010 there were the lowest number of working

7 Estonian Statistical Office, online data, www.stat.ee, authors calculations.

people during the last two decades: 570,900 (Brixiova et al., 2010). While aggregate outcomes increased from 2000–07, large inequalities persisted across regions, ethnic groups and workers with different skill levels (Brixiova, 2009).

Youth unemployment rates clearly echo the economic cycle (Figure 1). Unemployment risks vary according to educational achievement; the least educated being the most vulnerable. Unemployment data for tertiary graduates is missing for the economically better years as the number of unemployed tertiary graduates in age range 15–24 was too small to enable the calculation of the representative unemployment rate based on Labour Force Survey data. The two unemployment peaks are exactly ten years apart, in 2000 and in 2010. During both recessions the gap between educational groups increased and this has also been noticed in previous analyses in other EU countries (Gangl, 2003). As Estonia entered recession in 2008, the unemployment rate rose 2.4 times for young people with secondary and basic education. This was one of the biggest increases in the EU, only comparable with the youth unemployment increase in Spain, Ireland and the other Baltic States. The youth unemployment rate increased further in 2010, reaching almost 20 per cent for tertiary graduates, 30 per cent for secondary and 50 per cent for basic education graduates. It started to decrease in 2011.

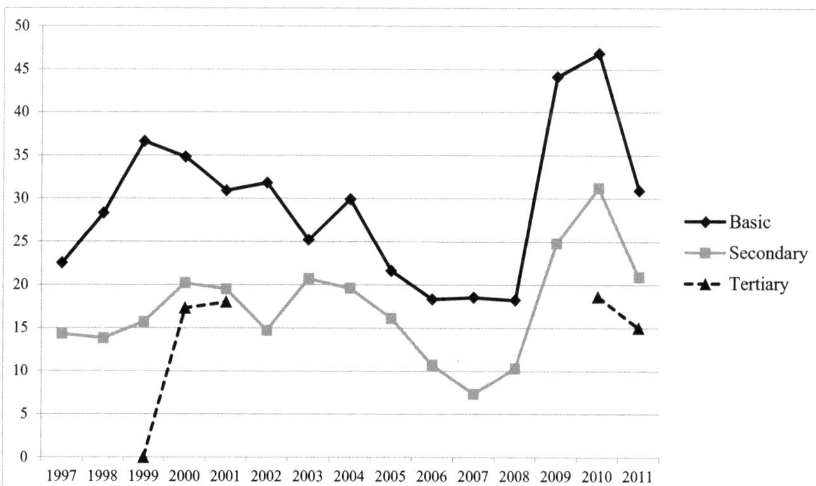

Figure 1. *Youth (15–24 years old) unemployment rates by education level in Estonia from 1997- 2011 (per cent)*

Source: Estonian Statistical Office, authors' calculations

Next, we considered the second major trend affecting the social positions of the young: trends in higher education. While vocational education at secondary and post-secondary levels became increasingly unpopular, tertiary education expanded rapidly as a result of the emergence of private institutions of higher education. Until the early 1990s, the system of Estonian higher education was highly centralised and institutionally homogenous. After that a considerable expansion took place through the establishment of new private universities and professional higher schools, the reorganisation of specialised secondary schools as public professional higher schools, and new legislation allowing foreign universities to establish departments in Estonia (Saar and Unt, 2011). Following the Bologna Process, in the 2002/2003 academic year, Estonia implemented a new system – the two-cycle (bachelor-master) structure, the so called '3+2 model'.

Figure 2 offers an insight into the overall number and profile of graduates from 1992 to 2010. In the 1990s, around 4,000 graduates entered higher education each year. After that a rapid expansion of higher education occurred from 1998 to 2005, when each year the number of graduates increased by almost 1,000. In 2004/2005, 11, 528 people graduated from tertiary institutions and since then the number of graduates has been about the same. It is also worth noting that the expansion of higher education mainly occurred before the implementation of the Bologna Process in Estonia.

In terms of the profile of graduates, almost all graduates obtained Bachelors degrees at universities in early 1990s. After the early 1990s the number of lower tertiary graduates started to increase rapidly. In parallel with the expansion of lower tertiary programmes, a growing number people opted for Masters level programmes. Based on typology developed by Arum,Gamoran, and Shavit (2007) we find that Estonia has had a diversified higher education system since the 2000s. While the primary tier consists of university courses, the secondary tier consists of both professionally and occupationally oriented programmes.

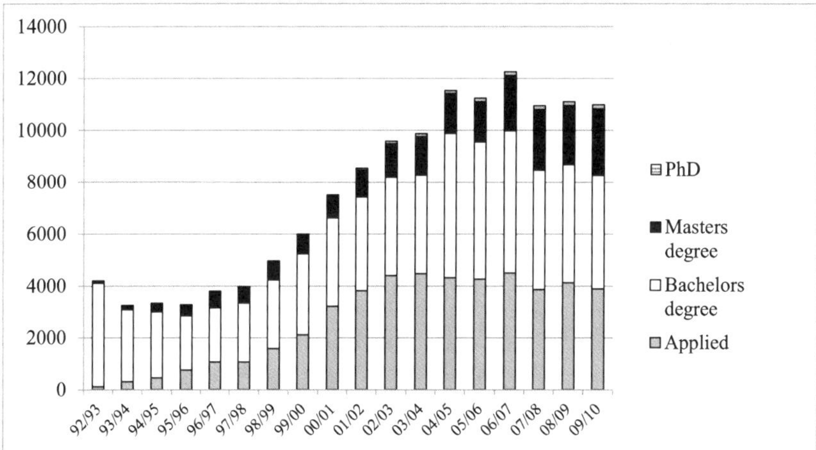

Figure 2. *Differentiation in higher education: graduates by type of higher education between 1992/93 and 2009/10, number*

Source: Tõnisson, 2011:7

With regard to gender differences, in the early 1990s there were equal numbers of male and female students. By 2010/2011 females outnumbered males at all levels of higher education. In applied higher education programmes 58 per cent were female; in Bachelor studies, 59 per cent; in Master studies 66 per cent, and in Doctor of Philosophy (PhD) studies 58 per cent (Tõnisson, 2011). The subject area preferences are traditional: the number of men is lowest in education (2010/2011: 10 per cent) and health (13 per cent) programmes. Men are in the majority in engineering, manufacturing and construction (Tõnisson, 2011).

Almost a third of the Estonian population belongs to an ethnic minority and many of these people are Russian-speakers (Statistics Estonia, 2012). From 1997–2011, it was possible to undertake secondary education for the large part in Russian. In 2010, graduates of Russian secondary schools continued on to higher education less often than those from Estonian secondary schools (54 per cent and 64 per cent respectively). Also a smaller proportion of them accessed state-funded places in tertiary education (Tõnisson, 2011:27). Higher education with Russian as the language of instruction is available mostly in private higher education institutions, where social sciences are often taught. Thus, graduates of Russian secondary schools more often continue their studies in social sciences than young Estonians (Saar, 2008b).

Previous studies have tried to classify the Estonian institutional regime in terms of linkages between the education system and the labour market. In the 1990s the Estonian institutional regime resembled that of liberal countries, such as the UK and Ireland. Here there are less institutionalised connections between education, training and the labour market, and there is potentially more open competition for the same positions between those with different levels and types of qualifications, i.e., there is a less segmented labour market (Saar, 2005; Täht, Saar and Unt, 2008). However, some Estonian features are similar to southern European countries, especially the strong 'insider-outsider' logic that decreases labour market flexibility (Täht and Saar, 2006). During the next few decades we expect that the Estonian pattern will combine elements present in both the ILM and OLM models, despite currently being more similar to the ILM context.

When analysing the social positions of graduates it is also essential to pay attention to the demand side, as referred to in the theoretical section. If we agree with job matching theories, the occupational achievement of graduates does not only depend on their educational achievement, but more on the types of jobs available in the labour market. Earlier research has shown that educational expansion and occupational up-skilling counterbalance each other. If there is a growing need for professionals and managers in the labour market, tertiary graduates easily find appropriate jobs. The other side of this is that the less educated are especially harshly pushed out of the labour market if these two processes take place in parallel (Gangl, 2003). If expansion of higher education takes place at a higher rate than the creation of new jobs at the top of the occupational ladder, then fresh graduates face more competition for the top positions. In all CEE countries, but especially in Bulgaria, Poland, Lithuania and Estonia, occupational up-skilling has taken place at a much slower rate than the expansion of tertiary education, which may have generated oversupplies of graduates and devalued degrees (Saar and Unt, 2012). Of course, increasing the numbers of highly qualified workers does not necessarily create an over-supply and devalue degrees when professionals and managers are under-qualified.

What does the occupational structure look like in Estonia? Estonia has a significantly higher proportion of unqualified workers and a noticeably lower proportion of white-collar workers than most other European countries (Saar, 2008a). In comparison with the European average, the current structure of the production sectors and the technology used in them in Estonia is heavily based on blue-collar workers. Data show that between 1990 and 2010 the percentage of lower white-collar workers (clerks and service workers) and elementary occupations increased, while the share of skilled workers decreased (Figure 3). However, there was practically no change in the percentage of jobs at the top of the occupational hierarchy (managers and semi-professionals) during the same period, except for professionals, whose share increased. The impact of the 2008 crisis hit the other occupations more, thus, the number of professional jobs was not so much expanding as holding its position. There are also remarkable differences in occupational positions by gender and ethnicity. Men are more likely to be either managers or blue-collar workers. Women dominate in professional, service and sales worker groups. Ethnic minorities work more as blue-collar workers and they are considerably less likely to occupy positions at the top of the occupational structure.

To summarise, the supply of educated labour has increased, but the demand for highly educated labour has not changed much. Thus, there is a conflict between the current economic structure, which needs less educated and cheap labour, and the relatively high educational levels of the new workers.

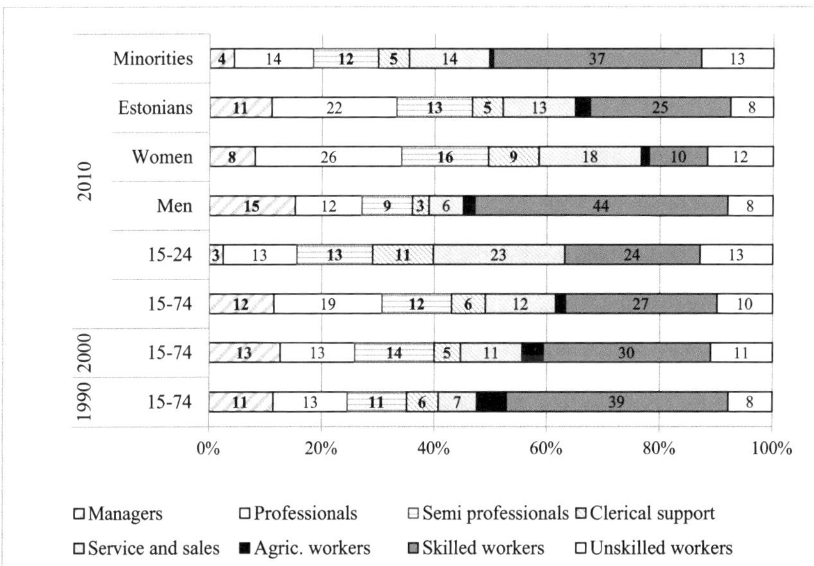

Figure 3. Occupational structure in Estonia 1990–2010 (per cent)

Source: Estonian Statistical Office, authors' calculations

What can we expect when analysing the social positions of graduates in Estonia? Due to the expansion of higher education and the shift from a unified higher education system to a more heterogeneous system, we expect to find growing differentiation in the social positions of graduates. Young people with applied (professional or vocational) higher education degrees should be less successful than those with Master's or Bachelor's degrees. They can be successful in finding a job if they accept lower positions, but they are less able to compete for top-positions in the occupational hierarchy compared to Bachelor and Master degree holders. In the case of educational expansion, and especially with the cumulative effect of economic recession and a growing supply of graduates, we suggest that young people with Bachelor degree holders will have lower chances of securing high level jobs and will, therefore, be more likely to continue their studies. However, we expect that young people with Master degree holders will have better chances of securing high level jobs as this is still a relatively small and select group, and thus their success in securing top positions is not as dependent on the year in which they graduated.

We expect that our reference group, young people with secondary education, will increasingly choose to continue their studies, due to the expansion of higher education. If they do not continue their studies, they will have a weaker labour market position than higher education graduates (i.e., higher risk of unemployment or low status jobs) and how much weaker will largely depend on the state of business cycle.

Pathways after graduation may be gender and ethnic specific. We suggest that ethnic minorities with Bachelor degree or applied higher education might experience more difficulty entering the labour market than Estonians, because, in general, ethnic minorities work less often in top positions (Figure 3). However, ethnic differences in pathways for graduates with Master degree are less likely because this level is more selective and the skills of graduates should lead to more success in the labour market.

It was mainly men who were studying in the areas that were particularly hit by the recession, i.e., engineering, manufacturing and construction (Tõnisson, 2011). We expect that this might also be reflected in the unemployment rate of recent graduates in the latest cohort 2008–2011, but no gender gap is likely for earlier cohorts. However, we believe that access to top positions (managers and professionals) does not depend on gender.

Data and method

Data

We used data from the Estonian Labour Force Survey (ELFS) 1999–2000 (1st half of the year) and 2002–2011. The ELFS covers the entire Estonian working age population (age 15-74 years). Based on the ELFS we made a new subsample of young people who had completed secondary or tertiary education within 2 years of the interview. We did not include young people with basic or lower education. The aim of the analysis was to find out how successful recent graduates with different higher education degrees were in securing different social positions. Also young people who had completed secondary education were included to see how their attainments varied compared to higher education graduates. Thus, we only included young people with no work experience and those who had found their first job 5 years before the interview at most. We only counted working careers which had started with a significant job (more than 6 months duration and at least 20 hours per week). The usual definition of 'young people' is people aged 15–24 years (e.g. Eurostat databases) but higher education graduates are often older. Thus, excluding people based on age would not best reflect the opportunities available after graduation from higher education. Thus, we focused on recent graduates (within 2 years) with less than 5 years of work experience. The total size of our subsample was 10,763 individuals. Most of them (99.6 per cent) were younger than 30 years old.

Variables

The dependent variable was the **social position** of the respondent at the time of the interview. We identified six social positions:

1) Management or professional: respondent's current job, groups 1–2 according to the International Standard Classification of Occupations (ISCO)-88;
2) Mid-level specialist: groups 3–4 on the ISCO-88;
3) Routine white-collar or blue-collar: groups 5–9 on the ISCO-88;
4) Unemployed: the respondent has no job and is actively looking for a job;
5) Inactive student: the respondent is studying but not working;
6) Inactive: the respondent is not working or studying.

Respondents who were working or unemployed might be also students. However, we were interested in how their current social position was influenced by their previous graduation from tertiary education or completion of secondary education. We took into account the highest level of education that a respondent had achieved within two years of the interview. We identified the following categories: (1) secondary education (which includes vocational secondary), (2) applied higher education, (3) Bachelor degree, (4) Master degree. There were too few recent graduates with doctoral degree to include them in the analysis.

Our definition of the educational cohorts was based on the expansion and contraction of the business cycle. Due to sample size limitations, we were not able to make a fine distinction between growth, peaks, recession, troughs and recovery within the business cycle. Thus, we divided the respondents into three **educational cohorts** according to the situation in the economy during the year of graduation. So, we had cohorts graduating (1) during the Russian crisis, from

1997–2000; (2) during the economic boom, from 2001–2007 and (3) during the global financial crisis from 2008–2011. Usually students finish their studies in June and we presumed that an individual's current social position depended on when they graduated and the labour market opportunities at that time. We also included the number of years between the interview and completion of education in our models. This measure shows **time after graduation** (to control for possible labour market experience).

We also analysed how the effect of education on social position depends on **gender** and **ethnic identity**. The respondents were asked about their ethnicity and based on this we formed two categories: (1) Estonian and (2) other ethnicity.

We took the respondents' current **place of residence** into account because social position might depend on the local labour market and the opportunities to continue studying. The variable 'place of residence' is divided into three categories: (1) Tallinn and the surrounding area, (2) Tartu and the surrounding area and (3) elsewhere in Estonia.

Unfortunately, we were not able to control for **social origin** or **abilities** as the ELFS does not collect this information.

Table 1 gives an overview of the educational level of respondents by gender and ethnicity. Many respondents only have secondary education because the sample included recent graduates (within two years of the interview) who had no work experience or less than five years of experience. Thus, our sample excluded about 15 per cent of recent graduates because they obtained their first significant work experience more than five years ago. For example, about 55 per cent of graduates with Master degree already had a job more than five years ago so they were not included in our sample. Table 1 shows that the educational achievements of different social groups were rather similar in the educational cohort 1997–2000. However, a gap between men and women appeared in the cohort 2001–2007 and was also evident for the cohort 2008–2011. Ethnic differences only appeared in the latest cohort and are conditioned by our sample restrictions. Estonians are more likely to have at least 5 years work experience when they obtain a Bachelor or Master degree. As a result, more Estonians are excluded from our sample.

Table 1. The educational achievements of different groups in the sample (per cent)

Cohort		Secondary	Applied higher	Bachelor's degree	Master's degree	Total
1997/2000	Women	91	3	6	1	100
	Men	92	1	6	1	100
	Minority	88	2	8	1	100
	Estonian	92	2	5	1	100
	Total	*91*	*2*	*6*	*1*	*100*
2001/2007	Women	80	4	13	2	100
	Men	89	3	7	1	100
	Minority	83	5	11	1	100
	Estonian	85	4	10	1	100
	Total	*84*	*4*	*11*	*1*	*100*
2008/2011	Women	73	5	16	6	100
	Men	83	3	9	4	100
	Minority	71	5	16	8	100
	Estonian	80	4	12	4	100
	Total	*78*	*4*	*13*	*5*	*100*
N		*8950*	*405*	*1150*	*258*	*10763*
Sample excludes: graduates with more than 5 years of work experience *(N=1819)*		20	24	39	17	100
Per cent excluded from all recent graduates		4	52	38	55	14

Source: Authors' calculations based on ELFS

Method

First, we analysed the distribution of social positions by educational groups. Then we used multinomial logistic regression to estimate the effect of education on social position. The reference group was managers and professionals. So, the model compared the probability of being in a different social position to managers and professionals. We also included interactions between cohort and education level to find out whether the effect of education on social position varied for different cohorts. We presented the regression results in terms of predicted probabilities. Other independent variables are fixed at their means.

The statistical significance of predicted probabilities is presented in the appendices. We were interested in:

1) Whether the probability of achieving a certain position had changed significantly over cohorts within educational groups. Appendix 1 shows separate models for graduates with secondary education, applied higher education, Bachelor and Master degree. These models show whether cohort significantly affects the success of the educational group.

2) Whether the probability of achieving a certain position varies significantly between educational groups within one cohort. In Appendix 2 separate models for three cohorts are presented. These models show whether the probability of a particular outcome differs significantly for graduates with secondary, applied, Bachelor and Master degree within one cohort.

We also conducted a separate analysis for recent graduates who are not currently studying. The aim was to see what position graduates achieve at the start of their working careers. Excluding students did not change the general picture much.

We also tested whether the effect of education on social position depended on gender and ethnicity. Our calculations were again based on a multinomial model but we added interactions (1) with gender, education and cohort for finding differences between the success of men and women and (2) with ethnicity, education and cohort for finding differences between other ethnicities and Estonians. The regression results were presented graphically as predicted probabilities. We only presented the predicted probabilities for the risk of unemployment and achieving a managerial or professional position. Appendix 3 shows the statistical significance of the differences between the groups. We estimated a separate model for every educational group and cohort (e.g. graduates with Bachelor degree in cohort 1997–2000, graduates with Bachelor degree in cohort 2001–2007). The aim was to find out the importance of gender and ethnicity for the success of graduates with different degrees in every cohort.

Results

The social positions of graduates by education during the last decade: descriptive approach

Figure 4 gives a descriptive overview of the social positions of recent graduates. It appears that young people with Master degree most often achieve managerial and professional positions. However, the proportion of those in top positions has decreased when comparing the cohorts 2001–2007 and 2008–2011 (in cohort 1997–2000 there were too few graduates with Master degree to analyse them separately) as they more often opt for mid-level specialist positions. At the same time it is worth noting that the risk of unemployment for graduates with Master degree did not increase nor did they accept lower level jobs more often. Thus, an Master degree was a successful buffer against the risk of unemployment and against taking a low qualified job during the last recession. However, graduates with Master degree increasingly have to accept semiprofessional jobs. The proportion of managers and professionals was considerably higher for those graduating during the boom years than for those graduating during the recession. On the other hand, it is also important to note that graduates with Master degree in the latest cohort have mostly graduated via 3-year Bachelor's studies, while in the earlier cohorts more graduates with Master degree completed 4-year Bachelor studies. Thus, the results might indicate that the perceived value of a degree from the 3+2 system is lower than that from the 4+2 system.

The decrease in opportunities is even more evident among young people who have attained Bachelor degree. In the 1997–2000 cohort more than half of the graduates with Bachelor degree secured managerial or professional positions. In the succeeding cohort, 2001–2007, young people with Bachelor degree secured top positions less often, while the proportion of mid-level specialists and those continuing to study increased. This trend continued in the latest cohort where less than a quarter of graduates with Bachelor degree were working as managers or professionals, and the percentages of routine white-collar and blue-collar workers increased. At the same time, more and more graduates with Bachelor degree postponed their labour market entry and continued with their studies. In the latest cohort about a third of the graduates with Bachelor degree continued with their studies. Thus, instead of working in a managerial or professional position an increasing proportion of graduates with Bachelor degree engaged in further study. This choice might be conditioned by labour market requirements and the opportunities open to graduates with Bachelor degree.

The situation for young people with applied higher education seems to be the most difficult. They experienced higher unemployment than young people with any other type of higher education. Almost a fifth of them were unemployed in the 1997–2000 and 2008–2011 cohorts, but this proportion was lower in the 2001–2007 cohort as the students in this group graduated during a period of economic growth. The proportion of inactive students was very low amongst applied higher education graduates for all of the cohorts. Thus, their opportunities for further study appear to be limited. In addition, their occupational positions are lower when comparing the 2001–2007 and 2008–2011 cohorts. The proportion of applied higher education graduates working in routine positions is highest in the latest cohort, while a smaller proportion of them in this cohort achieved top or mid-level specialist positions.

The position of secondary education graduates has changed little over time. In all cohorts, about half of them continued their studies after graduation. Those who entered the labour market usually started in routine service or sales positions. In addition, the proportion of unemployed was clearly the highest for the 2008–2011 cohort.

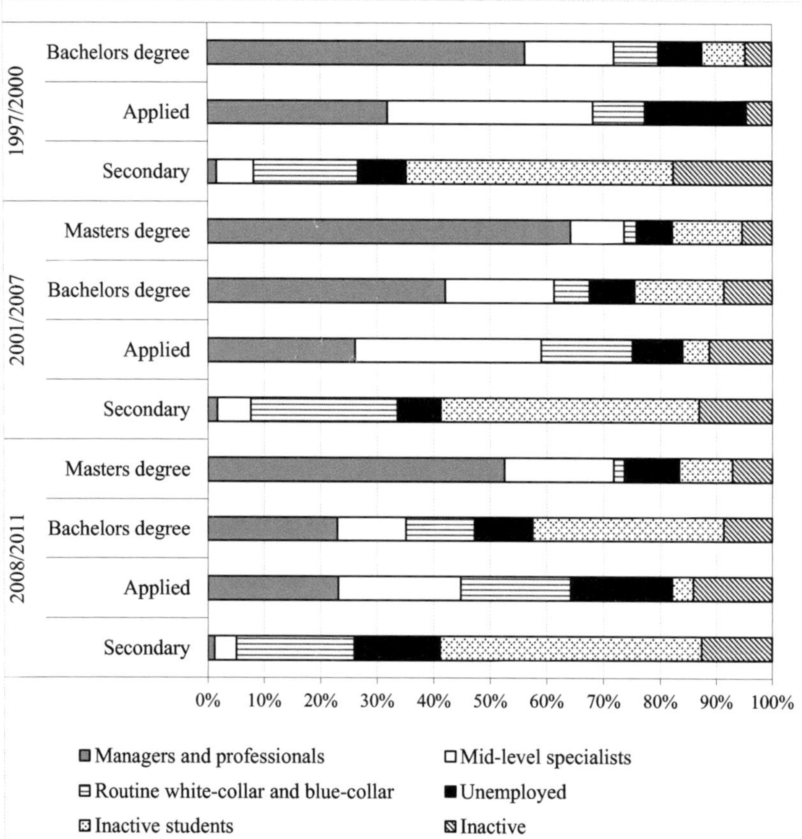

Figure 4. Social position by educational cohort and type of education, %

Source: Authors' calculations based on ELFS

The social positions of graduates during the last decade: the multivariate approach

The social positions that young people attain after graduation might depend on many factors as well as education. Thus, we estimated a multinomial regression model that included the variables education, cohort, gender, ethnicity, place of residence and time since graduation. We also added interactions between the type of education and cohort into our model. Based on this model, we calculated the predicted probabilities of belonging to different occupational position categories. Appendix 1 shows the statistical significance of changes over cohort within one educational group and Appendix 2 shows the significance of differences between educational groups within one cohort (see the Method section above). All the trends that we have described are statistically significant unless we state otherwise.

Figure 5 shows that after adding a set of controls, and this is similar to the descriptive results, young people with Master degree most probably secure managerial or professional positions. Their likelihood of being in top positions varies between educational cohorts. Young people who graduated during the last economic recession were less likely to secure a high occupational position than young people who graduated earlier, but their chances of becoming mid-level specialists increased (see also Appendix 1). The additional analysis that excluded inactive students gave similar results – the chance of securing a top position has decreased for graduates with Master degree (Figure 6). Thus, the economic recession and the growing number of Master students (with a decreased number of years of education in the latest cohort) has resulted in fewer opportunities to secure the highest labour market positions and young people have had to take second-best jobs as mid-level specialists. However, their risk of being unemployed, inactive or having to work in low-level jobs did not increase.

Compared to Master's degree holders, the tendency toward declining labour market opportunities is already visible in the earlier cohorts for young people with Bachelor degree. The opportunity to continue studying after a Bachelor increased significantly over the cohorts and was especially high for the latest cohort. Figure 5 shows that young people who gained Bachelor degree during the first recession in 1997–2000, had a high probability of securing a managerial or professional position despite the overall economic crisis. This probability decreased somewhat for graduates who had finished their Bachelor studies by the time of economic growth (although this decrease is not statistically significant) and the probability decreased further, and significantly, for the 2008–2011 educational cohort. Thus, it seems that despite good overall labour market conditions Bachelor's degrees started to lose some of their value. This trend is not explained by the increasing opportunities to continue studying at Master's level. Figure 6 shows that, even after excluding inactive students, graduates with Bachelor degree probabilities of securing top positions have clearly decreased for the last cohort. The reasons for this might be the growing number of graduates or changes in the organisation of higher education. In 1997–2000 all Bachelor students had to study for at least four years but for students starting their studies in 2002 the length of the programme was shortened to three years. In addition, the risk of unemployment, inactivity or of undertaking a routine white-collar or blue-collar position increased significantly for graduates with Bachelor degree in the latest cohort (see Appendix 1 and 2).

Figure 5 shows that young people who completed applied higher education were less successful compared to those with Bachelor degree. They were less likely to work in managerial or professional positions than graduates with Bachelor degree, although the difference was the smallest for the latest cohort (see also Figure 6). It also seemed that the probability of undertaking a routine white-collar or blue-collar worker position increased for every succeeding cohort. However, the difference between applied higher education graduates' and Bachelor degree holders' chances of working in routine or blue-collar positions has somewhat reduced for the latest cohort (see Appendix 2 and Figure 6). Despite the extensive expansion of education, in all cohorts, applied education graduates have a very low chance of continuing their education. The results indicated that young people who undertook applied higher education have also been affected by the economic cycle as their risk of unemployment was significantly higher in times of recession (Appendix 1). The reason for this might be that this type of education prepares young people for the industries that were hit hardest by the economic slowdown. The differences within applied higher education, in terms of specialisation or quality, might be important because the labour market outcomes of these graduates vary considerably.

Finally, Figure 5 indicates that the social positions of secondary education graduates have changed only slightly over three cohorts. Their risk of unemployment was higher at times of economic recession, and in addition, the risk of inactivity was significantly higher for the 1997–2000 educational cohort (Appendix 1). Figure 6 shows that young people who have only completed secondary education and who have not continued their studies are most likely to start their careers as routine white-collar or blue-collar workers.

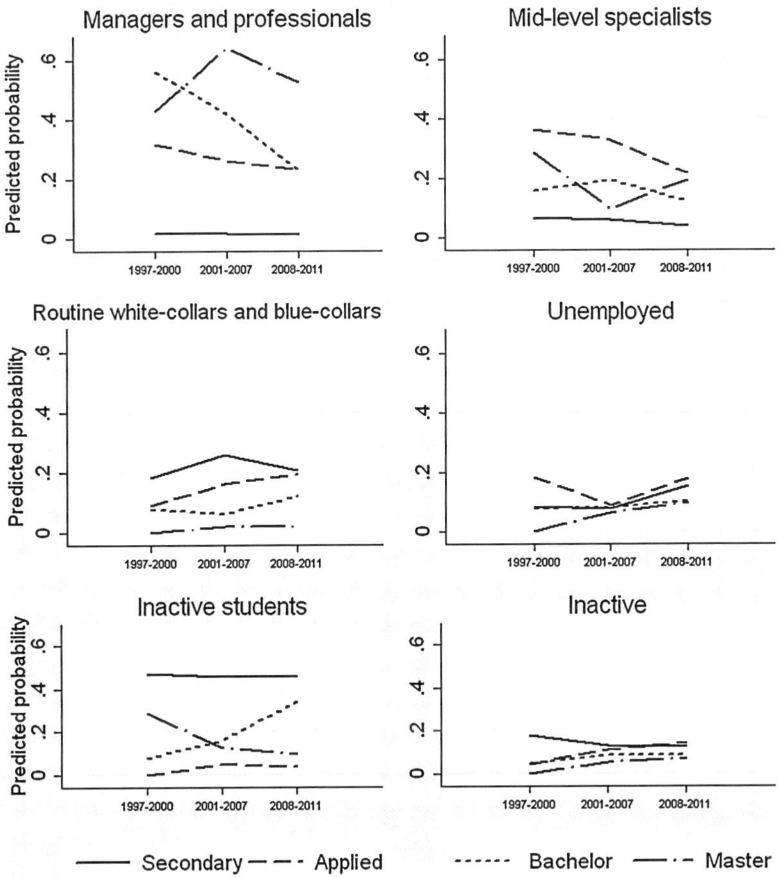

Figure 5. *The predicted probability of being in a different social positions by educational cohort and type of education (multinomial regression analysis, other independent variables are set to the mean, and the model includes interactions between type of education and cohort)*

Source: Authors' calculations based on ELFS

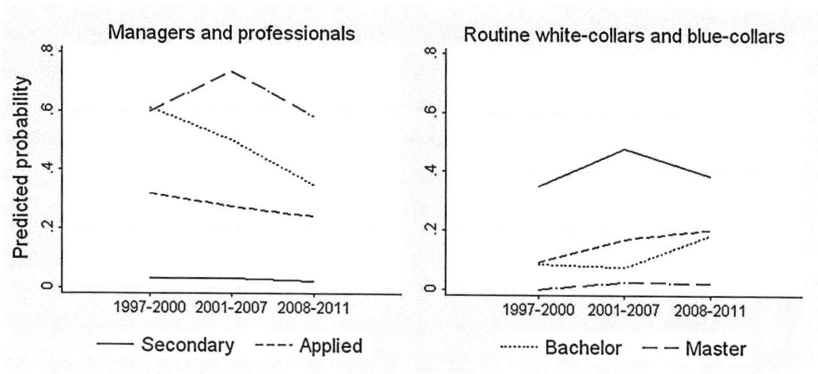

Figure 6. *The predicted probability of securing managerial and professional or routine white-collar or blue-collar worker positions by educational cohort and type of education (students are excluded, multinomial regression analysis, other independent variables are set to the mean and the model includes interactions between type of education and cohort)*

Source: Authors' calculations based on ELFS

The social position of graduates by gender and ethnicity

We also analysed whether the effect of education and cohort on the chances of attaining a high social position or being unemployed is moderated by gender and ethnicity. Unemployment has often been used as an indicator that the start of a working career has not been successful. In contrast, the most successful higher education graduates secure managerial or professional positions at the start of their working careers. Figure 7 shows the predicted probabilities of the risk of unemployment and Figure 8 shows the predicted probabilities of achieving the highest occupational positions for men, women and for ethnic groups. In general, the unemployment rate for all working age men was much higher during the last economic recession due to decline of the economic sectors which predominantly employed men (Statistics Estonia, 2012). However, this trend was not reflected in the unemployment rates of recent higher education graduates (Figure 7). It appears that there were no significant gender differences in unemployment patterns among graduates with applied higher education or Bachelor, Master degree in all three educational cohorts (Appendix 3).

As with the risk of unemployment, the probability of achieving top positions for graduates with different educational degrees did not depend on gender in any of the cohorts (Figure 8 and Appendix 3). Although the gender gap for the likelihood of achieving a high position looks very large for Master's degree graduates in the 1997–2000 cohort, it is not statistically significant due to the small number of Master's graduates in our sample. However, it seems that the chances of securing a managerial or professional position were almost equal for men and women who attained Master's degrees in 2001–2007. The opportunities for women with Master's degrees show a reducing, but not statistically significant, trend during economic recession while there was almost no change for men. At the same time, the number of women with Master's degrees has grown more quickly (Table 1). No gender differences in opportunities appear among graduates with Bachelor's degrees. However, men with applied higher education degrees were somewhat more likely to achieve top positions in 1997–2000 than women with similar degrees. However, such a gender gap was not visible for the later cohorts.

Figure 7 shows that the risk of unemployment clearly differs for ethnic groups. Estonian young people were less exposed to the risk of unemployment, regardless of their education, compared with ethnic minorities. In particular, minority young people with applied higher education degrees were more likely to be unemployed than Estonians in all cohorts. One explanation for this might be that some of the minority young people attained applied higher education degrees in Russian in private educational institutions. In 2005, about 15 per cent of all students in applied higher education were studying in private educational institutions with Russian as the language of instruction and 19 per cent were studying in private educational institutions with Estonian as the language of instruction. The respective figures for 2011 were 9 per cent and 15 per cent (Estonian Ministry of Education and Research, 2012). Thus, possible explanations for the higher risk of unemployment among minority young people are that they potentially lack Estonian language proficiency or employers might place less value on the Russian-language education in private educational institutions. In addition, minority young people who completed Bachelor's studies had a much higher risk of unemployment compared with Estonians with a similar education, especially during the last economic recession. Again, language skills might be a factor contributing to the disadvantage of the minority young people. There are few opportunities to attain Bachelor degrees in Russian. In 2011, about 5 per cent of all Bachelor students studied in Russian in private and public universities (Estonian Ministry of Education and Research, 2012). Among young people with secondary education, the probability of being unemployed also increased more for ethnic minorities than for young Estonians (see Appendix 3). Thus, it seems that economic recession has a greater negative impact on the labour market opportunities of ethnic minority young people than Estonians. Only those who manage to obtain Master's degrees do not face a higher risk of unemployment than Estonians.

The effect of ethnicity on the likelihood of recent graduates securing managerial or professional positions is somewhat weaker than the effect of ethnicity on the likelihood of being unemployment. Although Figure 8 shows that minority young people who secured Master's degrees in 2001–2007 were particularly successful in securing high occupational positions, this difference was not statistically significant from Estonians (Appendix 3). The number of young people with Master's degrees was still very small at this time (Table 1). Thus, the findings might not only show the positive effect of such a degree, but also prior selection. It is likely that more motivated and resourceful young people attain Master's degrees, especially among minority young people. Previous studies have shown that Russians are generally less likely to continue their studies in higher education even where parental resources are similar (Lindemann and Saar, 2011). On the other hand, Estonians with Bachelor's degrees were more likely to achieve managerial or professional positions than young people from other ethnic groups. This gap was visible in all cohorts. However, there are no ethnic differences in opportunities for young people with applied higher education degrees (Appendix 3).

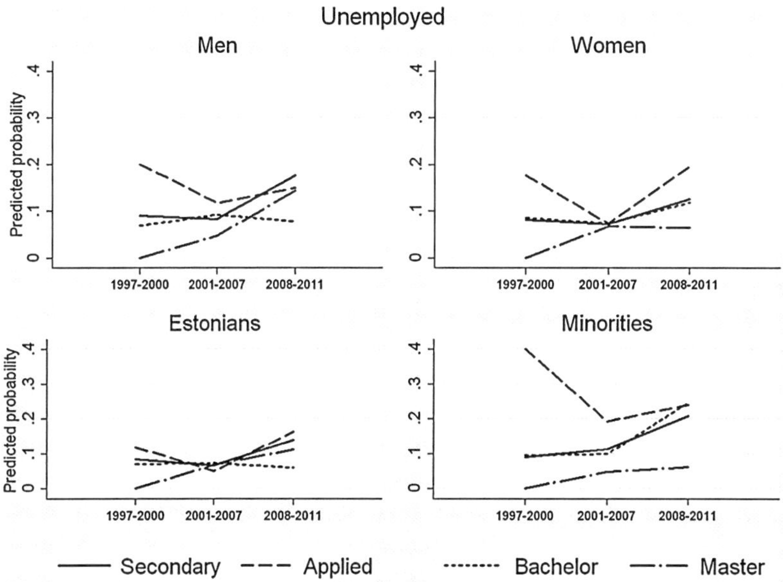

Figure 7. *The predicted probability of being unemployed by gender, ethnic group, educational cohort and type of education (multinomial regression analysis, other independent variables are set to the mean and the model includes interactions between type of education, cohort and gender/ethnicity)*

Source: Authors' calculations based on ELFS

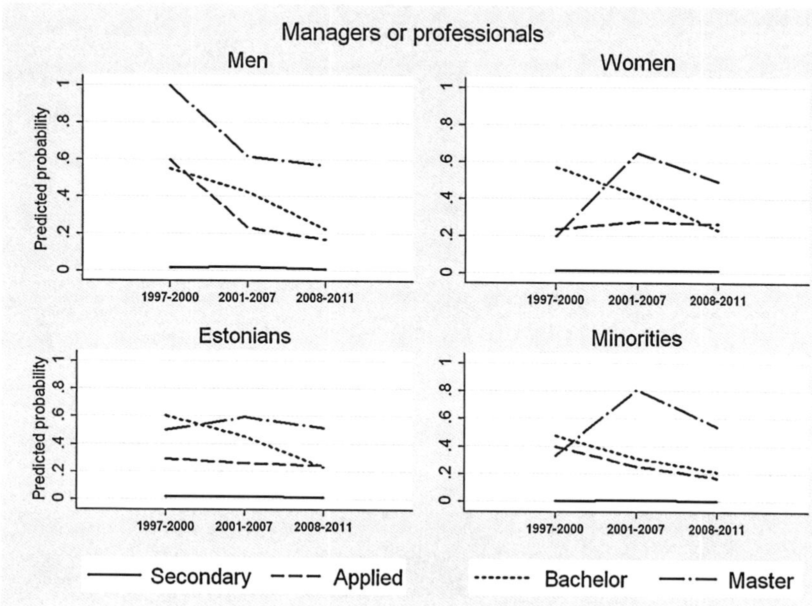

Figure 8. *The predicted probability of securing a managerial or professional position by gender, ethnic group, educational cohort and type of education (multinomial regression analysis, other independent variables are set to the mean and the model includes interactions between type of education, cohort and gender/ethnicity)*

Source: Authors' calculations based on ELFS

Discussion

Our aim was to give an overview of the social positions of graduates during the last decade in Estonia, a decade which has been marked by educational expansion, two severe economic recessions and one exceptional boom. We also explored gender and ethnic effects and their interaction with educational level in predicting employment status.

At the end of 1990s, around 4,000 students graduated annually (Figure 2). Ten years later, around three times more students graduated annually. During the economic boom, between 2000 and 2007, 77,600 new jobs were created, including 35,700 managerial and professional positions[8], however, the overall occupational structure changed only slightly. Therefore, as a growing number of graduates entered the labour market, their chances of obtaining high level positions decreased. Graduates from the last cohort faced a double problem as they had to compete for scarce jobs in a situation of economic crisis, (employment dropped by 85,600 between 2008 and 2010), as well as compete with fellows from particularly large birth cohort.

As we expected, it was possible to observe the difference in the social positions of graduates and the downward substitution process during the 2000's. Over 20 per cent of graduates with applied higher education degrees worked as managers or professionals in the last cohort. However, not all of them have been so lucky. For graduates with applied higher education degrees, in particular, unemployment has risen most rapidly and insecure jobs are relatively common. Many of those who graduated after 2008 have been pushed either to take lower level jobs or are still looking for work. It is surprising that despite the Bologna Process and the increase in various Master's level programmes during last decade, the probability of these students continuing their studies has not increased.

In addition, the value of a Bachelor's degree has decreased, and the signs of this were already visible during the boom years. In the first cohort, over half of the graduates secured jobs as managers or professionals shortly after graduation, while in the last cohort Bachelors graduates did not even do better than the applied higher education graduates. However, we must emphasise that a growing share of Bachelor graduates continue their studies at the Master's level without entering the labour market, so it may be the case that the educational system has absorbed some of these young people who would otherwise have had slim chances in the labour market, especially during the last recession. However, even if we analyse the labour market chances of those NOT continuing their studies, there is a clear tendency for every succeeding cohort to start their careers from lower positions than the previous cohort.

A Master's degree still seems to hold distinct value in the labour market. In the last cohort over half of the Master's graduates started in top positions shortly after graduation. It is still rather unlikely that Master's graduates would start in routine service or sales jobs, as is increasingly common for graduates with applied and Bachelor degree. However, even for Master's graduates the last economic recession reduced possibilities and almost one fifth of them, who during the boom years would have managed to find top positions, now have to accept second-best jobs as mid-level specialists.

8 Estonian Statistical Office, online data, www.stat.ee, authors calculations.

In addition to educational degrees, other characteristics might influence opportunities for recent graduates. Although men and women prefer different subject areas, we found almost no gender gap in unemployment risk or in the likelihood of being in a top position. Horizontal differentiation might also be important for ethnic groups, because it is possible to study in Russian in some higher education institutions. Our findings showed that ethnic minorities have a significantly higher risk of unemployment than Estonians, except for graduates with Master degree. In addition, minorities with Bachelor degrees were also less successful in achieving high positions than Estonians with a similar level of education. Thus, minority graduates are able to compete with Estonian graduates only if they reach the more selective Master's level.

To sum up, we observed clear signs of credential inflation as downward substitution in the social hierarchy occurred amongst all graduates; the most affected were people with applied higher education degrees and the least affected were graduates with Master degree. The two processes, the match shortages between supply from the educational system and demand in the labour market as well as the contraction trends due to the severe recession since 2008, have had a cumulative effect on the last cohort, who graduated 2008–2011. Also, in Estonia, flexible labour market structures do not alleviate the downward substitution process, as happens in occupational labour market systems where the occupational nature of job competition and available skills makes downward substitution processes less attractive (Gangl, 2002). In addition, the process of credential inflation is largely self-driven; it feeds on itself. A given level of education at one time gave access to élite jobs. As educational attainment has expanded, the social distinctiveness of a degree and its value in the occupational marketplace has declined; and in turn this will expand demand for still higher levels of education (Collins, 2002).

There are many possible ways to continue this analysis. One policy relevant possibility would be to undertake an in-depth analysis of the determinants of the education-job match among working graduates in Estonia. Here both a vertical mismatch of education, as a mismatch of the level of education and the job, as well as a horizontal mismatch, that is a mismatch of the field of study and the job, could be considered as an educational mismatch could have important consequences for the mismatched individual, employers and society. From a public policy perspective, both aspects are highly relevant given the substantial investment society puts into its postsecondary institutions, and the emphasis placed on education in economic development in all key strategic documents in Estonia.

Appendix 1. The probability of obtaining a certain social position; the significance of differences between cohorts inside educational groups; separate models for graduates with secondary, applied higher education, Bachelor and Master degree; multinomial regression coefficients

	Model for secondary education graduates	Model for applied higher education graduates	Model for Bachelor degree	Model for Master degree
Managers and professionals (vs. all others active in the labour market)				
Cohort (ref. 2001–2007)				
1997–2000	-.07	-.06	.39	-.90
2008–2011	-.29	.01	-.61***	-.69**
Mid-level specialists (vs. managers and professionals)				
Cohort (ref. 2001–2007)				
1997–2000	.21	-.08	-.57	1.62
2008–2011	-.06	-.42	.20	.94**
Routine white-collar or blue-collar (vs. managers and professionals)				
Cohort (ref. 2001–2007)				
1997–2000	-.11	-.54	-.22	-11.9
2008–2011	.08	.20	1.31***	.26
Unemployed (vs. managers and professionals)				
Cohort (ref. 2001–2007)				
1997–2000	.52*	1.26*	-.15	-11.7
2008–2011	.90***	.67*	.69***	.30
Inactive students (vs. managers and professionals)				
Cohort (ref. 2001–2007)				
1997–2000	.24	-12.4	-.93*	1.35
2008–2011	.31	-.59	1.31***	-.26
Inactive (vs. managers and professionals)				
Cohort (ref. 2001–2007)				
1997–2000	.94***	-1.01	-.69	-11.0
2008–2011	.01	.35	.53**	.63
N	*8950*	*405*	*1150*	*258*

Notes: Controlling for gender, ethnicity, place of residence and time after graduation

ref. Referent group

****effect significant at $p < 0.01$; ** effect significant at $p < 0.05$; * effect significant at $p < 0.10$*

Source: Authors' calculations based on ELFS

Appendix 2. The probability of obtaining a certain social position; significant differences between educational groups inside a cohort; separate models for cohorts; multinomial regression coefficients

	Model for cohort 1997–2000	Model for cohort 2001–2007	Model for cohort 2008–2011
Managers and professionals (vs. all others active in the labour market)			
Education (ref. Bachelor's degree)			
Secondary	-3.61***	-3.34***	-3.04***
Applied	-1.29**	-.99***	-.43*
Master's degree	.03	1.04***	1.01***
Mid-level specialists (vs. managers and professionals)			
Education (ref. Bachelor's degree)			
Secondary	2.71***	2.14***	1.80***
Applied	1.21*	1.11***	.52*
Master's degree	.72	-1.16***	-.30
Routine white-collar or blue-collar (vs. managers and professionals)			
Education (ref. Bachelor's degree)			
Secondary	4.51***	4.52***	3.41***
Applied	.94	1.43***	.38
Master's degree	-16.2	-1.44**	-2.82***
Unemployed (vs. managers and professionals)			
Education (ref. Bachelor's degree)			
Secondary	3.58***	3.15***	3.32***
Applied	1.43*	.43	.43
Master's degree	-17.2	-.62	-.98***
Inactive students (vs. managers and professionals)			
Education (ref. Bachelor's degree)			
Secondary	5.43***	4.33***	3.22***
Applied	-13.3	-.73**	-2.30***
Master's degree	1.32	-.76**	-2.17***
Inactive (vs. managers and professionals)			
Education (ref. Bachelor's degree)			
Secondary	4.89***	3.56***	3.29***
Applied	.48	.56**	.30
Master's degree	-15.8	-.97*	-.98**
N	*1067*	*6561*	*3135*

Notes: Controlling for gender, ethnicity, place of residence and time after graduation

ref. Referent group

****effect significant at p < 0.01; ** effect significant at p < 0.05; * effect significant at p < 0.10*

Source: Authors' calculations based on ELFS

Appendix 3. The probability of obtaining a certain social position; significant differences between men and women inside a cohort and educational group; separate models by cohorts and educational groups; multinomial regression coefficients

	Models for secondary education graduates and different cohorts	Models for applied higher education graduates and different cohorts	Models for Bachelor graduates and different cohorts	Models for Master graduates and different cohorts
Unemployed (vs. managers and professionals)				
1997–2000				
Men	-.19	...	-.39	...
Estonian	-1.59	...	-.43	...
2001–2007				
Men	-.28	.58	.08	-.36
Estonian	-1.17***	-1.35**	-1.04***	-15.4
2008–2011				
Men	.73*	.02	-.40	.24
Estonian	-1.80**	-1.54**	-1.50***	.52
Managers and professionals (vs. all others active in the labour market)				
1997–2000				
Men	0	2.95*	-.35	...
Estonian	1.86*	...	.58	...
2001–2007				
Men	.18	-.52	-.04	-.86
Estonian	.76***	-.18	.52**	.28
2008–2011				
Men	-.55	-.64	-.05	.43
Estonian	1.52**	.55	1.21***	-.37
N	*8950*	*405*	*1150*	*258*

Notes: Controlling for gender, ethnicity, place of residence and time after graduation

ref. Referent group

... Sample size is too small for calculating the model

****effect significant at p < 0.01; ** effect significant at p < 0.05; * effect significant at p < 0.10*

Source: Authors' calculations based on ELFS

Acknowledgements

The research presented has been undertaken within the project 'Labour Market Challenges to Higher Education: Estonia in European Context' supported by a Primus grant from the European Social Fund. Any errors and omissions are the responsibility of the authors alone.

References

Allmendiger, J. (1989). Educational systems and labor market outcomes. *European Sociological Review*, 5, 231–250.

Arum, R., Gamoran, A., and Shavit, Y. (2007). *Stratification in higher education: a comparative study*. Stanford, CA: Stanford University Press.

Becker, G. S. (1964). *Human capital: a theoretical and empirical analysis, with special reference to education*. New York: Columbia University Press.

Bell, D. N. and Blanchflower, D. G. (2010). Youth Unemployment: Déjà Vu? *IZA Discussion Paper Series*, 4705. Institute for the Study of Labor (IZA).

Bills, D. B. (2003). Credentials, signals, and screens: Explaining the relationship between schooling and job assignment. *Review of Educational Research*, 73, 441–449.

Bills, D. B. and Brown, D. K. (2011). New directions in educational credentialism. *Research in Social Stratification and Mobility*, 29, 1–4.

Boudarbat, B. and Chernoff, V. (2009). The Determinants of Education-Job Match among Canadian University Graduates. *IZA Discussion Paper Series,* 4513. Institute for the Study of Labor (IZA).

Brixiova, Z. (2009). Labour Market Flexibility in Estonia: What more Can be Done? *OECD, Economic Department Working Papers*, 697, 8.

Brixiova, Z., Vartia, L. and Wörgötter, A. (2010). Capital flows and the boom-bust cycle: The case of Estonia. *Economic Systems*, 34, 55–72.

Cedefop (2001). The Transition from Education to Working Life. Key Data on Vocational Training in the European Union. *Cedefop Reference series. Office for Official Publications of the European Communities*, Luxembourg.

Collins, R. (1979). *The Credential society: an historical sociology of education and stratification.* New York: Academic Press.

Collins, R. (2002). Credential Inflation and the Future of Universities. In Brint, S. (Ed.), *The Future of the City of Intellect: The Changing American University*. Stanford: Stanford University Press, 23–46.

Doeringer, P. B. and Piore, M. J. (1971). *Internal Labor Markets and Manpower Analysis.* Massachusetts: D. C. Heath and Company.

Estonian Ministry of Education and Research (2012). *Uuringud, statistika, andmebaasid* [Surveys, statistics, databases]. Available online: http://www.hm.ee/index.php?048055#k6rgharidus

Estonian Statistical Office, database. Available online: http://www.stat.ee

European Commission (2010). *Employment in Europe 2010.* Social Europe. Luxembourg: Publications Office of the European Union.

European Commission (2011). Youth Opportunities Initiative. COM 933, Brussels.

Gangl, M. (2002). Changing Labour Markets and Early Career Outcomes: Labour Market Entry in Europe Over the Past Decade. *Work, Employment & Society*, 16, 67–90.

Gangl, M. (2003). Explaining Change in Early Career Outcomes: Labour Market Conditions, Educational Expansion, and Youth Cohort Sizes. In Müller, W. and Gangl, M. (Eds.), *Transition from Education to Work in Europe*. New York: Oxford University Press, 25–276.

Habermalz, S. (2003). An Examination of Sheepskin Effects Over Time. *IZA Discussion Papers 725*. Institute for the Study of Labor (IZA).

Hampalová, D. (2003). Women and the Labour Market in the Czech Republic: Transition from Socialist to Social Democratic Regime. *GLOBALIFE Project Working Paper,* 46. Bamberg: University of Bamberg.

Kogan, I. and Unt, M. (2005). Transition from school to work in transition economies. *European Societies,* 7, 219–253.

Lindemann, K. and Saar, E. (2011). Ethnic inequalities in education: second-generation Russians in Estonia. *Ethnic and Racial Studies*, DOI:10.1080/01419870.2011.611890.

Mincer, J. (1974). *Schooling, experience, and earnings*. New York: Columbia University Press.

Müller, W. and Gangl, M. (2003). *Transitions from education to work in Europe: the integration of youth into EU labour markets*. Oxford; New York: Oxford University Press.

Noelke, C., Gebel, M. and Kogan, I. (2012). Uniform Inequalities: Institutional Differentiation and the Transition from Higher Education to Work in Post-socialist Central and Eastern Europe. *European Sociological Review*, DOI:10.1093/esr/jcs008.

Rei, T. (2009). From Crisis to Crisis or Estonia Now and 10 Years Ago. *Eesti Statistika Kvartalikiri*, 2, 18–22.

Saar, E. (2005). New entrants on the Estonian labour market: A comparison with the EU countries. *European Societies,* 7, 513–546.

Saar, E. (2008a). Expansion of higher education and opportunities in the labour market. In Heidmets, M. (Ed.), *Estonian Human development Report 2007*. Tallinn: Eesti Koostöö Kogu, 20–27.

Saar, E. (2008b). Haridus (Education). *Eesti Ühiskonna Integratsiooni Monitooring 2008* [Estonian Integration Survey]. Tallinn: Integratsiooni Sihtasutus ja Rahvastikuministri Büroo.

Saar, E. and Unt, M. (2011). Education and labour market entry in Estonia: closing doors for those without tertiary education. In Kogan, I., Noelke, C. and Gebel, M. (Eds.), *Making the transition: Education and Labour Market Entry in Central and Eastern Europe.* Stanford: Stanford University Press, 240–268.

Saar, E. and Unt, M. (2012). Labour Market Returns to Tertiary Education in Post-Socialist Countries. In Lambert, P., Connelly, R., Blackburn, R.M. and Gayle, V. (Eds.), *Social Stratification: Trends and Processes*. Farnham UK: Ashgate Publishing, 209–219.

Saar, E., Unt, M. and Kogan, I. (2008). Transition from Educational System to Labour Market in the European Union. *International Journal of Comparative Sociology*, 49, 31–59.

Sattinger, M. (1993). Assignment models of the distribution of earnings. *Journal of Economic Literature*, 31, 831–880.

Shavit, Y., Arum, R. and Gamoran, A. (2007). *Stratification in higher education: a comparative study.* Stanford: Stanford University Press.

Shavit, Y. and Müller, W. (1998). *From school to work : a comparative study of educational qualifications and occupational destinations*. Oxford, New York; Clarendon Press, Oxford University Press.

Shavit, Y., Müller, W. and Tame, C. (1998). *From school to work: a comparative study of educational qualifications and occupational destinations.* Oxford, New York: Clarendon Press, Oxford University Press.

Smyth, E. and McCoy, S. (2011). The dynamics of credentialism: Ireland from bust to boom (and back again). *Research in Social Stratification and Mobility*, 29, 91–106.

Sørensen, A. B. (2000). Toward a sounder basis for class analysis. *American Journal of Sociology,* 105, 1523–1558.

Statistics Estonia (2012). Statistical database. Available online: www.stat.ee

Täht, K. and Saar, E. (2006). Late careers and career exits in Estonia. In Blossfeld, H.-P., Buchholz, S. and Hofäcker, D. (Eds.), *Globalization, Uncertainty and Late Careers in Society.* London: Routledge, pp. 301–323.

Täht, K., Saar, E. and Unt, M. (2008). Changing mobility regime in Estonia? Young people's labor market entry and early careers since the 1980s. In Blossfeld, H.-P., Buchholz, S., Bukodi, E. and Kurz, K. (Eds.), *Young Workers, Globalization and the Labor Market. Comparing Early Working Life in Eleven Countries*. Cheltenham, Northampton: Edward Elgar Publishing, pp. 311–332.

Thurow, L.C. (1975). *Generating inequality: mechanisms of distribution in the U.S. economy.* New York: Basic Books.

Tõnisson, E. (2011). Kõrghariduse valdkonna statistiline ülevaade 2011 [Statistical overview of higher education 2011]. Tartu: Estonian Ministry of Education and Research. Available online and only in Estonian: http://www.hm.ee/index.php?048183

Wolbers, M. H. J., De Graaf, P. M. and Ultee, W. C. (2001). Trends in the occupational returns to educational credentials in the dutch labor market: Changes in structures and in the association? *Acta Sociologica*, 44, 5–19.

Chapter 14.
Why do social science graduates earn more than natural science graduates in Estonia?

Kerly Espenberg, Aivi Themas, Jaan Masso, Raul Eamets

Introduction

The type of employment that university graduates secure is of a great interest to academics and government representatives all over the world. It is well known that a university education plays a key role in the knowledge based economy. Factors such as increasing the proportion of white collar workers, knowledge spill-over, and shifts in the value chain, from low value-added to high value-added goods and services, are important for increasing the export capacity of an economy and thus also for improving its competitiveness, especially for small and open economies, and large economies with large domestic demand.

The labour market differences between hard (i.e. real) and soft (i.e. social) science graduates in Estonia have not previously been surveyed in detail, although Estonia has been included in some national comparative studies (see Reimer, Noelke, and Kucel, 2008). A recent study (Unt and Baranowska-Rataj, 2012) investigates graduates of social sciences and engineering. An earlier study by Kraut (2005) analysed the wage premiums of different study fields using tax office data. Our primary interest was to compare social sciences and natural sciences. In our opinion this is an important research question because there is a view that there is an overproduction of social science specialists while hard scientists are needed to guarantee sustainable growth in the economy. There is not much previous research in the economic literature about the soft-hard sciences wage gap in Estonia or in other countries. Previous studies have focused on different aspects of graduates entering the labour market, such as the female-male wage gap (Machin and Puhani, 2003; Goldberg and Hill, 2007; Livanos and Pouliakas, 2009), the effects of the quality of the university on labour market outcomes (Ciriaci and Muscio, 2010), and issues of over-qualification and the match between the skills required in the workplace and acquired in universities (Velasco, 2011). In some articles the income differences between postgraduates from different subject areas have been analysed (Finnie and Frenette, 1999; Black, Seth and Lowell, 2003; Thomas and Zhang, 2005; Bobbit-Zeher, 2007; Baranowska and Unt, 2011). See also the overview of literature in the section below 'Theoretical Background and Empirical Findings'.

At the European Union (EU) level much effort has been put into supporting the development of the hard sciences. In 2000 the EU set a target to increase the number of graduates in science and technology by at least 15 per cent by 2010 (Progress Towards…, 2009). Even though the proportion of graduates in these areas has increased in some countries (Estonia has exceeded the EU target for 2010), most European countries are still characterised by a low proportion of their young people choosing to study natural and life sciences. The main question of our study is: what are the factors that determine that? Although the adoption of natural and life science studies has increased in Estonia more than in many other European nations, it is possible that the factors that contribute to *not* choosing these fields of study in Estonia also apply elsewhere.

In Estonia hard science studies are supported by the government because they are seen as a critical prerequisite for the development of the knowledge-based economy. The Estonian government has supported studying in hard and technical sciences by providing state-funded university places, while the majority of social sciences students pay tuition fees. In 2009 about 84 per cent of social science students had to pay for their studies, while for hard sciences this figure was 25 per cent (Ministry of Education and Research). Despite this, many students prefer to study social sciences; engineering, manufacturing and construction or humanities (see appendix 1), and this is the case in other post-communist countries as well. In all Central European countries the proportion of students in social sciences was over 40 per cent (in Romania it was 56 per cent) in 2009, in the 'old' EU countries this figure was around 30–35 per cent or lower (in the UK 26 per cent, in Germany 26 per cent and in Finland 23 per cent, see Appendix 2). One potential explanation is the between-discipline differences in the cost of educating students. The liberalisation of the education systems and the formation of private education systems led to a very rapid increase in the number of students in the social sciences and humanities, where the cost of training is cheaper than in the natural and life sciences. Another reason was economic restructuring. There are many occupations that did not exist in the planned economies: e.g. real estate brokers, marketing managers, stock exchange brokers, PR specialists etc.

In this study we analysed how successful recent hard and social science graduates were in entering the labour market. We define 'hard sciences' as natural and life sciences and 'social sciences' as social sciences, economics and law. We analysed labour market status as well as wages a year after graduation. This comparison should shed a light on the question of whether immediate labour market effects are a reason why many students still prefer social sciences despite the policy efforts to support hard sciences.

The paper is empirical because of the empirical nature of the topic; there is no specific theoretical framework that explains hard and social science labour market differences. A general theoretical framework is Becker's human capital theory, which states that specific subject areas that develop specific skills can potentially produce higher wages than those subject areas which develop more general skills. In this sense hard sciences are certainly more specific than social sciences. Vila, Garcia-Aracil, and Mora (2007) find that employers prefer to hire those who have graduated in more specific fields with specific competence requirements, but specific study fields produce skills that are applicable to only a small number of firms in the labour market. This is particularly true for small countries. Therefore, subject areas that provide general training, widen the graduate's possible options in the labour market, but subject areas that provide specific training offer higher wages because the skills are more transferable (Thorson, 2005; Reimer et al., 2008).

Why are these issues particularly topical in the case of the post-communist economies? The available research evidence focusing on the experience of Western European countries suggests that young people with degrees from 'hard' fields of study such as engineering and hard sciences are relatively more successful at entering the labour market, whereas graduates who complete 'soft' subjects, such as humanities, face difficulties with the school-to-work transition. It is often assumed that the experience of Western societies can be easily translated into policies for Central and Eastern Europe countries. However, there are strong arguments to support the view that patterns of advantage and disadvantage relating to the field of study might differ across European societies. In a recent study Baranowska and Unt (2011) compare the labour market entry of Estonian and Polish graduates. The results indicate that in Poland and Estonia young people gain limited or no benefits from having a degree in engineering compared to the reference category of the most popular field of social sciences, business and law. Graduates from 'hard' fields of study do not tend to search for their first job sooner, or receive jobs with higher pay.

While generally the Central and Eastern Europe economies were characterised by a high level of general education[9], the fall of the Iron Curtain and the introduction of market economies led to drastic changes for certain occupations, which in turn affected the attractiveness of certain courses taken in

9 During the soviet time secondary education was compulsory (at least in the former SU). All levels and types of education were free of charge, including tertiary. Therefore, the proportion of people with tertiary and secondary education is higher in post-soviet countries than in EU-15 countries.

universities (Campos and Dabušinskas, 2009). However, another result was a general increase in the number of university students and the number of universities (for example, in Estonia the number of higher education institutions increased from 6 in 1990/1991 to 47 by 2000/2001 and decreased to 33 by 2010/2011). In Estonia over the last decade, the number of higher education students has more than doubled, from around 25,000 in the mid-1990s to approximately 70,000 in 2010 (Estonian Ministry of Education and Research). In Estonia the percentage of people with tertiary education in the 25–64 age group was 36 per cent in 2009. For comparison, the Organisation for Economic Co-operation and Development (OECD) average was 28 per cent in 2007.

Keeping in mind these developments, the purpose of this study was to compare the success of university graduates in social and hard sciences in the labour market of Estonia, as a case study of a small and open, post-communist economy. It is often debated in the media that there is an overproduction of social scientists in Estonia and therefore many of them face difficulties when entering the labour market after graduation. Based on Eurostat data, the percentage of graduates in social sciences, business and law in Estonia (38.9 per cent in 2009) is above the average of the 27 European Union (EU-27) countries (35.4 per cent in 2009) and the percentage of graduates in science, mathematics and computing is below the average of the EU-27 countries (8.9 per cent in Estonia and 9.1 per cent in the EU-27). Previous studies have concluded that graduates in some fields (especially law, business, engineering and health) have higher post-graduation incomes than graduates in other fields (e.g. humanities and social sciences). In our view, and as shown in their recent study (Baranowska and Unt, 2011), graduates from hard sciences do not have significant advantages in labour market entry compared to social science graduates, and our hypothesis is that young people with social science degrees obtain more general skills and fare better after graduation than their fellow graduates in hard sciences.

To analyse this we compared the labour market status and the wages of hard and social science graduates a year after graduation. We used data from the 2010 alumni survey (reporting 2009 graduates' data). People were surveyed a year after graduation. In total 14 universities were covered in the survey and the response rate was 22 per cent.

Another reason for the study was to analyse whether there is a demand-supply skills mismatch. As the number of graduates has increased over the past decade it has been hypothesised that the increased supply is not matched by demand which can create a problem of over-education. To test this hypothesis, we analysed the labour market positions of graduates a year after graduation. If there is a demand-supply mismatch we should observe quite a high unemployment rate among graduates, particularly as the depth of the economic crisis was experienced during 2009.

The rest of the paper is structured as follows. The second section gives a general overview of theoretical aspects and earlier empirical findings, the third part describes the Estonian education system; in the fourth section we introduce our data and in the fifth we present our results. In the last section we present our conclusions and suggest some resulting implications for practitioners and academics.

Theoretical background and earlier empirical findings

The links between subject areas and labour market outcomes have not been widely investigated in economics literature. Ten to fifteen years ago sociologists started to recognise the importance of the specific subject area of a degree on social stratification. They began to analyse its impact on labour market outcomes, such as employment status (Katz-Gerro and Yaish, 2003; Smyth, 2005), and income (Hansen, 2001; Bobbitt-Zeher, 2007, for Estonia Unt and Baranowska-Rataj, 2012), and on other aspects of labour market outcomes. The results indicate considerable differences in labour market outcomes associated with different fields of study. For instance, graduates from 'soft fields' such as the humanities or social sciences, are frequently found to fare considerably worse than their peers from the 'hard fields' such as the natural sciences and engineering (Marini and Fan, 1997; Arcidiacono, 2004) However, the results depend on the country and the outcome studied (Reimer et al., 2008)

Why are different fields of study valued differently in the labour market? From an economics point of view there are two major streams of literature. The first is related to human capital theory. It is argued that typical learning environments and acquired competencies and skills vary between different disciplines (van der Werfhorst and Kraaykamp, 2001). Certain fields can create more productive skills than others. Also, disciplines can vary in terms of how much they provide job specific skills versus general competences. Employers are interested in minimising training costs and, therefore, employees with more job specific training should have a more favourable position in the labour market.

The second approach is related to signalling. Spencer (1973) finds that the successful completion of degrees in some fields of study is assumed to be more strongly dependent on prior ability than in other disciplines. As result, fields of study effectively sort students by their ability, as more talented students choose more rewarding, more demanding fields of study. Employers learn about these distributional effects, and the more talented students from the more demanding disciplines get higher wages.

In sociology older studies of the relationships between education and the labour market tried to explain the differences between countries by using terms such as 'qualificational space' and an 'organisational space' (Maurice Sellier, and Silvestere, 1986). In qualificational space skills are learnt in a vocationally oriented schooling system, while in an organisational space work skills are acquired in the job, and education functions as a screening device. Van de Werfhorst (2004) argues that these approaches capture all kinds of important differences in secondary education. Today more and more people undertake higher education and therefore these classifications are not entirely accurate any more. Van de Werfhorst's main argument is that the transparency of education qualifications in higher education plays a crucial role for employers. If the system of competences is transparent the workers' control over their jobs are greater (Sorensen and Kalleberg, 1981) and they are able to make their employers pay higher wages in order to avoid the employees from looking for other jobs. In labour economics this concept is known as efficiency wage theory.

Van de Werfhorst (2004) finds some empirical support for his hypothesis that there are cross national differences in the effect of the field of study on occupational outcomes. He found that particularly in the Netherlands, a country with a highly developed secondary and tertiary vocational schooling system, without a bachelor – master structure and no minor major courses has the strongest educational effect on labour market outcomes is the absence of a bachelor or master's degree and any of the inherent minor or major courses. The fields of study in the Netherlands provide clear signals of specialisation, leading to advantageous positions compared to general schooling. In Norway and Australia these effects were much weaker.

However, there is also evidence from the literature that in countries with a 'weak' signalling function of education level (the UK for instance), the field of study is used as an additional selection criteria (Kim and Kim, 2003)

Reimer, Noelke, and Kucel (2008) argue that with increasing numbers of university graduates in the labour market, the signal value of a university degree from less academically challenging and less selective fields, like the humanities and social sciences, will deteriorate. Specifically, using data from 22 countries they found positive empirical support for their hypothesis that educational expansion is associated with worsening labour market chances for humanities graduates relative to other fields, both in terms of higher risks of unemployment and lower occupational status.

Arcidiacono (2004) estimated the monetary returns to particular majors (course subjects) of college graduates. He also tried to find the causes of ability sorting across the majors. He found that large monetary premiums exist for choosing natural science and business majors, even after controlling for selection. However, these large premiums, and the differential monetary returns to ability and college quality, cannot explain the ability sorting present across majors. Instead, virtually all sorting occurs because of differing preferences across abilities for majors, either in school or for the jobs associated with those majors in the workplace.

To conclude, from the literature there is no clear evidence about differences in labour market outcomes, particularly in social science and the natural sciences. If we believe the arguments of Reimer et al. (2008) then it can be assumed that increasing the number of graduates in social sciences would worsen their labour market positions relative to natural science graduates.

We can say also that, according to human capital theory, social science graduates should be in a less favourable position as they acquire more general skills compared to the more job specific skills acquired in the natural sciences. Studies in natural sciences also last longer as most jobs require master's degrees (five years of study), while in the social sciences many graduates will join the labour market after three years of study.

An overview of Estonian higher education and its funding system

At the beginning of 2011 there were 33 education institutions offering higher education in Estonia. Based on ownership and type of education provided, they can be divided as follows: 6 public universities, 3 privately owned universities, 10 public professional higher education institutions, 12 private professional higher education institutions and 2 public vocational education institutions.

Estonia signed the Bologna Declaration in 1999. This was a stimulus for large-scale changes in higher education – new study programmes were developed, the autonomy of universities was increased, a new study credits accumulation system based on student workload was established and an accreditation system was introduced. Since the academic year 2002/2003, the general structure of higher education has had three cycles that comply with the EU model: the bachelor's degree (or professional higher education diploma); the master's degree and the doctoral degree. In 2004 a Diploma Supplement and a degree recognising how qualifications awarded under different qualification systems correspond to current degrees, were introduced.

Studies at the higher education level within the scope of state-funded education are funded from the budget of the Ministry of Education and

Research. The funding system for state-funded study places is determined as follows: the total cost of a student place is calculated by multiplying the base cost of the student place by the co-efficient established for a field of study (or a study programme as an exception).

Public expenditure on higher education has been around 1 per cent of GDP in recent years. In 2009 this amounted to EUR 179 million (1.3 per cent of GDP, see Table 1).

Table 1. Total public expenditure on education

	2005	**2006**	**2007**	**2008**	**2009**	**2010**
Number of higher education institutions	39	35	35	34	34	33
Total public expenditure on education (EUR million)	554	626	753	839	831	NA
Share of GDP (%)	*4.96*	*4.73*	*4.82*	*5.22*	*6.06*	*NA*
Total public expenditure on higher education (EUR million)	101	111	161	172	179	NA
Share of GDP (%)	*0.91*	*0.84*	*1.03*	*1.07*	*1.30*	*NA*

Source: Estonian Ministry of Education and Research

Note: NA – data not available

In Estonia, some students qualify for state-funded study places. The ratio of students in state-funded to non-state funded study places has decreased significantly over the last 15 years (see Table 2). During the 2010/2011 academic year, 51 per cent of all students were funded by the state. In 1997 this figure was 72 per cent. There are remarkable differences between the social and the hard sciences too. While the vast majority of social science students have to finance their studies themselves (83 per cent in 2011), in hard sciences most places are state-funded (76 per cent in 2011). This reflects the government policy to support hard sciences.

Table 2. Number of social science and hard science students in state-funded (SF) and non-state-funded (NSF) places, 1997–2011

	Social science students			Hard science students			Total students		
	SF	NSF	Share of SF places	SF	NSF	Share of SF places	SF	NSF	Share of SF places
1997/1998	4688	7727	38	2892	28	99	24760	9782	72
1998/1999	4965	11074	31	3184	57	98	26342	14279	65
1999/2000	4921	15333	24	3422	352	91	28384	21190	57
2000/2001	5134	17100	23	3777	1106	77	30931	25506	55
2001/2002	5383	17679	23	4036	1501	73	31796	28613	53
2002/2003	5018	19011	21	4539	1860	71	32022	31603	50
2003/2004	4620	20411	18	4625	1955	70	31576	34083	48
2004/2005	4168	21618	16	5122	1903	73	31932	35828	47
2005/2006	4090	22515	15	5058	1802	74	31386	36901	46
2006/2007	4013	23326	15	5060	1769	74	31268	37499	45
2007/2008	3884	23509	14	5038	1527	77	31150	37018	46
2008/2009	3898	23210	14	5015	1480	77	31536	36863	46
2009/2010	3938	21174	16	5398	1793	75	33080	35905	48
2010/2011	3963	19370	17	5876	1836	76	35184	33929	51

Source: Estonian Ministry of Education and Research

Data and variables

We used the Estonian Graduates Alumni Survey, which reports data on graduates from 2009. The survey was conducted in 2010 and covered all major public and private Estonian universities (14 universities out of 18). University graduates were surveyed about one year after graduation. Both graduates and postgraduates, who had completed a master's or doctoral degree, were involved. The sample size was 2187 and we had a response rate of 22 per cent.

The survey included questions about working during studies and labour market status a year after graduation, as well as different aspects related to these issues: which channels were used to find a job, whether and to what extent the job taken was related to the previous field of study, current employment position, skills and level of education required for the position, gross wage and other income. More information about the data collection methodology can be found in Themas, Espenberg, Eamets (2011).

In our study we focused on comparing two graduate categories: students in hard sciences (i.e. natural and exact sciences, ISCED 97 fields of education classification, level 4) and social sciences (social sciences, economics and law, ISCED 97 fields of education classification, level 3). We excluded other student subject groups from the analysis.

The variables used in the analysis can be grouped into three categories: socio-demographic (gender, age), study-related (study level, university) and job-related (occupation, sector, location, firm size, tenure). Unfortunately our database did not include information about the family-related responsibilities of individuals (marriage status, number of children, etc) which may have an important influence on labour market decisions.

Age is defined in years not in age groups. In the analysis we made a distinction between study levels: bachelor's and applied higher education versus master's and doctoral graduates, because it was highly likely that there would be labour outcome differences between these categories. Compared to master's and doctoral graduates, bachelor's and applied higher education graduates have less work experience and their jobs are less related to the subject studied (Espenberg et al., 2012). For the university variable, we defined dummies for the each of the 14 universities included.

Occupation is defined based on the ISCO08 1-digit classification (i.e. 9 categories from managers to elementary occupations). Tenure is measured as the length of employment in the current job. In terms of location we distinguished between four Estonian districts: Northern, Central Eastern, Western and Southern Estonia. Firm size is the categorical variable having 6 values[10]. We controlled for the sector by including a set of dummies for the field of activity of the main job, corresponding mostly to the 2-digit sectors of the NACE classification.

Results

Working after graduation

There are notable differences when comparing the labour market status of social and hard sciences graduates a year after graduation. Social sciences bachelor graduates tend to enter the labour market, but hard sciences graduates tend to continue studying. In total, more than 80 per cent of social science first level[11] graduates, but only 65 per cent of hard science first level[12] graduates, are in

10 1 = 1–9 employees; 2 = 10–19 employees; 3 = 20–49 employees; 4 = 50–99 employees; 5 = 200–499 employees; 6 = more than 500 employees.

11 For the sake of brevity, in the empirical part we use the term '1st level' when talking about bachelor's and applied higher education graduates and '2nd level' for master's and doctoral level graduates.

12 For the sake of the shortness, in the empirical part we use the term '1st level' when talking about bachelor and applied higher education graduates and '2nd level' for master and doctoral level graduates.

work a year after completing their studies at that level. At the second level the percentages are about the same: about 90 per cent of both social and hard science graduates work. However, compared to hard sciences, a considerably higher proportion of social science graduates only work (without continuing their studies). This conclusion applies to both the bachelor's/applied higher education and the master's/doctoral level.

Continuing to study after completing a bachelor's/applied higher education degree is much more common among hard science graduates. Almost 70 per cent of them continue their studies (compared with 35 per cent of social science students). This is a reflection of the differences of employers' demands: in the social sciences, employers are often content to specify only 'higher education' among their qualification requirements, in hard science, a master's degree at least is often required to guarantee sufficient knowledge to successfully enter the labour market.

Only a small proportion of Estonian higher education graduates are unemployed (see Table 3). This is good news for university graduates, especially when comparing the results with Statistics Estonia data, which states that the general unemployment rate was 16.9 per cent and the youth unemployment rate 32.9 per cent in 2010, and 12.5 per cent and 22.3 per cent in 2011, respectively.

Table 3. Labour market status one year after graduation (per cent)

Level of study	Field of study	Work-ing	Studying	Working and studying	Unemp -loyed[13]	At home	Other	Total
Bachelor's or applied higher educational degree	Social sciences	54	9	28	3	6	1	100
	Hard sciences	29	31	36	1	1	3	100
Master's or doctoral degree	Social sciences	80	1	10	2	7	1	100
	Hard sciences	52	4	37	1	7	0	100

Source: Alumni surveys, authors' own calculations

When it comes to their current professions, social science graduates work more frequently as managers, legislators, senior officials and officials, and hard science graduates as professionals (see Table 4). As expected, the proportion of

13 This is not equal to the unemployment rate, because it reflects the share of graduates who are unemployed a year after graduation.

higher-rank workers is higher among those who completed master's or doctoral degrees, than among those holding bachelor's/applied higher education degrees. The share of blue-collar workers (ISCO08 levels 5–8, in the table marked as 'other') is low among graduates.

Table 4. Current professions of alumni (per cent)

Level of study	Field of study	Legislators, senior officials and managers	Professionals	Technicians and associate professionals	Clerks	Other	Total
Bachelor's or applied higher education degree	Social sciences	13	23	34	21	9	100
	Hard sciences	5	62	24	1	8	100
Master's or doctoral degree	Social sciences	17	56	21	5	1	100
	Hard sciences	5	66	25	3	1	100

Source: Alumni surveys, authors' own calculations

Compared to the social sciences, more hard science graduates have a job closely related to their degree subject (see Table 5). As expected, the mismatch is higher for the bachelor's and applied higher education levels than for the master's and doctoral levels. Therefore, we can conclude that while more social science graduates focus on working after finishing first level studies, their jobs are less often directly linked to the subject studied.

Table 5. The relationship between current job tasks and the subject studied (per cent)

		Very closely	Rather closely	To some degree	Not at all	Total
Bachelor's or applied higher education degree	Social sciences	39	23	23	15	100
	Hard sciences	52	19	19	10	100
Master's or doctoral degree	Social sciences	58	28	8	6	100
	Hard sciences	64	16	11	9	100

Source: Alumni surveys, authors' own calculations

There are two possible reasons for this: voluntary mismatches (i.e. due to a person's preferences) and involuntary mismatches (i.e. due to the labour market situation). If the involuntary mismatch is prevalent, this means that social science students face more problems finding appropriate jobs and accept jobs because they can see no better options in the labour market. We do not have an indicator that directly measures the volume of involuntary mismatch because the number of those who commented on mismatch and the reasons for it are too small to draw reliable conclusions.

However, the analysis of over- and under-qualification (i.e. mismatches between education level attained and that required for the job held) sheds a different light on this issue. At the bachelor's/applied higher education degree level there are signs of under-qualification and at the master's/doctoral degree level there are signs of over-qualification (see Table 6).

At the 1st level about 45 per cent of social science and 38 per cent of hard science graduates have a job that is in accordance with their degree; for 21 per cent of social science graduates and 13 per cent of hard science graduates their job requires less education, and for 5 per cent of social science graduates and 6 per cent of hard science graduates, they hold jobs that would normally require a higher level of education than they have actually achieved.

For those with 2nd level education the discrepancies are higher: 35 per cent of those with social science qualifications and 50 per cent of those from the hard sciences have a job corresponding to their education level. In general then, we can conclude that over-qualification is higher among social science graduates, but there are only small differences between the two groups.

Table 6. The relationship between actual education level and education level required in the current job (subjective evaluation by graduates) (per cent)

Level of study	Field of study	Education level is not important	Secondary (general)	Vocational	Applied higher	Bachelor's	Master's/ doctoral	NA	Total
Bachelor's or applied higher education degree	Social sciences	6	15	5	11	34	5	24	*100*
	Hard sciences	5	8	2	9	29	6	41	*100*
Master's or doctoral degree	Social sciences	2	3	1	2	40	35	17	*100*
	Hard sciences	2	2	1	4	27	50	14	*100*

Source: Alumni surveys, authors' own calculations

Wages[14]

According to Statistics Estonia, in 2010 the national average gross wage was 792 EUR per month. As can be seen from Table 7, a social science education pays off more than a hard science education, but only at the 2nd level where the proportion of those earning high salaries (more than 1,000 EUR per month) is considerably higher than hard science graduates. The proportion of those earning wages above the national average is higher among social science students at the master's/doctoral level. Interestingly, in hard sciences the proportion of those whose wage was lower than the national average was slightly higher amongst those with master's/doctoral degrees than those with bachelor's/applied higher education degrees.

Table 7. Wage distribution of 2009 graduates by education level and subject learnt (EUR per month)

EUR per month		...-300	300-500	500-792	792-1000	1000-1500	1500-...	TOTAL	less than national average (% of total)
Bachelor's or applied higher education degree	Social sciences	4.3	10.1	35.8	27	17	5.8	100	50.2
	Hard sciences	5	12.7	23.6	29.4	22	7.3	100	41.3
Master's or doctoral degree	Social sciences	0	2.4	17.6	17.5	41.2	21.3	100	20
	Hard sciences	4.9	15.6	24	14	25	16.5	100	44.5

Source: 2009 Alumni survey, authors' own calculations

Note: only university-based graduates, weighted data, upper and lower 2.5 per cent of wage scale excluded.

At the bachelor's/applied higher education degree level, the wages of social and hard science graduates are almost equal (the difference is not statistically significant); while at the higher degree level the difference is almost 25 per cent[15] (the difference is statistically significant, see Tabel 8). Moreover,

14 In this section we include only intramural graduates in the analysis to guarantee the comparability of the results. In the social sciences the share of extramural students is higher than in the real sciences, i.e. in the social sciences the higher share of students is obtaining the higher education while working, they have a longer tenure, etc.

15 We excluded 2.5 per cent at the lowest end and at the highest end of the wage distribution in each group from the analysis to mitigate the influence of outliers.

although a higher degree clearly has an impact in both groups, in the social sciences the influence is far more noticeable – the mean wage of someone who has a doctorate or a master's degree is about 45 per cent higher than those with a bachelor's degree in the social sciences. For the hard sciences the difference is about 10 per cent.

Table 8. Gross monthly salary of employed alumni a year after graduation (EUR per month)

Statistics		Bachelor's or applied higher education degree		Master's or doctoral degree	
		Social sciences	Hard sciences	Social sciences	Hard sciences
N		855	262	267	223
Mean		822	876	1183	963
Median		793	893	1150	895
Std. Deviation		346	385	442	508
Minimum		256	256	320	243
Maximum		2556	2301	2556	2512
Percentiles	1	256	256	320	243
	5	345	345	617	286
	95	1534	1534	2045	2016
	99	2045	2301	2556	2512

Source: 2009 Alumni survey, authors' own calculations

Note: only university-based graduates, weighted data, upper and lower 2.5 per cent of wage scale excluded.

In what follows we will introduce the results of the Oaxaca-Blinder decomposition in order to shed light on which variables explain the social and hard sciences wage gap in Estonia. We applied a step-by-step approach when adding explanatory variables to the analysis. Model 1 only includes the level of study (bachelor's/applied higher versus master's/doctoral). Model 2 includes the level of study and personal characteristics (university, age, gender). Model 3 includes all variables included in Model 2 plus an occupational variable. Model 4 has a sector variable added and in Model 5 the location of the enterprise, firm size and tenure are added.

As a first step, a probit model was estimated[16] and, based on the results of the probit model, an Oaxaca-Blinder decomposition was performed. To decompose the graduate wage gap, we used the widely accepted Blinder (1973)

16 Estimation results are not presented here, but are available from the authors upon request.

-Oaxaca (1973) decomposition (subscript *s* marks social and subscript *r* hard sciences):

$$\Delta \equiv lnw_s - lnw_r = (X_s - X_r)\beta_s + (\beta_s - \beta_r)X_r$$

The first part of the right-hand side, the 'explained gap', is the part of the pay gap due to observed differences in X-variables between the social and hard sciences graduates. The second part, the 'unexplained gap', is a residual that arises due to differences in the returns to the X-variables between the two groups. Sometimes the second term is regarded as discrimination against females; however, since the interpretation of the unexplained gap depends on whether all of the relevant differences between the two groups are taken into account, one has to be cautious when interpreting the explained and unexplained gaps.

Table 9. Oaxaca-Blinder decomposition of the wage (EUR per month) gap between hard and social sciences graduates: gross wage

Variables	**1**	**2**	**3**	**4**	**5**
Social sciences	885	885	885	885	885
Hard sciences	847	847	847	847	847
Wage gap (log difference)	4.5%	4.5%	4.5%	4.5%	4.5%
Explained	-5.8%	-17.0%	-19.4%	-18.8%	-17.0%
Unexplained	10.3%	21.5%	23.9%	23.4%	21.5%
Explained part by factors					
Level (first/second level)	-0.058 (-3.82)	-0.046 (-3.33)	-0.027 (-2.4)	-0.038 (-3.21)	-0.033 (-2.94)
University		-0.087 (-4.32)	-0.067 (-3.66)	-0.051 (-3.03)	-0.051 (-3.16)
Age		-0.053 (-3.09)	-0.039 (-2.46)	-0.027 (-1.87)	-0.013 (-0.94)
Gender		0.016 (1.46)	0.005 (0.53)	0.009 (0.93)	0.015 (1.53)
Occupation			-0.066 (-3.33)	-0.058 (-3.08)	-0.05 (-2.71)
Sector				-0.023 (-0.57)	-0.043 (-1.13)
Location					0.02 (1.51)
Firm size					-0.017 (-1.75)
Tenure					0.001 (0.32)
Observations	544	544	544	544	544

Not: Z-statistics are in parenthesis. In order to control for possible measurement errors we excluded the lower and upper 2.5 per cent of observations from the calculations. Only university-based students are included in the analysis. Both graduates with master's and bachelor's degree are included in the calculations. The sample size is the same in all estimations as we chose to sample the observations with non-missing values in all relevant variables. All estimations are weighed with sample weights.

The reported numbers and different factors show the contribution of each factor to the explained part of the wage gap. The estimated regression coefficients of the underlying wage regressions are not reported to save space.

As can be seen, the social science-hard science wage gap observed is largely due to factors not included in the analysis. The unexplained gap is remarkably high and positive in all models and increases when additional explanatory variables are added. The explained part of the gap is large too, but, unlike the unexplained part, it is negative. This means that, based on the socio-demographic and job-related characteristics that we used as explanatory variables in the analysis, we should observe a considerable wage gap in favour of hard science graduates, but there are factors not included in the analysis that give the opposite result. What those factors are is still unknown. They probably include personal characteristics like empathy, motivation, and there are probably some family-related characteristics which have an effect but which we do not have information about in the data set. One possible explanation could be that the variables as defined in our data are too general. In the case of occupation, for example, we have 9 occupational dummies (at the 1-digit level occupational code). Most university graduates are employed in white-collar jobs and the issue is rather, how different white-collar jobs are paid (e.g. marketing clerks versus engineers), and we are unable to capture that with this data.

For the explanatory variable, the most important factors are the university, occupation and sector. Other variables are either not statistically significant or close to zero.

Conclusions

The aim of this study was to compare the labour market outcomes of graduates in the hard sciences (i.e. natural and exact sciences) with those in the social sciences (i.e. social sciences, economics and law). We used data from a recent (2010) alumni survey to analyse labour market activity and the wages of the two groups. Despite the lack of state-funded places, social science degrees are far more popular than hard science degrees in Estonia, even though the Estonian government has declared the latter a priority in order to guarantee sustainable development. In our study we surveyed the reasons for this tendency.

The comparison with the professions and incomes of hard and social science graduates showed the popularity of the latter. First, a considerably higher proportion of social science students entered the labour market compared to their hard science counterparts. This can be explained by the fact that the skills obtained in social sciences are more general and, therefore, it is easier for the social science graduates to find a job after finishing the first higher education level. However, in hard sciences the graduate's jobs and the subject that they studied are more closely linked, indicating that it is easier for the hard science graduates to find jobs closely linked with the subject that they studied. At first glance these facts contradict existing theory. As mentioned in the theory section, more job specific skills should give an advantage in a job search, but they can also be a disadvantage. If the labour market is rather limited, then those graduates, with skills applicable across a range of different industries, will have more chance of finding a suitable job. Earlier studies about Estonia show that the largest spread across industries was in social sciences, while the smallest was in education and health (Kraut, 2005).

The proportion of blue-collar workers was low in both groups. Social science graduates tend to be found more often in legislators, senior officials and managers' positions and hard science graduates in professional positions.

The wage analysis indicated that while there is no difference between the average wages of social and hard sciences graduates at the first higher education level (i.e. bachelor's/higher applied education), at the master's/doctoral level the wages of the social sciences graduates are clearly higher. This explains the continuing popularity of the social sciences – labour market prospects for social scientists are better. The earlier study of Praxis (Kraut, 2005) also indicates that tax office data showed that the largest wage premiums are earned in the social sciences in Estonia. Why is this? There are no clear answers. As we have seen, human capital theory does not work in the Estonian case, and signalling theory has little to say. If we assume that the social sciences are only accessible to the most talented students, then signalling theory could explain the situation. However, we know that the majority of students in the social sciences are self-financing. We could say that those who have money to pay for their studies should have more able parents who can afford their study costs, but this is not always true, as it is also well known that the majority of students work during their studies. One explanation is provided by Unt and Baranowska-Rataj (2012) who studied graduates in Poland and Estonia. They focused on engineering and social sciences and argued that European countries differ with respect to the level of restrictions to entry into a given occupation, which is regulated by means of licensing. In Central and Eastern European countries, licensing in the engineering occupations is particularly strict. Their results demonstrate that in Poland and Estonia, young people derive limited or no benefits from having a diploma in engineering compared to their reference category, the most popular field, social sciences, business and law.

These kinds of institutional factors could influence certain occupations in natural sciences as well. Why do wage differences remain high even at the master's level? If we assume that, according to human capital theory, the returns to education are dependent on the number of years of schooling, then why do the wage differences between the two disciplines increase? One explanation is the high proportion of open-university graduates in the social sciences. Different types of Master of Business Administration (MBA) programmes are very attractive for those who already have a good job with a good salary. First labour market entrants from natural sciences with master's degrees cannot compete with those who already have many years of experience.

The decomposition model revealed that the wage gap in favour of social sciences was not explained by the variables used in the analysis (level of study, university, sex, age, occupation, sector, firm size, location, tenure). We should have observed a significant wage gap in favour of the hard sciences based on those variables. In other words, we find that real sciences graduates are working in sectors and occupations where higher wages are paid. So, the determinants of the wage gap in favour of social sciences remain an open question. There are probably self-selection effects that cannot be captured in an explicit way, but have an important influence of the differences observed.

Acknowledgements

The research presented has been undertaken within the project 'Estonian higher education alumni survey 2010' supported by a Primus grant from the European Social Fund. Any errors and omissions are the responsibility of the authors alone.

References

Arcidiacono, P. (2004). Ability Sorting and the Returns to College Major, *Journal of Econometrics,* 121, 343–75.

Baranowska, A., and Unt, M. (2011). Is it Worth Becoming an Engineer in Central and Eastern Europe? The Evidence from Poland and Estonia. *Tallinn University, TööKõrgEEL, Working Paper*, No 8.

Black, D., Seth S. and Lowell, T. (2003). The economic reward for studying economics. *Economic Inquiry*, 41, 365–377.

Blinder, A. S. (1973). Wage Discrimination: Reduced Form and Structural Estimates. *Journal of Human Resources*, 8, 436–455.

Bobbitt-Zeher, D. (2007). The Gender Income Gap and the Role of Education. *Sociology of Education* 80, 1–22.

Campos, N. F. and Dabušinskas, A. (2009). So many rocket scientists, so few marketing clerks: Estimating the effects of economic reform on occupational mobility in Estonia. *European Journal of Political Economy*, 25, 261–275.

Ciriaci, D. and Muscio, A. (2010). Does university choice drive graduate's employability? *University Library of Munich, MPRA Paper, 22846.*

Espenberg, K., Themas, A., Masso, J., Eamets, R. (2012). Does university degree pay off in Estonian labour market? *Studies for Learning Societies*, 2, 46–60.

Finnie, R. and Frenette, M. (2003). Earning differences by major field of study: evidence from three cohorts of recent Canadian graduates. *Economics of Education Review,* 22, 179–192.

Goldberg D. and Hill, C. (2007). Behind the pay gap. *AAUW Educational Foundation.* Available online: http://www.aauw.org/learn/research/upload/behindPayGap.pdf

Hansen, M. N. (2001). 'Education and Economic Rewards. Variations by Social-Class Origin and Income Measures', *European Sociological Review* 17, 209–231.

Katz-Gerro, T. and Yaish, M. (2003). Higher Education: Is More Better? Gender Differences in Labour Market Returns to Tertiary Education in Israel, *Oxford Review of Education,* 29, 571–592.

Kim, A. and Kim, K.-W. (2003). Returns to Tertiary Education in Germany and the UK: Effects of Field of Study and Gender, working paper no. 62, Mannheimer Zentrum für Sozialforschung (MZES).

Kraut, L. (2005). *Kõrghariduse omandanute ja katkestanute võrdlus töötasult laekunud tulumaksu põhjal: lõpparuanne* [The comparison of the university graduates and dropouts based on the income tax: survey report]. Praxis, Tallinn.

Livanos, I. and Pouliakas, K. (2009). The gender wage gap as a function of educational degree choices in an occupationally segregated EU country. *IZA Discussion Papers, 4636.* Available online: http://ftp.iza.org/dp4636.pdf

Machin, S. and Puhani, A. P. (2003). Subject of degree and the gender wage differential: evidence from the UK and Germany. *Economics Letters*, 70, 393–400.

Marini, M. M. and Fan, P.-L. (1997). The Gender Gap in Earnings at Career Entry, *American Sociological Review,* 62, 588–604.

Maurice, M., Sellier, F. and Silvestere, J.-J. (1986). *The Social Foundations of Industrial Power: A Comparison of France and Germany.* Cambridge MA: MIT Press.

Progress Towards the Lisbon Objectives in Education and Training. Commission of the European Communities, 2009, 181.

Reimer, D., Noelke, C. and Kucel, A. (2008). Labor Market Effects of Field of Study in Comparative Perspective: An Analysis of 22 European Countries. *International Journal of Comparative Sociology,* 49, 233–256.

Smyth, E. (2005). Gender Differentiation and Early Labour Market Integration across Europe, *European Societies,* 7, 451–479.

Sorensen, A. B. and Kalleberg, A. L. (1981). An Outline of a Theory of the Matching of Persons to Jobs, in I. Berg (ed.) *Sociological Perspectives on Labour Markets*, 49–74. New York: Academic Press.

Spence, M. (1973). Job Market Signaling, *Quarterly Journal of Economics,* 87, 355–74.

Themas, A., Espenberg, K. and Eamets, R. (2011). Estonian Universities' Graduates Survey. Research report. Tartu: University of Tartu.

Thomas, L. and Zhang, L. (2005). Post-baccalaureate wage growth within 4 years of graduation: the effects of college quality and college major. *Research in Higher Education*, 46, 437–459.

Thorson, A. (2005). The effect of college major on wages. *The Park Place Economist*, 13, 45–57.

Universities UK (2010). Recession to recovery: Changes in student choices and graduate employment. Research report. Available online: http://www.universitiesuk.ac.uk/Publications/Documents/ChangesInStudentChoicesAndGraduateEmployment20100907.pdf

Unt, M. and Baranowska-Rataj, A. (2012). Is it Worth Becoming an Engineer in Central and Eastern Europe? The Evidence from Poland and Estonia, European Sociological Review, published online June 25.

van de Werfhorst, H. G. (2004). Systems of Educational Specialization and Labour Market Outcomes in Norway, Australia, and the Netherlands, *International Journal of Comparative Sociology,* 45, 315–335.

van de Werfhorst, H. G. and Kraaykamp, G. (2001). Four field-related Educational Resources and Their Impact on Labor, Consumption, and Sociopolitical Orientation, *Sociology of Education,* 74, 296–317.

Velasco, M. (2011). Evidence on graduate over-qualification in Europe: underutilization of educational skills and unrealized expectations. Universidad de Granada, Spain, mimeo. Available online: http://www.alde.es/encuentros/anteriores/xeea/trabajos/s/pdf/044.pdf (last accessed 27.03.2012).

Vila, L., Garcia-Aracil, A. and Mora, J. (2007). The distribution of job satisfaction among young European graduates: does the choice of study field matter? *The journal of Higher Education*, 78, 97–118.

Appendix 1. Students in social sciences, business and law (per cent of total number of students, 2009)

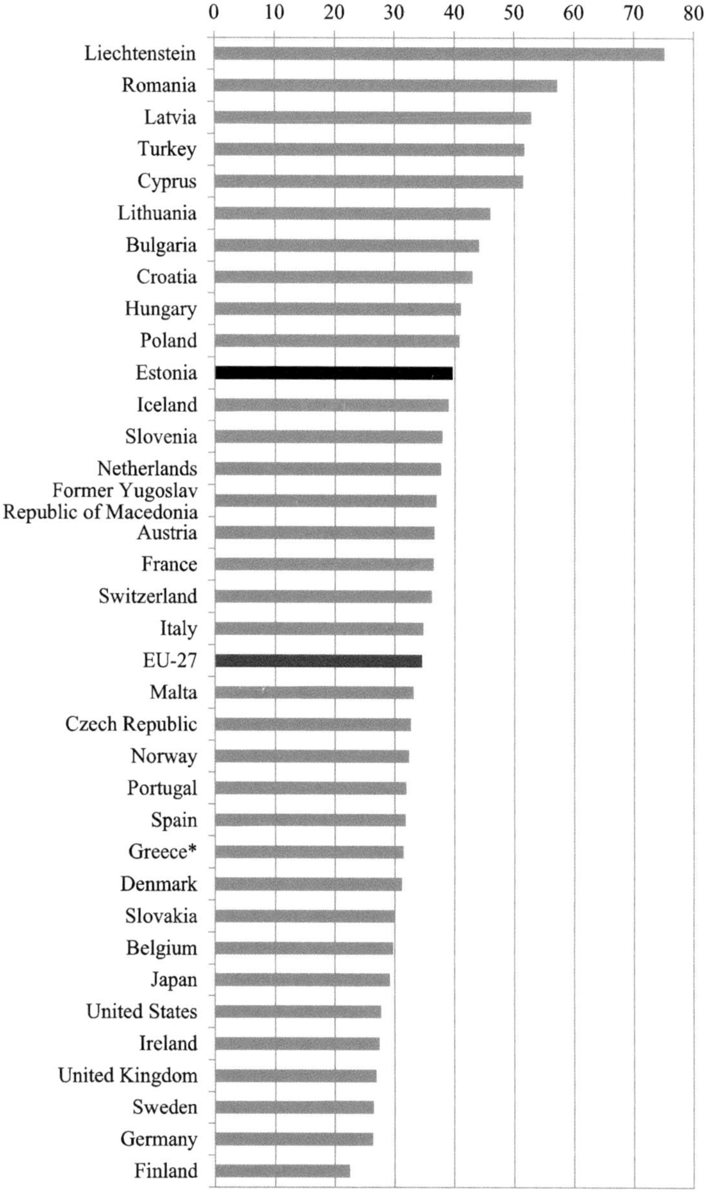

Source: Eurostat, authors' own calculations

Appendix 2. Number of students in social and real sciences faculties in Estonia, 1995–2011

	Social sciences		Real sciences		Total
	No of students	Share from all students	No of students	Share from all students	No of students
1993/94	6 439	26%	2 140	9%	25 064
1994/95	7 220	28%	2 249	9%	25 483
1995/96	8 883	33%	2 289	8%	27 234
1996/97	10 286	34%	2 303	8%	30 072
1997/98	12 415	36%	2 920	8%	34 542
1998/99	16 039	39%	3 241	8%	40 621
1999/00	20 254	41%	3 774	8%	49 574
2000/01	22 234	39%	4 883	9%	56 437
2001/02	23 062	38%	5 537	9%	60 409
2002/03	24 029	38%	6 399	10%	63 625
2003/04	25 031	38%	6 580	10%	65 659
2004/05	25 786	38%	7 025	10%	67 760
2005/06	26 605	39%	6 860	10%	68 287
2006/07	27 339	40%	6 829	10%	68 767
2007/08	27 393	40%	6 565	10%	68 168
2008/09	27 108	40%	6 495	9%	68 399
2009/10	25 112	36%	7 191	10%	68 985
2010/11	23 333	34%	7 712	11%	69 113

Source: Estonian Ministry of Education and Research

Share of students by the field of study

	1998/99	2008/09
Education	10,0	7,0
Humanities	12,3	12,3
Social sciences	39,5	39,6
Natural sciences	8,0	9,5
Engineering, manufacturing and construction	13,8	13,3
Agriculture	2,3	2,2
Health and welfare	8,3	8,3
Services	5,8	7,8

Source: Estonian Ministry of Education and Research

Chapter 15.
The expansion of higher education: devaluation or differentiation? The Estonian case

Marge Unt, Kadri Täht, Ellu Saar, Jelena Helemäe

Introduction

After the global financial crisis of 2008, the demand for labour dropped in most countries (European Commission, 2010). One of the central elements of the financial crisis was the housing bubble. In a similar way to housing, higher education (HE) has rapidly expanded in many developed countries during the last decade (Shavit, Arum and Gamoran, 2007). What are the consequences of these developments? Is there also a HE 'bubble' leading to its devaluation, as argued by Thiel, one of the founders of PayPal and an investor in Facebook (Swail, 2011)? Or has HE kept its distinctive power despite its expansion? The aim of this work was to study the outcomes of expansion in terms of the perceived role and meaning of HE and these were studied from the perspective of labour market prospects, particularly the meaning and importance of HE in job recruitment.

Many authors have suggested that if a considerable proportion of people undertake HE, it loses its distinctive power (Collins, 1979; Seidman, 1984; van der Ploeg, 1994) and that this may lead to *devaluation*. Here 'devaluation' is used to mean that a HE degree loses most of its value as a 'rare and distinctive sort of capital', and it could be argued that this has happened in the majority of European countries. This has meant that formal qualifications (including HE) have become more of a basic requirement rather than a tool.

In contrast, other researchers consider that the expansion of HE results in a shift towards an internal *differentiation* of HE (Davies and Guppy, 1997; van de Werfhorst, 2002; Gerber and Cheung, 2008). This differentiation can take place in awarded degrees (diploma, Bachelor's, Master's), subject areas, or types of HE institutions and their selectivity.

In a similar way to many other European countries, Estonia has experienced HE expansion, which is characterised by a dramatically increasing number of (private) HE institutions and growing numbers of students (Tõnisson, 2011). Previous studies have shown that graduates of HE enjoy clear advantages in the labour market, both in terms of status and job security. This may also explain why so many young people aim for a HE degree. However, HE has expanded in Estonia at a much greater rate than the upgrading of the occupational structure. Some studies indicate that HE may have lost some of its advancement-power: its 'safety-net-character' against downward mobility has weakened, and many university graduates enter the labour market over-educated.

In parallel with its expansion, the Estonian HE system has gone through various changes. During the socialist period (1944–1991), universities and other institutions of HE involved 4 to 6 years of studying. At the end of the 1990s, the Bologna Declaration was implemented, the 3+2 curriculum was adopted and provisions for professional HE studies were drafted. Changes in HE have been accompanied by the creation of certificate and degree requirements for several professions when hiring and promoting staff. All these changes may affect the way that HE is seen and perceived, by sending mixed or confusing signals to the different parties involved, i.e. graduates, employers and universities. Therefore, the aim of this study was to investigate the role and meaning given to HE in labour market recruitment by different parties in Estonia.

Earlier research on the role of education in the labour market in Estonia has mainly been either or both quantitative (Saar, 2008; 2011, see also Chapter 16) and focused on the labour market outcomes of HE graduates compared to other educational groups (Unt, 2011). However, little is known about the demand aspect, that is, the employers' perspectives, and there are even fewer studies where the perceptions and views of different parties are analysed and considered. So, the current study analysed and contrasted the perceptions and understandings of the three main groups – the graduates, the employers, and the HE institutions. We used a qualitative approach that allowed examination of the selection mechanisms and criteria applied by the employers and the respective strategies and expectations of the HE graduates and HE institutions.

The expansion of higher education and the changing role of higher education credentials

The expansion of HE has resulted in a proliferation of HE credentials, which, as argued by various authors (Collins, 1979; Seidman, 1984; van der Ploeg, 1994), may lead to their devaluation. When the attainment ratio is small, the value of HE credentials is also small because employers do not use them in the recruitment process. The value increases as the proportion of people with HE grows, because employers use HE more frequently as a selection criterion (van der Ploeg, 1994). The expansion of HE means that it becomes a threshold for access to many jobs with some potential candidates not even coming to the attention of the employers because they do not have HE credentials. As HE expands, the value of the credentials in the labour market tend to decrease again because as the supply of HE graduates prevails employers give less weight to their credentials than when they were in shorter supply. This means that the signalling role of HE credentials reduces. This decrease is an example of credential inflation: the employer practice of increasing hiring standards over time (Collins, 1979). On the other hand, the proliferation of HE credentials may cause the absence of them to serve as an indicator of 'unqualification' and send a negative signal to an employer (Olneck and Kim, 1989; van der Ploeg, 1994).

Other research suggests that HE expansion does not devalue all HE credentials, but introduces qualitative differentiation (Lucas, 2001; Arum, Gamoran and Shavit, 2007), either vertically or horizontally. Vertical differentiation refers to the situation where the credential, either a diploma, Bachelor, Master or doctoral degree, will differentiate the graduates' chances in the labour market. It might be, for instance, that the labour market value of a diploma or Bachelor degree may devalue in the process of expansion, but Master degree and doctoral degree degrees might still hold a distinct value for applying for high status positions. Horizontal differentiation refers to the growing importance in later labour market outcomes of field of study, or type of HE institution and how selective it is (Davies and Guppy, 1997; van de Werfhorst, 2002; Gerber and Cheung, 2008). While differentiation is commonly regarded as a consequence of expansion, it may also contribute to expansion, as new places become available in new segments of the education system (Arum et al., 2007). Some researchers suggest that HE expansion is a process of diversion, whereby members of lower classes are diverted from élite universities and are channelled to lower-tier HE institutions (Brint and Karabel 1989; Gamoran and Mare, 1989). This means that even when the overall inequality of access to HE decreases, horizontal differentiation in HE increases (Gerber and Cheung, 2008).

With the proliferation and diversification of HE qualifications, it is suggested that their role in labour markets is diversifying as well, and interpretations of this role are expected to have complex, context- and time-dependent characteristics. Credentials from highly respected institutions may become more important in the recruitment process during a tightening economic situation.

The link between education and job assignment and the role of education credentials in this have been explained in various ways. *Human capital theory* assumes that education provides marketable skills relevant to job performance. The employers' aim is to maximize productivity, which makes the more highly educated applicants more valuable to employers. Close to human capital theory is *signalling or screening theory*. Employers screen workers on the basis of the signals sent out by applicants. More schooling is not seen as direct proof of productivity but rather as an indicator of some latent, desirable but unobservable trait (for example ability, trainability, commitment, cognitive endowment etc.) (Spence, 1973; Arkes, 1999).

At the other end of the continuum is *symbolic theory* which stresses the importance of education as a symbol *per se* (Bridges, 1996). This idea is supported by *credentialist theory*, which assumes that education functions as a legitimised means of closure. Entry to certain occupations is closed to those not having the required credentials, thus, what matters is the formal recognition of the completion of a certain educational level. This means that normatively defined threshold points become valued in their own right. For instance, education may be rewarded because access to occupations is regulated on the basis of qualifications. Other authors have shown that employers often overstate the level of education they state in their formal requirements for work positions (Berg, 1971; Collins, 1979). Students might also adopt this strategy (of being overqualified) in order to compete at the labour market.

The way that employers use education in the recruitment process depends on the relation between the supply and demand for education. The liberal human capital theory assumes that the *expansion of HE* reflects the rising demand for qualified workers that are required for a steadily increasing and technologically advancing economy (Blau and Duncan, 1967; Brown, Lauder and Ashton, 2008). Whilst several studies have shown that the knowledge-based economy does not necessarily produce an increase in high-skilled positions to match the rate of the expansion of HE, other researchers emphasise demand resulting from the decisions of prospective students and their families (Collins, 1979). The incentives to attend university rise because individuals compete for access to the best jobs. Regardless of the specific mechanism, these theories share the assumption that expansion is demand-driven.

Under conditions of the proliferation of higher education, qualifications decline in a value as a signal, and employers need to look for alternative or supplementary signals (Jackson, Goldthorpe and Mills, 2005). Some of these signals are education-related, for example the type of HE institutions, as suggested above. Other non-educational signals (for example such ascribed characteristics as social background, ethnicity etc.) may supplement or even supplant education-related signals (Brown, 2003) and may indicate the devaluation of HE credentials.

The background to job assignment: the case of Estonia

In recent decades, HE in Estonia has gone through various important changes. One of the biggest changes is the expansion of the sector: the number of students in HE in Estonia has almost tripled over the last decade. At the beginning of the 1990s the number of students was about 25,000, by 2010/11 it had reached almost 70,000 (Tõnisson, 2011:3).

The increase in the number of students has taken place in both the academic (Bachelor, Master and doctoral degree) and professional HE tracks. Compared to the early 1990s, the absolute increase in the number of students has been greater in the academic track, while in relative terms the increase has been greater in professional HE, which has always been proportionally smaller. The proportion of academic track students is slightly over 60 per cent of all HE participants and has remained quite stable in recent years (Tõnisson, 2011:6).

When looking at the changes in the number of students across the study levels in HE, the decrease has mostly been in the proportion of first level (professional HE, bachelor and integrated master studies) students, while a clear increase can be observed in the proportion of Master and doctoral students. In 1993/94, the proportion of first level students was 93 per cent, by 2010/11 it was only 77 per cent of all students (Tõnisson, 2011:8). This is at least in part a result of the Bologna reform, which shortened first level studies and aimed to direct students to continue their studies at the master's level.

The deregulation policies of HE led to the creation of private HE institutions. New admissions into private HE institutions as a proportion of all admissions into the HE sector increased from 5 per cent in 1995 to 22 per cent in 2005. However, unlike the prestigious private institutions in the USA most Estonian private HE institutions are financially weak and have relatively poor reputations. Another sign of horizontal differentiation is the increase of the proportion of students paying tuition fees, which increased from 7 per cent in 1993 to 49 per cent in 2010 (Tõnisson, 2011). Seventy per cent of the increase of the total number of students can be attributed to students paying tuition fees and only 30 per cent of the increase to state financed places (data taken from Tõnisson, 2011:7). However, private HE institutions were not alone in introducing tuition fees, as all public universities also did. Moreover, majority of paying tuition students are studying in public universities.

According to the criteria offered by Arum et al. (2007) in their typology, Estonia has a diversified HE system. While the primary tier comprises public university courses, the secondary tier comprises both professional HE programmes as well as more academic programmes in private universities. First tier institutions are typically selective in terms of academic staff and students ('status seekers') and enjoy higher prestige; the less-selective, less-prestigious second tier consists of many private institutions, which rely on tuition fees for revenue ('client seekers').

When turning to the demand aspect of the factors shaping the job recruitment process, Estonia can be characterised as a case of 'market radicalism' (Helemäe and Saar, 2011). This is due to the lack of negotiated industrial relations, low union density, uncoordinated wage bargaining, and the low collective bargaining coverage rate, which have not led to innovation but to specialisation in the low-tech or the low-skilled parts of the high-tech sectors. Exports are based on labour intensive traditional industries and services which are controlled by highly mobile transnational corporations. These corporations, rather than significantly investing in local facilities, usually subcontract production (Eamets, 2008). Estonia has a significantly higher proportion of unqualified workers in the workforce and a lower proportion of white collar workers than most European countries (Saar, 2008). Compared to the European average, the current structure of the production sectors, and the technology used in them in Estonia, is heavily based on blue-collar workers (Cörvers and Meriküll, 2007; Eamets, 2008). Data show that between 1990 and 2008 the percentage of lower white collar workers (clerks and service workers) and elementary occupations increased, while the proportion of skilled workers decreased (Helemäe, 2011). However, there was practically no change in the percentage of jobs at the top of the occupational hierarchy (those of managers and professionals) during the same period. No radical changes have occurred in the occupational structure since 2008[17]. There were almost 50,000 fewer jobs in 2011 than there were in 2008. Whereas the proportion of managers and skilled workers in the occupational hierarchy during this period decreased by almost 2 per cent; the proportion of professionals increased by 6 per cent[18]. The aggregated proportional changes among workforce groups in the occupational structure account for less than one per cent.

---

17 Data from www.stat.ee, authors' calculations.

18 This might be partially due to a technical reason, that is, the change in the coding rules for the professional's subgroup, specialists in business and administration. Looking at absolute numbers, there appeared to be almost 30,000 more jobs for professional workers from 2008-2011. Most of the increase can be attributed to the single sub-group of business and administration professionals (18,300 new jobs). However, it is striking that the number of mid-level specialists in the same area, business and administration, has decreased by around the same number (16,400) during the same time period. This needs further investigation to see if there are real changes in occupational structure or if the change is a result of coding changes.

Thus, we can conclude that the supply of educated labour has increased at a much higher rate than the demand for educated labour, which has not significantly changed.

Methodology and data

The empirical analysis of this study was based on semi-structured interviews with the three different parties that play important roles in the labour market success of higher level education graduates: the graduates, the employers, and the representatives of HE institutions. The 'sample' for the qualitative interviews was shaped according to the main dimensions to be considered in the analysis of the evaluation and differentiation of education: the level of study, the field of study and the type of HE institution (public *versus* private).

The data representing the HE **graduates** came from different sources. First, we carried out focus group interviews with mixed groups of business and engineering graduates in order to show the similarities and differences between the fields of study in live discussions. The fields of study were defined based on the International Standard Classification of Education (ISCED) 1997 (Eurostat, 1999). The two fields – business and administration (ISCED 34), and engineering and engineering trades (ISCED 52) – were chosen as one represents a field of study prioritised by the state, while the other represents fields that have mainly expanded due to student demand. Engineering subjects are on the agenda in strategic documents and the highest proportion of state-supported students study either engineering, manufacturing or construction (22 per cent of all state-supported study places) (Tõnisson, 2011). The subject of business and administration is one of the most popular among students. Forty per cent of students study the social sciences, law or business, generally covering their fees themselves (ibid.). Despite more and more students opting for this field, the state has decreased its support. Also, the choice of these two areas allows the opinions of graduates from more generally oriented curricula (here business administration) to be compared with those of graduates from more occupation specific curricula (here engineering).

The graduates in the focus group interviews represented HE institutions with different types of degrees and ownership. There were graduates from private and public professional HE institutions, as well as from private and public universities. Fourteen focus groups (11 in Estonian and 3 in Russian) were carried out in the second half of 2009 with a total of 63 graduates, 41 of whom were from the business field and 22 from the field of engineering. Nine focus groups were in the mixed group of different fields, while 5 focus groups had representatives from one study field only. The focus groups were organised as semi-structured interviews, although the order of the main topics and the exact set of subtopics varied according to the dynamic of the specific focus group. The graduates were asked about their motives for entering HE, and about their studies and experiences on entering the world of work.

As a continuation of the graduate study, in 2011, additional interviews were held with professional level graduates (n=7) who had experienced unemployment after graduation from university. The interviewees were the same two study fields as those in the focus groups: business field (n=4) and engineering (n=3).

Two selected time points were of crucial significance for the graduates' interviews. The focus group interviews were carried out in 2009 when the Estonian labour market had only recently been affected by the global crisis, which meant that many of the graduates entered the labour market before the crisis, i.e., in a situation of economic boom and a shortage of labour supply. The interviews in 2011 took place in the context of a radically changed labour market and a dramatic increase in unemployment. The number of unemployed young people with tertiary education was too small to allow the calculation of a representative unemployment rate before the global economic crisis. However, by both 2009 and 2011 a significant proportion, around 15 per cent, of economically active young people[19] with tertiary education were looking for jobs in Estonia.

In the **employer survey** the 'Development of Competences in the World of Work and Education' study from the 'Higher Education as a Generator of Strategic Competences' (HEGESCO) project (for details see http://www.hegesco.org) was used as a methodological starting point. The interviews focused on topics such as employers' perceptions of graduates and their qualifications; recruitment strategies and cooperation with HE institutions. Based on NACE Rev.2 (Eurostat, 2008) employers were selected from amongst the biggest employers in all sectors from the Estonian Business Registry. In Estonia most companies are microenterprises and only 2 per cent of companies can be classified as big, having more than 250 employees[20] in Estonia. Therefore, despite our selection criteria, we have among the biggest employers companies of different sizes, including small and medium size enterprises. All sectors were covered, except agriculture, forestry and fisheries, and mining and quarrying, as very few graduates start their careers in these sectors. Altogether, 15 interviews were car-

19 The Statistical Office uses the age group 15–24, however, graduates are usually over 21 years old.

20 Estonian Statistical Office, www.stat.ee, authors' own calculations.

ried out in 2010 and there were both private companies and public institutions in the sample. The private companies were based on local as well as international capital. In the larger companies a specialised department deals with human resource (HR) questions and therefore, most interviews were carried out with the head of the HR department; only one interview was with the company owner. The backgrounds of the interviewees varied: they were graduates of physics, law, economics, communication, etc. The reason for their mixed backgrounds was mainly because they work in an area that is new to Estonia: there were no HR curricula taught in universities before the 1990s.

For the study of the HE institutions, in 2011 seven semi-structured interviews with deans or vice-deans of faculties at different HE level education institutions were carried out. The sample covered the different types of HE institutions: 2 public universities, 1 state-financed vocational HE institution, 1 private university, and 2 private schools of vocational training. Five were representatives of the field of business, and 2 were from the field of engineering. Also, the semi-structured interviews with the heads of the institutes or faculties were used as a method of data collection. The interviews focused on the experiences, problems and perspectives of HE from the point of view of the respondent institutions (for further details about sample and interview topics, see Reiska, 2012).

In the analysis, we focused on the role and function of HE in the recruitment process by reflecting on and comparing the views and experiences of the three parties. We considered how, and if, members of the different parties viewed the changed value of HE. To do this we compared the perceived values of diplomas, Bachelor's and Master's degrees and the transition to the 3+2 system. A coding scheme of the relevant topics and aspects emerging from the interviews was developed for the analysis. The interviews were then coded by independent coders and the analysis was carried out using the software Nvivo 8. In the text we use direct quotes from the interviews. These are word-for-word transcriptions, reflecting the spoken language.

Analysis

Degree is a norm – higher education as a selection criterion and a 'sign'

Throughout the interviews, the HE graduates pointed out that, according to their perceptions, having a Bachelor's degree has become a norm – without a HE degree they would be out of the selection pool.

> I guess higher education is already the standard. To get on the court, to even have a chance to try and score, you need to have it.
>
> Graduate: Bachelor degree in Economics; Public University

Even the field of study seemed to be not as important as having a HE degree.

> …at some places you just need higher education. … Definitely they just checked whether you had higher education or not… it wasn't important just what kind of higher education you had, as long as you had it. As it would show that you are a highly educated person and have been able to make something of yourself.
>
> Graduate: Bachelor degree in Economics; Public University

The employers also pointed out the importance of having completed HE for getting a job.

> Let's just say that in certain fields, higher education is definitely very important… I guess that about 70 per cent of our jobs are such that higher education is certainly important there.
>
> HRM, real estate

The importance of having a degree seems to have increased over recent years. During the economic downturn and in periods of high unemployment, employers had the opportunity to choose employees from a significantly higher number of job seekers. Having a degree is in this situation was often used as a pre-selection criterion or as a requirement. In this way the role of HE in the recruitment process has increased even more. A university graduate with unemployment experience explained her viewpoint that she did not get a job because at the time of applying she did not have a diploma.

> I guess it is because I didn't have a diploma yet. That's the first thing they look at when there are many candidates. If some have diplomas and others don't – no matter whether you haven't written your thesis or you have more stuff left to do – having a diploma is decisive.
>
> Graduate: Bachelor degree in Economics; Public University

Higher education is perceived to be the primary filter with respect to a number of occupations. The lack of a diploma, especially in the economic fields, may exclude applicants from getting past the screening stage. Where there are a large number of candidates, human resource managers (HRM) initially look for formal indicators, for example a HE degree. This activity, in Estonian context, does not indicate a lack of interest in the candidate's other expertise, abilities and motivation.

The use of the requirement for a HE degree as a selection criterion can be observed particularly in situations where this type of qualification is stated as required in the job advertisement while it is not actually necessary for the tasks to be carried out in the job.

> The majority required higher education but I don't know if it's really necessary for doing that job. Secretaries, for instance… they do hire people without higher education, don't they. I guess it's there to somehow sort out the better ones. As there will be high demand, let's add this higher education thing.
>
> Graduate: Bachelor degree in Economics; Public University

One of the reasons for this behaviour is explained as the 'signal' that having a HE degree gives, which both graduates and employers understand. The view here is that the HE degree requirement helps to select the 'better ones' – in situations where there are a large number of applicants, a degree has become a quick 'sorting criterion'. Moreover, various skills and personal characteristics such as the ability to think, take responsibility, trust, independence, etc., are often associated with having gained a HE degree, which explains again the situation where the presence of a degree is more important than the field of study and/or specialisation.

> This also screens out those who are persistent and everything else. That you have in spite of everything been able to get a higher education, and it makes no difference in what field, you know. That you have something in your head.
>
> Graduate: Bachelor degree in Economics; Public University

> But if you are looking for an employee and also you know, that he has a higher education, it means that he is capable of thinking independently. Exactly for that reason, that someone might think about me in the same way, I decided to get a diploma.
>
> Graduate: Bachelor degree in Economics; Private HE institution

In line with the previous arguments, the view of evaluators was that failure to get a HE degree was an indicator of intellectual failure. Even though some employers and graduates recognised the limitations of this first sorting criterion, they still believed that this was the most rational way of dealing with large numbers of job applicants.

> Especially right now, I suppose, yeah, if there are 100 applications that come in, then the first thing I do, I immediately get rid of those who don't have any higher education, because in any case about twenty of them do have a higher education and if they already have it then it implies that they have pursued it and they want to be better than the others. Perhaps I do throw to the side someone who would be awfully good; however, he hasn't been successful in getting a diploma ... but you just have to make a choice.
>
> Graduate: Diploma in Professional Technical Engineering; Public HE institution; employed as a manager

> You don't get any idea about a person's expertise only on the basis of a CV. Rather it's just an indicator or some kind of filter, on the basis of which in general to invite someone to an interview and more specifically to find out, whether he has those real areas of expertise or not. But that pile, that big pile of CVs which just swamps the managers ... and you can't completely find out about everyone and then you need that first filter just to move them along and when a person has a high-school education or a higher education then you make that [choice-author's addition] quickly and then move forward.
>
> Graduate: Bachelor degree in Economics; Public University; employed as a manager

Not all degrees are the same

Differentiation across educational levels

Although the view that a HE degree (irrespective of the field) is crucial in the recruitment process is strongly felt by both graduates and employers, some differentiating criteria could be observed which were presented by employers, graduates and representatives of universities. One of these differentiation aspects was the level of HE achieved – whether it was a diploma, Bachelor's or Master's degree.

All the key actors were very critical about the Bologna process and especially the transition from the 4-year Bachelor's programmes to the 3-year Bachelor's programmes. Many graduates felt that their 3-year Bachelor's degree gave them fewer competencies than the 4-year Bachelor's programme of former graduates.

> These three years are really not enough, and I don't think that this 3+2 system is suitable at all, that you should have five years straight away.
>
> Graduate: Bachelor degree in Economics; Public University

Representatives of the HE institutions saw, in the 3-year Bachelor's programme, a decrease in the content of education and of the competencies obtained during the studies.

> Now they [Europe] want the majority to have higher education, so willing or unwilling they had to lower the requirements and with these three years you somehow make it, you study the general and introductory subjects and to more specific subjects you actually never make. And then enters the labour market a vainglorious person who can do basically nothing. In principle those people could still continue in Master's studies, but as we know very well, the majority does not. [...] In that sense we can talk about important devaluation.
>
> Private HE institution, economics

> In the society it is assessed that higher education has changed due to the 3+2 system. That the first level is in a sense like used to be the higher professional training. And the word higher education studies, and the people who do not know the system that well for them there is a gap, that the content of higher education has changed. It has definitely or at least for me changed. It has been devalued.
>
> Public University, economics

Some employers also pointed out the differences between the 3-year and 4-year Bachelor's programmes. They felt that students need more time to acquire a certain skill level and, as a result, in the recruitment process they often prefer young people with Master's degrees over those with Bachelor's degrees.

> Here we sense indeed a very clear distinction between an old four-year baccalaureate and today's three-year baccalaureate, [...] that they have started to form their own opinions, that they already know something, but actually with a three-year baccalaureate in today's business there is very little for us to do.
>
> HRM, electricity, gas, steam and air conditioning supply

> We equalize how it in general is, which is the old 4-year and current 5-year program. Meaning at the moment we have more people with former 4-year or current Master's degree, and those with three years you basically do not find here. In this respect we do differentiate, meaning that our expectation is the 5-year program in case there is a higher education requirement.
>
> HRM, electricity, gas, steam and air conditioning supply

We can see that representatives of HE institutions and some employers share the view that the Bologna process has, by default, devalued the new 3-year Bachelor degree.

In the case of the graduates, two groups seemed to exist – (a) those who did not experience any major difficulties entering the labour market and who managed to establish their labour market position quickly; and (b) those who did not manage to enter the labour market, or only managed with difficulty (for example those who experienced unemployment at the beginning of their working careers). During the interviews, graduates who had no problems finding a job rarely talked about the devaluation of HE in the recruitment process. They thought that the importance of a Master's degree may increase in future, but that at present it was more important to have a Bachelor's degree.

> In the future, a Master's will definitely be more important, if today it's a Bachelor's, then in 10 years when there's a big crowd, they'll say, "Oh, you've got a Master's, we'll take you.
>
> Graduate: Bachelor degree in Economics; Public University

Graduates with experience of unemployment, thought the opposite, that just having a 3-year Bachelor's degree was not sufficient for successful recruitment.

> ...whether you have got this piece of paper, and preferably higher than a Bachelor's. That's because competition among Bachelors is so intense that the value has been somewhat devalued.
>
> Graduate: Bachelor degree in Economics; Private University

> I do think that a Bachelor's is not so important any more – so many people have got it already. Maybe an advantage when compared to people with secondary school education, but not as big an advantage as having a Master's.
>
> Graduate: Bachelor degree in Economics; Public University

They saw clear vertical differentiation in HE as a result of the expansion of the sector. Attaining a Master's degree was seen as improving labour market opportunities. The graduates were of the view that continuing to study and obtaining a Master's degree could be seen as a sign of perseverance, ambition, and a higher level of competencies.

> ...Every other person has a BA in Estonia. It takes more persistence and work to acquire a Master's degree. If I were an employer, I'd definitely prefer a person with a Master's degree. ... A Bachelor's is unfinished education.
>
> Graduate: Bachelor degree in Economics; Public University

> ...A Master's degree is worth more than a Bachelor's degree.... When someone has a Master's, it shows that he is interested in this field, or he wouldn't have gone to get that Master's degree.
>
> Graduate: Bachelor degree in Economics; Private University

> There are lots of courses that go in depth, these will come only on the Master's level. You will get a foundation during the BA studies, some kind of an idea of a direction to follow, and you'll like go further during your Master's studies.
>
> Graduate: Bachelor degree in Technical engineering; Public University

However, a Master's was also perceived as purely instrumental, as a way to stand out from the crowd. The graduates also emphasised that in order to secure some positions or to participate in public procurement applicants should have Master's degrees.

> Because in my opinion it is somehow valued much higher when you can tick the box that you have a Master's degree. Then you will be immediately valued higher than those without Master's degree.
>
> Graduate: Bachelor degree in Technical engineering; Public University

Despite the fact that a Master's degree is perceived as something useful and therefore valuable, having such a degree does not necessarily guarantee success in the job market. Essentially, a Master's degree is a prerequisite for entering the job market with the high level probability of a successful outcome.

> ... most secondary school graduates go to university; most of them receive at least their Bachelor's. Fewer go to get their Master's. In fact, bachelors are all over the place. It's essentially the same as if nobody went to college at all. Competition is so intense because everyone has the same education. To stand out from the masses or to show that you're smarter or have invested more into your education, you have to get a Master's degree. Although even this won't guarantee a thing...
>
> Graduate: Bachelor degree in Economics; Private HE institution

However, what does seem to matter is the timing of the interview, in terms of the state of the economy – during the economic recession, the labour market opportunities reduced dramatically and applying for a job became much more competitive. For that reason it was especially important to 'be different', i.e. to stand out from all of the other young people with Bachelor degrees, but also to 'be better' than other young people with Bachelor degrees.

Some HE graduates and representatives of HE institutions blamed the employers for not seeing any differences between Bachelor degrees and Master degrees and graduates.

> Unfortunately the employers do not differentiate between Bachelor's and Master's degree. We can emphasize the difference and say that 3-year Bachelor is unfinished higher education, but the employers just sees that has been to university that's all
>
> Public University, economics

> Well, when you look at the job adds, it is rather rare, meaning they ask for higher education. When they require Master's degree then they point it out, but this I required very rarely.
>
> Graduate: Bachelor degree in Technical engineering; Public University

However, some graduates indicated that there are big differences between public and private enterprises, as well as between large and small ones.

> ... In some large companies such as banks, the person who decides to employ a new person distinguishes between different degrees. At the same time, there are those medium-size businessmen, and in Estonia most companies are medium or small, fewer than 5 or 10 employees. That manager is significantly older than us and has received his education during the Soviet time or has no education at all. Thus he may not make such a sharp distinction between degrees.
>
> Graduate: Bachelor degree in Economics; Public University

> It depends on the company that is hiring. ...The current situation is certainly such that private companies do not distinguish BAs and MAs. But if you go to a ministry, the Bank of Estonia, or research institutions, you'll definitely need a Master's degree.
>
> Graduate: Bachelor degree in Economics; Public University

In the interviews with the employers, the attained level of education (3-year Bachelor, 4-year Bachelor, Master degree) did not always stand out as the main criterion in the recruitment process. The majority of employers did not mention different degrees or different lengths of study, which indicated their low awareness or the low value they attributed to vertical differentiation within HE. These findings are in line with those of Eamets, Krillo and Themas (2011). However, this was not the full story. In some cases the level of education was noted by employers in the service sector, and this was connected with the signalling value rather than associated with better skills or knowledge. Master's studies were seen as a sign of personal characteristics rather than an indication of better skills or more knowledge.

> I rather look at what it tells me about the candidate, that once a person has finished Master's studies, it shows that he is persistent and hard-working, not necessarily his knowledge, that I don't know.
>
> HRM, real estate

Another case is when the level of education is given relevance when it is required by law (for example holding an Master degree is a requirement for teachers in secondary education) or when it shows certain qualification criteria (for example, a Master's degree is required in order to be accredited as an engineer).

> Teachers must definitely be qualified, that is, have a Master's degree in education. And beyond that, in this sense, work experience is certainly beneficial, but that again is not the kind of condition that we couldn't go without. And the third and the most important one is the person himself.
>
> HRM, education

> According to the law, only a Master can become a lawyer. …I do think that Bachelors are good for nothing. If they don't go for their Master's degree, then a lawyer with a three-year Bachelor's degree, well, I couldn't do anything with him.
>
> Owner, public administration and defence, compulsory social security

Some companies in the secondary sector of economic activity (manufacturing and construction) also differentiated between the levels of degree attained. However, their reasons differed from those in the service sector, where different degree levels were associated with different personal traits. Those in the manufacturing sector claimed that the current BA does not provide the same level of knowledge and skills as the previous 4-year Bachelor degree and they often considered the old four year Bachelor degree to be equivalent to the current Master degree. The current Bachelor degree was not considered to be at a HE level.

> We equalize how it in general is, which is the old 4-year and current 5-year program. Meaning at the moment we have more people with former 4-year or current Master's degree, and those with three years you basically do not find here. In this respect we do differentiate, meaning that our expectation is the 5-year program in case there is a higher education requirement.
>
> HRM, electricity, gas, steam and air conditioning supply

Horizontal differentiation across higher education institutions

Another differentiation criterion was the type of HE institution from which a degree was obtained. Both graduates and employers pointed out that the value of a degree in the recruitment process may well depend on the type of HE institution from which it was obtained. The fact that one has a degree from a particular university may turn out to be essential in getting a job interview invitation. Graduate respondents have commented that some job advertisements openly state that only degrees from certain HE institutions will be considered.

> I myself saw on the CV website that some firms were offering work and underneath was written: those who have graduated from X or from Y universities [private higher education institutions], please do not call. So blunt and to the point. What kind of university you go to is essential.
>
> Graduate: Bachelor degree in Economics; Public University

One graduate of a private HE institution considered it necessary to emphasise that their HE institution was not a mediocre school but one with quite a high reputation among employers.

> I'm quite satisfied with education from W (a private university). Later I have heard from employers that the reputation of W is not as bad as some may think. That some good people have come from there…
>
> Graduate: Bachelor degree in Economics; Private HE institution

Employers considered the diversification of the HE system to mean 'diversification of educational quality' and they responded to the uncertainty brought about this diversification by relying more on information conferred by the educational credential. They introduced the source of the credential as an additional criterion to sort out 'inappropriate' candidates. In the opinion of the graduate respondents, this behaviour has several causes. First, possible earlier good or bad experiences with specific university graduates influenced the recruiter's future decisions. Second, depending on the job content, those who have a professional HE degree are sometimes preferred, while at other times those who have an academic HE degree are preferred. Employers also highlighted the 'two-tier' system of Estonian HE: more competitive public universities versus client-seeking private universities. For a senior position, employers usually expect an applicant to have a degree from a public university. It is noticeable that the employers who prefer graduates from the more prestigious competitive public universities do not connect the preferred degree with better skills, but rather with the sorting power of the staff in these HE institutions. This logic suggests that the public universities' 'standard' for admission is higher and that their students are seen as 'smarter'.

> Somehow it has turned out that Z (a public university) is more trusted. It may even be that the education is not necessarily better but… people trust it more. A better known and larger school – and the more reliable for that.
>
> Graduate: Bachelor degree in Economics; Public University

> We still prefer this kind, not quite these, well, maybe we have taken some /from a private university/, but we have tried to avoid the totally suspicious universities. Public universities are still our priority anyway. Many people have come to our economic development department like from let's say the University of Tartu. Somehow it has become like a tradition, too. Then we have had many public administration ones from Tallinn University, and thus it's always those public universities.
>
> Owner, public administration and defense, compulsory social security

The employers admitted that it is often hard to assess and judge the quality of the numerous new HE institutions and, as a result, their qualifications and their graduates are not so highly regarded.

> If we rank the schools, then for me, all these unknown private schools have, well, a negative connotation the whole bunch of them, I don't know whether some of them are accredited or not. I don't even know that so exactly.
>
> HRM, real estate

Representatives of HE institutions are more aware about quality differences between HE institutions. The head of one private professional HE institution indicated that

> There are certainly still some poor ones among private schools and also among public schools, but competition has weeded them out much more quickly here.
>
> Private HE institution, economics

In addition to being an indicator of potential intellectual deficits, the decision to go to a private HE institution was perceived as evidence of moral failing, such as faulty judgment or a lack of foresight on the part of the student.

> The one who hasn't gotten in /..../ like into proper universities, in that case raises the question of whether he has some shortcoming or why. Well surely a diploma alone does not give any kind of guarantee, but it is a prerequisite that shows that this person by being admitted and by persisting in school has been perhaps a little bit better

> than the one who has thrown up his hands and given up and well, wasted his time and money studying somewhere in W [a private higher education school].
>
> Owner, administration and defence, compulsory social security

However, the use and interpretation of educational prestige were couched in the evaluators' own frames of reference. There was also a notable exception by an HR manager, who pointed out that there is not a big difference between graduates from different schools. He had graduated from a private HE institution and this suggests the possibility that managers tend to trust those graduates who have a similar educational background to their own. Also, the larger universities (which are the state universities) are better known, while the smaller (private) universities are known only by those who have attended them.

> But when I put well-known and good schools next to each other, then there isn't such a big /difference/ in the sense that when you have a candidate with an economics degree /from a public university/ and let's say a candidate with an economics degree /from a private professional higher education institution/ then I can't say that one is somehow better than the other. Then it doesn't play as important a role anymore. Then you like want to see those other things that go with it. Although schools compete for their image quite hard, at the end, at the moment when you have two persons with higher education who have both graduated well, their school does not play such an important role there. We have a lot of people from /private professional higher education institutions/ precisely because we had, I don't know whether they had it, specialized in real estate economics. /…/ It somehow is the kind of place from where such people come with whom you see right away that they are /private professional higher education institution/ boys. That they are not like /public university/ and not like /public university/.
>
> HRM, real estate

The majority of employers and graduates agreed that using the additional criterion of source of qualification was well-grounded, but for different reasons. On the basis that the credentials obtained were from the less competitive educational institutions, the employers tended to jump to far-reaching conclusions, not only about skills and trainability, but also about personality. The graduates thought that an employer's use of the additional sorting criterion was a way of dealing with uncertainty, but did not recognise that employers were using this not to search for information but to rank institutions based on their prestige. The graduates were also hardly aware of the negative aspects attributed to applicants from 'low' ranking HE institutions by some employers.

The representatives of the public universities did not worry about the success of their students in the job market, because these universities are well known and they are highly rated by both the public and employers. A representative of a private HE institution was aware of the need to improve the image of the school.

> People come to study here when we have this image that when you graduate from this school, you will find a job, a job on the market.
>
> Private HE institution, economics

Representatives of the HE institutions referred to the absence of clear signals from the institutions of HE to employers which may increase uncertainty for all involved.

> …the education system does not give very clear signals as to what will become of you when you graduate. To lure more students, universities have pushed their way to the playing field of professional higher education and professional higher education institutions want to become universities. I guess that things have kind of cooled down on the side of professional higher education institutions, they have settled down, such ambitious private universities have been closed by now. The ones that in reality gave professional higher education but wanted to give academic higher education…
>
> Public University, economics

Discussion

Higher education in Estonia expanded dramatically through the 1990s and into the first decade of the 2000s. The labour market failed to keep pace with this expansion, by not offering enough 'university-level' jobs. Although having a HE credentials has given clear advantages in the Estonian labour market, both when applying for jobs and in career development and stability, recent studies show that job and career prospects have worsened for university graduates (Täht, Saar and Unt, 2008). The aim of the current research was to study the views of employers, graduates and representatives of HE institutions about the possible devaluation of HE in Estonia as a consequence of the expansion of the sector. For this, university graduates, employers and HE institutions were interviewed.

The findings of the current study suggested that when referring to the upper part of the occupational ladder, the idea of a schooled society (Baker 2011; Meyer, 1977) is strongly present in Estonia. Having a HE degree has become a norm that is shared by all three of the aforementioned parties. Being without a HE degree may lead to negative signals and de-selection – even in positions where this level of education is not actually needed, the possession a HE degree gives clear advantages in the recruitment process. Thus, as the credentialist theory explains the HE is becoming the mean of closure. HE is considered to be a pre-requisite for labour market entry irrespective of whether or not the job requires it. In order to enter the labour market, the key issue is the formal completion of a certain level of education. In addition, having a HE degree carries a certain 'sign' and meaning for the graduates and employers, such as having certain personal characteristics and abilities (independence, trustworthiness, ability to learn, etc).

Even though a HE degree was considered very important as a pre-selection criterion, the interviews with the three parties indicated that vertical differentiation exists in the HE field, suggesting some devaluation of HE in Estonia. As having a HE degree is already so widespread, it was felt that having only a Bachelor's degree did not allow the applicants to stand out from the 'crowd', and this was especially felt by those who had experienced unemployment at the beginning of their careers. Also the HE representatives were critical of the low level of skills and knowledge attained in the 3-year Bachelor's degrees. At the same time, for the employers, the differentiation between a Bachelor's and a Master's degree was not always clear. The Bologna process and changes in the HE system have created confusion for many employers (especially those in small and medium size enterprises and in the private sector) in distinguishing between different types of HE degrees. As a result, often other or additional criteria, such as the institutional status, were applied for selecting the 'best' candidate'.

As there is an increasing range of HE credentials available, employers seem to rely more on institutional status because of their uncertainty about the value of the various credentials, and this indicates the importance of horizontal differentiation in HE. Using institutional status is a fast and efficient way to reduce the list of applicant to a short list of possible candidate. The graduates were, like the other two parties, aware of the prestige of different HE institutions by perceiving public universities as more trustworthy and acceptable than most new private HE institutions. This means that, under conditions of HE expansion, the credentials from private HE institutions lose their capacity to 'make a difference'. This type of hiring process seems to resemble a filtering model (Arrow, 1973), where HE serves as a screening device because it sorts out individuals of differing abilities, so that employers get better workers. The interpretations by employers are also in line with Arrow's proposition (1973) that HE offers a double filter, forcing graduates to signal their productive capacity twice: first, by being admitted to the 'right' HE institution and second, by graduating from it.

Thus, the current analysis showed that in the context of strategies of higher education expansion, those that are individually reasonable may result in collective outcomes that undermine individual outcomes. In the interviews, the graduates often emphasised the instrumental value of education. When talking about their motives for undertaking higher education they often referred to the possibility of securing a better job afterwards. A higher education certificate as a preselection criterion in the recruitment process was widely used by employers. Thus, we can conclude that the certifying role of higher education has increased, or in other words, the costs of not having higher education have increased. People not having a higher education certificate may not even come to the attention of employers. In parallel, the differentiation of higher education has increased. This seems to indicate the problem of the 'opportunity trap': 'as opportunities for education increase, they are proving harder to cash in' (Brown, 2003:149–150). Even when higher education still has its 'magic power' and gives advantages in the labour market in Estonia, the kind of higher education it is becomes increasingly more important. In terms of vertical differentiation, the degree seems to be most important and in terms of horizontal differentiation, the type of higher education institution attended seems to be most important.

In this study we have only looked at the beginning of a professional career, but the meaning and role of the higher education undertaken may change throughout a career.

Acknowledgements

The research presented has been undertaken within the project "Labour Market Challenges to Higher Education: Estonia in European Context" supported by a Primus grant from the European Social Fund. Any errors and omissions are the responsibility of the authors alone.

References

Arkes, J. (1999). What do educational credentials signal and why do employers value credentials? *Economics of Education Review*, 18, 133–141.

Arrow, K. J. (1973). Higher education as a filter. *Journal of Public Economics*, 2, 193–216.

Arum, R., Gamoran, A. and Shavit, Y. (2007). More inclusion than diversion: expansion, differentiation, and market structure in higher education. In Shavit, Y., Arum, R. and Gamoran, A. (Eds.), *Stratification in higher education*. Stanford: Stanford University Press, 1–35.

Baker, D. P. (2011). Forward and backward, horizontal and vertical: Transformation of occupational credentialing in the schooled society. *Research in Social Stratification and Mobility*, 29, 5–29.

Blau, P. M. and Duncan, O. D. (1967). *The American occupational structure*. New York: John Wiley & Sons.

Bridges, W. P. (1996) Educational Credentials and the Labour Market: An Inter-Industry Comparison. In Kerckhoff, A. (Ed.) *Generating Social Stratification. Toward a New Research Agenda*. Oxford: Westview Press, 173–199.

Brint, S. G. and Karabel, J. (1989). The diverted dream: community colleges and the promise of educational opportunity in America, 1900–1985. Oxford: Oxford University Press.

Brown, P. (2003). The opportunity trap: education and employment in a global economy. *European Educational Research Journal*, 7, 131–147.

Brown, P., Lauder, H. and Ashton, D. (2008). Education, Globalisation and the Future of the Knowledge Economy. *European Educational Research Journal*, 7, 131–156.

Collins, R. (1979). The credential society: an historical sociology of education and stratification. New York: Academic Press.

Cörvers, F. and Meriküll, J. (2007). Occupational structures across 25 EU countries: the importance of industry structure and technology in old and new EU countries. *Economic Change and Restructuring*, 40, 327–359.

Davies, S. and Guppy, N. (1997). Fields of study, college selectivity, and student inequalities in higher education. *Social Forces*, 75, 1417–1438.

Eamets, R. (2008). Economic structure, labour market and education. In Heidmets, M. (Ed.) *Estonian Human Development report 2007*. Tallinn: Eesti Ekspressi Kirjastuse AS, 97–102.

Eamets, R., Krillo, K. and Themas, A. (2011). *Eesti kõrgkoolide 2009. Aasta vilistlaste uuring*. [Study of graduates of Estonian higher education institutions in 2009]. Tartu: SA Archimedes.

European Commission (2010). Employment in Europe 2010.

Gamoran, A. and Mare, R. D. (1989). Secondary school tracking amd educational inequality – compensation, reinforcement, or neutrality. *American Journal of Sociology*, 94, 1146–1183.

Gerber, T. P. and Cheung, S. Y. (2008). Horizontal Stratification in Postsecondary Education: Forms, Explanations, and Implications. *Annual Review of Sociology*, 34, 299–318.

Helemäe, J. (2011). Intragenerational mobility under conditions of rapid neoliberalization. In Saar, E. (Ed.) *Towards a normal stratification order. Actual and perceived social stratification in post-socialist Estonia*. Frankfurt: Peter Lang, 83–110.

Helemäe, J. and Saar, E. (2011). An Introduction to Post-Socialist Transition in Estonia. In Saar, E. (Ed.) *Towards a normal stratification order. Actual and perceived social stratification in post-socialist Estonia*. Frankfurt: Peter Lang, 13–32.

Jackson, M., Goldthorpe, J. H., Mills, C. (2005). Education, employers and class mobility. *Research in Social Stratification and Mobility*, 23, 3–33.

Lucas, S. R. (2001). Effectively maintained inequality: education transitions, track mobility and social background effects. *American Journal of Sociology*, 106, 1642–1690.

Meyer, J. W. (1977). The effects of education as an institution. *American Journal of Sociology*, 1, 55–77.

Olneck, M. R. and Kim, K. (1989). High school completion and men's incomes: an apparent anomaly. *Sociology of Education*, 62, 193–207.

Reiska, E. (2012). Metoodika [Methodology]. In Reiska, E., Roosalu, T., Tamm, A., Täht, K. and Unt, M. (Eds.), *Kõrghariduse tähendused ja kõrgkoolide koostöö tööandjatega* [The meanings of higher education and cooperation between universities and employers]. Available online: http://primus.tlu.ee/tehtud-tood/Sunteesraport.pdf

Rivera, L. A. (2011). Ivies, extracurriculars, and exclusion: elite employers' use of educational credentials. *Research in Social Stratification and Mobility*, 29, 71–90.

Saar, E. (2008). Expansion of higher education and opportunities in the labour market. In Heidmets, M. (Ed.) *Estonian Human Development Report*. Tallinn: Eesti Koostöö Kogu, 20–27.

Saar, E. (Ed.) (2011). *Towards a normal stratification order. Actual and perceived social stratification in post-socialist Estonia*. Frankfurt: Peter Lang.

Seidman, R. H. (1984). The logic and behavioral principles of educational systems: social independence or dependence. In Archer, M. S. (Ed.), *The Sociology of Educational Expansion*. Beverly Hills: Sage, 267–292.

Shavit, Y., Arum, R. and Gamoran, A. (2007). Stratification in higher education: a comparative study. Stanford, CA: Stanford University Press.

Spence, M. (1973). Job market signaling. *The quarterly journal of Economics*, 87, 355–374.

Swail, S. W. (2011). The College Bubble. *Educational Policy Institute/EPI International*. Available online: http://etwus.wordpress.com/2011/05/13/the-college-bubble/

Täht, K., Saar, E. and Unt, M. (2008). Changing mobility regime in Estonia? Young people's labor market entry and early careers since the 1980s. In Blossfeld, H.-P., Buchholz, S., Bukodi, E. and Kurz, K. (Eds.), *Young Workers, Globalization and the Labor Market. Comparing Early Working Life in Eleven Countries*. Cheltenham, Northampton: Edward Elgar Publishing, 311–332.

Tõnisson, E. (2011). *Kõrghariduse valdkonna statistiline ülevaade 2011* [Statistical overview of higher education 2011]. Tartu: Estonian Ministry of Education and Research. Available online and only in Estonian: http://www.hm.ee/index.php?048183

Unt, M. (2011). Youth entry into the labour market and early career outcomes. In Saar, E. (Ed.), *Towards a normal stratification order: actual and perceived social stratification in post-socialist Estonia*. Frankfurt am Mein: P. Lang, 111–142.

van de Werfhorst, H.G. (2002). Fields of study, acquired skills and the wage benefit from a matching job. *Acta Sociologica*, 45, 287–303.

van der Ploeg, S. (1994). Educational expansion and returns on credentials. *European Sociological Review*, 10, 63–78.

Chapter 16.
The graduate gender pay gap in Estonia

Kerly Espenberg, Aivi Themas, Jaan Masso

Introduction

Equal pay for equal work is one of the founding principles of the European Union (EU). Enshrined in the Treaty of Rome in 1957, it was the subject of a 1975 directive 75/117/EEC, which prohibited all discrimination in all aspects of pay between women and men for the same work or for work of equal value. Although there has been considerable progress towards equality, and there are now fewer cases of direct discrimination, according to Eurostat data, there are still important differences between men's and women's earnings in the EU.

The gender pay gap is linked to a number of factors that are frequently interrelated. The reasons can be divided into two broad categories (UNDP, 2006): first, direct discrimination: this occurs when people who have the same level of education and amount of work experience are treated differently because of their gender – different pay levels for the same work or different job requirements for the same pay; and second, objective discrimination: this occurs as a result of occupational gender segregation in the labour market – the concentration of women and men in different sectors and occupations and the lower human capital of women (due to lower job tenure). It has been widely observed and agreed that the prevalence of discrimination has decreased due to the development of international regulations by the International Labour Office (ILO), United Nations (UN) and EU.

The focus of this study was on gender segregation in different subject areas in Estonian higher education, the male-female wage gap among recent graduates and the main reasons for the gap. Estonia is a particularly interesting case because it has the largest raw (i.e. unadjusted) gender pay gap of all European Union (EU-27) countries[21]. Our research contributed to the existing literature in this field in several ways. First, we gave an overview of gender segregation in higher education by subject types for last 20 years based on data from the Ministry of Education and Research and previous research. Second, while there are several recent studies focusing on working among students (Mägi et al., 2011; Saar and Unt, 2011) and the general gender pay gap in

21 Eurostat online-database: Gender Pay Gap Statistics http://epp.eurostat.ec.europa.eu/statistics_explained/index.php/Gender_pay_gap_statistics.

Estonia (Anspal, Kraut and Rõõm, 2010), in our work we focused on the existence of the gap shortly after entering the labour market. There is a growing interest in this field and our study will add valuable knowledge to it. For the wage gap analysis we used data from a recent survey of university graduates (Themas, Espenberg and Eamets, 2011). We used several multivariate statistical analysis methods, including regression analysis and decomposition, to analyse which factors explain the gender wage gap among higher education graduates and to what extent.

The rest of the paper is structured as follows. In the second part of this paper we give a short overview of previous studies in this field; in the third part we introduce the econometric framework and in the fourth part the data and variables used. The results are presented in the fifth section and in the final section we present our conclusions.

Determinants of the gender pay gap

There is a large body of literature focusing on the gender pay gap and its determinants in various countries. In this section we give a short overview of studies, which have focused on the graduate wage gap and its causes. Traditionally, within the context of human capital theory, differences in pay are explained by differences in individual characteristics, like age, education and work experience. Evidence from different studies (Plantenga and Remery, 2006; Anspal et al., 2010) suggests that these differences only play a minor role in the persistence of the gender pay gap.

The gender pay gap is found to be lowest or non-existent for young employees[22], and it increases with age as a result of the career breaks taken (or potential career breaks due to family obligations) by women during their working lives (Beblo and Wolf, 2000; Datta Gupta and Smith, 2002; Belgian Presidency Report, 2010). The wages of women of child-bearing age may be lower than those of men because employers assume that during a certain period of their lives women will not participate in the labour market due to having children. There are potential costs to employers for this (seeking and training substitute employees), so they compensate during wage negotiations by offering women of child-bearing age lower pay than they would offer to men. In addition to the negative impact of direct discrimination, this can also have an indirect

22 This is confirmed by a clear increase in the gender pay gap with age in the EU-27, from 3.1 per cent for employees younger than 30 years to 17.5 per cent for those 30–39 and 23.8 per cent for those 40–49 years old in 2006. It decreases slightly, however, for those of 50 years and older (21.8 per cent).

effect on women's wages as they will also have fewer opportunities to undertake specific training and to move up the career ladder. The differences in women's and men's wages in various groups indicate that discrimination is one of the reasons for the gender pay gap in Estonia. The wage difference between women and men is the greatest in the age range 25–54 years, during which time having a family and raising children is most likely (Anspal et al., 2010).

Educational differences once played a major role in the gender wage gap. However, today this is not as significant as it used to be because more and more women undertake higher education. In most EU countries women's education levels are at least comparable to men's, and even tend to be higher among the younger generations (Pothieux and Meurs, 2005). Educational attainment affects both female participation in the labour market and their level of earnings. The Eurostat data shows that the situation varies among EU member states; in some countries the gender pay gap is much higher for people with a higher level of education than for those with a lower level of education (e.g. Czech Republic, Greece and France), in other countries the opposite is true (a lower wage gap for those with higher education, for example in Belgium and Lithuania) while in others the gender pay gap is less dependent on educational attainment (e.g. Bulgaria, the UK).

A study of the gender wage gap in Estonia (Anspal et al., 2010) suggests that although an increase in educational level will decrease the gender pay gap, wage differences for highly educated workers have not changed significantly over the years. Even though, in most EU countries, women have higher educational qualifications than men, they remain under-represented – because of educational segregation – in the most valued subject areas (engineering, science and so forth) (O'Dorchai, 2008).

Human capital theory states that the incentive to invest in education depends on the time a person expects to work over their lifetime. In turn, the education acquired in schools and on-the-job training determines their earning potential. The more years worked, the greater the opportunity to reap the benefits of higher earnings. However, dropping out of the labour force (for example, to take care of children) reduces the years worked during a lifetime, which in turn decreases the potential rewards from human capital. Thus, all other things being equal, the less a person participates in the labour force over their lifetime, the lower the benefits of the investment, and hence the smaller the incentive to invest in training. Since, on average, women work fewer hours throughout their lives than men, one would expect women to purchase less human capital investments than men. Lower human capital investments relative to men translate to lower hourly wages for women. Hence the male-female wage gap widens (Polachek, 2004; O'Dorchai, 2008).

A key indicator related to the complex underlying factors affecting the situation of women in the labour market is their participation–employment rate and working hours. Eurostat data[23] shows that in most of the EU countries where the female employment rate is low (e.g. Malta, Italy, Greece, Poland, Hungary, Romania, Slovakia), the pay gap is lower than EU average, which may reflect the small proportion of low-skilled or unskilled women in the workforce. A possible explanation could be the self-selection effect, i.e. mainly those women who can expect high earnings participate in the labour market, and they are concentrated in sectors or jobs where wages are particularly high. Countries in which a significant proportion of women work part-time (e.g. Netherlands, Germany, UK, Austria, Sweden, and Luxembourg) tend to have a relatively high gender pay gap as women with low-pay perspectives enter the labour market via these part-time jobs.

Part-time work, which almost exclusively involves women, leads to a significant gap in working hours, and consequently, in earnings (Manning and Petrongolo, 2006; O'Dorchai, 2008; Belgian Presidency Report, 2010). Often the labour market is significantly divided in terms of the types of jobs that are available full-time and those that are offered as part-time employment. Part-time jobs are more often found in the low skill jobs and low pay sectors, and make up a significant proportion of the low productivity parts of the economy. It has also been found that women who work part time have, on average, lower educational qualifications than their full time counterparts, are more likely to be married or co-habiting, and have more and younger children.

In 2010 in the EU, 29 per cent of women 'in the age range 25–49 years worked part-time[24]. Of all workers in the EU, 19.2 per cent worked part-time in 2010. Part-time work was most common among working women in the Netherlands, Switzerland and Germany. Statistics Estonia finds that part-time work is not widespread in Estonia. In 2010, 10 per cent of women and only 4 per cent of men aged 25–49 worked part-time. Compared to women in Estonia, the number of women aged 25–49 and working part-time was even smaller in Greece, Lithuania, Slovakia and Bulgaria. Men working part-time were also rare elsewhere in the EU. In 2010 in the EU only 6 per cent of men aged 25–49 worked part-time (only in the Netherlands was the corresponding indicator above 10 per cent).

---

23 Eurostat: Gender Pay Gap Statistics, http://epp.eurostat.ec.europa.eu/statistics_explained/index.php/Gender_pay_gap_statistics.

24 Eurostat online database: Employment Statistics, http://epp.eurostat.ec.europa.eu/statistics_explained/index.php/Employment_statistics.

Women also spend more time out of the labour force or work part-time due to family obligations (e.g. to take care of children, elderly or disabled family members) and this also lowers their wages relative to men who tend to work full-time (Olsen and Walby, 2004; Datta Gupta et al., 2006; O'Dorchai, 2008). There is an important role for the state to ensure that childcare services for children under three years old are available, and that parental leave is adequate, for example. All these factors have an important effect on the labour market participation rate of women with small children, and they can either encourage or discourage the participation of women in employment, particularly in full-time work. Other family characteristics (e.g. having a partner, having children and the number of children) can also affect the participation rates of women in employment (Pothieux and Meurs, 2005).

It is generally assumed that wage gaps will be smaller in the public sector since the mechanism for setting pay is highly regulated and established in pay scales with few individual salary components. This also means that the wage system is based more on the measurable characteristics of the employees (such as length of working experience and educational level), which means that it is less likely that people working in the same job with the same qualifications will earn different wages. The public sector is heavily represented in female employment in EU-27 countries according to the Belgian Presidency Report (2010). In all countries (except Finland and Sweden) average salaries in the public sector were higher than those in the private sector, for both women and men. However, the size of the wage gap varies greatly depending on the country and sector concerned – generally the wage gap found in the public sector is lower than that found in the private sector, with some exceptions (e.g. Bulgaria, Finland, Greece and Hungary). Part of the pay gap in the public sector is explained by the lack of females in senior management roles (NJCHES 2010). Lucifora and Meurs (2006) examine public-private pay determinants for three European countries, France, Great Britain and Italy in 1998, and show that, on average, low-skilled public sector workers are paid higher wages than their private sector counterparts, whilst the opposite is true for highly-skilled workers. They also found that the public sector pay premium is greater for female public sector employees than for males. The proportion of women employed in the public sector in Estonia is higher than that of men[25] (See Table 1). Anspal et al.(2010) find that, on average, the gender pay gap is lower in the public sector than in the private sector (in 2000–2008 accordingly 23 per cent for public sector and 31 per cent in private sector) in Estonia. Wage differences

25 Statistics Estonia shows that 36.9 per cent of women in employment worked in the public sector in 2010, but only 17.7 per cent of men.

in the public sector compared to the private sector are smaller, not only in Estonia, but also in the EU as a whole (Plantenga and Remery, 2006; European Commission, 2009a).

In contrast to human capital theorists, other researchers look to job-related variables to explain the existence of the wage gap. Some of them have focused particularly on the relationship between sex segregation in the workplace and women's comparatively low wages. Segregation encompasses the clustering of women and men in different occupational groups, in different occupations within these groups, in different jobs within these occupations, and in the same type of job in different industries or firms.

Anspal et al. (2010) indicate that part of the gender pay gap in Estonia is derived from horizontal and vertical segregation[26]. The possible reasons for the gender segregation of the Estonian labour market are the high employment rate for women which is above average compared to other EU member states[27], and the size of the sectors in which women predominate, e.g. education, health care and other social services. The hourly wage data shows that women and men earn different wages even within the same occupation (and, on average, the gender pay gap in the same occupation is 13 per cent). Therefore, the concentration of women and men in different sectors and occupations measurably impacts on the gender pay gap in Estonia, but does not fully explain it.

Highly segregated labour markets mean that employment for women is more concentrated in a restricted number of sectors and/or professions (countries with the highest sector segregation include Estonia, Latvia, Lithuania, Ireland, Slovakia, Finland, Bulgaria, Lithuania and Cyprus) and this tends to result in higher pay gap statistics. Previous research shows (Olsen and Walby, 2004) that the higher the proportion of males in an occupation the higher the wages, so the fact that women are more concentrated in occupations with fewer males means that their average wages are lowered by this factor. The results of a recent European-wide study reveal that Estonia is at the top of the list of countries with the highest occupational and sectoral gender segregation (European Commission, 2009b). Key factors identified in the large volume of literature on segregation are comparative biological advantages, lower investment in human capital by females, different family roles, preferences and

---

26 Concentration in different sectors (e.g construction, health care, education) is called horizontal segregation, and vertical integration is the concentration in different occupational levels in the same sector (e.g. managers, clerks).

27 Eurostat, Employment rate by gender, age group 15–64, http://epp.eurostat.ec.europa.eu/tgm/refreshTableAction.do?tab=table&plugin=1&pcode=tsiem010&language=en

prejudices, socialisation and stereotypes, entry barriers and organisational practices. Gender stereotypes are cultural and social attitudes towards what are traditionally considered to be 'male' or 'female' roles and functions. They may influence women's and men's choices of studies and jobs, and may lead to a gender-segregated labour market. These stereotypes influence the unequal shares of working time between women and men, and income and family responsibilities; they also constitute barriers to the career advancement of women and their appointment to decision-making positions (European Commission, 2009c). In recent research, priority is given to four sets of factors: the choice of study field, stereotypes, the demand for shorter or flexible hours of work because of the unequal care burden and different family roles, and covert barriers and biases in organisational practices, including collective bargaining procedures (European Commission, 2009b).

Vertical segregation, or the lack of women at senior board and in executive level roles, has proved to be a difficult area for improvement. Manning and Petrongolo (2006) suggest that the 'glass ceiling' may be a critical factor contributing to the rapid increase in the gender pay gap in later working life. The relatively low representation of women in management positions may explain why the gender pay gap rises steadily with age and peaks for women in their 40s. Vertical segregation is also related to caring responsibilities and is influenced by both the impact of years out of the labour market and the lack of suitable, flexible management positions for women with childcare obligations. The 'sticky floor', which refers to the inability of women to progress from low-paid positions, is also often mentioned in the literature with regard to vertical segregation, and it is largely linked to the lack of progression opportunities in part-time jobs.

When analysing differences in the labour market returns for male and female higher education graduates, it is necessary to relate human capital investment not only to the vertical differentiation in the different degree levels attained, but also to the horizontal dimension of higher qualifications (different fields) as a further dimension of educational achievement (Garcia-Aracil, 2007; Triventi, 2011). When looking at the data clear differences can be seen in the subject areas that men and women choose to study for their degrees. Furthermore, there are clear wage differentials by degree subject. The gender pay gap and its relation to the field of study has been researched based on higher education graduates when they enter the labour market (Machin and Puhani, 2003; Garcia-Aracil, 2007; Goldberg and Hill, 2007; Livanos and Pouliakas, 2009). It has been found that graduates in particular subject areas (law, business, engineering, and health) have higher post-graduate incomes

(Finnie and Frenette, 2003; Black, Seth and Lowell, 2003; Kanep, 2005; Thomas and Zhang, 2005; Norton, 2008).

Napari (2006) finds that by using more detailed major categories (up to 241) instead of a few categories, the contribution of subject areas to the gender wage gap increase remarkably. Though there are some variations in the estimated size of the contribution of these major categories with the level of education (Bachelor's vs. Master's) and with the stage of a career (new entrants to the labour market vs. more experienced workers), the contribution of these major categories to the gender wage gap is remarkably large.

The different value of subject areas is also addressed in the literature. It is argued that the typical learning environment, as well as the acquired competencies and skills, vary between subject areas. The wages for individuals graduating in subject areas providing specific training should exceed those graduating in more general areas. However, particular subject areas that create specific skills only produce skills applicable to a small number of firms in the labour market. Study programmes that provide general training, on the other hand, should allow an individual to find employment in a wider range of firms because the skills that they possess are more transferable (Thorson, 2005; Reimer et al., 2008).

In their recent study of the gender wage gap in Estonia, Anspal et al., 2010 find that there is no one dominating factor that can be considered to be the main reason for the large gender pay gap in Estonia. The pay gap has developed as a result of the joint impact of many factors which cannot always be measured. The regression analysis showed that the unexplained wage difference made up approximately 85 per cent of the general pay gap in 2008. In general, the pay gap is smaller for people with higher education, for ethnic Estonians, single people, childless people, and for those who work in the public sector: these factors explained 15 per cent of the variance in the gender pay gap (Anspal and Rõõm, 2010:23–24). However the field of study did not reduce but increased the unexplained wage differences, since women have more frequently graduated in subject areas that ensure a higher than average wage than men.

Econometric framework

To decompose the graduate wage gap, we used the widely accepted Blinder (1973)-Oaxaca (1973) decomposition:

$$\Delta \equiv \ln w_m - \ln w_f = \underbrace{(X_m - X_f)\beta_m}_{\textit{explained gap}} + \underbrace{(\beta_m - \beta_f)X_f}_{\textit{unexplained gap}}$$

The first part on the right-hand side, 'explained gap', is the part of the gender pay gap due to observed differences in X-variables between males and females. The second part, 'unexplained gap', is a residual that arises due to differences in the returns to the X-variables between men and women. Sometimes the second term is regarded as discrimination against females; however, since the interpretation of the unexplained gap depends on whether all relevant differences between men and women have been taken into account, one has to be cautious when interpreting the explained and unexplained gaps.

The key question is which variables to include among the X-variables. Human capital variables like age, education and field of study, and work-related variables like occupation, industry, region, part-time and public sector, are often used.

In our calculations we used the programme developed by Jann (2008) for the implementation of the Blinder-Oaxaca decomposition for Stata.

Data and variables

In our analysis we used data from a 2010 alumni survey which covered 14 Estonian universities. The survey was conducted in a web-based format[28]. Among other issues, the questionnaire included information about the labour market status and wages of the respondents a year after graduation. The response rate for the survey was 22 per cent. The total number of respondents was 2187. The results were weighted across the following variables: the institution, field of study and level of degree to ensure the validity of the results. The data was calibrated by university and degree.

University graduates were surveyed about one year after graduation, i.e. the survey covered those who graduated in 2009. The distribution by subject area in the sample closely follows the distribution of all graduates (see Table 1).

28 In 2010 the questionnaire was adapted slightly, i.e. the 2007 and 2010 questionnaires are not identical.

Table 10. Distribution of graduates by subject area in the population and the survey sample

	Graduates (population)		Graduates (sample, weighted)	
	Males	Females	Males	Females
Education	5.8	94.2	8.0	92.0
Humanities and arts	19.8	80.2	14.4	85.6
Social sciences, business and law	24.7	75.3	16.4	83.6
Science	53.8	46.2	43.9	56.1
Engineering, manufacturing and construction	67.6	32.4	59.2	40.8
Agriculture	44.1	55.9	39.4	60.6
Health and welfare	7.5	92.5	7.3	92.7
Services	39.4	60.6	31.3	68.7
Total	29.8	70.2	24.6	75.4

Source: Estonian Ministry of Education and Research, Alumni survey 2010, authors' own calculations

Whereas the survey thoroughly mapped study- and work-related aspects, there were several limitations of the survey that influence our research possibilities. For example, we did not ask about working hours so we cannot adjust wages according to hours worked in order to use full-time equivalent wages in the analysis. However, since the incidence of part-time work is low in Estonia, this is not a major problem and should not create bias in the results.

The variables used can be grouped into three categories: socio-demographic (sex, age), study-related (field of study, study level, university) and job-related (occupation, sector, location, firm size, tenure). Unfortunately our data does not include information about an individual's family-related responsibilities (marriage status, number of children, etc) which may have an important influence on labour market decisions.

Age is defined in years not in age groups. In the analysis we make the distinction between study level: bachelor and applied higher education versus master and doctoral graduates because it is highly likely that these categories are not similar. Compared to master/doctoral graduates, bachelor and applied higher education graduates have less work experience and this work is less related to the subject studied (Espenberg et al., 2012). For the university variable, we defined dummies for the each of the 14 universities included.

Occupation is defined based on the ISCO08 1-digit classificatory (i.e. 9 categories from managers to elementary occupations). White-collar staff are defined as ISCO08 categories 1–4 and blue-collar workers as ISCO08 categories 5–9. Tenure is measured as the length of employment in the current job position. In terms of location we distinguished between five Estonian districts: Northern, Central, Eastern, Western and Southern Estonia. Firm size is a categorical variable having 6 values[29]. We controlled for the sector by including a set of dummies for the field of activity of the main job, corresponding mostly to the 2-digit sectors of the NACE classification.

Empirical evidence – gender segregation in Estonian higher education and the wage gap of recent graduates

Gender segregation in Estonian higher education

As we have already observed (see Table 10), the Estonian higher education system is clearly gender-segregated. Females clearly dominate in education, humanities and arts, social sciences, business and law, and health and welfare. Males dominate in science and engineering, manufacturing and construction. The only two areas where the number of men and women are quite equally distributed are agriculture and services.

However, against the background of the increasing overall proportion of females undertaking higher education, the male-female segregation division between study fields has changed quite remarkably over the last two decades (see Figure 1). This is particularly true for services, where the proportion of females who had studied at a higher education institution was less than 30 per cent in the mid-90s, but it had increased to almost 50 per cent by 2011. The female proportion has also increased significantly in health and welfare (15 per cent), and in social sciences, business and law (10 per cent).

29 1 = 1–9 employees; 2 = 10–19 employees; 3 = 20–49 employees; 4 = 50–99 employees; 5 = 200–499 employees; 6 = more than 500 employees.

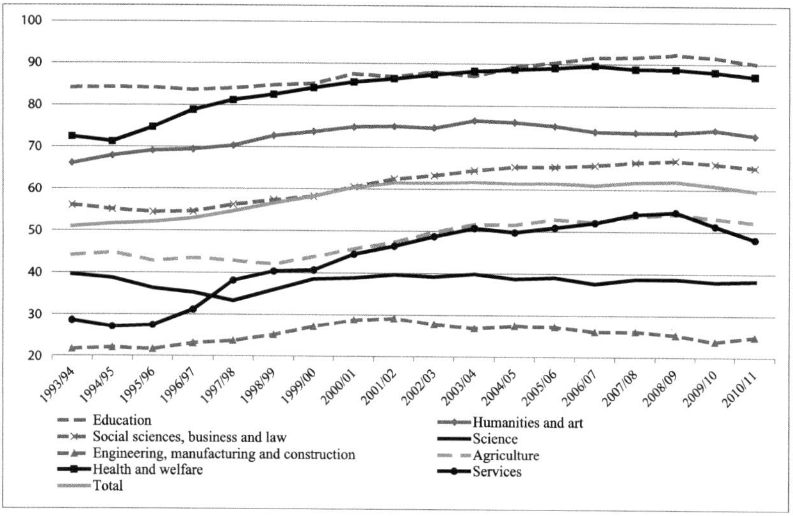

Figure 1. Female proportion of all students by study fields (per cent)

Source: Estonian Ministry of Education and Research

Another dimension important in this regard is the concentration of males/ females in particular study fields (see

Table 11). Over 50 per cent of men study social sciences, business, law, engineering, manufacturing or construction. For females the picture is a bit more mixed, but still more than a third are studying social sciences, business or law.

	Males	Females	Total
Education	1.8	11.2	7.4
Humanities and arts	9.2	16.7	13.7
Social sciences, business and law	29.1	36.9	33.8
Science	17.1	7.1	11.2
Engineering, manufacturing and construction	26.8	6.0	14.4
Agriculture	2.7	2.0	2.3
Health and welfare	3.0	13.6	9.3
Services	10.2	6.4	8.0
Total	**100.0**	**100.0**	**100.0**

Table 11. Division of male and female students by study fields in Estonia in 2010

Source: Estonian Ministry of Education and Research

Wage gap[30]

The raw (i.e. unadjusted) gender pay gap in Estonia is the largest of all of the EU-27 countries. Eurostat data shows that, on average, women earned only 72.4 per cent of what men would earn in Estonia in 2008, i.e. the size of the gender pay gap was 27.6 per cent, whereas the EU-27 average was 18 per cent (see Figure 1).

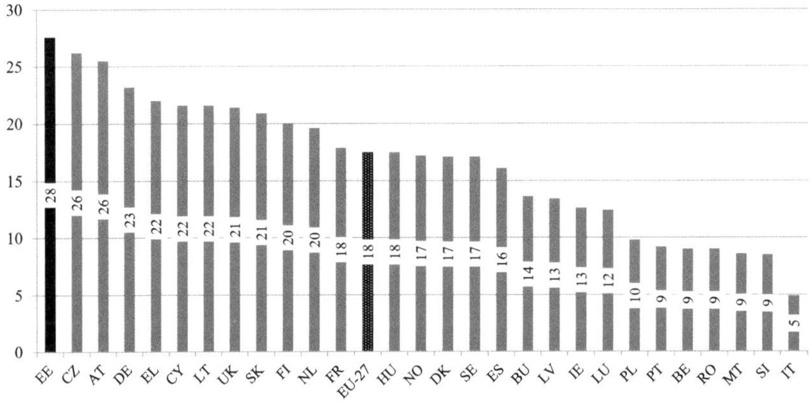

Figure 2. The gender pay gap in EU-27 countries and Norway in 2008

Source: Eurostat

Note: EE – Estonia, CZ, Czech Republic, AT – Austria, DE – Germany, EL – Greece, CY – Cyprus, LT – Lithuania, UK – United Kingdom, SK – Slovak Republic, FI – Finland, NL – Netherlands, FR – France, HU – Hungary, NO – Norway, DK – Denmark, SE – Sweden, ES – Spain, BU – Bulgaria, LV – Latvia, IE – Ireland, LU – Luxembourg, PL – Poland, PT – Portugal, BE – Belgium, RO – Romania, MT – Malta, SI – Slovenia, IT – Italy.

The Estonian alumni survey shows that the raw gender pay[31] gap among recent graduates is at just about the same level as the whole economy: 24.7 per

30 In the analysis we use gross wages. The top and bottom 2.5 per cent of the wage scale was excluded to neutralise the effects of the outliers.

31 Our monthly wage variable has not been adjusted for different working hours as that information is missing from our data. This may not be a probleem as part-time work is not common in Estonia (e.g. in 2008 just 7.2 per cent of those in employment worked part-time).

cent. However, there are considerable differences between graduates from different subject areas.

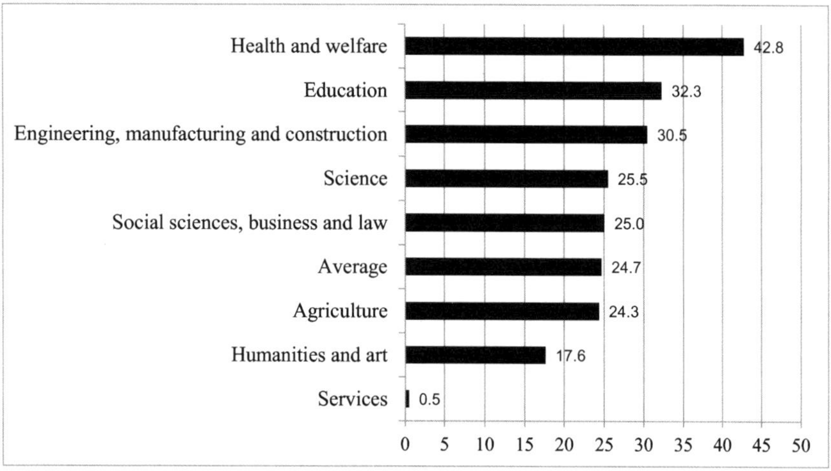

Figure 3. The gender pay gap of 2010 graduates by subject area

Source: Alumni survey (Themas, Espenberg and Eamets 2011), weighted, authors' own calculations

We used ordinary least squares (OLS) wage regressions to analyse which factors influence the wages of male and female recent graduates. As the results in Table 12 show, when all other variables are equal, white-collar workers earn more than blue-collar workers[32]; however, the effect is double that for females compared to males and it is statistically significant. Thus, one important conclusion to be drawn is that there are no significant wage differences for recent graduate male white-collar and blue-collar workers, as in those occupations regarded as 'blue-collar',wages tend to be quite high in 'male areas' (for example, construction and engineering), but this result does not apply to 'female areas' (for example, female blue-collar workers in shops, etc.)[33].

32 In total, 8 per cent of respondents worked as blue-collar workers (weighted data).

33 As the explanatory variable explaining the wage gap, weal so tried using the dummy variable for the current job being very closely, or closely, related to the field of study. Those peole working in a job related to their field of study do have some what higher wages (by 16 per cent), yet that variable is only slightly lower among hard science graduates (67 per cent) than among social science graduates (75 per cent), which perhaps

As expected, educational level also plays an important role: master's/ doctoral degree graduates earn more than bachelor's/applied higher education degree graduates, and those with longer job tenure earn more than those with less experience (but the effect is only statistically significant for females). The University from which they graduated also has an effect for females only.

The influence of the region where the job is located plays a role for females only: jobs in Northern and North-Eastern Estonia pay more than in any other region. Age has a positive and almost linear association with wages (as shown by the negative squared term). In terms of sectors, for females wages are higher in hotels and restaurants, which may seem surprising given that these are usually regarded as low-wage sectors, but we need to take into account here that we have a sub-sample of graduates of higher education institutions.

Table 12. Wage equations for male and female graduates

Variable	**Males**		**Females**	
	Coeff.	T-stat.	Coeff.	T-stat.
Age	0.125	(2.83)***	0.037	(2.07)**
Age squared	-0.002	(-2.68)***	-0.000	(-1.79)*
District (ref. Southern Estonia)				
Northern Estonia	0.151	(1.63)	0.309	(7.59)***
Central Estonia	-0.017	(-0.09)	0.080	(1.17)
North-Eastern Estonia	0.077	(0.16)	0.217	(2.30)**
Western Estonia	-0.028	(-0.10)	0.116	(1.83)*
Master	0.120	(1.68)*	0.152	(4.91)***
University (ref. other)				
University of Life Sciences	0.117	(0.44)	0.173	(1.95)*
Tallinn University of Technology	0.186	(0.79)	0.370	(4.72)***
University of Tartu	0.064	(0.26)	0.326	(4.25)***
Tallinn University	0.140	(0.58)	0.186	(2.55)**
Tenure (*ref. up to 3 months*)				
Tenure 4-12 months	0.173	(1.34)	0.075	(1.33)
Tenure 12-36 months	0.099	(0.89)	0.139	(2.61)***
Tenure more than 3 years	0.184	(1.55)	0.192	(3.41)***

---

explains why it turned out to be statistically insignificant in all the decomposition exercises.

Table 3. Continued

Variable	Males	Females	Variable	Males
Occupation (*ref. blue-collar*)				
White-collar	0.232	(0.83)	0.443	(6.36)***
Sector (*ref. agriculture*)				
Construction	0.099	(0.53)	0.053	(0.33)
Sales and trade	-0.501	(-1.52)	0.084	(1.03)
Hotels and restaurants	0.028	(0.13)	0.292	(3.01)***
Transport	-0.013	(-0.03)	0.015	(0.12)
Finance	0.253	(1.31)	0.194	(2.15)**
Other business services	0.145	(1.11)	0.271	(4.07)***
Public services	-0.041	(-0.54)	0.103	(2.70)***
Constant	6.851	(8.52)***	7.524	(24.66)***
Number of obs.	207		608	
R-squared	0.270		0.376	

Note: the dependent variable is the natural log of the wage variable. The category 'white-collar' includes legislators, senior officials and managers, professionals, technicians and associate professionals.

Source: Alumni survey data (2010), weighted, authors' own calculations

As the final step of the analysis, we also performed the Oaxaca-Blinder decomposition[34] of the wage difference between male and female graduates. The purpose of this exercise was to discover the extent to which the gender pay gap can be accounted for by different factors. We also analysed which part of the wage gap was linked to differences in the characteristics (i.e. an explained or objective gap) and which part was related to the differences in returns to these characteristics (i.e. an unexplained or a subjective gap).

Figure 4 shows the Kernel density functions for wage distributions. It is clear that male graduates have higher wages than female graduates, and that is consistent with the overall gender pay gap observed in Estonia. In the case of females, the highest wage earned was about 8000 kroons[35], in case of males it was 10000–15000 kroons.

34 In the sample used in the decompositions, 38 per cent were graduates of hard sciences.

35 1 EUR=15.6466 kroons.

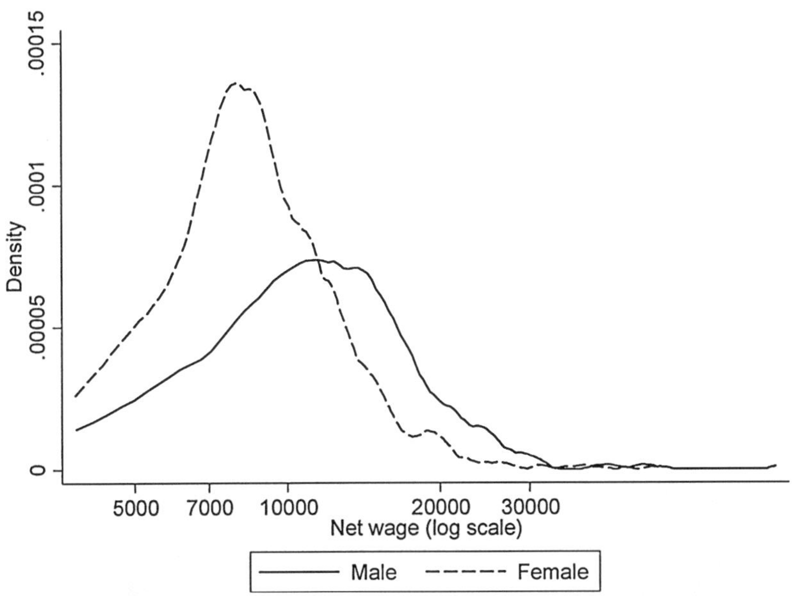

Figure 4. *Kernel density for wage distribution (in EEK): gross wages, lower and upper 2.5 per cent observations dropped.*

Source: Alumni survey data (2010), weighted, authors' own calculations

Table 13 shows the results of the Oaxaca-Blinder decomposition. The explained component has a negative sign which means that variables used in the model explain the higher wages of males, which was also seen in the raw data. To observe the effects of the different variables on the wage gap, we used a step-by-step approach when adding the factors into the analysis. There are five separate models. The first includes only the level of study (bachelor/applied higher educational versus master/doctoral degree). The second model incorporates university, age and occupation, and the third and the fourth include factors that were found to be important determinants of wage differences in previous studies. The last model includes all previous variables plus firm size and tenure.

Table 13. Oaxaca-Blinder decomposition of the wage gap between the men and females

Model	1	2	3	4	5
Average wage (female)	10712.6	10712.61	10712.6	10712.6	10712.6
Average wage (male)	14600.1	14600.1	14600.1	14600.1	14600.1
Wage gap (log difference)	-31.0%	-31.0%	-31.0%	-31.0%	-31.0%
Explained	-2.7%	-13.2%	-16.6%	-19.8%	-18.0%
Unexplained	-28.2%	-17.8%	-14.4%	-11.1%	-13.0%
Explained part by factors					
Level (master/ bachelor)	-0.027 (-2.79)	-0.024 (-2.6)	-0.018 (-2.35)	-0.019 (-2.48)	-0.018 (-2.39)
University		-0.04 (-2.66)	-0.035 (-2.48)	-0.027 (-1.99)	-0.02 (-1.65)
Field of study		-0.041 (-1.48)	-0.039 (-1.44)	0.015 (0.56)	-0.02 (-2.55)
Age		-0.027 (-3.11)	-0.022 (-2.88)	-0.026 (-3.25)	-0.054 (-4.39)
Occupation			-0.052 (-4.1)	-0.052 (-4.22)	-0.085 (-3.62)
Sector				-0.089 (-3.68)	-0.006 (-0.97)
Location					0.017 (0.63)
Firm size					0.011 (1.44)
Tenure					-0.004 (-0.99)
Observations	718	718	718	718	718

Note. Z-statistics are in parenthesis. In order to control for possible measurement errors, we excluded the lower and upper 2.5 per cent of observations from the calculations. Graduates with bachelor's, applied higher educational, master's and doctoral degrees are included in the calculations. In all estimations the sample size is the same as we chose to include in the sample the observations with non-missing values in all relevant variables.

Source: Alumni survey data (2010), weighted, authors' own calculations

The total wage gap is around 31 per cent in favour of males. Note that the raw gap here differs from the numbers reported above because the calculations include only the observations with non-missing values of the variables included in the model. About 58 per cent of the wage gap is explained by the variables included in the model.

The results of the decomposition indicate that, of the different factors, occupation is the most important determinant of the wage gap – it explains almost half of the explained gap. Age is also very important – it explains about a third of the explained gap. Smaller effects come from university, field of study and degree (there was a higher representation of males among those with master's degree). Enterprise-specific factors, like sector, location and size, are relatively unimportant and not statistically significant. Our results are fairly similar to those of Finnie and Frenette (2003) who show that occupation and sector are fairly highly correlated with field of study and adding those variables to the model will capture some of the effects of the subject field.

Conclusion

During last two decades, the proportion of females has increased in almost all study fields, especially in services, health and welfare, social sciences, and business and law. Estonian higher education is clearly gender segregated. Male students dominate in hard science (science, engineering, manufacturing and construction), female students in the social sciences and humanities (education, humanities and arts, social sciences, business and law), and health and welfare. Both genders are quite equally represented in services and agriculture. However, females tend to be more successful in finishing their studies – even in the study fields dominated mainly by men, the female proportion of graduates is higher than the female proportion of students.

We used data from a recent (2010) alumni survey to analyse the size and causes of the gender wage gap among recent graduates from 14 Estonian public and private universities. The survey covered graduates of all educational levels (bachelor's, applied higher education, master's and doctoral). Graduates were surveyed a year after graduation.

We found that there is a wide gender wage gap among recent graduates in Estonia. On average the raw wage gap (i.e. the unadjusted wage gap) is around 25 per cent, but there are large discrepancies between study fields. The male-female gap is highest in health and welfare (more than 40 per cent), education and engineering, and manufacturing and construction (more than 30 per cent). There is no gender wage gap observable in services. The probable explanation is the differences in the occupations that men and women hold – in health and services most low-paid jobs (like care workers and nurses) are held by women; men are mostly in higher-paid positions, like doctors. The same applies to education, where women are much more likely to be in the lower-paid jobs than men. The significant influence of the study field on the wage gap corresponds to previous studies, such as Finnie and Frenette (2003), Machin and Puhani (2003), Napari (2006) and Garcia-Aracil (2007). However, there may be other factors affecting the gender pay gap not related purely to differences in productivity. There could be indirect discrimination based on sex, stemming from cultural stereotypes and traditions, and general opinions about the role of females in the labour market.

The wage regression and the Oaxaca-Blinder decomposition analysis indicate that 58 per cent of wage gap is explained by the factors used in the analysis. Employer-related factors like sector, size and location do not play a significant role in the graduates' gender pay gap. The most important factor, that explains about half of the female pay penalty, is occupation. This stresses the importance of occupational segregation on the male-female wage gap of graduates in Estonia. The results are in accordance with previous studies that have taken the wage gap at a more general level into consideration. As with our study, other recent studies in Estonia find occupation-related variables to be important in explaining the pay gap (Rõõm and Kallaste, 2004; Anspal et al., 2010) and this is the case in other countries as well (Triventi, 2011). Another important determinant of the explained gap is age. We found the relative importance of the explained and unexplained components to be quite different from the earlier Estonian studies using the labour force survey data. For instance, Rõõm and Kallaste (2004) find that in a total gap of 30 per cent for 1998–2000 the explained part was 8 per cent and the unexplained part 21.3 per cent; Krillo and Masso (2010) find the explained component to be 5 per cent and the unexplained component to be 24 per cent for 2005–2007. It needs to be stressed that our sample was just a segment of the total labour force, consisting of relatively well educated and well qualified workers. It could be that the issues of gender based discrimination are more important for the less educated labour force.

References

Anspal, S., Kraut, L. and Rõõm, T. (2010). *Sooline palgalõhe Eestis: empiirline analüüs. Uuringuraport* [Gender pay gap in Estonia: empirical analysis. Survey report]. Eesti Rakendusuuringute Keskus CentAR, Poliitikauuringute Keskus PRAXIS, Sotsiaalministeerium.

Anspal, S. and Rõõm, T. (2010). *Gender Pay Gap in Estonia: Empirical Analysis.* Tallinn: Sotsiaalministeerium. Available online: http://www.sm.ee/fileadmin/meedia/Dokumendid/V2ljaanded/Publikatsioonid/2011/Gender_pay_gap_Estonia_analysis.pdf

Beblo, M. and Wolf, E. (2000). How much does a year off cost? Estimating the wage effects of employment breaks and part-time periods. Discussion Paper No 00-69. Zentrum für Europäische Wirtschaftsforschung.

Belgian Presidency Report (2010). The gender pay gap in the Member States of the European Union: quantitative and qualitative indicators. Available online: http://register.consilium.europa.eu/pdf/en/10/st16/st16516-ad02.en10.pdf

Black, D., Seth S. and Lowell, T. (2003). The economic reward for studying economics. *Economic Inquiry*, 41, 365–377.

Blinder, A. S. (1973). Wage Discrimination: Reduced Form and Structural Estimates. *The Journal of Human Resources*, 8, 436–455.

Council Directive 75/117/EEC of 10 February 1975 on the approximation of the laws of the Member States relating to the application of the principle of equal pay for men and women. Available online: http://eur-lex.europa.eu/LexUriServ/LexUriServ.do?uri=CELEX:31975L0117:EN:HTML

Datta Gupta, N. and Smith, N. (2002). Children and career interruptions: The family gap in Denmark. *Economica*, 69, 609–629.

Datta Gupta, N., Verner, M. and Smith, N. (2006). Child care and parental leave in the Nordic countries: A model to aspire to? *IZA Discussion Paper*, 2014.

Espenberg, K., Themas, A., Masso, J. and Eamets, R. (2012). Does a university degree pay off in the Estonian labour market? *Studies for the Learning Society*, 2, 46–60.

European Commission (2009a). Equality between Women and Men – 2009. Report from the Commission to the European Parliament, the Council, the European Economic and Social Committee and the Committee of Regions.

European Commission (2009b). Gender segregation in the labour market: Root causes, implications and policy responses in the EU.

European Commission (2009c). Report on Equality Between Women and Men 2009.European Commission, Directorate-General for Employment, Social Affairs and Equal Opportunities.

Eurostat online database, http://epp.eurostat.ec.europa.eu/portal/page/portal/statistics/search_database

Finnie, R. and Frenette, M. (2003). Earning differences by major field of study: evidence from three cohorts of recent Canadian graduates. *Economics of Education Review*, 22, 179–192.

Garcia-Aracil, A. (2007). College Major and the Gender Earnings Gap: A Multi-country Examination of Postgraduate Labour Market Outcomes. *Research in Higher Education*, 49, 733–775.

Goldberg D. and Hill, C. (2007). Behind the pay gap. *AAUW Educational Foundation.* Available online: http://www.aauw.org/learn/research/upload/behindPayGap.pdf

Jann, B. (2008). A Stata implementation of the Blinder-Oaxaca decomposition. *ETH Zurich Sociology Working Paper,* 5.

Kanep, H. (2005). *Analüüs erinevate koolitusvaldkondade lõpetanute seisundite kohta tööturul ametialade, haridustasemete ja majandusharude lõikes* [The analysis of the status of the graduates of different fields on the labour market by jobs, education and economic sectors]. Poliitikauuringute Keskus Praxis. Available online and only in Estonian: www.hm.ee/index.php?popup=download&id=9022l/documents/Genderpaygap2006.pdf

Krillo, K. and Masso, J. (2010). The part-time/full-time wage gap in Central and Eastern Europe: The case of Estonia. *Research in Economics and Business: Central and Eastern Europe*, 2, 47–75.

Livanos, I. and Pouliakas, K. (2009). The gender wage gap as a function of educational degree choices in an occupationally segregated EU country. *IZA Discussion Paper*, 4636.

Lucifora, C. and Meurs, D. (2006). The public sector pay gap in France, Great Britain and Italy. *Review of Income and Wealth*, 52, 43–59.

Machin, S. and Puhani, A. P. (2003). Subject of degree and the gender wage differential: evidence from the UK and Germany. *Economics Letters*, 70, 393–400.

Manning, A. and Petrongolo, B. (2006). The Part-time Pay Penalty for Women in Britain. *IZA Discussion Paper*, 2419.

Ministry of Education and Research, www.hm.ee

Mägi, E., Aidla, A., Reino, A., Jaakson, K. and Kirss, L. (2011). *Üliõpilaste töötamise fenomen Eesti kõrghariduses. Uuringu lõpparuanne* [The phenomenon of the working among university students. The final report]. Tartu: Sihtasutus Archimedes.

Napari, S. (2006). Type of Education and the Gender Wage Gap. *Helsinki Center of Economic Research Discussion Paper,* 128.

Norton, T. (2008). Graduate employment and earnings: Are universities meeting student expectations? Research report.

O'Dorchai, S. (2008). Pay inequality in 25 European countries. *Département d'Economie appliquée (DULBEA) Working Paper*, 08-06.RS.

Oaxaca, R. (1973). Male-Female Wage Differentials in Urban Labor Markets. *International Economic Review*, 14, 693–709.

Olsen, W. and Walby, S.(2004). Modelling gender pay gaps. *EOC Working Paper*, 17.

Plantenga, J. and Remery C. (2006). The gender pay gap – Origins and policy responses – A comparative review of thirty European countries. *Office for Official Publications of the European Communities*.

Polachek, S. W. (2004). How the Human Capital Model Explains Why The Gender Wage Gap Narrowed. *IZA Discussion Paper*, 1102.

Pothieux, S. and Meurs, D. (2005). The gender wage gap in Europe: Women, Men and the Public Sector. *Institut National de la Statistique et des Etudes Economiques (INSEE) Working Paper*, F0502.

Reimer, D., Noelke, C. and Kucel, A. (2008). Labor Market Effects of Field of Study in Comparative Perspective: An Analysis of 22 European Countries. *International Journal of Comparative Sociology*, 49, 233–256.

Rõõm, T. and Kallaste, E. (2004). Men and women in the Estonian labour market: an assessment of the gender wage gap. *PRAXIS Center for Policy Studies Policy Analysis*, 8.

Saar, E. and Unt, M. (2011). Education and labour market entry in Estonia: closing doors for those without tertiary education. In Kogan, I., Noelke, C., and Gebel, M (Eds.), *Making the Transition: Education and Labour Market Entry in Central and Eastern Europe*. Stanford University Press, 240–268.

NJCHES (2010). The Gender Pay Gap – A Literature Review. *New Joint Negotiating Committee for Higher Education Staff(NJCHES) report*. Available online: http://www.ucea.ac.uk/download.cfm/docid/39012615-27AC-42CA-9FE9EC1B5F23B422

Themas, A., Espenberg, K. and Eamets, R. (2011). Estonian Universities' Graduates Survey. Research report. Tartu: University of Tartu.

Thomas, S. L. and Zhang, L. (2005). Post-baccalaureate wage growth within 4 years of graduation: The effects of college quality and college major. *Research in Higher Education*, 46, 437–459.

Thorson, A. (2005). The effect of college major on wages. *The Park Place Economist*, 13, 45–57.

Triventi, M. (2011). The gender wage gap among recent European graduates. *Alma Laurea Inter-University Consortium Working Paper*, 32.

United Nations Development Programme (2006). The Gender Pay Gap over Women's Working Lifetime. UNDP Working Paper.

Chapter 17.
Wishing Welcome to the Non-traditional Student: How Institutions Create Barriers for Returning to Higher Education

Ellu Saar, Kadri Täht, Triin Roosalu, Auni Tamm

Introduction

Is there place for adult students in higher education system in Estonia, and how difficult is it for them to claim this place? How, at all, could we measure the institutional barriers in access to education, and are they high or low? These are the main concerns of this chapter.

The mainstreaming of the ideas of lifelong learning in policy as well as practice (Jarvis, 2007, 2010) has contributed to the creating of lifelong learning societies in Europe (Holford et al, 2008; Riddell, Markowitsch and Weedon, 2012; Saar, Ure and Holford, 2013). While most advanced countries have moved to having a mass higher education system (Schoefer and Meyer, 2005), educational expansion has brought about segmentation and differentiation in higher education (Shavit, Arum and Gamoran, 2007). As part of those processes of expansion and differentiation, one important shift has been the entrance of non-traditional students, traditionally excluded from or underrepresented in higher education. Also, the decreasing birth rate of aging societies has forced educational institutions to look at other ways of maintaining recruitment (Bowl, 2001). Overall, this means that the profile of the student population has changed and the number of adult students has increased (Morey, 2004; Darmody and Smyth, 2008). Several European Commission documents refer to the need to ensure the provision of flexible, relevant and innovative programmes in higher education targeting a diversified student population and the need to establish alternative routes to higher education (see for example European Commission (2012).

Although there are difficulties in defining the term 'adult students' (Schuetze and Slowey, 2002), several concepts of adult students have been identified (see Kasworm, 2003; Wyatt, 2011). These are based on: (1) age (typically defined as twenty-five years of age and older); (2) entrance or re-entrance to higher education with a prior major break in their educational path; (3) mature life experience gained through work, family and community involvement; (4) status of responsibility. We use the second concept in this paper, defining adult students as people who have left full-time formal initial education – e.g. to enter the labour market – and who, after at least two years, have re-entered the educational system at the level of higher education.

A greater number of adult students in higher education also calls for a different perspective with regard to practices and policies, which should be reflected in entry routes, modes of study, provision of higher education, teaching methods, and in policies at the national level. Some studies (Spanard, 1990; McGivney, 1996; Chao, DeRocco and Flynn, 2007) however argue that the needs of adults have not been adequately represented in higher education.

Much research has been focused on the question why adults do not participate in education and how we should understand the barriers to participation (Cross, 1981; Darkenwald and Valentine, 1985; Valentine and Darkenwald, 1990). However, most research so far is centred on individual and psychological attributes, without reference to external factors (Blair, McPake and Munn, 1995). Some studies have nevertheless attempted to examine a variety of societal factors that are associated with participation in educational programmes (Gooderham, 1993; Babchuk and Courtney, 1995). Still, there are a few studies that have analysed also the impact of structural factors on participation of adults in higher education, as well as the impact of meso level factors that are under control of the educational system itself (Jung and Cervero, 2002; Schaffer, 2010). However, these have not focused on understanding the actual impact of these factors on the effective barriers to adults' participation in higher education.

The current study is thus founded on the need to discuss the barriers to participation of adults in higher education from a sociological perspective in order to better understand the impact of supply side factors, i.e., conditions pertaining to education provision on formation of barriers. We concentrate our attention on the institutional barriers perceived by adults participating in higher education programmes and the impact of institutional factors on the formation of these barriers.

The main research questions are:

- How to describe the level of institutional barriers in Estonia? To what extent does the level of institutional barriers to participation of adults in higher education differ cross-nationally?
- How accessible, flexible and affordable are higher education programs for adults in Estonia? To what extent do accessibility, flexibility and affordability of these programs for adults differ cross-nationally?
- What is the relationship between factors characterising accessibility, flexibility and affordability of higher education programs and the institutional

barriers perceived by adult students? Based on this relationship, how does the Estonian higher education system compare to the other national systems?

In Estonia, during the Soviet era, the 1960s and the 1970s marked a period when the involvement of adults in higher education institutions was quite high (see Helemäe and Saar, 1999). In the 1980s, the proportion of adults in higher education decreased steadily. However, with the structural change from the Soviet Union to independence, the previously well-established institutionalised systems, including those for adult education and lifelong learning, were discontinued. When, at the beginning of the societal transformation, there was a lack of resources, attention was paid to other aspects of regime construction and state building. Development of institutions such as those of adult education took more time and was dependant on the economic growth and opportunities that were opened up with the EU accession process, which was completed in 2004. At the same time previous research shows complex changes in terms of meanings attached to learning (e.g. constantly high evaluation of values of self-development, rapidly increasing adherence to values related to economic rewards) (Aava, 2010; Roosalu and Roosmaa, 2010). It is thus important to look at how these societal changes are reflected in the institutional settings of the higher education system.

The structure of the chapter is as follows. We first review previous literature on this topic, secondly, we briefly describe the data, variables and methods we use in the analysis and finally we report the main findings and discuss the results.

Barriers to participation

Our theoretical starting point is the bounded agency model formulated by Rubenson and Desjardins (2009). The premise of the model is the assumption that the nature of institutional arrangements and broad structural conditions can affect a person's capability to participate through the way these institutional arrangements construct structural conditions and helps individuals overcome both structurally and individually based barriers (Rubenson and Desjardins, 2009).

Adults as Learners (Cross, 1981) remains the most frequently cited work on barriers to participation in education. Analysing her research and that of others, Cross categorised the obstacles most commonly cited by adults as barriers to their participation in learning activities. She identified three categories: situational, institutional and dispositional. Situational barriers are related to a person's life situation at a given point in the family life cycle and working life. Institutional or structural barriers include institutional practices and procedures that discourage or prevent participation, such as lack of provision or opportunity, timing of provision, high fees or entry qualifications, general lack of flexibility. Dispositional barriers refer to personality traits, or personal qualities acquired through early school experiences, concerns about own ability to succeed, belief that one is too old to go back to school. It may be easier for the education system to help the potential students to overcome the problems related to institutional barriers, rather than those originating from the situational barriers of each individual learner or their dispositional barriers. The latter are usually closely related to the wide range of internalised norms in the social structure of the society, while the institutional barriers are originating more clearly from within the education system, if not from within each specific school in question. Therefore, in this paper we concentrate mostly on those institutional barriers, which Cross (1981) categorized into five thematic problems: (1) scheduling problems; (2) problems with location or transportation; (3) procedural problems related to enrolment; (4) lack of information regarding procedures or the programs of study. Spanard (1990) added to this list a further thematic problem: (5) fee structures (cost). However, it is important to underline here that the majority of research on barriers has been conducted through questionnaire-based surveys of individual learners. Therefore, the findings may not be actual indicators of why adults do not participate, but individual perceptions of those things they themselves feel would be barriers.

Schuetze and Slowey (2000) studied the changes in adults' participation in higher education in ten countries, and they managed to identify six institutional factors, which appeared to be particularly influential with regard to the participation of adults. These are: (1) institutional differentiation – the extent to which various types of institutions encourage or discourage participation of adults; (2) flexible or open admission for those without traditional entry qualifications; (3) mode of study – the availability of modes of study that accommodate the particular needs of adult learners, especially the extent of distance learning and part-time studies, modular courses, policies for assessment of prior learning; (4) financial and other support; (5) institutional governance and control – the extent of institutional flexibility with regard to the organization of studies, contents or curricula and programs; (6) continuing educational opportunities – the availability of short courses or non-credit programs that serve as gateway activities to engaging adult learners.

In the literature about higher education participation, access remains one of the most cited and studied variables (Adelman, 2007). Access may be considered by proximity and availability of an institution of higher education to potential student. Several studies have indicated that institutions tend to engage more adult learners when they: have open admission practices (Mancuso, 2001; Schuetze and Slowey, 2002); deliver distance learning opportunities (Chao, DeRocco and Flynn, 2007); recognise life and work experience and use prior learning assessment programs (Knowles, Holton and Swanson, 2005); and have lower tuition fees (McGivney, 1993; Heller, 1999). The level of need-based financial assistance may play an important role in influencing adult participation (Long, 2008).

These basic assumptions, derived from previous studies, provide a broad context for development of our hypotheses. Namely, we suppose that all these factors may impact on the institutional barriers perceived by adult students. Adults studying in higher education may have less institutional barriers in countries with higher diversification of higher education, with higher percentage of higher education institutions with open admissions, with prevalence of distance learning, with opportunities for earning credit for prior experience, with affordability of higher education, with availability of financial aid.

Data, variables and methods

As the first step, to describe the body of adult students in higher education and to indicate the level of different barriers in the society for the potential adult learners, we rely on the data from European Adult Education Survey (AES), conducted by Eurostat in 2007 in all European countries. To analyse the perceptions of adults in formal education we will use the data from the Survey of Adult Learners in Formal Education (ALiFE) carried out in the project 'Towards a Lifelong Learning Society in Europe: The Contribution of the Education System' (http://LLL2010.tlu.ee) with co-funding from European Commission in the 6th Framework Programme. The survey was also conducted in 2007 in 13 European countries, from 5 geographies: Anglophone – England, Scotland, Ireland; Northern European – Norway; Continental Europe – Austria, Belgium; Central and East European (CEE) – Bulgaria, the Czech Republic, Hungary, Slovenia; Post-Soviet Republics – Estonia, Lithuania, Russia. In some countries, the survey was conducted regional either because education is regionalised as in the UK (England, Scotland, Northern Ireland) and Belgium (Flanders) or because the country is very large e.g. Russia. Within each country, a stratified multi-stage sample was drawn with effective response targeted by level of education (ISCED). A three-stage selection procedure was used to select learners: first, a number of institutions were selected within each of the four strata to represent the variety of types of providers (colleges, academies, providers of distance education etc.). Next, within each selected institution, one or more fields of study were selected. A last stage was to select respondents within each field. We are using the subsample of adults studying at higher education institutions comprising a total of 3943 respondents (for sample description see Appendix).

The questionnaire included questions about the characteristics of the institution in which respondents attend courses: questions about entry requirements, exemptions, preparatory programmes, time use, teaching modes and organization of the programme; about the costs of the course: questions about the party that pays the costs, the amount of the fee, extra costs, grants, paid leave and services, questions about the learning process: the classroom environment, support received, barriers and satisfaction. Based on our research question, we then composed specific indicators to best reflect the various institutional factors that affect adult learners' participation in formal education. Table 1 summarises the variables that we will use in our empirical analysis.

Table 1. Description of variables

Factor	Variable	Description
Access	Diversification	Country type according to level of diversification: 1 – low diversification 2 – medium diversification 3 – high diversification
	Entry requirements	Entry on the basis of a certificate or diploma: 0 – no, 1 – yes
		Entry on the basis of an admission test: 0 – no; 1 – yes
Flexibility	Delivery of distance learning oportunities	Distance education using an electronic learning platform or written materials: 0 – never, rarely; 1 – occasionally; 2 – often, very often
	Attendance of school	During evenings or the weekend: 0 – no; 1 – yes
		Weekly frequency: 1 – less than once a week; 2 – once a week; 3 – twice a week; 4 – three times a week; 5 – more than three times a week
		Hours in a week: 1 – 0/9 hours; 2 – 10/19 hours; 3 – 20/29 hours; 4 – 30/39 hours; 5 – 40 hours or more
	The use of prior learning assessment programs	APEL: 0 – no; 1 – yes
		APL: 0 – no; 1 – yes
Affordability	Payment of the enrolment fee	Self-paid: 0 – no; 1 – yes
	Financial assistance	Use of student grant: 0 – no; 1 – yes
		Use of student loan: 0 – no; 1 – yes

Our analysis consists of two parts. First, we compare cross-nationally the level of institutional barriers mentioned by adult students as well as characteristics of access, flexibility and affordability of higher education for adult students. Secondly, we use linear regression analysis to estimate the impact of different variables characterising access, flexibility and affordability of higher education for adult students on perceived institutional barriers. The dependent variable is the mean of three institutional barriers fixed in the questionnaire: studies scheduled at an inconvenient time, financial problems and transportation problems.

In addition to this comparative statistical analysis, we will further illustrate Estonian results using interviews with the representatives of higher education institutions, to analyse how the institutions shape their student bodies and thus create different barriers – or help to overcome them – in Estonia. In 2011, seven interviews were carried out among the representatives of academic administrations in five higher education institutions in Estonia within the Primus programme research project 'Labour Market Challenges to Higher Education: Estonia in European Context'. These enabled us to further explore the institutionalised attitudes towards inclusion of non-traditional students – see further details on approach and methods in the research report (Reiska et al., 2012). In 2011, another nine interviews with the coordinators of the study programmes were carried out in five higher education institutions within the Primus project 'Lifelong Learning in Higher Education: Supportive Learning Environment' (see further information in Saar et al., 2012), to reflect the multilevel approach to adult students in higher education. We will use the sections from those interviews to explore some of our concepts and to illustrate how the actors in the field of higher education make meaning of those concepts we use.

Empirical results

Institutional barriers for adult students

In developing our argument, let us first have a look at the level of participation of adults in higher education (see Figure 1). A quick overview shows there is high variance across countries. In 2007, only a quite small proportion of Estonian adults, 4.2 per cent, attended formal higher education, which is more than in Bulgaria, Hungary and the Czech Republic, but considerably less than in Norway or Slovenia.

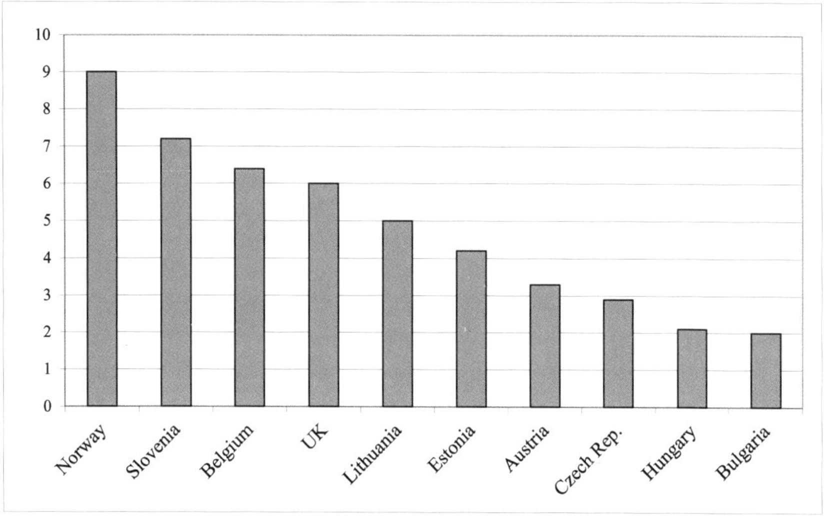

Figure 1. Participation of adults (25–64 years old) in higher education in 2007(per cent)

Source: authors' own calculations, Adult Education Survey 2007

How do the adults in higher education perceive institutional barriers? Which barriers are perceived as most prominent, and which less so? Does Estonia stand out from the cross-national comparison? In order to answer these questions,

we first calculated how many adult students in each country reported to having one of the institutional problems: difficulties in getting transportation to their higher education institution; financial problems of some kind or another; or felt studies were scheduled at inconvenient times. We then calculated the mean value, combining all these institutional problems.

When looking at what adults perceive as the biggest challenges in participating in formal education in Estonia (Table 2), the most frequently experienced are restrictions related to financial situations. Almost half of the respondents say that they have experienced financial problems during their studies. A slightly smaller number of adult students have experienced time-related barriers, such as studies being scheduled at inconvenient times. Although transportation-related problems are the least frequent of the three barriers characterized and analysed in this paper; one in four adult students confirms that they have experienced problems related to transport during their studies.

The situation of adult learners in Estonia resembles their peers in other post-Soviet countries, Lithuania and Russia, in which the most frequently experienced barrier is related to financial problems. On average, post-Soviet countries show a very high share of institutional problems, while the Anglophone countries have the lowest. Adult learners in Anglophone countries (especially England and Scotland) quite rarely experience either transportation problems or inconvenient study schedules. Transport-related problems occurred more frequently in Austria, Hungary and the Czech Republic and studies have been scheduled inconveniently most frequently in Belgium-Flanders and Slovenia.

In summary, the post-soviet countries Russia, Estonia, and Lithuania are the countries with highest level of perceived institutional barriers in higher education, joined by Austria. These countries were among those with the lowest level of adults' participation in higher education. By contrast, adult learners from Anglophone countries, and those in Belgium and Norway reported the least problems. UK and Norway together with Belgium and Slovenia were also the countries with highest participation rates.

Table 2. Institutional barriers to higher education, 2007 (per cent)

	Studies scheduled at an inconvenient time	Financial problems	Transportation problems	Institutional problems, mean
Anglophone				
England	7	22	12	0.14
Scotland	5	36	7	0.16
Ireland	22	39	24	0.28
Northen European				
Norway	39	31	18	0.29
Continental European				
Austria	39	39	**37**	**0.39**
Belgium-Flanders	**43**	21	19	0.27
CEE countries				
Slovenia	44	40	20	0.34
Hungary	21	40	**34**	0.32
Czech Rep.	34	29	**35**	0.33
Bulgaria	28	**45**	25	0.29
Post-Soviet countries				
Estonia	**42**	**49**	24	**0.38**
Lithuania	25	**52**	29	0.35
Russia	26	**62**	29	**0.39**

Source: authors' own calculations, ALiFE 2007

Characteristics of higher education programmes

Having set out the conceptual framework of our paper, we will now explore the main characteristics of higher education programmes that are relevant for adult students: diversification of education system; accessibility of educational programme; flexibility of the organisation of the studies; and financial affordability of the higher education programme. We are most interested in studying the education system Estonia compared to other EU countries.

Diversification

In determining the level of diversification of formal education provision for adults, we rely on the approach developed by Günter Hefler within the research project LLL2010 (see Hefler 2010). Hefler's approach analyses a national education system based both on the variety in the length and content of programmes covered by formal adult education and on the variety of institutions providing formal adult education. This enabled Hefler (2010) to distinguish three groups of countries characterised as having high, medium or low diversification of formal education (see below in Figure 2).

In the context of the diversification of the formal education system, the higher education system in Estonia has low diversification, which means that the duration of the studies is strictly regulated and there is little variation and also that the variety of institutions providing formal adult education is rather small. This means that adults who are interested in participating in formal education have little choice both in terms of different education institutions offering formal adult education as well as in finding programs meeting their needs in terms of the intensity and duration of studies. Normally, in Estonia the regulated duration of higher education program is 3 or 5 years and few alternatives are available to complete it within a different time frame. The lack of variation here as a barrier to enter higher education in Estonia has been pointed out also by representatives of higher education institutions:

> But (one of our programs) is with integrated study, meaning that you have to study 5 years in a row. You would not even get a certificate if you have passed some of, so that you could present it to your employer. This way there is less interest in participating in this program.

Estonia is similar to other post-socialist countries (Russia, Lithuania, Bulgaria), while adult learners in English-speaking countries (Scotland, England, Ireland), by contrast, have the best opportunity to choose programs most suitable to their needs and interests both in terms of content as well as duration.

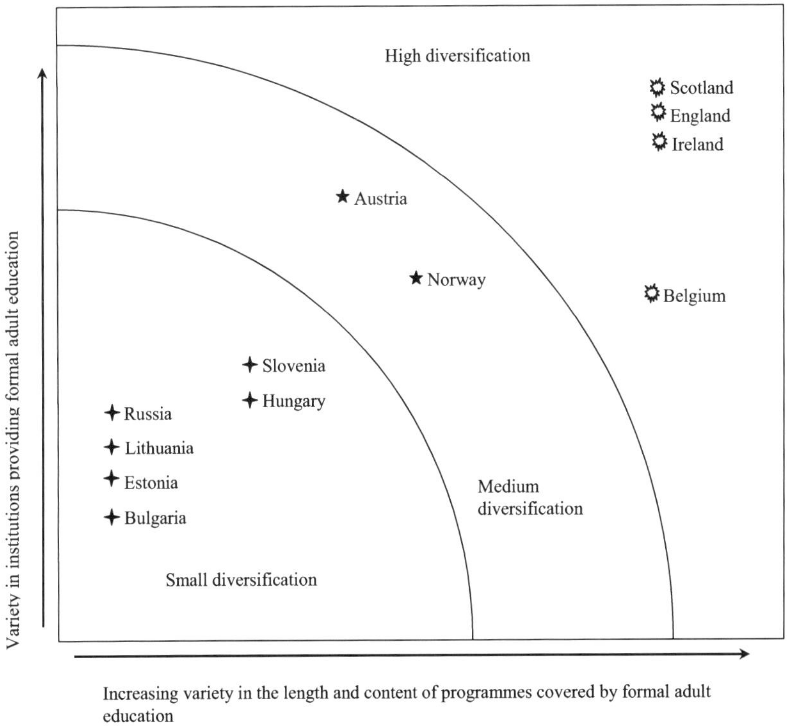

Figure 2. Diversification of formal education systems in the 21st Century

Source: Hefler 2010:57

In summary, we see a correlation between greater flexibility in learning programmes and higher participation rates of adults in higher education.

Access and flexibility

Accessibility to formal education for adults in terms of formal requirements differs remarkably across countries (see Table 3). Estonia has one of the strictest systems with 92 per cent of the respondents stating that one of the entry requirements to their current studies was possession of an educational diploma and 59 per cent having to take a pre-entry test or exam.

Table 3. Characteristics of higher education system for adult students: access and flexibility, 2007(per cent)

Country	Access		Flexibility						
	Diploma requirements	Test	APEL[1]	APL[2]	Distance learning	Weekend or evening classes	Modular courses	Attendance of school: >3 times per week	Class hours: >20 per week
Anglophone									
England	55	6	13	10	13	26	-	15	13
Scotland	63	9	12	13	39	16	-	39	8
Ireland	44	17	7	13	32	54	73	49	21
Northen European									
Norway	86	13	-	92	96	…	65	41	32
Continental European									
Austria	62	71	40	48	38	68	32	54	30
Belgium-Flanders	90	9	10	43	25	46	41	30	11
CEE countries									
Slovenia	96	3	24	20	84	66	16	42	5
Hungary	91	52	22	23	24	57	91	29	24
Czech Rep.	58	54	…	…	45	…	67	4	11
Bulgaria	90	53	5	22	24	34	25	24	41
Post-Soviet countries									
Estonia	92	59	17	27	83	57	81	21	23
Lithuania	98	7	20	48	64	54	89	51	42
Russia	86	76	23	27	59	77	18	71	42
Average	78	33	15	29	48	43	46	36	23

1 APEL – Accreditation of Prior and Experiental Learning

2 APL – Accreditation of Prior Learning

Source: authors' own calculations, ALiFE 2007

The need to pass a pre-entry test shows a divide in the institutional understanding of the entry process to higher education in Estonia. Private education institutions mostly share the view that everybody who wants to enter should have the chance, whereas the public universities argue that only 'the best' should be accepted and consequently selection 'tools' such as pre-entry exams are necessary. Furthermore, as the passing of a threshold in state exams has not proven to be efficient as a selection tool, any 'pre-entry' selection criterion (test, interview) is necessary.

> This is of course a point of discussion. But I think that entrance exams are not such a bad idea at all. State exams could form of course part of it, but on top of that could be also entrance exams and maybe even oral exams as there used to be. This shows also person's self-expression abilities, etc. I think this unified state exam system has been exhausted. Because everybody has [...] put the threshold lower or made the 'gate' wider [...] in order to attract more students. In other words, the general movement towards mass-university.

The characteristics of Estonia's higher education system for adult learners are more similar to Russia, Hungary and Bulgaria although another CEE country, Slovenia and post-Soviet republic, Lithuania differ significantly from Estonia and are more similar to each other as well as Belgium and Norway. By contrast, the Czech Republic, another post-socialist country in Europe, is systematically different, with access criteria being much more open and similar to Austria. Higher education programmes in Anglophone countries seem excel in their open access, making it easier for adult students to fulfil the formal criteria and get the right to become a student. There is no legislation referring to alternative entry into higher education in the UK, but higher education institutions commonly accept non-traditional candidates who do not comply with standard entry requirements (European Commission, 2012:86).

In addition to access criteria, another barrier to starting studies as an adult is the flexibility of the education system. Several issues are prevalent: can previous study or work experiences be evaluated as part of the study program; whether or not studies can be attended as distance-learning; whether or not the study programme is part-time, evenings or weekends; whether or not the programme is delivered regularly throughout the academic year or in a format of short periods of intense teaching or modules. In the context of the acceptance of previous experience (APEL and APL), Estonia, compared to other countries, occupies a middle position. (17 per cent of adult learners have APEL experience, 27 per cent have APL experience) (see Table 3). The statistics for students integrating their previous studies into current study programmes are 92 per cent (Norway), almost 50 per cent for Austria, Belgium and Lithuania. In Austria, 40 per cent of adult learners were able to integrate both their previous study and work experience into their current studies. One of the reasons for still low use of APEL and APL in the Estonian education system is the ambivalent feeling towards this practice:

> APEL is very attractive. This is used by more and more students. Still, there are teachers and heads of programs who have not yet accepted it. This I find many times problematic. I have to explain to heads of programs, talk to them, but they do not take it into practice. I have to find solutions, because students have right for APEL. There have been cases where I had to 'bypass' the head of the program and take the requests directly to the head of APEL committee.

The issue of greater flexibility can be observed in the way teaching is organized in Estonian higher education institutions. Distance learning accounts for more than two thirds of adult students in only 3 of the 13 surveyed countries; Norway – 96 per cent; Slovenia – 84 per cent and Estonia – 83 per cent. Another way to achieve greater flexibility is to schedule classes for the weekends or evenings. This type of flexibility has been used by more than half of adult learners (57 per cent) in Estonia, which is about the average in the cross-country comparison. Modular courses are the most popular way of increasing flexibility in Estonia with 81 per cent of adult learners having attended them during their studies.

Although attending higher education has been made more attractive and easy for adult learners in Estonia by these various teaching time flexibility options, there still exist various obstacles and limitations. Moreover, the organization of teaching differs a lot across higher education institutions. For example, the practice of distance studies or intense study periods might be incompatible with work of the learner. According to law, adult learners in Estonia have a right to take (partially paid) study leave or a (non-paid) break for studies from their job. However, in practice it requires negotiation with the employer, and not all are tolerant towards such requests. At the same time, higher education institutions are trying to find ways to make the time schedules more convenient for students.

> In most programs, the classes start at 16:00 hours. During the day hours, only when teachers are not willing to lecture in the evening or there are no classrooms available. We have to find ways so that students can come to classes. Most students from the bachelor studies have flexible agreements with their employers. They work part-time or they work from home.

Another obstacle for distance or weekend studies is often child-care, which in nonstandard working hours has to be arranged mostly by the adult learners themselves.

> Q: Do you offer any childcare facilities to teachers or students?
>
> R: No. But I have had cases where in the evening classes kids are with me and drawing. There is no formal childcare.

Another important aspect considered by adult learners is the weekly attendance hours of the study programme. In Estonia the practice is towards having fewer teaching sessions and fewer hours, only about a fifth of Estonian learners attend more than 3 sessions and 20 hours per week. The comparable figures for Austria, Lithuania, and Ireland are more than 50 per cent. Only in the Czech Republic and England do students attend classes even less frequently. The situation in Estonia can be explained by the increasing popularity of e-studies.

> Next to modular studies we are trying more and more to introduce e-studies, because it is difficult to come to classes when you are working.

At the same time, extensive use of e-studies has raised concerns related to the quality of studies – teachers have little control over how the materials have been processed and the level of in-put by a student in their contribution:

> Those who are not very interested have it easier this way. As the exam takes place in a virtual environment, then they sit together around the table and do it. The question here is the quality. Teachers try to include various compulsory elements – discussions, opinions – just to be sure about contribution.

Affordability

Estonia, Slovenia and Lithuania have the highest mean fees for higher education programmes (see Table 4) and moreover, a large percentage of students in these three countries have to pay (Self-paid) for their education, Estonia (65), Slovenia (70) and Lithuania (90). In Estonia, two thirds of the adult learners reported that they pay themselves the tuition fee. Although a high proportion of students in other countries are 'self-paid', their tuition fees are significantly lower.

Table 4. Characteristics of the affordability of national higher education systems for adult students, 2007

Country	Affordability				
	Self-paid enrolment or tuition fee (%)	Mean Self-paid enrolment or tuition fee (€)	Students with study grant (%)	Students with study loan (%)	Direct public-sector support to students*
Anglophone					
England	60	861	16	46	31.2**
Scotland	11	924	12	42	
Ireland	0	0	24	9	12.7
Northen European					
Norway	60	374	18	24	44.1
Continental European					
Austria	25	363	12	4	17.4
Belgium-Flanders	76	438	12	1	13.2***
CEE countries					
Slovenia	70	1477	5	8	23.2
Hungary	47	261	8	21	14.3
Czech Rep.	73	827	1	2	4.9
Bulgaria	69	303	15	3	6.7
Post-Soviet countries					
Estonia	65	1397	16	46	7.4
Lithuania	90	1275	6	3	14.1
Russia	62	579	6	7	...

* *Direct public-sector support (grants and loans) to students at tertiary level as a percentage of total expenditure on education, 2008 (Key Data on Education in Europe, 2012:101)*

***UK*

****Belgium*

Source: authors' own calculations, ALiFE 2007; Key Data on Education in Europe, 2012

Our interviews showed that higher education institutions see costs related to studies as important obstacles for adult learners, which include not only the enrolment and tuition fees, but also materials, transport, accommodation, reduced salaries (if applicable), etc.

> Many students come from outside Tallinn. It is difficult to pay in addition to the fee also for accommodation etc. There is for example one person from Haapsalu who is

> close to graduation and comes every day. There is also somebody from Pärnu. People come with their own car. This is impressive. There have been also people from Tartu. And they graduate. They have families back home, but ...

Against the backdrop of high study-related costs, the issue of (financial) support becomes highly important. While only 16 per cent of adult students in Estonia reported they received a study grant, 46 per cent have taken a study loan. This pattern of low incidence of study grants and a high uptake of study loans is prevalent in Estonia, England, Scotland, Norway and Hungary. Even if an Estonian adult student is able to get a study loan (in 2007 capped maximum of 25000 kroons, or 1602 EUR), it is unlikely to cover both the tuition fee, as well as the other study-related expenses throughout the programme. This seems to be very different from other cases in this group of countries: in England and Scotland the average tuition fee in 2007 was just about less than half the size of that in Estonia, and in Norway and Hungary it is just one fourth of it. It is plausible to suggest that adult learners did not really find the loans very helpful or even try to avoid to take them.

> As many have families and previous loans etc, they try to avoid taking study loans. They try to find other ways. Now the situation is a bit better already. But in the beginning of economic depression could be clearly seen how students took massively a break from the studies. Many lost jobs or were afraid to lose it. Like if I go to school on Fridays then maybe it is me who will be laid off as next. School became secondary.

The quality and strength of the student support system is related to the amount of money made available through the public budget. Direct student support from the public sector, which should if necessary act as a safety net for students in financial difficulties, amounts to 7.4 per cent of the national education budget (amongst the lowest in the survey). This leaves adult learners in a very vulnerable situation,

> There are not many options to react. There are no financial resources to support students. Study grants are small and it is not possible to make the ends meet only with a study grant. What we can offer is that study fee is paid in parts. We make payment schedules, so that one does not need to give out the whole sum in the beginning of the course. Once delaying the payment, students will not be exmatriculated immediately. We keep students.

Moreover, many student grants in Estonia are not means-tested, which means students have to compete for them. Research indicates that the likelihood of paying fees is not greatly affected by receiving public funding (European Commission, 2012:95). In Estonia students who do not to pay fees are much more likely to receive public support. It means that such support system may increase social inequalities. Also, the bureaucratic process involved in asking for aids is complicated and reduces the uptake of grants.

> It is rather sophisticated to apply for financial aid. One has to submit declarations, documents for parents' salaries. I think it has been made too complicated. Students do not want to reveal the data of their parents. Of course who really needs applies for it.

In other countries with low options for student grants and high takeout of student loans that have lower average tuition fees the statistics of receiving financial support in 2007 are more encouraging: 31 per cent in UK and even 44 per cent in Norway. Even Hungary's direct public support for students (14 per cent) is, proportionally, twice as high as Estonia's.

Using all the different characteristics of higher education institutions that could determine their suitability for adult learners that we described above – diversification, access, flexibility and affordability – we can rank the countries based on how their adult students experience these characteristics (Table 5). The comparison suggests that Estonia, together with other post-socialist countries, has 'weakest' performance in three of the four characteristics.

Table 5. Relative ranking of countries by institutional factors in higher education, 2007

	Degree			
	Low	Low-Medium	Medium-High	High
Diversification	Estonia, Lithuania, Russia, Bulgaria, Czech Rep., Hungary, Slovenia	Norway, Austria		England, Scotland, Ireland, Belgium
Access	Hungary, Bulgaria, Estonia, Russia	Austria, Czech Rep.	Belgium-Flanders, Lithuania, Slovenia, Norway	England, Scotland, Ireland
Flexibility	Scotland, England, Ireland, Belgium-Flanders, Bulgaria, Russia	Austria, Slovenia, Hungary, Czech Rep.	Lithuania, Estonia	Norway
Affordability	Estonia, Lithuania, the Czech Republic, Russia, Bulgaria	Ireland, Belgium-Flanders, Hungary, Austria, Slovenia	Scotland, England	Norway

Source: authors' own classification

The low diversity of the system of educational offers, difficulties in accessing the programmes, and low affordability of studies mean that adult students in Estonia face more barriers than in many other countries. Despite the recognition that in complex systems, like education, weaknesses in one aspect can be compensated by strengths in other aspects, there is also recognition that measures and practices are not always suitable for every system. For example, Estonia excels in the flexibility in organisation of studies, which enables adult students who are able to overcome the financial barrier, to arrange their schedule of attendance according to their other life domain responsibilities. This suggests, however, that the institutions and lecturers as well as the adult learners themselves are supposed to prioritise their other commitments, mostly those related to paid employment, over their studies. Consequently, difficulties in reconciling the different spheres of life, ensure learning activities often become of secondary importance.

It appears the best countries for adult students are – or, according to our study, were in 2007, before the global financial crisis – Norway, together with England, Scotland and Ireland, followed by Belgium. Note, however, that even the countries with highest suitability for adult learners may in fact be far from ideal, but just perform better than others.

Effects of characteristics of higher education programmes on perceived institutional barriers

We now look at the impact of various meso-level institutional characteristics on the perception of institutional boundaries in attending formal education as an adult. We performed linear regression analysis, with the cumulative average value of institutional barriers as dependent variable and indicators of access, flexibility, and affordability of the learning programmes as independent variables. The results are presented in Table 6.

Table 6. Impact of meso-level characteristics on perceived institutional barriers to higher education: linear regressioon analysis

		Beta	T statistic
Access	Diversification	-.110***	-4.491
	Entry on the basis of a certificate or diplom	-.011	-.496
	Entry on the basis of the test	.037	1.744
Flexibility	Delivery of distance learning oportunities	.043**	2.029
	Evening or weekend attendance of programme	.074***	3.555
	Weektime attendance of programme: times a week	-.039*	-1.881
	Programme hours	.063***	2.909
	APEL	.007	.722
	APL	.050**	2.422
Affordability	Paid self	.054**	2.521
	Study grant	.036	1.190
	Study loan	-.020	-.643
Adjusted R square		.058	

**** significant at level 0.001; ** significant at level 0.05; * significant at level 0.10*

Source: authors' own calculations, ALiFE 2007

The analysis suggests that in general, the more diversified the education system, the less likely are institutional barriers perceived in attending formal education as an adult. In other words, having greater variety of modes and arrangements of attendance as well as bigger choice of higher education institutions with programs for adult learners makes it more likely that adults continue their educational careers.

The regression results also indicate a relationship between affordability and perceived barriers: self-paid students are more likely to perceive institutional barriers. This is in line with our expectation, since the economic burden of education costs is often high. Adult students cannot put aside their other family and work-related duties aside for the period of their studies. It is likely that those paying their own tuition fees did accept the institutional challenges related to attending educational programs because they considered it feasible. At the same time, in order to be able to pay tuition fees, they have to stay committed to their working career and working schedules.

When looking at the various aspects of flexibility arrangements for adult learners, we receive a rather diverse picture. While there would be a natural expectation that more flexibility would result in fewer institutional barriers, our findings suggest the opposite. One explanation is that the adult learners' decision to start their higher education in 'flexible study' mode reflects their awareness of their own situational difficulties. This awareness enables them to evaluate their perception of potential barriers based on previous experience and to evaluate the system in a more critical way, as their expectations towards the educational institution were shaped during their previous study experiences. In order to test this idea, researchers need a different type of data, in which the changes in study modes and respective perceptions could be followed over a long period of time.

Summary and conclusions

In this chapter, we developed a new holistic measure consisting of four key aspects (indicators) to analyse how suitable education systems for adult students are in different countries. We then described and compared the countries based on both these indicators and the level to which adult students in those countries perceive different kinds of institutional difficulties. Finally we analysed to what extent the indicators we had chosen relate to the level of perceived institutional barriers by students.

Based on our analysis of data from 13 European countries in 2007, we can say that diversification of higher educational offers and affordability of higher education can predicate fewer institutional barriers for adult learners. In the context of both these measures (indicators), Estonia's higher education system has among the weakest in Europe. Due to the high level of diversification of higher education, recognition of prior learning is not used as a pre-selection tool for access to higher education. However, the flexibility of the organisation of studies, an aspect where Estonia outperforms most of the other surveyed countries, is not necessarily the way to lessen barriers to participation in adult higher education. It seems the influx to higher education of non-traditional students who prefer flexible schedules should make the institutions more open to their needs and preferences throughout the educational organisation. Flexibility may act as a trigger, attracting adults into higher education, but this is apparently insufficient to help them cope with other institutional barriers.

Estonia inherited from the Soviet period a poorly diversified formal adult education system, which worked quite well when the role of the state was crucial in the process of lifelong learning. Later, this low level of diversification combined with marketization and liberalization in education brought about a sharp increase in inequality of participation because individuals are mainly responsible for their own educations.

Despite a high level of adult participation in higher education institutions, strategies for promoting lifelong learning are incipient in Estonia and there are no provisions to allow entry into higher education on the basis of a person's assessed competencies instead of formal qualifications. The question remains as to whether or not the national higher education policy gives sufficient priority to these issues. The OECD report about higher education in Estonia formulates some challenges for higher education institutions and higher education policy: to widen opportunities for lifelong learning by increasing the flexibility of provision (e.g. part-time and distance provision), by providing financial support to address the difficulties facing low-income workers, by reviewing the suitability of education and training alternatives and by recognition of prior learning (OECD, 2007). .

The Estonian higher education situation is comparable, according to our analysis, to other post-socialist or sometimes even just post-Soviet countries. The social transformation brought about realignment from the goals of learning as enlightenment per se and contributed to the instrumentalisation of education and knowledge as something relevant mostly for the productive sphere (Saar et al., 2013). This paralleled with the abolition of the previously functioning support systems for adults returning to education, as institutional arrangements that had been developed by the end of the socialist period were mostly destroyed during the state-building processes (Bunce, 1999). Lack of resources not only financial but also those capable of legitimising the possible strengths of the previous education system eventually led to the weakness of the new decentralised and market-based system, increasing inequalities in participation and the role of the formal education system in catering for those of disadvantaged backgrounds.

It is worthwhile to remember that data from 2007 forms the basis of our study, which means it does not show the effects of the ongoing economic crisis. To the contrary, this reflects the educational ideology which was prominently neoliberal (see Aava, 2010), and it is possible that with the global crisis new discursive space become available to criticise the neoliberal agenda. Even in line with the neoliberal agenda, countries may have opted to invest more in preparing their human capital better to the new challenges of restructuring economy, while it is just as likely that governments might have cut their expenditure on education systems because of the austerity measures. It would therefore be very interesting to see how the system has changed during the 2008–2012 global economic crisis, and what does it mean for the non-traditional students. That is the future direction of our research.

References

Aava, K. (2010). *Eesti haridusdiskursuse analüüs. Tallinna Ülikooli Sotsiaalteaduste dissertatsioonid 44* [The Analysis of Estonian Educational Discourse. Tallinn University Dissertations on Social Sciences 44]. Tallinn: Tallinn University.

Adelman, C. (2007). Do we really have a college access problem? *Change: The Magazine of Higher Learning*, 39, 48–51.

Babchuk, W. A. and Courtney, S. (1995). Towards a sociology of participation in adult education programs. *International Journal of Lifelong Learning*, 14, 391–404.

Blair, A., McPake, J. and Munn, P. (1995). A new conceptualisation of adult participation in education. *British Educational Research Journal*, 21, 629–644.

Bowl, M. (2001). Experiencing the barriers: non-traditional students entering higher education. *Research Papers in Education*, 16, 144–160.

Bunce, V. (1999). *Subversive Institutions: The Design and the Destruction of Socialism and the State*. Cambridge: Cambridge University Press.

Chao, E. L., DeRoccoo, S. and Flynn, M. K. (2007). *Adult learners in higher education: Barriers to success and strategies to improve results.* Washington, D. C.: US Department of Labor.

Cross, K. P. (1981). *Adults as learners: Increasing participation and facilitating learning.* San Francisco, CA: Jossey-Bass.

Darkenwald, G. G. and Valentine, T. (1985). Factor structure of deterrents to public participation in adult education. *Adult Education Quarterly*, 35, 177–193.

Darmody, M. and Smyth, E. (2008). Full-time students? Term-time employment among higher education students in Ireland. *Journal of Education and Work*, 21, 349–362.

European Commission (2012). *The European Higher Education Area in 2012: Bologna Process Implementation Report*. Eurydice.

Gooderham, P. N. (1993). A conceptual framework of sociological perspectives on the pursuit by adult access to higher education. *International Journal of Lifelong Education,* 12, 27–39.

Hefler, G. (2010). *The qualifications-supporting company – The Significance of Formal Adult Education in Small and Medium Organisations*. Krems: Danube University Krems.

Helemäe, J. and Saar, E. (1999). The Estonian Education System in the Second Half of the 20th Century: Opportunities and Choices for the Cohorts. In Vetik, R. (Ed.), *Estonian Human Development Report 1999*. Tallinn: UNDP, 84–92.

Heller, D. E. (1999). The effects of tuition and state financial aid on public college enrollment. *The Review of Higher Education*, 23, 65–89.

Holford, J., Riddell, S., Weedon, E., Litjens, J. and Hannan, G. (2008*). Patterns of Lifelong Learning: Policy & Practice in an Expanding Europe*. Vienna: Lit Verlag.

Jarvis, P. (2007). *Globalisation, Lifelong Learning and the Learning Society: Sociological Perspectives*. London: Routledge.

Jarvis, P. (2010). *Adult Education and Lifelong Learning: Theory and Practice*. London: Routledge.

Jung, J.-C. and Cervero, R. M. (2002). The social, economic and political contexts of adults' participation in undergraduate programmes: a state-level analysis. *International Journal of Lifelong Learning*, 21, 305–320.

Kasworm, C. E. (2003). Setting the stage: Adults in higher education. *New Directions for Student Services*, 102, 3–10.

Key Data on Education in Europe (2012). Eurydice.

Knowles, M. S., Holton, E. F. and Swanson, R. A. (2005). *The adult learner: The definitive classic in adult education and human resource development, 6th edition.* Burlington, MA: Elsevier.

Long, B. T. (2008). *What is known about the impact of financial aid: Implications for policy.* New York, NY: The National Center for Postsecondary Education.

Mancuso, S. (2001). Adult-centered practices: Benchmarking study in higher education. *Innovative Higher Education*, 25, 165–181.

McGivney, V. (1996). *Staying or Leaving the Course: Non-Completion and Retention of Mature Students in Further and Higher Education.* Leicester: NIACE.

Morey, A. I. (2004). Globalization and the emergence of for-profit higher education. *Higher Education,* 48, 131–151.

OECD (2007). *OECD Reviews of Tertiary Education. Estonia.* Paris: OECD.

Reiska, E., Roosalu, T., Tamm, A., Täht, K. and Unt, M. (Eds.) (2012), *Kõrghariduse tähendused ja kõrgkoolide koostöö tööandjatega* [The meanings of higher education and cooperation between universities and employers]. Available online: http://primus.tlu.ee/tehtud-tood/Sunteesraport.pdf.

Riddell, S., Markowitsch, J. and Weedon, E. (Eds.) (2012). *Lifelong Learning in Europe: Equity and efficiency in the balance*. Bristol: Policy Press.

Roosalu, T. and Roosmaa, E.-L. (2010). Back At School: Do They Really Have Nothing Else To Do? Lifelong Learning Ideologies. In Kozlovskiy, V., Vöörmann, R. and Roosalu, T. (Eds.), *Learning in Transition: Policies and Practicies of Liflong Learning in Post Socialist Countries.* St Petersburg: Nauka, 41–65.

Rubenson, K. and Desjardins, R. (2009). The Impact of Welfare State Regimes on Barriers to Participation in Adult Education. A Bounded Agency Model. *Adult Education Quartely*, 59, 187–207.

Saar, E., Ure, O. B. and Holford, J. (Eds.) (2013). *Lifelong Learning in Europe: National Patterns and Challenges*. Cheltenham: Edward Elgar.

Saar, E., Tamm, A., Roosalu, T. and Roosmaa, E.-L. (2012). *Mittetraditsiooniline tudeng kõrgkoolis* [Nontraditional student in higher education]. Tartu: SA Archimedes.

Schaffer, J. M. (2010). *Accessibility, affordability, and flexibility: The relationship of selected state sociopolitical factors and the participation of adults in public two-year colleges.* Doctoral dissertation. University of Montana.

Schoefer, E. and Meyer, J. W. (2005). The Worldwide Expansion of Higher education in the Twentieth Century. *American Sociological Review*, 70, 898–920.

Schuetze, H. G. (2006) International concepts and agendas of lifelong learning. *Compare*, 36, 289–306.

Schuetze, H. G. and Slowey, M. (2002). Participation and exclusion: A comparative analysis of non-traditional students and lifelong learning in higher education. *Higher Education,* 44, 309–327.

Schuetze, H. G. and Slowey, M. (Eds.) (2000). *Higher Education and Lifelong Learners. International Perspectives on Change*. London: Routledge.

Shavit, Y., Arum, R., and Gamoran, A. (2007). Stratification in higher education: a comparative study. Stanford, CA: Stanford University Press.
Spanard, J.-M. A. (1990). Beyond intent: Re-entering college to complete the degree. *Review of Educational Research*, 60, 309–344.
Valentine, T. and Darkenwald, G. G. (1990). Deterrents to participation in adult education: profiles of potential learners. *Adult Education Quarterly*, 41, 29–42.
Wyatt, L. G. (2011). Non-traditional student engagement; increasing adult student success and retention. *The Journal of Continuing Higher Education*, 59, 10–20.

Contributors

Liina Adov is a master's student at the University of Tartu in the Department of psychology. In her masters studies she is focusing on educational psychology, in specific on students' self-efficacy, self-esteem and self-concept in different levels of education.

Jüri Allik received his PhD from Moscow University (1976) and also from Tampere University, Finland (1991). He is the professor of experimental psychology at the University of Tartu and served there as the Dean of the Faculty of Social Sciences from 1996 to 2000. He was the chairman of the Estonian Science Foundation (2003-2009). He is a member of Estonian Academy of Sciences (2010) and a foreign member of the Finnish Academy of Science and Letters (1997). His primary field of research is visual psychophysics, especially perception of visual motion. Recent research, however, is more concentrated on personality, emotions, intelligence, and cross-cultural comparison. With Robert R. McCrae, he edited 'The Five-Factor Model of Personality Across Cultures' (Kluwer Academic/Plenum Publishers, 2002).

Dr. Raul Eamets is professor of macroeconomics at the University of Tartu, Estonia. Currently he is the head of the Institute of Economics and Chairman of the Council of EuroCollege at the University of Tartu. He is also director of the PhD Programme at the faculty of Economics. In 2004-2009 he is a member of the Board of the Bank of Estonia. He has been short-term research visitor at Birkbeck College (London), IZA, CERGE-EI (Prague) and CLS (Aarhus). He received his PhD in economics from Tartu University in 2001, half of his PhD time he spent in Aarhus University. His main interests are in the area of labour market flexibility issues like labour market flows, firm entry and exit, educational economics, flexicurity, industrial relations, employment protection and labour policy issues. His publications include articles in *Post-communist Studies, European Journal of Industrial Relations, Transfer and Baltic Journal of Economics*.

Kerly Espenberg (MA) is a deputy head of the University of Tartu's Centre for the Social Sciences, Estonia. She is finishing her PhD studies in the University of Tartu in economics. Her main research area is labour economics. She has participated in many national research projects and has also been involved as a researcher in a number of international comparative studies concerning employment and labour market funded by European Commission and ILO.

Dr. **Jelena Helemäe** is a senior researcher at the Institute of International and Social Studies at Tallinn University. Her main research focuses are related to stratification and its perception. She has published chapters in books published by prominent international companies, including Palgrave McMillan, Edward Elgar Publishing, Peter Lang Publishers House.

Dr. **Krista Jaakson** is a researcher in the Faculty of Economics and Business Administration in the University of Tartu. She has published in Cross-Cultural Management: an International Journal, Journal of Management Development, Baltic Journal of Management, Atlantic Journal of Communication and elsewhere. Her research interests include organizational and individual values, management, industrial relations, and organizational behavior.

Dr. **Larissa Jõgi** working as associate professor in adult education and as the head of Department of Adult Education in the Institute of Educational Science at Tallinn University. Her current research and professional interests include teaching and learning in university; professional development, learning and identity of adult educators; adult learning in the life course; emotional learning experiences; narrative and visual research. Larissa Jõgi is an editor of journal *Studies of the Learning Society*, member of advisory boards of *European Journal for Research on Adult Education and Learning* (EJRAEL) and *Adult Education Discourses*. She is is a member of steering committee of European Society of Research in Adult Education (ESREA) and one of the convenors of the ESREA network 'Adult Educator, Trainer Professional Development'; also she is a member of International Society of Comparative Adult Education (ISCAE), member of Nordic-Baltic Network in Higher Education, member of the Estonian Adult Education Council and expert of the European Union Educational Programme SOCRATES, sub-programme 'Grundtvig'.

Dr. **Mari Karm** is a senior lecturer at the Institute of Education, University of Tartu, Estonia. Her research interests include professional identity, reflective practice and professional learning of academic staff.

Kristiina Krabi is a lecturer of Adult Education in the Institute of Educational Science at Tallinn University, Estonia. She is a PhD student in Educational Sciences. Her research interests include adult learning, philosophy and theory of education, higher education, qualitative research methodology, academics' identity. Her main publications are 'Raamat õppimisest: õppides täiskasvanuks – õppimine erinevates perspektiivides perspektiivides' [The Book of Learning: learning to be an adult – learning in different perspectives] (Jõgi and Krabi, 2011) and also papers published in *Studies for Learning Society*.

Dr. **Kairi Kreegipuu** is a senior researcher at the Institute of Psychology, University of Tartu, Estonia. She is an experimental psychologist studying sensory and cognitive processing in normal and special conditions including fatigue or